1912–2012
100
YEARS

AME BC

Association for Mineral Exploration British Columbia

© Association for Mineral Exploration British Columbia 2011

Library and Archives Canada Cataloguing in Publication

Davis, Chuck, 1935-2010
    Into the mountains : celebrating 100 years of mineral
exploration advocacy, 1912-2012 / Chuck Davis.

Includes bibliographical references and index.
ISBN 978-0-9738395-4-8

    1. Mineral industries—British Columbia—History. 2. Mineral
industries—Economic aspects—British Columbia—History. 3. Mining
corporations—British Columbia—History. 4. Mineral industries—
British Columbia—Employees—History. 5. Association for Mineral
Exploration British Columbia—History. I. Association for Mineral
Exploration British Columbia II. Title.

HD9506.C23B725 2012   338.209711   C2011-908564-X

Cover photograph by John Fleishman
Design by Dead Famous

Printed and bound in Canada by Hemlock Printers Ltd.

ASSOCIATION FOR MINERAL EXPLORATION BRITISH COLUMBIA

formerly the British Columbia & Yukon Chamber of Mines

Into the Mountains

1912 ~ 2012

Celebrating 100 Years of Mineral Exploration Advocacy

Chuck Davis

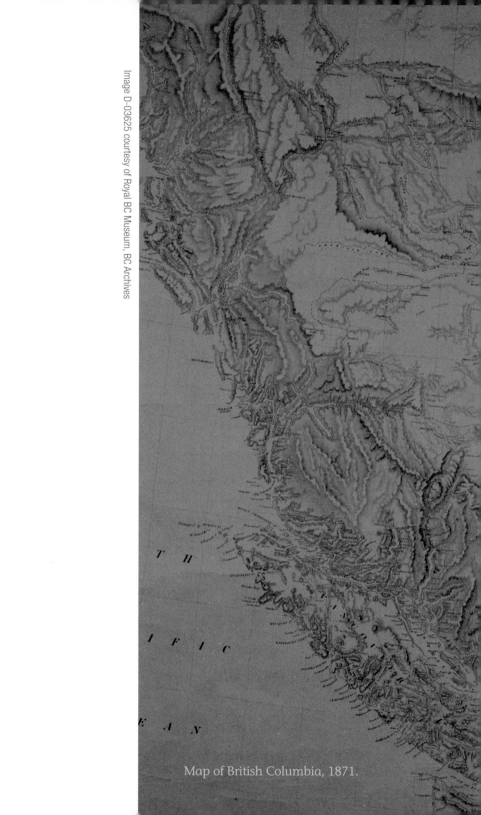

Map of British Columbia, 1871.

Preface
Bob Dickinson

Raeff Miles

At this writing, July 2011, British Columbia hosts the largest assembly of mineral exploration and development companies in the world. The TSX Stock Exchange and TSX Venture Exchange list over 1,600 mining companies, of which more than half are based in Vancouver, and this does not include mining-related service and research companies. How did this impressive concentration of corporate, scientific, technical and financial talent come to reside on Canada's West Coast?

History, notably the gold rushes of the 1800s, played a central role in establishing B.C.'s political structure. The province's geological endowment is among the richest in the world, resulting in the development of countless mines over the decades.

B.C.'s location in Canada — a vast country with a variety of geological environments that have provided a foundation for both a globally competitive mining sector and a strong national economy — has also played a key part. Far distant from the corridors of power and money in Central Canada, it is perhaps not surprising that B.C.'s pioneering

and self-sufficient spirit led to the development of a venture capital market that has fueled the growth of mineral exploration and development in the province and internationally.

British Columbia's challenges have also been its strengths. The lay of the land, mountainous and daunting in much of the province, has led to innovation in the ways that mineral claims are staked and deposits are discovered and developed.

A combination of history, natural endowment and a penchant for innovation, risk-taking and self-sufficiency has spawned a cluster of mineral exploration and development companies that has made Vancouver and B.C. the biggest and most dynamic world centre for mineral exploration and development.

The economic importance of mining is not always well understood, or even perceived. Perhaps the hidden nature of mineral deposits causes their importance and the contributions of those who seek them to be overlooked.

Hence the need for an association to ensure that development of B.C.'s mineral wealth is a priority for government, industry and communities; and to ensure that such development occurs in a manner that generates wealth and opportunity while preserving important environmental, social and cultural values. This is the story of just such an organization.

Over its 100-year history, the British Columbia & Yukon Chamber of Mines (now known as the Association for Mineral Exploration British Columbia, the Association or AME BC) has brought together all the diverse elements of the mineral exploration and development sectors.

AME BC's membership includes prospectors, junior companies and major integrated mining conglomerates. Some member firms comprise a single geologist or engineer. Others are major international consultancies. There are claim-stakers and those committed to developing better exploration and discovery tools. There are academic researchers and scientists; geophysical and geochemical specialists; and applied technologists focused on deeper drilling, developing more precise analytical tools, or designing computer models to determine how valuable mineral deposits can best be developed.

Beyond these technical experts are the lawyers who assist mining companies in securing land holdings and negotiating partnerships. There are auditors, investor relations advisors, brokers and other financial specialists who help companies access the capital they need to find and develop new orebodies. There are equipment providers and logistics specialists who get exploration teams and their tools in to the field. And there are those who establish and maintain B.C.'s geological surveys and the world-class database of mineral occurrences. These skilled, dedicated men and women live and work in communities throughout British Columbia and Yukon and contribute in untold ways to Canada's economic and cultural life.

As part of this fraternity of explorers, I treasure the knowledge I have gained about British Columbia, its geology, geography, environment and people over four decades as a working geologist. I have had the good fortune to work with exceptional people: Colleagues, business partners and citizens from communities throughout B.C., all of whom have helped develop and share the benefits that come from mineral wealth.

AME BC has provided an invaluable voice for our industry with politicians, regulators, other land and resource users and the public which ultimately owns B.C.'s mineral resources. As the needs and perceptions of these audiences have changed over the years, so has the organization changed to ensure widespread understanding of the importance of mineral exploration and mining.

Today, although mining is B.C.'s most important primary industry, the Association is still providing a valuable service: educating; advocating; wherever possible, lending support to the industry.

On the occasion of the hundredth anniversary of AME BC, it is my privilege to write the foreword to this commemorative volume. It stands testament to the remarkable contributions of all those men and women who came before us to build B.C.'s minerals industry. Of course, it also marks an important centennial milestone for the Association.

Perhaps most importantly, it is my hope that this book provides a compass for those who will lead mineral exploration and development in British Columbia for the next 100 years, important work supporting the development of a nation's economy, providing the materials necessary to build and maintain a modern society, while preserving important environmental and cultural values.

Bob Dickinson is Chairman of HDI.

Acknowledgements

Many people contributed to this volume. AME BC wishes to thank and recognize the hard work and leadership of the Commemorative Book Task Group. Numerous people, too many to mention here, contributed helpful ideas, comments and suggestions; they also deserve thanks.

The following made specific contributions:

John S. Brock: Junior Mining Companies in British Columbia

Jonathan Buchanan (with **Julie Domvile**): A Safe Day, Everyday – 30 Years in the Making

Nicholas Carter: British Columbia Iron Mining: 1951 to 1984; Uranium in British Columbia and the Impacts of Provincial Government Policies; contributions to Porphyry Deposits in British Columbia and Yukon

Bob Cathro: Porphyry Deposits in British Columbia and Yukon; plus other contributions

Vivian Danielson: The Long Road to Aboriginal Engagement; The Role of Global Miners, Oil Giants and Consulting Firms; Noranda Mines Limited; Innovation and Leadership; Women in Mining; plus other contributions

Gavin E. Dirom – Contributions to Porphyry Deposits in British Columbia and Yukon; plus other contributions

Julie Domvile: AME BC's Roundup – 25 Years (with Shari Gardiner); Endako profile; Jerry Asp profile

Bob Gale: Gavin A. Dirom profile

Shari Gardiner: Contributions to The 2000s; AME BC's Roundup – 25 Years; Eldorado Mountain – The Lucky Jem Story; Women in Mining; plus other contributions

Rick Higgs: Contribution to The 1970s

Mary Hughes: Granby profile

Ed Kimura: The Bre-X Scandal; B.C. Assay Laboratories 1960s to Present; contributions to Porphyry Deposits in British Columbia and Yukon

Denis Lieutard: Claims Staking in British Columbia

John Murray: The Lardeau District; Rossland; Sandon – The "Sunless City," Misfortune's Playground; plus other contributions

Don Mustard: Contribution to The 1970s

Bill Smitheringale: Contribution to Britannia Mine Museum

Laurence Thomson: Eldorado Mountain – The Lucky Jem Story; profiles of Jim Morin and Ross Beaty; contribution to Coal and Metallurgical Coke; plus other contributions

This book came into being largely through the urging and energy of Chamber past president, Don Mustard (1979-1981). Through his persistence and gentle prodding, beginning in early 2005, an editorial committee was formed and the members of the work group set about recording this history for future generations.

The book owes much to the detailed chronology, prepared by long-time manager Tommy Elliott, which covers the years 1912 to 1980; afterwards it often relies on *Mining Review* (renamed *Mineral Exploration* in 2006) as the organization's primary work of record.

In early 2009, AME BC commissioned Chuck Davis, popular author of more than a dozen books on Vancouver, to write this history. Chuck began work with typical gusto. He immediately developed a passion for learning about the history of the Association, along with mineral exploration and mine development. His enthusiasm and wit enrich the book. Even when battling the cancer that would take his life, he remained cheerful and alert to the book's progress. In recognition of his outstanding service to AME BC, he received the Frank Woodside Past Presidents' Distinguished Service Award in the fall of 2010. He died shortly thereafter.

At Chuck's suggestion, business journalist and author Jim Lyon was engaged to assist the editorial committee – a coterie of learned and civilized zealots – in the book's completion. Jim thanks task group members for their patience and inexhaustible professionalism. He also acknowledges the help and many courtesies he received from AME BC staff, in particular the Association's Director, Communications & Public Affairs, Jonathan Buchanan.

Early in 2011, it became clear that an enterprise as ambitious as *Into the Mountains* – calling upon the talents, insights, memories and written contributions of industry leaders, past and present – needed a dedicated project manager. Laurie Thomson was recruited for that role and displayed rigorous attention to detail and an intuition into unsung aspects of mineral exploration and development and their societal importance. Laurie thanks Gavin C. Dirom, President & CEO, and Rick Conte, Vice President, AME BC for their contributions; and Kathleen Brow, Archivist, AME BC for cataloguing and scanning the historical images used in this book.

Chuck Davis upon receiving the Frank Woodside Past Presidents Distinguished Service Award for his work on the history of AME BC.

Contents

Contents

Contents

BRITISH COLUMBIA CHAMBER OF MINES MINERAL EXHIBIT

Chamber of Mines exhibit at the Canada Pacific Exhibition (now PNE), ca. 1930s

AME BC/photographer: Dominion Photo Co.

Introduction

Jack M. Patterson

The year 1912 was great for business in British Columbia, particularly for the City of Vancouver. It was also a good year for the mining community, made better by the formation of the Vancouver Mining Club. Many location and name changes later, this became the Association for Mineral Exploration British Columbia, as we know it today. Created to foster mining and in particular exploration in British Columbia, the Chamber, as it was called from 1912 to 2005, soon realized that its primary purpose was to inform and educate.

The Chamber became an information collection and distribution centre. It grew from conversations at the Vancouver Mining Club, through its collection of geological maps, publications and annual reports, to the highly successful annual Roundup convention, now attended by thousands. Public education was always important. This component of its work began with public lectures in the early 1900s and led to the popular Placer Mining and Prospecting Schools, attended by hundreds over the years. A necessary educational aid was the creation of an

excellent display of mineral, rock and ore specimens, generously donated by individuals and companies. In the year 2000, a joint venture was set up with the British Columbia Institute of Technology (BCIT).

Safety in mineral exploration also became an educational objective and resulted in the publication of a safety manual for explorationists in the Canadian Cordillera, later modified to address worldwide exploration needs.

The Chamber's information and education focus embraced the political arena. Representatives made frequent visits to both Victoria and Ottawa. Submissions almost always included requests for more geological mapping with rapid publication, practical land use regulations for mineral exploration, and recognition of the depleting nature of ore deposits.

Cooperation with other regional mineral exploration and mining associations located in British Columbia, Yukon and the Northwest Territories (NWT), as well as national organizations, was established and maintained. The mineral exploration and development scene changed dramatically with the growth of land use issues, in particular the creation and designation of parks and pseudo-parks (where mineral exploration was banned) in the 1990s. This appropriation without consultation came to a peak in June 1993 with the creation of the Tatshenshini-Alsek Park. During this period the Chamber's arguments fell on deaf ears.

Although its primary purposes was to foster mining in British Columbia, many in the Vancouver-based mineral exploration community also explored in Yukon, NWT and what is now Nunavut. Consequently, the Chamber's mandate was extended and efforts were made to foster mineral exploration in these areas. When Vancouver grew into a centre for worldwide mineral exploration

in the 1990s, the Chamber responded positively, providing data and assistance to Canadian exploration companies as well as to officials of foreign host countries. The Association has always maintained that, through good times and bad, a strong mineral exploration community must be maintained in Vancouver for the continued development of B.C. mineral resources. Vancouver has one of the finest, if not *the* finest, mineral exploration communities in the world.

Readers may ask how all this was accomplished by an organization with only a few dedicated employees and limited funds. The answer: through equally dedicated, hard-working, long-lasting volunteers supported by their respective employers. If a volunteer was needed for teaching, committee

work, fund-raising, special events and so on, the Chamber had only to ask. There was always someone willing to contribute.

How successful has the Chamber been in meeting the needs of its members and society as a whole? Being alive and well after 100 years shows it must be doing something right. One can only imagine what remarks its first president, Robert R. Hedley, might make reading this volume. To him and all the men and women who are, or have been, associated with the Association, this volume is dedicated.

Jack M. Patterson was Manager of the Chamber of Mines from 1980 to 1998.

AME BC

The Chamber's prize-winning exhibit at the Northwest Mining Association convention, Spokane, 1923

Chamber of Mines building at 840
West Hastings Street, Vancouver, 1959

Seeking a hidden resource – the More Creek Valley in northwestern British Columbia

Why Is It So Hard to Find a Mine?

A mineral property that has little or no economic potential today can be tomorrow's mine as more geologic information becomes available; measurement or extractive techniques improve; infrastructure evolves; and commodity markets strengthen.

One of the most common misperceptions about mineral exploration and mining is that B.C. has been prospected and explored for 150 years so surely whatever there is to be found has been found already.

It is easy to forget that mineral exploration is an iterative process; that we can't examine a property and know once and for all whether or not there is a mineral deposit there. In fact, we can **never** definitively say "…there is no valuable mineral deposit here…" even after multiple stages – and even years or decades of exploration. The best we can say is we haven't found it, yet.

Sometimes years of fieldwork, diligent prospecting, thorough and often creative geological interpretation, and a little luck are needed to create a viable mineral project.

Unlike other natural resources; minerals lie truly hidden. And the mineral exploration and development process does not lend itself to land use planning as people generally understand that concept today; unlike forests, where the trees can be physically seen and counted; or agriculture where the arable land is known, and so are their yields; or even fish, which can be (roughly) counted too.

Our mineral resource really **is** different. We can't plan discoveries; but we certainly **can** plan **against** the possibility of discovery – and far too often we do exactly that in our approaches to land use.

Mining history is replete with examples of areas once considered to have low potential that eventually produce very valuable mines.

As an example, up until the late-1980s, the conventional wisdom of geologic experts was that there were no – repeat no – mineable diamond deposits in Canada! But, today, Canada is a leading producer of conflict- free diamonds. Moreover, not so very long ago, geologic expert advice was not to bother looking for gold in granitic intrusions. Yet today much of B.C.'s gold production comes from just such geologic environments (as a by-product of copper mining).

In summary, mines are hard to find because each mineral deposit is unique, often defying conventional wisdom as to its geological setting and associated host rocks. Some mines produce metals and minerals that weren't recognized a century ago, such as rare earths that power today's high-technology world. Mines are also hard to find because nature hides them well, sometimes at depth under extensive overburden or glacial cover, and often in remote, rugged and geologically complex areas that are challenging to explore.

Advanced exploration techniques and geological concepts have contributed to recent discoveries, however, as later pages will show, there is still no substitute for old-fashioned "boot-and-hammer" prospecting as the first step in the discovery of new mines.

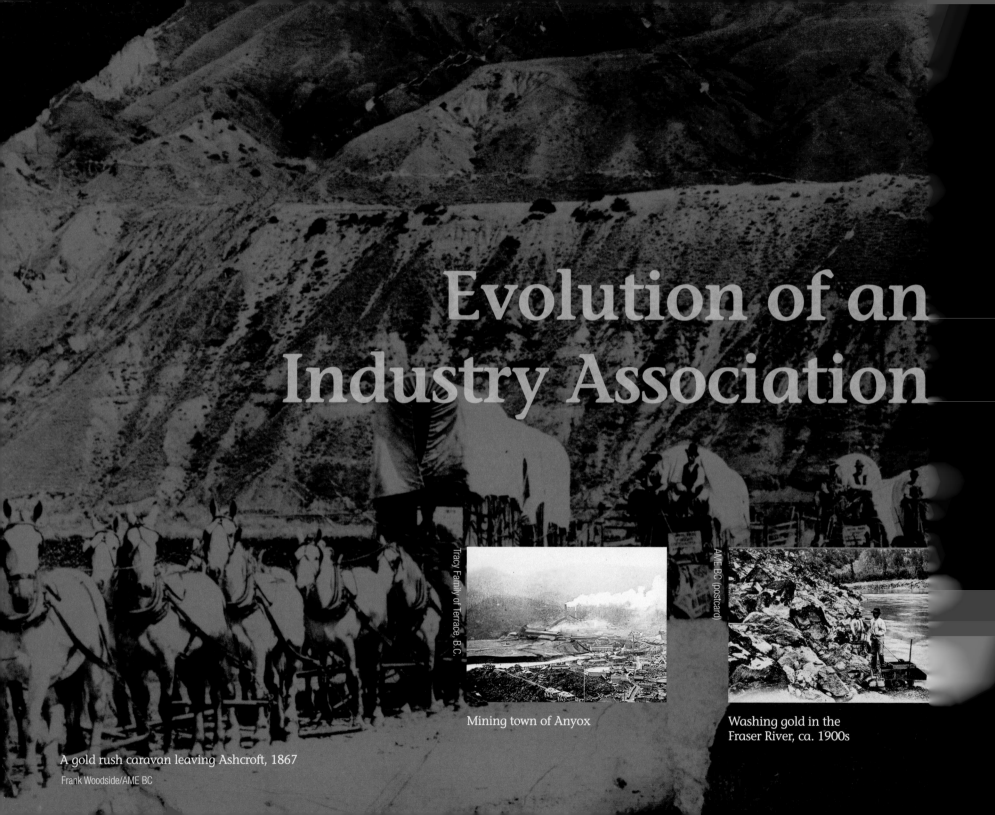

Evolution of an Industry Association

Tracy Family of Terrace, B.C.

AME BC (postcard)

Mining town of Anyox

Washing gold in the
Fraser River, ca. 1900s

A gold rush caravan leaving Ashcroft, 1867

Frank Woodside/AME BC

A First Nations family pans in a river at Lillooet.

The Early Years

~ The Origins of Mineral Exploration and Mining in B.C.

The quest for metals and minerals was driven by necessity as humans settled the West Coast of North America following the retreat of huge glacial ice-sheets 10,000 years ago. A typical hunting-and-gathering family would benefit enormously from the use of sharp stone tools, which were stronger and superior to implements hewn from wood or bone. Their odds of survival increased further as metal tools were introduced. Daily life was also enhanced as rocks and minerals were fashioned into jewelry and household artifacts.

Archaeological evidence shows that mining and mineral exploration took place many thousands of years ago at early Aboriginal settlements across British Columbia. In Coast Salish territory, a 3,500-year-old site at the mouth of the Fraser River revealed copper ornaments and sculptured stone bowls among other ceremonial artifacts, suggesting a vibrant cultural life. The Similkameen bands near present-day Hedley mined extensive chert beds, a source of flint for weapons and tools, along with ochre and traded them across the West. The Haida, known for their large coastal settlements and rich culture, mined black slate for tools at a site on

Gold nuggets found in 1935

Haida Gwaii (formerly the Queen Charlotte Islands) that is still mined today to create argillite art pieces seen in museums around the world.

And in the far northwest is one of the oldest mining sites, Mount Edziza, north of Terrace. The second largest volcanic complex in Canada, Mount Edziza's glacier-covered peak (at 2,590 meters high) looms above the traditional lands of the Tahltan people. According to studies by the Geological Survey of Canada (GSC), the first phase of eruptive activity began seven million years ago, followed by four additional phases, with numerous eruptions within the last 10,000 years. Some Tahltan elders remember stories about families who had to move camp hurriedly because of the volcanic activity. But there was a benefit too; as hot, thick dark lava chilled in the northern air to form sheets of black volcanic glass known as obsidian.

The Tahltan people began to mine the obsidian many millennia ago, breaking off chunks to fashion into tools, ornaments and, sometimes, weapons for their own use and for trading with other tribes. Obsidian has long been valued for its cutting qualities. It breaks into pieces with razor-sharp edges. Even today, scalpels made of obsidian are used in some surgical procedures where extremely fine cutting action is required. An obsidian knife, still sharp, found in the Stikine River area, is estimated to have been fashioned 2,000 years ago. Archeological evidence has shown that Mount Edziza obsidian was traded in ancient times with other First Nations people from Haida Gwaii to Alaska.

iStockphoto

Imagine a typical family: mom, dad and a young boy and girl. They could live in Vancouver, Whitehorse or Wawa, or down the street in your neighborhood.

Dad shaves with an electric razor he just got for his birthday while his BlackBerry beeps on the granite counter; mom takes eggs from the fridge and chops onions and peppers for the omelette she's cooking; the little girl is already wearing a fancy hairclip and necklace although her school concert is still hours away; and first her parents must drive her young brother to hospital for a fresh x-ray on the arm he broke in a nasty fall a week ago.

We could describe a whole day in the life of this family; or a week, or a year. Already, we can see a common element in their lives, an element none will shed if they live to be a hundred. It

is their dependence, their utter, inescapable reliance, on metals and minerals that smart men and women wrestle from the earth and turn into objects of utility, often beauty. Dad's electric razor and electronic gadgets, mom's stainless steel kitchen appliances, the girl's pretty ornaments, the family car and the hospital x-ray machine all derive from mineral exploration. Almost everything they touch has some link to mined metals or minerals, including food grown with help of fertilizers, tilled by mechanized equipment and transported to markets by road, rail or ship.

To borrow from philosopher Thomas Hobbes: Without the fruits of mining our lives would be "…nasty, brutish and short…," truly barren and unproductive.

AME BC

Early prospectors with their gold pans.

Even now in the early 21st century, the Tahltan are still chipping away at the mountain to understand its past secrets. Vera Asp, Tahltan band member and archaeologist, studies the use of obsidian by her ancestors. And other scientists — following in the footsteps of GSC researchers Jack Souther and Catherine Hickson — continue to study the Mount Edziza volcanic complex as one of the largest areas of young volcanic activity in Canada.

❧

The desire to own metal objects is persistent and universal. Spanish explorer Juan Perez discovered just that when he landed at Nootka Sound on the Pacific Coast in 1774 as part of an expedition to explore for new trade routes and investigate rumoured incursions by Russian fur-traders. The commander of the *Santiago* had brought along iron knives to trade with local Aboriginal tribes for furs and carved boxes, but was surprised to discover they had iron already! A friar traveling with Perez wrote: "We were interested also to see that the women wear rings on their fingers and bracelets of iron and copper …"

In a 1938 paper, Thomas A. Rickard, who wrote extensively on the history of mining, quotes John Meares (at Nootka in 1788): "The pure malleable lumps of copper ore seen in the possession of the natives, convince us that there are mines of this metal in the vicinity of this part of the Western coast … We had also occasionally seen necklaces and a sort of bracelet worn on the wrist,

which were of the purest [copper] ore, and to all appearances had never been in the possession of a European." Rickard himself writes: "The Tsimshian Indians, on the Skeena River, in northern British Columbia, have a tradition of fire that fell from heaven and was transformed into copper. This suggests the finding of copper in nugget form, like a drop of molten metal from the sky."

This "native copper," one of the few metallic elements to occur in uncombined form as a natural mineral, would be fashioned, among other things, into copper shields, which British Columbia's early First Nations esteemed.

As for the iron, several possible origins have been suggested. Rickard writes: "We have good reason to infer that the indigenes on this northwestern coast made their first acquaintance with iron, as the South Sea Islanders did, by means of drift-wood, brought by the oceanic winds and currents, both moving persistently eastward from the Asiatic shore to the American mainland." He provides instances of metal-studded flotsam washed ashore from wrecked vessels.

Iron may have come from Russian traders in exchange for prized sea-otter pelts. And there is significant evidence to support that the natives of Canada's West Coast were visited and traded with the huge Chinese treasure fleets of Admiral Zheng He of the early 1400s (before Columbus!) and perhaps much earlier.

But evidence also suggests that some tribes were mining native copper and other metals for tools and artifacts — and trading such items far and wide — long before the Europeans arrived. They were truly Canada's "First Miners."

Gold and coal

The discovery of minerals and metals intensified with the arrival of Europeans in greater numbers.

Scots botanist, David Douglas, after whom the Douglas fir is named, is said to have made the first discovery of gold by a European in British Columbia. While on an expedition under the auspices of the Hudson's Bay Company (HBC) in the summer of 1833 he apparently found enough gold on the shores of Okanagan Lake to make a seal. Douglas roamed the Pacific Coast, seeking specimens for Britain's Royal Horticultural Society.

Simon Winchester notes in *A Crack in the Edge of the World*, that Douglas met an early death in Hawaii. He fell into a hole and was gored by a bull that had fallen in first.

A few years later, a momentous discovery was made on Vancouver Island: Coal. The native people around Port Hardy, on the island's northeast coast, already knew about it. They told Dr. William Tolmie, a young surgeon working for the Hudson's Bay

Company. (One story tells of a group of men who were amused to see a local blacksmith using coal imported all the way from Wales, when they knew there were mountains of the stuff nearby.) Tolmie told his employers about the coal, and HBC sent its steamer *Beaver* to check the report.

It took some years after *Beaver's* visit but what they found persuaded the company to begin mining the coal. That was the small beginning of what has been described as "...the oldest established and most important industry of Vancouver Island...." HBC carried on intermittent mining for several years and then abandoned the project. Newly-arrived Scot Robert Dunsmuir revived mining at Nanaimo in 1851; it has continued, off and on, ever since. The Dunsmuir family – whose own background was in coal mining in Scotland – would come to dominate the industry for many years.

Gold was back in the spotlight by 1849, when the discovery of gold nuggets in California led to a mass influx of people from others states, Europe, Australia and Asia. The big attraction for the thousands of newcomers was that gold was "free for the taking" under a claim-staking system. Claim-jumpers were treated with the same disdain as bandits.

Interest in gold spread to other areas in the West including Fort Victoria following an 1850 government dispatch to London that made note of a "...very rich specimen of gold ore said to have been brought [to HBC] by the Indians of Queen Charlotte Islands...." HBC, which then controlled the colony of Vancouver Island, sent one of its vessels, the *Una*, on an expedition to the island chain in 1851. Historic reports state that about 60 ounces of gold was obtained, mainly by barter, but also note that the natives "soon got an exaggerated idea of its value." Reports that one native had demanded "...1,500 blankets for a 21-ounce lump of nearly pure gold..." may have been embellished, but added to interest in the region. News of the gold find spread, despite HBC's efforts to keep it under wraps.

In 1852, several boatloads of American miners landed in the islands intent on finding the mother lode, but the Haida were hostile. Tensions between the Haida and the Americans escalated to the point where James Douglas, Governor of Vancouver Island, sent in a gunboat to assert British sovereignty and the rights of the Crown to all precious metals. He also took the first steps toward government regulation of miners and mining.

The mini-rush to the Charlottes was largely over by the time gold was discovered on the Pend d'Oreille River, a tributary of the Columbia, near present-day Trail in 1855. Then, in 1857, it was discovered on the Thompson River, and miners began to come in from Washington and Oregon. In 1858 it was found along the Fraser River, which led to a mass outbreak of gold fever fueled by bullish newspaper reports. An estimated 25,000 gold-seekers, mostly Americans, including experienced miners from California, headed for the Fraser River by sea through Victoria, or by trekking overland along an old trail to the Okanagan.

On August 2, 1858 Governor Douglas – alarmed by all those Yankees – proclaimed that the British

Gold Nuggets

In the British Columbia's gold rushes, some really struck it rich. Nuggets of astonishing size were discovered.

An all-gold nugget of about 60 ounces, worth $800, was found at Dease Creek in 1875. Imagine the celebrations at McDame Creek in 1877, when the largest known nugget in the province was found, weighing 72 ounces with a value of $1,300 at the time. In mid-August 2011, the McDame Creek nugget might have commanded a price exceeding $131,000. (On August 19, 2011, gold was selling at $1,824 per troy ounce).

A quartz and gold nugget, found on Spruce Creek in 1899, weighed 85 ounces; and in 1901 one weighing 36.6 ounces was found. In 1931 one weighing 73 ounces and valued at $1,200 was found on Birch Creek. Germansen Creek in 1935 yielded a nugget of about 24 ounces. In 1937, a nugget weighing 52.7 ounces was found on a tributary of Wheaton (Boulder) Creek. One weighing 46.25 ounces was discovered on Squaw Creek. A nugget valued at $900 was found

Columbia mainland to be a British colony, soon to be united with the Colony of Vancouver Island. Gold had created a province.

An historical sidelight: In 1858 a man named Alfred Waddington arrived in the Fraser River area, lured by its gold potential. He thought there was still much gold to be found on and around the river, even though miners were beginning to abandon what they thought were worked-out claims. Waddington produced a book called *The Fraser Mines Vindicated*. We mention it because this was the first book published in British Columbia.

A little book published 100 years later, entitled *Mining in Focus*, by the late Bruce Ramsey, is subtitled *An Illustrated History of Mining in British Columbia*. (See Mining in Focus, page 143). In it, Ramsey writes that many Chinese immigrants "…moved to the Cariboo to become miners or set up businesses such as laundries and restaurants. An estimated 6,000 to 7,000 Chinese immigrants had come to B.C.…." Gold was changing the province's ethnic makeup.

The Cariboo Gold Rush

There was another rush in 1859 when Peter Curran Dunlevy discovered gold at Little Horsefly Creek in the Cariboo.

Then there was the discovery of placer gold deposits in the Cariboo in 1860 and, that same year, yet more gold was found in the Similkameen district, near Princeton, and on the Stikine River the year after. That latter led to the establishment of what was called "Stikeen Territory." HBC authority was taken away, and Douglas took over as administrator. In 1863 the territory was absorbed into British Columbia.

As discovery followed discovery it is no exaggeration to say that gold – or more precisely the quest for gold – led to creation of the province and its early growth.

The Cariboo Gold Rush actually started in 1860 when placer miners discovered the south end of

the extensive goldfield. The major producing creeks to the north were all discovered the following year. Initial mining was in shallow deposits but within a year it had extended to depths of 20 metres. Production peaked in 1863 and has continued intermittently to the present day. Lode gold deposits were found early in the gold rush but were not viable until cyanide treatment became available much later.

We must mention the Douglas Trail, built from Fort Douglas at the north end of Harrison Lake to the Interior in 1859 at the command of Governor Douglas. Three years later demand for a better route would lead to the construction of the Cariboo Trail, which would stretch 650 kilometres through the Fraser Canyon from Yale to Barkerville to provide a wagon route to the Rock Creek goldfields. The Alexandra Bridge was built across the Fraser – the first bridge across that river. To the east, in 1865 the 720-kilometre Dewdney Trail from Hope to Wild Horse Creek in the east Kootenays would open, again to facilitate passage to and from the gold fields. Now gold was changing the map.

---

on Lockie (Boulder) Creek in 1887; another weighing 32 ounces was found about five miles up the Bridge River. The largest recorded nugget from the Cariboo was found in 1864 on Butcher Bench, Lightning Creek and weighed 30.1 ounces. Wild Horse River yielded a nugget weighing 37 ounces.

Imagine what such a sum would buy in the nineteenth century. Here are a couple of random examples of

prices then. In early-1858, at the start of the Fraser River gold rush, passage by ship from San Francisco to Victoria cost $15. Soon, as gold fever struck, the trip cost many times that. In Victoria, immediately before the gold rush, the land office was selling lots for $50 in the most desirable part of town. Speculators quickly pushed the price up to $5,000. One lot was flipped in three days from $5,000 to $6,200.

Bricks and nuggets from Atlin, B.C. ca. 1901

"The wagon road through the [Fraser River] canyon," Ramsey wrote, "was to remain the sole economic lifeline to the Interior until the Canadian Pacific Railway was built. Even today it is a crucial economic link for the province. Once it was built the prices of all goods dropped radically, and more importantly it meant that now families with women and children rode into the Cariboo to join in the gold rush and the development of the province." Gold was changing our social structure.

∽

By 1874, British Columbia had its first mines minister. He was John Ash and on March 8 he submitted his first report: "Productive mining in B.C. is, at the present time, restricted to mining for gold in many widely separated districts of the province; and to mining for bituminous coal, which is confined to Nanaimo and its immediate vicinity. The indications of the existence of other metals and minerals of great economic value are frequent throughout the country."

"The number of miners employed in B.C.," Ash went on, "is estimated. . . [at] Whites 2,248; Chinese 620," and, he added: "With regard to the actual annual yield of gold, as this is the first time that any attempt has been made in the history of the province to collect mining statistics, numerous obstacles have prevented full information being obtained, foremost among which is the disinclination on the part of the miner, both white and Chinese, to furnish information which might

The Klondike Gold Rush

The stampede to the Klondike was the last great placer gold rush of North America

The gold discovery that sparked the excitement was made on Rabbit Creek, a tributary of the Yukon River, in the summer of 1896 by George Carmack, the son of an American forty-niner; his Tagish Indian partners, "Skookum" Jim Mason and Dawson (or "Tagish") Charlie; and Nova Scotia prospector Robert Henderson. As reports of "…raw gold lying thick…" in Yukon creeks and rivers spread, almost 100,000 fortune-seekers from across North America and around the world headed for the remote northern territory. Only about one-third of them completed the arduous journey and only a few thousand found gold.

At the peak of the stampede, Dawson City was home to more than 30,000 residents. By the turn of the century, the population had dropped to a few thousand hardy souls. But the Klondike gold rush and its predecessors in B.C. created wealth that helped build the territory and province while also laying the foundation for the modern mining industry.

Anyone who searches for gold will find Ernest Ingersoll's book Gold Fields of the Klondike *a fascinating read. It was originally published in 1897 as* Gold Fields of the Klondike *and the* Wonders of Alaska, *and brought out in 1981 in an abridged edition (with the shorter title) by a Langley publisher named Mr. Paperback. Its 128 illustrated pages are packed with information aimed at gold seekers headed for the Klondike, which, in this case, took in Yukon and Alaska. One contemporary reviewer described it as "…a masterly and fascinating description of the newly-discovered gold mines, how they were found, how worked, what fortunes have been made, the extent and richness of the gold fields, how to get there, outfit required, climate, the natives…." It was written while the Klondike gold rush was happening, so it is lively and immediate, also very well written.*

Among the interesting facts: Some native porters nonchalantly carried weights of well over 100 pounds; one native man, hired by a music-loving gold-seeker, carried a 220-pound organ on his back over the mountains. Men would leave their belongings beside the trails that led to the goldfields, trails used by thousands of other men on the same quest. The goods could be left there to be retrieved later, their owner confident they would not be stolen.

Conditions were different once on the claims; your gold might be taken by "midnight miners."

Typical of the yarns that circulated amongst the gold camps, he tells the story of a man who used a moose

to pull his goods and what happened when a "tenderfoot" shot the moose, thinking the animal was wild.

Another wonderful tale is of a prospector, whose backpack contained explosives, who stopped for a rest unaware that the sun's rays were concentrated on his backpack. He smelled smoke, realized the pack was on fire, and tore it off to throw it aside as he ran. The explosives went off, and the miner crept back to discover that the blast had exposed a vein of gold that made him rich.

Canadian author Pierre Berton has also documented this fascinating period of mining history in his books: Klondike: The Last Great Gold Rush and The Klondike Quest.

AME BC

Klondike prospectors, ca. 1900s

be relied upon, the prevalent idea being that such information can only be sought with the view of imposing some new tax."

Gold was not the sole generator of rushes. In August of 1886, brothers Osner and Winslow Hall, from Colville, Washington found the Silver King copper-silver deposit, which started a rush to Toad Mountain and led to the birth of the city of Nelson.

The next quarter-century saw a steady succession of discoveries: Fairview, north of Oliver; Britannia, on Howe Sound near Vancouver; LeRoi, near Rossland; North Star, at Kimberley; the Sandon camp; Mother Lode, at Greenwood; Sullivan, at Kimberley; St. Eugene and North Star, at Moyie; Lenora and Tyee, near Duncan; and on and on. This feverish activity led to the realization that some sort of organization was needed to speak on behalf of the prospectors and developers, and keep track of what was going on.

In 1898, a Chamber of Mines was founded in Vancouver.

The group has long since disappeared and seems to have no connection to present-day AME BC. Thanks, however, to newspaper reports of the time, we do know its aims:

(a) *To promote and protect the mining interests and industries of British Columbia;*

(b) *To consider questions connected with the mining industry and promote public discussion thereon;*

(c) *To promote measures affecting the mining industry;*

(d) *To collect and circulate statistics and other information relating to the mining industry; and*

(e) *To communicate with and exchange information on mining matters with chambers of mines and government departments of mines in the Dominion of Canada and other countries.*

When a new Chamber of Mines, now AME BC, began in earnest in 1912 (originally as the Vancouver Mining Club), its aims were virtually identical and they have changed little since.

Impetus for the Vancouver-based organization was probably similar to that of the formation of the Nelson Prospectors Protective Association in 1921 (which became Chamber of Mines of Eastern B.C. in 1925). Part of its function was to both represent mining interests to government and to protect prospectors from sharp promoters and con men! An unknown hand wrote that its purpose was "…to act as a lobby of government legislation, advise on best handling of properties and help get capital to develop them; an organization whereby prospectors, often uneducated and unsophisticated (in those days) could protect themselves from unscrupulous promoters of those early days…."

Panorama view of the town of Hedley, B.C.

1912 to 1920

~ Inauguration Through World War One

In the Charles S. Ney Library at AME BC offices is a dog-eared, yellowing copy of the 1919 Year Book of the British Columbia Chamber of Mines. What makes this 98-page booklet valuable is its look at the early history of the Chamber, beginning with its inception. "On April 23, 1912," it reads, "the Vancouver Chamber of Mines came into existence, following a meeting held in the Council Chamber of the Vancouver City Hall. The real purpose of that gathering was to form what was called a Mining Men's Club."

One can see the reason for the Chamber's formation in 1912. For the preceding 10 years the annual value of minerals mined in the province had ranged from $17 million to $26 million. In 1912 it jumped to $32 million, with indications that this level of production would continue. (These were 1912 dollars. A typical wage in those days was $2.50 for a 10-hour day.) Gold was particularly strong: $6 million's worth was mined in B.C. in 1912. Copper was even stronger, with a value of more than $8.4 million.

Mining was not isolated in its success. The year 1912 was terrific for British Columbia business, particularly in Vancouver. The city was bursting with vitality. The World Building (what we now call the Old Sun Tower) was built, and so was a beautiful new CPR station and, in the West End, the Sylvia Apartments, later to become the famous hotel. Construction started on the Birks Building and the Vancouver Club. A brand-new newspaper, the *Vancouver Morning Sun*, appeared.

The first professional hockey game was played in Vancouver's Denman Arena that year. It was the first artificial ice rink in Canada and was reportedly the largest ice rink in the world. The Vancouver Millionaires defeated the New Westminster Royals 8 to 3.

The Pacific Great Eastern Railway was created and so was the municipality of West Vancouver. The first passenger on an airplane flight in B.C. was flown for six miles in eight minutes. The brave soul soared up to 600 feet while riding on a board strapped to the lower wing. Sharp and Thompson, architects, won the contract to design the new Point Grey campus for the University of British Columbia.

The formation of the Chamber of Mines was part of this exciting time. At the end of its initial meeting, presided over by Mayor James Findlay, the name of the group was fixed as The Vancouver Mining Club. The name of the organization would change many times . . . almost as many times as the addresses it would rack up. In fact, very shortly after the first meeting the name was changed to the Vancouver Mining Club and Bureau of Information. Then, in November 1912, it was changed yet again to the Vancouver Chamber of Mines. Three name changes in seven months. (Not until 1921 would it become the British Columbia Chamber of Mines.)

The biggest initial expense was rent. Vancouver's boosterish Progress Club offered the Chamber space in its own offices at 437 West Hastings at $150 a month.

The Year Book told its readers that the Chamber was a non-profit-earning institution, organized to foster mining in British Columbia. "The necessity of a reliable centre in Vancouver," it said, "where mining men can meet, exchange views, and discuss matters relating to mining, was recognized long ago. A big city is the natural mecca of the miner and prospector, the logical place for him to gravitate to in the hope of attracting capital either to buy or develop his prospect. When he arrives amongst the multitudes of the city, if no reliable centre exists to attract him, he is like a ship without a rudder; his time is spent hanging around hotels, infested with plausible parasites who fatten on such men…"

The Chamber's first president was Ontario-born Robert R. Hedley, 49, who had been manager of the Hall Smelter in Nelson, which had thrived for years – shipping its matte copper to Wales for refining – but which was now declining. (It closed in 1907, shortly after Hedley quit.) Hedley was well known and respected in the mining fraternity, and had grubstaked many prospectors. The town of Hedley, B.C. was named after him.

In addition to Hedley, the following officers were elected for one year: Vice president, A.B. (Arthur Bryant) Clabon; secretary-treasurer, H.B. Cameron; executive committee: B.A. Laselle, Leander Shaw, C.Scott Galloway, I.I. Rubinowitz, R.S. Lennie, R.D. Morkhill and W.H. Armstrong.

Laselle was a well-known name in the Cariboo mining community; a 1907 newspaper report identifies him as manager of the Bear Hydraulic Mining Company. In 1898 Shaw was associated with a silver mine at Ainsworth. Galloway was one of the owners of the town site of Greenwood (in fact, he named it).

Finances for the Chamber were tight. In fact, there were times when it seemed the vigorous little group was on the brink of collapse.

B.C. suffered the effects of a world-wide financial recession in 1913 that would last for two years. Construction, which had been red-hot for some years, slowed way down. Still, the Pacific Great Eastern Railway began, with hopes to open up the interior by establishing a line from North Vancouver to Prince George. The Pacific Highway opened as a gravel road running from the Fraser River to the U.S. border. The mining industry was hard hit.

Lytton W. Shatford, Member of the Provincial Parliament, was elected president for the second year of the Chamber's existence. One suspects the members chose a sitting politician in hopes that he would open a pipeline to the legislature. Shatford, born in Nova Scotia, had come to B.C. some years earlier with his brother Walter to open a general store in the gold mining town of Fairview, near Oliver. They also owned a shop in Hedley, so he knew the mining industry well. Shatford, 40 when he became president, had been elected as a Conservative in 1903.

Shatford and Hedley went to Victoria to ask for a grant of $2,500 to assist the Chamber in its work. They likely looked forward to a favourable response from Premier Sir Richard McBride, who had been the minister of mines (at age 30) in 1900, and again from 1903 on, when he was both minister of mines and premier. Surprisingly, McBride turned them down.

The Chamber was formally incorporated as the Vancouver Chamber of Mines in April of 1913 and, at the same time, relocated to the Fee Building at 570 Granville Street, its home for the next six years.

Despite the economic gloom, there was still much to be hopeful about. A study shows that by 1913 only one-ninth of B.C.'s land mass had been surveyed. At that time, a little over 200,000 hectares were closed to mineral exploration.

The town of Smithers was established this year as a railway division headquarters for the Grand Trunk Pacific Railway and soon became a supply centre for mining activity in the surrounding area.

The following year, the railway, with its eastern terminus in Portland, Maine, completed construction to Prince Rupert, with the last spike ceremony held one mile east of Fort Fraser on April 7. The Grand Trunk Pacific was not a success, its president and prime mover, Charles Melville Hayes, dying in the 1912 Titanic disaster, and would eventually be taken over by the CNR. The third CPR station—today the home of SkyTrain, the SeaBus and West Coast Express—opened on Cordova Street in Vancouver.

Two major events happened in 1914 that would have an effect on the industry, although not immediately. One was the opening of the Panama Canal on August 15; the other was the outbreak of World War One. On August 4, Britain declared war on Germany, and Canada, as a colony, automatically became a combatant.

In May 1914 the Chamber, which had briefly suspended its activities for lack of funds, sent a message to Premier McBride: "Unless the Government . . . can render substantial assistance

to the finances of the Chamber of Mines, it will be necessary to . . . close down this most useful rendezvous and bureau of mining information for mining men, capitalists and geologists. We feel that this course will be a most serious setback to the increasing activity of the mining industry of this rich mineral Province. The deficit is practically $2,000 up to date which is only a small item when compared with the useful work already done."

The premier promised that the government would give a grant of $1,000 provided the Chamber handed over its mineral exhibit to the Vancouver Board of Trade. The Board agreed, free of expense, to take charge of the mineral exhibits until such time as the Chamber renewed its activities. There was good news also from Vancouver City Hall: Alderman Walter Hepburn, the chairman of the Civic Finance Committee, recommended a grant of $1,000 to the Chamber.

The CPR had produced nearly a million tons of poor-quality coking coal in the previous few years at Hosmer (on the Crowsnest Highway just northeast of Fernie) and shipped it to the Consolidated Mining and Smelter (later known as Cominco) at Trail, but was forced to close the mine in 1914. Some locals say: "The ghostly ruins of CP's operations still lurk in the bush around Hosmer."

The Britannia Mine on Howe Sound was struck by tragedy in March 1915 when a rockslide at Jane Camp killed 54 people, and demolished many buildings. This slide was only one of a series of

UBC Archives

Dr. Reginald Brock

natural disasters to hit Britannia over the years. Mining operations began there at the Jane surface discovery in 1905; the mill was built five years later. (See Britannia, page 153).

The war had an early impact on the Chamber. Reginald Brock, elected president for the 1915 term, was "called to the colours" with the 72nd Seaforth Highlanders of Canada. He would serve in Palestine and Syria with the Egyptian Expeditionary Force as a geologist and special intelligence officer for the British Army.

His departure was a painful loss to the Chamber, not only because he was personally popular. Brock was one of Canada's leading geologists. He graduated from Queens with an MA in geology, was Director of the Geological Survey of Canada from 1907 to 1914 and one of the first four teachers hired by UBC president Frank Wesbrook. Brock had been named Dean of Applied Science but the war took him away before he could begin his duties. After hostilities ended, he was reinstated as dean and head of Department of Geology where he would serve until his death in 1935 in a plane crash at Alta Lake, while en route to Bralorne.

John Moncrief (Jake) Turnbull, 38, well known in the mining fraternity, was elected president in 1915 to replace Brock. A graduate of McGill, Turnbull had just arrived to begin what ultimately became a 30-year tenure as head of UBC's Mining Department. Mount Turnbull in the Kootenays is named for him and he was given the Chamber's Gold Pan Award in 1977. In 1979, aged 101, he paid his last visit to UBC and lectured on the province's mining history at the turn of the 20th century.

Not all the news was happy. Arthur Clabon, elected president of the Chamber for 1918, was killed later that year when he fell from a bluff above a creek near the northeast end of Mount Revelstoke National Park. The creek was subsequently named for him.

With the economic depression easing, in December the CPR opened its five-mile Connaught Tunnel beneath Mount Macdonald at Rogers Pass. The second Hotel Vancouver (a spectacular building that would have a short life) opened that year and industrial construction began on Granville Island.

The Chamber maintained persistent appeals to Victoria for financial support. The premier offered a grant of $2,500 "…provided the City of Vancouver and its businessmen contributed an equal sum or whatever balance was necessary to run an efficient Chamber." The city made a grant of $1,000.

By 1918 the Chamber was beginning to thrive and its influence on the mining industry began to make itself felt. More inquiries were received than in any previous year since the Chamber came into existence, and they came from all parts of Canada and from the United States, with a considerable number from Great Britain.

The Chamber's public lectures, which dealt with all phases of the mining industry proved popular. Twenty were delivered during the winter, all by UBC professors.

In October 1918, just days before the armistice ended the Great War slaughter, the mining industry was greatly affected by a terrible marine tragedy: the loss of at least 350 lives in the sinking of the CP vessel *Princess Sophia* in Lynn Canal, Alaska while en route from Skagway to Vancouver. The vessel, the last to head south before winter's bitter cold descended on the Klondike, was crowded with prospectors; mine workers and developers; river and lake boat crews; Alaskan pioneers of the Klondike gold rush days; women, children and babies; almost all were involved with mining in one way or another.

The disaster had a major impact on the development of the North. The loss of many experienced and seasoned prospectors and mining men deprived

the Klondike – and Canada – of much valuable expertise at a critical moment, just as the Chamber was getting established.

Not only was mining expertise lost, so was a significant part of the transportation and logistical knowledge.

World War I had created hard times in the North, drawing manpower and investment capital away. And, with the coming demobilization of the armed forces, there would be a need for economic development and jobs.

The *Sophia's* loss was the worst maritime disaster in B.C. history. The exact number on board is still uncertain. There were definitely 350 people who boarded *Sophia*; there could have been as many as 360.

B.C. mineral production in 1918 was valued at just over $41 million, a near all-time record. The increase was almost entirely from the products of the collieries: outputs of both coal and coke were away up. Coal was selling, on average, at about $5 per ton; coke at about $7 per ton.

War's end caused difficulties for mining in B.C. The Chamber's minutes note: "The transition between war conditions and peace leaves the metal market in an entirely unsettled state. At present copper has a nominal market price of 26 cents a pound, but since the armistice there has been no market and no buyers." That was expected to change: The return of peace would quicken the development of B.C.'s mineral resources, with many more prospectors and much more development money.

A 1918 crew from Sullivan Mine

Chamber President Frank Woodside holds a mineral specimen.

The 1920s

~ The Great War's Aftermath

Nineteen-twenty was memorable for the creation of Garibaldi Park and for the Chamber's reaction. The park opened officially August 13. The subject had been discussed earlier by the Chamber's executive. Aware that minerals had been found within the park boundaries, the Chamber told the mines minister it supported the park's creation but wanted mineral rights reserved for development.

The minutes make no mention of a minister's response but, if we skip ahead 20 years, we find an article about mining in Garibaldi by geologist Victor

Dolmage in the April 1940 issue of *The Miner.* He writes: "In recent months a number of mineral claims have been staked in the southern portion of Garibaldi Park, one or two of which have yielded a few tons of high grade gold ore." But Dolmage goes on to say, "There is in the Garibaldi Park Act a clause dealing specifically with …natural resources…" Stripped of legalese, the clause stated that ultimately the provincial cabinet controlled park activities.

Dolmage warned that limited guarantee of title might discourage large mining companies from developing properties in the park. Hence, prospectors would

likely have trouble obtaining mining capital. Dolmage suggested prospectors devote their efforts to vast areas outside the park that were equally promising and free from restrictions.

In 1922, the ruggedly beautiful Kokanee Glacier Provincial Park was set aside. Located north of Nelson, it is one of the oldest parks in the province. It sits mostly above 1,800 metres elevation and has three glaciers – Kokanee, Caribou and Woodbury – which feed over 30 lakes and are the headwaters of many creeks. Access to the park and most of the present-day hiking trails were developed from old mining and forest roads. Several mines paid quite well, but most were worked out after only a few years. "Today we can only marvel at the tenacity of those prospectors, who clung to steep rock faces throughout the park while trying to scratch a living from their mining claims," the Park's website remarks.

Canada was getting smaller in 1920: In October, the first plane to fly across the country arrived in Richmond from Halifax. It had taken 10 days to get here. On October 20, 1920 there was an event that cheered many: the end of Prohibition in B.C. – three years and 19 days after it began. Perhaps, in the modest offices of the Chamber of Mines, a few quiet glasses clinked in celebration.

In January 1921 it was decided the organization should change its name from the Vancouver Chamber of Mines to the British Columbia Chamber of Mines. Perhaps the Chamber's finances prompted the name change to one that indicated province-wide endeavour.

Meantime, the Chamber elected as president a man who would hold that post for an unprecedented six years. His name was Frank Woodside, and he would eventually come to be called "Mining's Grand Old Man." But that was years ahead, he was just 47 when he took the reins as president. He would be associated with the Chamber for more than 40 years.

By 1923, the Chamber was becoming known for the quality of its mineral displays. Its exhibit at the Northwest Mining Association Convention in Spokane, including samples from 250 mines from different parts of the province, won first prize for the finest mineral display. And some 98,000 people visited the Chamber's mineral exhibit at the New Westminster Exhibition.

There was excitement in B.C. in June 1924 with the visit from Britain of *HMS Hood*. She was the largest warship in the world and thousands converged to see her. In July, Chamber President Woodside presented samples of various ores being mined in British Columbia to Vice-Admiral Sir Frederick L. Field, commanding the visiting Special Naval Service Squadron. *Hood* would become tragically famous on May 24, 1941 when she was sunk by the German battleship *Bismarck*. Of her 1,418 crew, only three survived. Eight days later *Bismarck* would, herself, be sunk in a relentless British attack.

In 1924, M. Y. Williams, associate professor of paleontology and stratigraphy at UBC, began the collection that became the university's Geological Museum, now called the Pacific Museum of the Earth. The museum itself was founded by Reginald Brock (Chamber president in 1915), and had been included in the preliminary plans of the Applied Sciences Building (now the Geography Building) in 1923. The building was completed and the museum began in 1925.

Williams, a friend of the Chamber, had given talks to its members and the general public. In 1936, he would be appointed head of the Department of Geology and Geography, and would remain in that position until his retirement in 1950.

In 1924, an increase in the Chamber's activities led to a decision to raise the secretary's salary to $200 per month, generous at that time.

What has been described as the beginning of a new era for mining in B.C. occurred in 1925: A branch of the Chamber was established at Stewart and an American mining syndicate inaugurated fly-in exploration in northern B.C. and Yukon. Using Dease Lake as a base, an amphibious Vickers Viking IV aircraft flew prospectors to various sites. The aircraft was destroyed in September 1932 when a fuel line broke while airborne. The pilot, J. Scott Williams, landed in the Strait of Georgia and he and the occupants got out safely.

The minutes for 1925 that showed the Chamber was now in high gear; active, engaged, and connected with the community. A contribution of $1,000 was received from the Canadian National Railway, and it was reported a further $9,592

M. Y. Williams

had been collected from a special drive for funds. The Chamber's bank balance stood at $17,108. Vancouver Mayor Louis D. Taylor attended the executive meeting on January 14 and expressed his support for the Chamber's activities in encouraging mining development in the province.

At the request of A. H. Gerhardi, who controlled the Toric Mine, strong representations were made by the Chamber to the B.C. Minister of Mines to take action to re-open the Dolly Varden mine. An 18-mile narrow-gauge railway was built between 1917 and 1920 to haul silver ore from mine site to a waterside ore bunker on Alice Arm.

One of the matters dealt with in 1926 was the "Hope-Princeton Trail and proposed Road" which would connect with the coast. William Dornberg, a mine developer in the area, was reported to have already built 24 miles of road and he recommended that its completion should be investigated. Dornberg, from Spokane and well known in the silver-mining field, got his wish: The highway, which was mostly two lanes, was officially incorporated in 1932. It finally opened in 1949, mainly following a mid-19th century gold rush trail originally traced out by engineer Edgar Dewdney.

On the wall of the Association's offices on West Pender Street in Vancouver hangs a large relief map of British Columbia. It has hung on the wall of AME BC and its predecessors for more than 80 years, donated to the Chamber of Mines in 1927 by Major General F. A. Sutton.

To encourage young people's understanding of the importance of British Columbia's mineral resources, the Chamber organized a province-wide, high school essay competition on the subject. The first prize was $20, 2nd prize $10, and 3rd prize $5. (Remember, this is 1927. You could buy a man's suit; jacket, vest, and two pairs of pants, for $18.)

Harry N. Freeman, a coal mining engineer "…of vast experience in all departments of the industry and with all types of coal…." addressed the executive committee on coal production; methods of using it and its by-products; the distillation of oil from coal, shale, tar sands, sawdust etc., particularly in connection with an exhibit of a patented machine on display at the Chamber of Mines. He suggested a research bureau should be organized to investigate coals and encourage their greater use throughout the province.

It was Freeman who arranged 1927's mineral display at the Pacific National Exhibition at Hastings Park. The exhibit attracted many visitors, including the Prince of Wales and his brother Prince George, who expressed keen interest in the exhibit of British Columbia ore samples. The Prince of Wales would later become King Edward VIII (who abdicated); his brother Prince George became King George VI.

Also in 1927, high school graduate Tommy Elliott was taken on staff. He would be with the Chamber for his entire working life, and become one of the most influential voices in B.C. mining history. He was appointed Chamber secretary-manager in 1954 and

retired as manager in January 1975 although he remained an active participant on the mining scene for many years. Readers will encounter Elliott's name often in these pages.

The Chamber had no difficulty in attracting local publicity. Public lectures on mining at the Board of Trade Hall drew larger crowds than ever and the annual prospectors' training classes were well attended and considered to be one of the Chamber's most important activities. And hundreds of notices were mailed throughout the province alerting the public to the forthcoming Hastings Park Exhibition (Aug. 8 to 18, 1928) and asking for new mineral specimens and photographs of properties.

Attention was drawn to the interest that the Consolidated Mining & Smelting Co. was taking in locating deposits of potash-bearing minerals in B.C. A collection of four of these minerals had been sent to the Chamber for exhibit together with pamphlets describing their occurrence. "Potash" first appeared in the Chamber minutes in 1929; the second occurrence was not until 1960.

The Chamber was busy in 1929 seeking information about the properties of new mining companies listed in the *B.C. Gazette* and asking for ore samples. This information helped the Chamber answer an increasing volume of inquiries.

An important harbinger of future activity occurred Oct. 7, 1929, when Mr. S. Mitsuda, a mining engineer representing the Japanese mining and smelting company Mitsui Mining, visited the Chamber's mineral exhibit and information centre. He was given a representative collection of British Columbia minerals. Mitsuda was the first Japanese representative to visit the Chamber. Many more followed and Japan went on to become an important market for B.C. mineral products.

The Chamber and the industry it served grew in strength and stature during the Roaring Twenties, despite a slow start to the decade. By 1926, B.C. was Canada's leading silver producer, beating Ontario, which held that status for years, and the nation's largest producer of lead, copper and zinc.

The decade was a period of technical innovation at B.C. mines, notably Sullivan, owned by Consolidated Mining & Smelting (CM&S, later Cominco). The silver-lead-zinc mine was transformed by the introduction of differential froth flotation, a new processing method adapted to the ore by in-house research. (See Teck, page 242). CM&S benefitted from its early use of hydro-electric power, which allowed its inland, energy-intensive Trail smelter to be globally competitive.

During the early twentieth century, B.C.'s mining industry was becoming important by world standards. Garnet Basque, in *West Kootenay – The Pioneer Years*, notes that the Ymir Mine was the largest gold mine in the British Empire and the 80 stamp mill, built in 1897, was also the largest in the Empire.

B.C. had other star performers in the 1920s, including Britannia on Howe Sound, then the largest copper

mine in the British Empire; and Granby Mining's Anyox copper mine north of Prince Rupert.

A booming economy also contributed to the industry's growth. The value of B.C. mine production reached a high of $68.24 million in 1929, smashing the record set in 1926, with coal and building materials adding to the overall value.

Mining companies used their robust profits to acquire and develop mineral prospects across the province, which benefited prospectors, small companies and mining syndicates. Credit was easily available too for both businesses and consumers.

Trading on North American exchanges reached frenzied levels in the late 1920s, particularly on Wall Street, where million of Americans played the stock market. This was a time when the public could invest in exciting new technologies such as radio, telephone and power utilities, as well as banks and blue-chip companies for as little as 10 per cent down. As stock prices rose more people invested. But as prices peaked and fell the buying stopped abruptly, leading to a market crash in October. Indebted investors panicked and sold their stocks for whatever they could get.

By the end of 1929 stock values had dropped an estimated $15 billion or by 90 per cent. U.S. brokerages had lent an estimated $8.5 billion to investors, more than the total of U.S. currency circulating at the time. This crisis led to the mass failure of over-leveraged and poorly managed

businesses and banks. The contagion spread from Wall Street to financial centres in the Western World, including Toronto, Montreal and Vancouver. Capital dried up almost overnight, leaving many companies struggling for survival.

The economic slump was so swift and severe that desperate governments imposed tariffs and regulations to protect the industries underpinning their economies, which in turn led to a drastic decline in foreign trade. Millions of people were thrown out of work as companies closed their doors and governments slashed spending.

B.C.'s mining industry faced an uncertain future as it ushered in the 1930s, as did the Chamber of Mines. Tough times lay ahead for everyone.

AME BC/photographer: Artray Limited Photographers

Tommy Elliott

Harry Warren

The Chamber of Mines at the Canada Pacific Exhibition in 1938

The 1930s

~ The Great Depression

Victor Dolmage, elected president in 1930, was faced with the early fall-out of the 1929 stock market crash, which devastated mining companies. For example, Newmont Mining Company was one of the world's leading copper producers, earning $32 per share in 1927. Its stock, which reached a peak price in 1929 of $236, was selling for only $3.87 in 1932.

With one eye over his shoulder, Dolmage dealt with management issues by appointing five committees: Finance; Exhibitions and Conventions; Lectures; Legal and Legislative; and Subscriptions and Membership.

The Chamber once again stated its opposition to placing restrictions on prospecting for minerals in park areas and came out strongly against the suggestion of a park reserve between Pitt Lake and Alouette Lake.

In February 1931, with the recession escalating into the Great Depression, the Chamber sought federal financial assistance for prospectors. For the next few years the Chamber received numerous inquiries regarding placer and lode gold deposits. As many individuals were interested in trying to survive the depression by placer mining, the Chamber published a booklet, *Elementary Methods of Placer Mining*.

In 1932, the Great Depression really began to work its way into the Chamber's deliberations. A threat of the loss of its annual grant from the provincial government was in the air, along with a reduced grant from the City of Vancouver. The Chamber had to raise temporary operating funds from merchants and business firms in Vancouver, as well as from individual membership fees of $5 per year.

At the Chamber's request, unemployed men were allowed to obtain a government certificate to stake a placer claim free of charge. "Many of these men are working the gravels along gold bearing streams in an endeavour to earn a living," it was noted. The Chamber was doing everything possible to assist these healthy, young men to find a useful occupation. It was estimated 150 men, many of them from the Prairie Provinces, had come calling.

Professor Harry. V. Warren took over the Chamber's annual Prospector's Training classes in the fall of 1932. Warren would continue to lecture at the school on mineralogy, geochemistry and other subjects until 1981.

Many businessmen assisted in financing the activities of placer and lode gold prospectors. This activity helped in reducing the number of unemployed living in Vancouver "and is creating a market for a variety of manufactured goods, thereby helping improve the overall economy," the Chamber minutes observed.

To aid the novice in outfitting when preparing to go into the hills, the Chamber compiled a free list of equipment and supplies necessary for a 90-day prospecting trip. It advised inexperienced men about the mining tools, camping equipment, food, cooking utensils, clothing and personal effects they would require.

A resolution sent to the Chamber by Andrew Shilland of New Denver recommended that the provincial government should "vest all mining recorders with discretionary power to exempt assessment work on mineral claims, providing ... that the recorder is satisfied that the applicant for exemption was unable to bear the cost of such work." Shilland reported that not a single mine was working in the whole of the Slocan, and that men once employed in mining were earning a bare existence working on government wagon roads.

A letter from the Chamber of Commerce at Port Arthur (now Thunder Bay), Ontario invited the Chamber to join them in urging Canadian railways to charge unemployed prospectors a reduced rate of one and one-half cents per mile of travel during 1933.

B.C. Minister of Mines W. A. McKenzie announced plans to establish placer mining training camps throughout the province. Unemployed men would be allowed to attend the camps without charge. The government also announced that *bona fide* prospectors on relief in B.C. would be given two months' supplies in advance "...to enable them to engage in their regular calling and lighten relief rolls to that extent." The Alberta Relief Commission was reported to be planning the placement of unemployed men in B.C. placer gold areas, "under government care."

Free mining lectures, by government geologists and others, at Victory Hall, 535 Homer Street, Vancouver were particularly successful, with attendance often exceeding 500 people.

During 1933 and 1934, much of the Chamber's efforts focused on gold and concentrated on prospecting, production and sales. The Chamber submitted recommendations to government regarding proposed changes to the "Mineral" and "Placer" Acts as well as to the "Security Fraud Prevention" Act. By this time, an estimated 12,000 people were using the Chamber's services each year.

Cariboo Gold Quartz Mining Co., Ltd. principals with first two gold bricks poured at their pilot mill in Barkerville; L to R: O.H. Solibakke, J.R.V. Dunlop, Fred M. Wells; W. B. Burnett.

Frank Woodside and others at the Chamber of Mines exhibit at the PNE, ca. 1930s

At the end of 1933, Provincial Mineralogist John D. Galoway published the following somber evaluation of British Columbia's mining industry:

"After three years of depression, mineral production in 1933 was down to $28 million. With the dawn of the New Year it is but natural that we should scan the horizon in an endeavour to determine the promise of the future of our mineral industry. The world is sick industrially and until definite remedial measures for trade and finance are amplified more than at present, the mineral industry of the world must mark time. Three years of depression have served to emphasize the interdependence of the world and the fact that no real prosperity can come until all countries share in it. British Columbia is almost entirely dependent on outside markets to dispose of her production of silver, copper, lead and zinc. In this respect, increased international trade is essential for our mining industry."

Fortune smiled on gold mining companies in February 1934 when President Franklin Roosevelt persuaded the U.S. Congress to increase the gold price to $35 from the previously fixed $20.67 an ounce. AME BC Past President Bob Cathro discussed Roosevelt's decision and its effects in a 2010 article on the history of economic geology in the CIM Magazine. The following is adapted from Cathro's article:

The President's decision was certainly not made to help struggling mining companies; it was the final step in a desperate strategy that began a year earlier, immediately after his inauguration. The United States was on the gold standard, under which both banks and the government guaranteed to redeem their notes and deposit liabilities at $20.67 per ounce. The United Kingdom had abandoned the gold standard in September 1931, near the start of the Depression. The U.S. was forced to do the same when a banking crisis developed just as President Herbert Hoover's term was ending. Both foreign and domestic depositors and note-holders were rushing to cash in their dollars for gold, resulting in a run on the U.S. banks. The fear was that many banks would fail because there was insufficient gold to cover demand and the U.S. gold reserves would be depleted. Speculation that the U.S. might end the gold standard worsened the crisis as people rushed to obtain gold while they could.

The gold standard had to be abandoned quickly. Roosevelt took office on March 4, 1933, and the process began three days later. New laws were passed hurriedly to give the federal government the right to purchase all the gold in private hands at the old price and become the sole owner of gold in the U.S.

At the beginning of February 1934, the U.S. established the new $35 price. This stabilized the banking system by creating a large inflow of gold into the country. The Treasury made a huge profit (almost $3 billion) by purchasing gold at $20.67 prior to its revaluation to $35. Next, the U.S. re-adopted a limited form of the gold standard. From January 31, 1934 to August 15, 1971, the Treasury purchased gold from all sellers at $34.9125, but sold gold only to foreign monetary authorities and licensed industrial users at $36.0875.

Lewis Green, in his book *The Great Years – Gold Mining in the Bridge River* Valley paid eloquent tribute to the role that gold played in British Columbia's troubled mining sector during the Dirty Thirties. He wrote:

"Gold mining was one of a few industries, legal or otherwise, that boomed throughout the Great Depression, its salvation an unlimited demand for a product selling at a fixed price. In contrast, British Columbia's base metal mines, victims of falling prices and poor demand, struggled to survive with the value of their 1932 production falling to less than a third the 1929 figure. Gold's lure drew the venturesome to remote mining camps, some in hopes of a job and others on the lookout for business opportunities or the chance to prospect for their own motherlode."

Dr. W. B. Burnett was elected Chamber president in 1935 and served until 1940. A Vancouver physician, Burnett was president of the Cariboo Gold Quartz Mining Co. He had been one of the shrewd backers of prospector Fred Wells, who against almost all expectations had found a motherlode in 1930 near the town that now bears his name. The town of Wells also provided an example of how the Depression affected Newmont Mining Corporation. The company successfully transformed itself from a copper giant into a major gold company by acquiring control of the main lode mines in California's Mother Lode district. Newmont also acquired control of six small gold mines in Canada including the Island Mountain deposit at Wells

in 1932 from C. J. Seymour Baker. The company operated the mine from 1934 until 1954.

Burnett immediately became involved in plans for a Mining Week from July 20 to 25, 1936. This was a year of tremendous celebration for the City of Vancouver: its Golden Jubilee. Chamber minutes describe Mining Week as "…one of the most elaborate and interesting attractions…" of the celebration. The Chamber clearly saw the Jubilee as an opportunity for publicizing and strengthening the industry. The price tag was large, with a budget set at $4,500. Since mining had played a vital role in building up the City of Vancouver, other organizations were invited to help. One highlight was a Gold Rush Parade through the city centre. Tommy Elliott wrote: "It was a fascinating sight to see the team of oxen, stagecoaches and pack trains, being driven down Georgia Street past the old Medical Dental Building!"

Much of the activity took place in Stanley Park. Entertainment included an operating placer mining exhibit set up near Lumberman's Arch, a rock drilling competition between teams from different mining camps and an out-door dance with old-time music. An elaborate Cariboo Gold Rush display included: A fully-equipped pack train of 10 horses; a bull-team with four yoke of oxen with driver and swamper; a 10 horse jerk line freight outfit; six horse stage outfit with old-time Cariboo coach and deluxe Dufferin Coach; and many relics of the early days. Teams also competed in mine rescue demonstrations. There was an exhibition of British Columbia minerals with special emphasis

on gold ores. Professor J. M. Turnbull arranged an open house at the UBC mining department. Major D. R. MacLaren of Canadian Airways demonstrated the use of the aeroplane for transporting equipment into mines.

The minutes record: "Mining Jubilee Display was one of the most interesting and time-consuming efforts ever arranged by the Chamber and its many friends. Frank Woodside and his staff had an exceptionally busy year."

The Chamber continued its efforts to help men become prospectors and placer miners during this period. During the late-thirties, vigorous opposition was raised against several naive and ill-judged amendments to existing mining legislation, resulting in their being set aside. The most objectionable amendment called for the blazing of four lines around the boundaries of, and placing a post at the corner, of each claim. Chamber minutes note: "It is the general opinion among prospectors and practical mining men that in many of the rugged mountain areas of British Columbia, it is almost impossible to blaze four straight lines around the boundary of a mineral claim."

In 1933, international news turned ominous. In January, German President Paul von Hindenburg appointed Nazi leader Adolph Hitler as Chancellor; in March, the Reichstag made Hitler dictator; in April, the Gestapo was established; in May, Hitler banned trade unions while the Nazis staged massive book burnings and banned all non-Nazi parties; in October, physicist Albert Einstein fled to the U.S.

Elliott's minutes note: "Another of British Columbia's old-timers recently passed away [in 1933] with the death of R. D. "Bob" Henderson, who was the first man to discover gold in Yukon during the Spring of 1896." Henderson certainly played a major role in finding the huge lode that ignited the Klondike rush, yet prospectors, historians and government officials have long disputed who made the first discovery. In 1999, the Canadian Mining Hall of Fame gave Henderson shared credit with American George Carmack and local natives "Skookum" Jim Mason and Dawson "Tagish" Charlie.

But not all the year's news was depressing. The movie *King Kong* premiered at Radio City Music Hall; Karl Jansky detected radio waves from the centre of the Milky Way galaxy, triggering radio astronomy; Wiley Post became the first person to fly solo around the world in 7 days, 18 hours and 45 minutes; Americans repealed Prohibition and the board game *Monopoly* was invented.

In 1934, Canada's Governor General, the splendidly named Vere Brabazon Ponsonby, 9th Earl of Bessborough, visited Vancouver. The Chamber's minutes record that during his visit, Major D. R. MacLaren of Canadian Airways presented to "His Excellency," on the Chamber's behalf, "…an attractive collection of British Columbia gold ores…" that the Chamber had prepared. What happened to the gift, the minutes do not state.

Lord Bessborough was the only prominent British businessman ever to be Canadian Governor General. Despite his aristocratic background, he had a solid mining connection as a former deputy chairman of De Beers. Born into the Irish peerage and trained as a lawyer, he was a soldier, Member of Parliament in Westminster and subsequently sat in the House of Lords. In Canada, he inaugurated the Dominion Drama Festival. As a gesture of sympathy with Canadians at the height of the Great Depression, Lord Bessborough took a 10 per cent pay cut. When the Dominion Women's Amateur Hockey Association was founded in 1933, Lady Bessborough donated a championship trophy.

In 1935, much attention was paid to silver. Large purchases by the American government were reported to be mainly responsible for rapid worldwide price increases to 75 cents an ounce. In Canada, the first issue of the new silver dollars had been immediately absorbed, apparently held as souvenirs. A Chamber campaign to boost their distribution met with considerable success. The minutes note that contact was made with W. F. Kennedy, head of the B.C. Liquor Control Board; John M. Watson, president of the Retail Merchants' Association; A. S. Rupert of Safeway Stores; W. R. Dowrey of the Piggly Wiggly Stores and the heads of large department stores, urging them to use silver dollars when giving change. The Chamber also wrote to all chamber branches as well as up-country boards of trade suggesting they take charge of the campaign in their respective districts. "It was felt that this campaign would help to establish silver as a medium of exchange and bring substantial benefit to the silver mining industry."

An estimated 100,000 people visited the Chamber's 1935 mineral exhibit at the Pacific National Exhibition at Hastings Park. It was believed the exhibit encouraged the flow of much foreign capital into local mining ventures.

Chamber president Burnett attended a special dinner of the West Coast Mineral Association in Seattle during Mining Institute Week along with mining men from all parts of the Pacific Northwest. The president noted that in the early gold rush days, Seattle had been the distributing centre for mining supplies; Vancouver was rapidly taking over that enviable position.

1937 was a year of bridges. Construction began on the Lions Gate, then the longest suspension bridge in the British Empire. In San Francisco, the Golden Gate was officially opened. In November, the Pattullo Bridge across the Fraser River also opened to traffic. Premier Duff Pattullo wielded a welder's torch to cut a metal chain across the roadway. Several services had been installed beneath the bridge deck, the heaviest being water mains for the municipalities to the south. A crossing toll of 25 cents on the $4 million bridge would not be removed until 1952.

Ottawa awarded a contract for eleven Blackburn Shark warplanes to be built by Boeing at Coal Harbour for the Royal Canadian Air Force. Britain had built 238 Sharks for the Royal Navy. They served on aircraft carriers and as catapult seaplanes on battleships. In response to increased tensions in Europe, the RCAF created two torpedo-bomber squadrons. Some planes were built in England, the remainder in Vancouver. The B.C.-built aircraft had enclosed canopies and were equipped with floats.

The public's interest in mining remained keen. The Chamber arranged a show of pictures of prominent British Columbia mining camps, including Zeballos, Cariboo, Bridge River, Hedley, Portland Canal, Nelson and Slocan, taken by Howard T. Mitchell, editor of the *Financial News & Merchantile Review*. An estimated 1,100 people turned up at Victory Hall; 400 were turned away owing to lack of seating.

In October 1938, the first Canadian airmail service between Vancouver, Winnipeg and waypoints was inaugurated. The Chamber marked the occasion by sending letters with best wishes to chambers of mines in other provinces.

The Dirty Thirties ended for Canada with its declaration of war on Germany in September 1939. Tumultuous years lay ahead.

Jubliee Cariboo Gold Rush Parade of 1936

End of shift at Burrard Shipyards, Vancouver, 1944

The 1940s

~ *World War Two*

Canada declared war on Germany in September 1939, precipitated, as was Britain's declaration days earlier, by the Nazi invasion of Poland. The country hurriedly prepared for hostilities. Vancouver, with its huge harbour, seemed an especially inviting target for enemy attack. Gun emplacements, set up during the First World War above Siwash Rock in Stanley Park, were quickly put back into service to protect the port. Engineers built new emplacements with six-inch guns at the First Narrows and at Point Grey. More guns were set up on the North Shore west of the Lions Gate Bridge to guard the harbour

entrance. Searchlights were installed to illuminate potential targets.

With the onset of war the Royal Canadian Navy took over the port's management. The Navy set up a controlled zone inside English Bay. Ships approaching the port had to slow and signal their identity with flags to two patrol craft. Suspect ships were ordered to anchor for inspection within range of Stanley Park's guns. Another examination station was established at Steveston to guard against attack up the Fraser River.

As the war progressed, the Vancouver's shipyards played a crucial role in the Allies' war effort. The

demand for shipping was huge, with thousands of tons lost to enemy action in the early war years. To fill government orders for ships, Burrard Dry Dock expanded into two facilities, Burrard North and Burrard South, with some 11,000 workers. West Coast Shipbuilders hired more than 5,000 workers for its yards on False Creek. Many of the shipyard workers were women; at the peak of construction 1,495 women were employed at the various yards.

All this activity had a serious impact on mining. It was reported in 1941 that the province suffered from a severe shortage of experienced miners, possibly numbering 1,000, as many men quit their jobs to find higher paid work in the shipyards and other industries.

War work was a great magnet that attracted workingmen to the Pacific coast from Eastern Canada, the prairies and the B.C. Interior. The men sought employment in the shipyards, in aircraft construction industries and in new factories, manufacturing aluminum castings for aircraft and boilers, winches and windlasses for naval vessels. At peak production, the shipyards in Victoria and Vancouver hired more than 30,000 workers. In the aircraft plants near Vancouver International Airport there was immense activity, even at nighttime.

War production spread throughout the province. Huge Sitka spruce trees were logged in the Queen Charlottes to make light wooden frames for Mosquito bombers. Prospectors searched in the hills for bismuth, cadmium, mercury and other rare and precious metals. CM& S converted its fertilizer plant to production of munitions grade ammonium nitrate and other chemicals for the production of war materiel. By 1942, the smelter was turning out 700 tons of refined lead and 470 tons of refined zinc daily to aid the war effort. There was new interest in harnessing the rivers of B.C. for waterpower.

British Admiralty officials contacted the Chamber for information about magnetite iron ore, particularly deposits on Texada Island, for possible use as ballast in large maintenance ships being built in Vancouver. The Chamber's staff drew attention to samples of pure barite from a deposit located at Parsons, B.C., owned by the Summit Lime Co. of Lethbridge, Alberta. They told the officials this barite was chemically inert and would better suit their purpose. Later, a contract was awarded to Northern Construction Co. of Vancouver to mine and transport some 50,000-60,000 tons of the barite from Parsons to Vancouver for use as ballast.

The shipyards were not only engaged in new construction. They were also kept busy with ship repair and refitting. Unusual sights at Burrard Dry Dock were American aircraft carriers whose flight decks were being extended.

By war's end in 1945, West Coast shipyards had launched 255 of Canada's 354 10,000-ton cargo ships. The yards also launched 15 frigates, 10 corvettes, 22 minesweepers and three landing ships.

The sad internment of Japanese Canadians in the wake of Japan's attack on Pearl Harbour in December 1941 indirectly impacted the Chamber. Manager Frank Woodside reported in April 1942 that the Dominion government had taken over the entire grounds at Hastings Park in Vancouver to house Japanese fishermen and their families, before transferring them to Interior points. As a result, there would be no Pacific National Exhibition that year. At the request of the Hastings Park management, all of the ore samples in the park's Mining Building had been packed in boxes and stored elsewhere. Subsequently, Tommy Elliott noted: "Unfortunately …the mineral storage building was allowed to deteriorate into a very poor condition and the bulk of the ore samples were ultimately bulldozed into an area of low-lying ground. This was a great loss to the Chamber of Mines and the industry." [Hastings Park would remain under military control until 1946].

At the Chamber's annual meeting in 1941, W.H.S. McFarland, General Manager of the Yukon Consolidated Gold Corporation, described his company's gold dredging operations at Dawson in Yukon. The company's proved dredging reserve stood at approximately 89,000,000 cubic yards, containing gold at an estimated value of $41 million.

After a long and concerted effort by the Chamber, the federal government ruled that draglines for use in alluvial gold mining would be allowed duty-free entry to Canada since such equipment was not manufactured in the country. The Chamber believed that "a substantial number" of dragline dredge operators in the western part of the United States were prepared to move their units into Canada, mainly B.C. and Yukon, to work placer gold bearing gravels.

In its representations to Ottawa, the Chamber had argued Canada's need to produce more gold to assist the war effort and pay for other foreign expenditures. The federal government responded; gold miners were protected from the draft and gold mines had priority in supplies until the lend-lease agreement with the U.S. was signed and gold was no longer needed to purchase war materiel. The focus shifted to base metals production for the war effort.

Chamber minutes note: "During the years to follow, several of these dredging companies did move their equipment into western Canada, creating a substantial number of jobs mining placer gold, and providing a market for … locally manufactured goods and services. It was an exceedingly worthwhile effort. One of the large dredging companies built the initial road from the Alaska Highway, south of the McDame Creek area, opening up a section of the province that eventually produced the famous Cassiar Asbestos lode mine."

In January 1945, members decided to rename the association "The British Columbia & Yukon Chamber of Mines" and to open branches in Whitehorse and Dawson. The decision was based on the fact that the organization was so closely affiliated with the Yukon mining industry and so many of the large exploration companies active in Yukon maintained their exploration offices in Vancouver. In addition, many Yukon prospectors wintered in the city and had taken an active role in the affairs of the Vancouver organization.

At war's end, large-capital mining companies such as Kennecott Copper Corporation, American Metal Co. of Canada Ltd., New Jersey Zinc Co., Noranda Mines and Anaconda Copper Co. opened offices in Vancouver. The Chamber now served unofficially as an employment office for miners, muckers, geologists and engineers. By 1948, the increasing price for base metals (zinc 15.5 cents per pound; lead 21.5 cents per pound; copper 23.5 cents per pound and silver 76 cents per ounce) brought predictions of a base metal

boom. The Chamber proudly claimed that increased mining activity in western Canada was in no small way due to its efforts over the previous thirty years.

As ex-servicemen returned home, the Chamber worked hard to help them get back into the mining industry. A number took the Chamber's Prospecting Training School course and some 300 fully-trained prospectors were soon reported to be in the hills.

In 1948 Howard Firth, Secretary of the Dawson City branch of the Chamber, accompanied by Wilfrid

"Wop" May, of Canadian Pacific Airlines, visited the Chamber seeking support for the airline's request for improvements to the airports at Mayo and Dawson City. It was proposed to develop the airline's service with an extension to Fairbanks, Alaska. May said that a request had also been made to have mail flown from Fort St. John to Whitehorse and thence to Dawson City and Mayo. For Yukon to develop as a mining territory, speedier mail service would have to be provided. The Chamber endorsed the airline's efforts.

AME BC

Stripping muck from the dredging area at Yukon Consolidated Gold Corp. Ltd.

John W. Hogan worked as a summer student at a Yukon placer mine during this post-war period. This account of his experiences provides rare insight into the working lives of hardy northern miners.

My father was E. A. Hogan who was a Yukon councillor for the Klondike District (1912-1915). A Lake Hogan in the Peel River was named for him. He started working for Yukon Consolidated Gold Corporation (YCGC) in 1935. This led me to getting a summer job in the late forties.

So here we were, two university students happily heading for Dawson City to help pay for our studies. Our joy was stopped when we were told in Whitehorse that the field at Dawson was out (spring break-up, a weather phenomenon – not a Mexico trip). Since we were students, we did not have any cash. YCGC put us up for two weeks. The manager of the hotel gave us money to buy two beers every Friday. Our daily walks once led us to the base of a hill going up to the airport. Obviously this [hike] was a challenge and as we crested the top and started walking down the runway there were lights and sirens in the distance that did not bother us until we realized that they were coming at us. It was a military airport in those days. We were soundly reprimanded and booted out.

We were at last at Sulfur Creek (not my Dad's camp) and found out that our pay was $1.05 per hour –

minus $2.50 per day room and board. I had a much more superior job than my friend because I got paid an extra hour for walking four miles to my shift.

My job was running a monitor on the stripping phase of dredging. Gold placers were covered by gravel and muck in valley bottoms that were dissected to form V shapes. This area of the Yukon was not glaciated, which would have scoured U shaped valleys, so that a dredge could have pumped from side to side.

Now, on top of this scenario comes the permafrost. How man's ingenuity springs into motion. My job was to spray surface temperature water over the frozen surface. In summer, maybe six inches would melt in a week, so that with a few dozen monitors set up over a wide area, one could mobilize to remove the dirt and ultimately bring ground level to creek level. The 90 pounds-per-square-inch pressure through a 4 ½" nozzle is awe inspiring. I could snap four-inch pilings off at a one-hundred-foot distance.

My walking to work entailed the end of afternoon shift and the start of graveyard shift – both shifts by myself. Lots of fun because bears smelling my lunch bucket would follow me in the bush.

It's about time we got back to my friend. This lowly creature ended up with the most difficult job known to man. He was on the thawing crew, which involved driving up to forty feet of pipe (circulating water) down through permafrost gravel to the level that the dredge would dig. This involved twisting and sledging for the length of the shift. If your pipes were going down as

fast as your neighbour's you were chastised by the foreman. Many people only lasted a few days. My friend survived.

Our camp life was work-eat-sleep. I took many walks in the bush and was fascinated by the many 18-inch stumps that were left from the gold rush days. The main cursed entertainment was to go to Granville and play baseball in a field with many dips and knobs that resulted in so many sprains that games were cancelled after two attempts.

The most interesting part of camp life was bizarre. Our outhouse was a twenty-foot one-holer. There was a board to sit on in front and a board to lean on in the back. If things were busy people would squeeze together to make room for you. Need I say more?

Finally comes the beautiful ending to a fascinating summer. We boarded the DC-3 in Dawson and the pilot said we were making a nonstop flight to Vancouver down the coast…. The DC-3 has no oxygen system so we were low level all down the coast as compared to the 30,000 feet nowadays.

P. S. – A good day on a dredge in the Yukon was 100 ounces.

Chamber prospecting school, Vancouver, 1958

The 1950s

~ Recovery and Growth

The 1950s were marked by irregular cycles of optimism and alarm. As the decade began, asbestos attracted prospectors' attention. The minutes of October 2, 1950, note "…another non-metal mineral discovery of considerable importance…" — a deposit of high-quality chrysotile asbestos — had been found at McDame Creek, in the Cassiar Mountains of northern British Columbia.

Canadian Johns-Manville Co. at Asbestos, Quebec had sent samples of first-class asbestos to the Chamber, which was now receiving numerous inquiries about the mineral.

In addition to Cassiar, other important events this decade included exploration of what would become the Granduc mine, also in remote and hostile terrain; the development of low-grade copper deposits such as Bethlehem, which marked the birth of porphyry copper mining in B.C. and the Phoenix Mine, a skarn deposit. Also, Kennco Explorations, the Canadian subsidiary of Kennecott Copper, initiated geochemical exploration methods as part of its exploration programs in B.C., a major pioneering step.

Many firms, believing that a potential market for magnetite ore was developing in Japan, bombarded the Chamber with inquiries about iron ore deposits along the B.C. coast. Preparations were soon under way for shipping iron ore from Texada Island and from Quinsam Lake, on Vancouver Island, to Japan; and from Texada Island, where the Hugo Neu Corporation, of New York, was diamond drilling known iron deposits. Meanwhile, Consolidated Mining & Smelting Co. was considering the establishment of an iron and steel industry in Kimberley.

In 1951, B.C.'s mining industry was booming; the Chamber's minutes trumpeted "a banner year" with 14 new mills planned for construction.

For years much speculative capital from Vancouver and other parts of B.C. had helped support the development of gold mines in Ontario and Yellowknife, NWT. Alberta oil fields had also benefited from this outflow of B.C. capital. Now, a "goodly portion of this money," plus considerably more from elsewhere in Canada and the United States, was being invested in developing base metal deposits in B.C. In 1952, the Emerald tungsten mine at Salmo became Canada's leading producer of this valuable metal. (See Placer, page 234).

Despite much general optimism about the future, the industry experienced difficulties in 1953. In October, it was reported: "The mining picture in British Columbia and Yukon is generally a clouded one. A drop in zinc and lead prices, plus the continued low price being paid for gold, on the one hand, and steadily increasing costs of mining, on the other hand, are making it more and more difficult to profitably operate mines in this section of Canada." Regardless, interest in the search for, and development of, new mineral deposits remained unabated. The Chamber knew of at least 19 large companies that would soon be searching for mineral deposits in B.C. and Yukon.

The prospectors' school went from strength to strength and the Association's minutes were glad to trumpet its graduates' achievements. Early in

the decade Tom McQuillan and Einar Kvale re-discovered an interesting prospect in the Unuk River area of northern B.C.; this property turned out to be a large copper-silver-gold discovery that went on to become the Granduc mine. In 1955, the year's prospectors' classes were said to be the most successful of the past 37 years with more than 200 people registered at King Edward High School. The school was attaining wide acclaim; *The New York Times* published an excellent story on it that year.

The Chamber was obliged to move house twice during this decade. In 1954, the landlord of the Angelus Hotel Building at 790 Dunsmuir Street asked the Chamber to move out of the premises so he could put in a cocktail bar. The Chamber found a new location, at the same rent of $300 per month, across the street at 751 Dunsmuir, but its lease expired at the end of the decade. Facing the doubling of its rent, the Chamber decided to buy its own building in 1959.

By 1954, the mining industry showed renewed vigour. The prices of lead and zinc were increasing gradually; silver was still selling at 85 cents per oz.; copper was in good demand at 29 cents per lb., mercury had moved up from a low of $96 to $255 per 76-lb. flask.

Exploration remained active in Yukon, where Hudson's Bay Mining & Smelting planned to have 75 men working on its Wellgreen nickel-copper property at Kluane Lake. Conwest was drilling a new copper showing at Carmacks, and

Prospector's Airways Co. was diamond drilling its Vangorda zinc-lead-silver deposit near Ross River. In B.C., the Cassiar asbestos mine was expanding and a road was being surveyed to Stewart, where Granduc Mines was obtaining favourable results. In addition, Torbrit Silver was progressing well and U.S. Steel Corporation was continuing its search for iron ore. In total 35 large companies were engaged in the search for new mineral deposits.

The hunt for copper continued unabated. In 1954, Kennecott Copper Corporation had several parties in the field using biogeochemistry to detect orebodies. The technique, championed by Professor Harry Warren of UBC, analyzes plant life and other vegetation for possible metal content.

By mid-decade, British Columbians were seriously bitten by the mining bug. A curious feature of the mining scene in 1955 was the general public's involvement in the search for new mines, particularly uranium. An estimated 500 searchers headed into the field with Geiger counters and many samples were brought into the Chamber's offices to be identified and tested for uranium. Mr. J. Edgar Tretheway of Haney, found a radioactive substance in seven-inch high grass growing in loose earth. The minutes record: "This material gave quite a kick on the Chamber's Geiger counter!"

One of the most significant Chamber events was the retirement of manager Frank Woodside, who was replaced by Tommy Elliott as secretary-manager.

Mineral explorer with early Geiger counter

The Chamber wrote to Ottawa protesting that the export tax on gold mined in Yukon was an injustice to producers. It was argued that, while the tax introduced in the 1897 gold rush may have been justified historically, it had now become discriminatory as practically all the placer gold mined in Yukon was shipped to the Royal Canadian Mint in Ottawa. The tax increase was an added burden on an industry that was barely surviving. Subsequently, the federal government reduced the tax on Yukon gold exports from 2.5 per cent to 1.5 per cent. This meant a considerable saving for Yukon miners.

Towards the end of the 1956, it was estimated that about 50 exploration companies and a thousand prospectors had been active in British Columbia and Yukon. The government issued 7,686 Free Miner's Certificates and 20,082 mineral claims had been staked up to the end of August. Some 30 helicopters were used in mineral exploration work and at least 600,000 feet of core drilling was completed before the year ended.

Important developments included: the discovery of a new mercury deposit by Cominco at Pinchi Lake, near Fort St. James; revival of the old Greenwood-Phoenix copper camp by Granby; and the start of production from the Bethlehem Copper mine in the Highland Valley, near Ashcroft. In addition, there was an important lead-zinc-silver discovery on Copeland Creek, near Revelstoke, exploration of copper-iron deposits in the Queen Charlottes, more good results from the Granduc copper mine near Stewart, and the discovery of another important asbestos deposit by Cassiar Asbestos at Clinton Creek, 30 miles from Dawson, Yukon.

The success of the Bethlehem mine in the Highland Valley caused a staking rush and the Mining Recorder's office in Kamloops was overwhelmed with mineral claims. Prospectors working in the Ashcroft-Kamloops area complained that the office had fallen about six weeks behind in issuing titles, which held up exploration. The Chief Gold Commissioner sent in extra staff after an urgent call from the Chamber.

There was other welcome news. The federal finance minister lifted all restrictions on the export of gold. Canadian gold miners were now allowed to ship their gold out of Canada for sale at the world price.

In 1957, Mines Minister Ken Keirnan decided to bring in royalty legislation and a tax on iron ore in the ground. Chamber president Chris Riley recommended that a group, separate from the Chamber and AME BC, should join to fight the proposed legislation. As a result, the Vancouver Exploration Group (MEG) was formed with about 20 members to provide assistance to the Chamber, resulting in the withdrawal of the proposed legislation by the provincial government. The modern MEG organizes geological talks at luncheon meetings during the winter that regularly attract 300 to 500 attendees.

The year 1957 proved difficult. A drop in world metal prices and the continuing high cost of mine operations dampened provincial mineral production. Prospecting and exploration activity was well down. Mineral claims staked and recorded dropped 60 per cent. By mid-September, they numbered only 8,000 versus more than 20,000 at the end of August 1956.

Prospectors were hurt as the flow of speculative capital from eastern Canada and the U.S. fell sharply. A robust Canadian dollar hurt base metal producers. U.S. threats of increased duties on lead, zinc and copper, protested by the Chamber, didn't help either.

But there was good news too. Japan had emerged as a significant market for B.C. raw materials. The local representative of a Japanese mining and smelting company, anxious to obtain nickel concentrates, visited the Chamber and was advised about local deposits.

Later, Japanese officials said they had examined the Wellgreen deposit in Yukon and hoped to negotiate a deal with its owner, Hudson Bay Mining & Smelting Co.

In June, the Chamber borrowed a yacht, courtesy of Harry Dennison of Straits Towing Ltd., to entertain visitors from forty large Japanese iron and steel companies. The guests showed a keen interest in buying B.C. iron ore and a variety of other minerals and metals, including coking coal. During a tour of Vancouver harbour, Chamber representatives described available opportunities and stressed the need for venture capital to develop the province's mineral resources.

The Chamber arranged a mining display at the first British Columbia International Trade Fair at Hastings Park. This display was made possible through the co-operation and financial assistance of Boyles Brothers Drilling Co. Attractive samples of ore; pictures of mines; a scene depicting a prospectors' camp in the mountains; cards telling of the importance of mining; together with a number of Boyles' large diamond drills, attracted considerable attention.

Consolidated Mining & Smelting Co. decided to proceed with plans for a $5 million steel smelter at Kimberley, using pyrrhotite tailings from the Sullivan Mine to produce pig iron. Also, the provincial and federal governments agreed to share the cost of constructing the Stewart-Cassiar Road in northern British Columbia, which the Chamber had urged for several years.

The difficulties of 1957 intensified in 1958. As the end of the year approached, Tommy Elliott reported that the past summer had "…been one of uncertainty, recession and gradual readjustment…" for the B.C. mining industry. Faced with a severe drop in world metal prices and higher operating costs, a number of mines had been forced to close. These included Britannia, Western Nickel, Silver Standard, Sunshine Lardeau, Emerald Tungsten and Fernie Coal. Later, it was reported that 1958 mineral production dropped by $23 million to $149 million.

There were bright spots, other than continued growth in the asbestos industry. In the Highland Valley district, intensive exploration and development activity indicated it would become one of British Columbia's most important mining areas. An important tungsten discovery in the Northwest Territories would ultimately become one of the most significant tungsten mines in North America, operating as the Canada Tungsten Mining Corporation (Cantung).

Also, the provincial government ordered the lifting of the reserve on iron and manganese in the Vancouver, Victoria, Nanaimo, Alberni and Skeena Mining Divisions. The Chamber had advocated this for some years.

Present-day Highland Valley Copper

Bethlehem Mine, 1963

1960s Japanese Steel visit

The 1960s

~ Japan Emerges, Beginnings of a Boom

During the 1960s, the Chamber coped with several new initiatives and challenges. These included renewed interest in B.C. metals by Japanese companies, market abuses on the Toronto Stock Exchange, land-use conflicts, and a sharp increase in exploration activity and the development of new operating mines.

In the early sixties, visits by Japanese interests increased as the nation's interest in B.C.'s iron ore deposits intensified. Japanese investments in new mines on Vancouver Island grew significantly after the provincial government eliminated most of the objectionable features of the legislation relating to iron ore staking, mining, and export in 1960. (See Iron Mining, page 116). New investments in the province's increasingly important porphyry copper mines and projects were also welcomed.

A 1961 article in the *George Cross News Letter* about B.C. mineral exports to Japan caused jubilation at the Chamber. It stated that existing contracts between the province's mine operators and Japanese buyers were worth $220 million. "A very appreciable sum!" Tommy Elliott wrote. He said the Chamber could take great pride in the work it had done, possibly more than any other organization, to encourage this trade in mineral products. The activity first got under way seven or eight years previously. Since then, numerous Japanese firms had called on the Chamber for help in finding local suppliers. In 1963, two Japanese company representatives were appointed to the Honourary Advisory Board, marking a milestone in the Chamber's history.

As British Columbia's population increased and other industries grew and expanded, mining ran into increasing land-use conflicts. Elliott reported in 1962 that the rights of free miners were being jeopardized more than ever, threatening the industry. One area of conflict involved the logging industry, which questioned the rights of prospectors and exploration people to work in vast Tree Farm Licences and use the logging roads for access. Another issue involved proponents of parks and recreation, who wanted to ban all mining in large park areas. In addition, fishing interests pressured governments to restrict placer and lode mining. Elliott said the Chamber was continually involved in fighting for the rights of free miners to carry on their activities. Persuading governments and others of the need to develop mineral resources wherever they might occur was a time-consuming task. (As later minutes show, such conflicts are not easily resolved and remain a challenge).

To counter the ongoing challenges to explore within the province's vast parks system, the Chamber continued, with renewed vigour, its work of elevating the public profile of mining. Elliott led the PR battle but the Chamber hired public relations consultant Gus Sivertz on a monthly basis in 1965. For many years Sivertz had been a reporter on the *Vancouver Sun*. His work was to assist in publication of articles dealing with the importance of mining to British Columbia.

The public relations effort paid off. Sivertz probably had a hand in writing a report entitled *1966 – A Record Year for Mining*, which was widely distributed among newspapers and various mining and financial journals across Canada and the United States. The *Vancouver Sun* and *Province*, the *Journal of*

Commerce, *The Northern Miner* and many other influential publications gave the report wide coverage. In addition, *The American Metal Report*, a widely circulated trade daily, gave considerable publicity to the Chamber's release on mining activity as well as a B.C. Hydro booklet on mining. As a result, inquiries were received from at least 40 leading U.S. mining and metal buying firms.

Tommy Elliott heard many complaints about mining stock promotions. "It appears mining promotion is not held in a very good light these days, with a number of disconcerting events taking place, which reflect on the whole of the industry," he commented. It was important, he said, that strong public participation in mineral exploration and development be retained. It was his opinion that unless steps were taken to stamp out questionable promotions they would ultimately destroy public confidence in all mining activity and the industry would suffer.

The warning was apropos as interest in Canadian mining stocks had grown dramatically following a string of discoveries ranging from porphyry copper deposits in B.C.'s Highland Valley to uranium deposits in Ontario's Blind River region. Yet regulations to protect investors from promotional excesses were weak and rarely enforced at the time. This led to a proliferation of broker-dealers, mostly concentrated in Toronto, who specialized in "penny" mining stocks with little regulatory oversight.

Franc Joubin, credited with the Blind River uranium discoveries, noted the popularity of penny stocks in

his book, *Not for Gold Alone*. "Practically all forms of lotteries or games of chance were then illegal, save for official racetrack wagering and modest church or charity-sponsored fund-raising." As a result, he wrote, "in many circles, discussion of penny stocks was often as common as discussion of the weather."

Against this backdrop, it was hardly surprising that trading volumes on the Toronto Stock Exchange (TSE) smashed all records in April of 1964, after Texas Gulf Sulphur reported a zinc-copper-silver discovery near Timmins, Ontario that later became the famous Kidd Creek mine.

Timmins was then a prolific gold camp, but Texas Gulf wondered why no other deposit types had been found. The company conducted a geophysical survey capable of detecting deep-lying electromagnetic anomalies in the region, which led to the discovery of an anomaly indicating a large mineralized body, later confirmed by drilling. Prospecting had not detected the deposit because it was covered by a swamp and overburden.

News of the discovery sparked a large staking rush, with more than 20,000 claims filed by 146 mining companies, including Windfall Oils & Mines, which was led by the well-known mining couple of Viola and George MacMillan. Shares of Windfall soared from 56 cents to $5.70 a share on speculation that it had also made a major discovery. After several months of silence, the company reported that "no commercial assays were obtained." The stock tumbled to pennies again, taking other penny stocks and the fortunes of many investors down with it.

The "Windfall Scandal" was investigated by a royal commission that pointed fingers in all directions. Viola MacMillan bore the brunt of the consequences that followed, with her reputation badly damaged despite many past contributions to the industry, including her long-time service as president of the Prospectors & Developers Association of Canada (PDAC).

The TSE was criticized for acting more as a "private gaming club" than as a watchdog. The Ontario Securities Commission (OSC) came under attack for its lack of action to protect investors. The end result was a dramatic change in Ontario capital markets, with more clearly defined roles for the TSE and a new focus on blue-chip stocks and investment-grade securities. The OSC enforced new regulations under a strengthened Securities Act.

The TSE actions discouraged speculative mining investment, despite past successes, within a few years, most of the junior exploration companies and their promoters had moved to the Vancouver Stock Exchange (VSE). The Chamber advocated policies to protect investors from promotional abuses so that responsible companies could continue to attract exploration investment.

In 1966, the VSE experienced its own flurry of investor excitement on news of a rich lead-zinc discovery at Pine Point, on the south side of Great Slave Lake east of Hay River, NWT. The speculative activity on the VSE grew so intense that it drove Pyramid Mines from a penny stock to more than $4 before any holes had been drilled. The B.C. Securities Commission, obviously mindful of the Windfall Scandal, took extraordinary steps to ensure that there would be no leaking of news as Pyramid drilled the first exploratory hole. Security measures were so strict that even the drillers were not allowed to see the core before it was boxed and sent out for assaying. When the assays were finally released, confirming a major deposit, Pyramid shares soared to $24 a share, rewarding patient investors. The Pine Point discovery lent credibility to Vancouver's emergence as a centre for venture capital financing.

A similar flurry of exploration and stock market activity took place in Yukon at the same time after Dynasty Exploration discovered the Faro zinc-lead-silver deposit near the Vangorda deposit in the Ross River district.

The Carter Royal Commission on Taxation released recommendations for elimination of the three-year tax exemption for new mines, removal of the depletion allowance and a proposed tax on capital gains. The latter proposal caused a furor among prospectors, whose "once in a lifetime" gain from the sale of a discovery would now be subject to tax. The Chamber and its members were adamantly opposed to taxation of a prospector's gains and wrote hundreds of letters to Finance Minister Edgar Benson on the subject.

New federal tax policies to begin taxing capital gains and eliminate the three-year tax-free period for new mines were adopted at the end of the decade, effective at the end of 1972. The elimination of the tax-free period had a major affect on B.C. mining because a number of porphyry-type mines were being advanced toward a production decision. For tax reasons, these plans were accelerated for several deposits, with the result that four new large mines began production in 1972. Luckily, copper and molybdenum remained strong and none of the mines suffered from the hasty production decisions. (See Porphyry Deposits, page 102).

Among the development and production highlights, the Cariboo Gold Quartz Mine at Wells produced its one-thousandth gold brick in 1961. The Wells Board of Trade feted Vancouver physician Dr. W. B. Burnett, an original backer of the project, and other directors. The mine had been in production for 30 years. (See Fred Wells, page 210). At the Bralorne camp, the three-thousandth gold brick was poured in 1963.

Another momentous event also occurred in 1963 when the dynamic Keevil Mining Group (which later evolved into Teck Resources Limited) arrived from Toronto, bent on making a little history of its own.

December 1962 was highly significant for British Columbia mining: the start of production by the Bethlehem Copper Company. The following year, Bethlehem staged an official mill opening at its large property in the Highland Valley area, near Ashcroft. Four hundred people attended the event and poured praise on prospector and company president, H. H. "Spud" Huestis, for his distinguished role in discovering the orebody and bringing the mine into production. Another important event was the official opening of the Endako Mines mill in 1965. (See Endako, page 221; see Porphyry Deposits, page 102).

In regular Chamber activities, one of the highlights was the additional work related to the growth in the industry. As a result, the Chamber produced a directory of mining and mining supply companies and exploration companies. It was the first directory of its kind and was later emulated by the other organizations in Canada and the U.S. In addition, manager Tommy Elliott began compiling information each year for the *Chamber's Annual Review of Mineral Exploration Activities.*

With the professional assistance of land surveyors McElhanney & Associates, the Chamber prepared a well-received map of Canada's Pacific Northwest, showing the location of most of the active mines and some of the more promising new properties.

The Chamber's golden anniversary *Prospecting & Exploration Conference* in 1962 was hugely successful. Some 485 people registered, many of them coming from outlying areas. As well as prospectors and exploration people, there were representatives of equipment, supply and service firms. Chamber minutes record: "The technical sessions were excellent and the luncheon, dinner, entertainment and dance most enjoyable. Everyone appeared to have a good time!"

Among new companies entering B.C. in 1963 was the Anaconda Copper Co. , one of the largest U.S. producers, which purchased the Britannia Mine on Howe Sound. Other large American mining companies engaged in exploration in B.C. in the early 1960s included Kennco (Kennecott), Southwest Potash (AMAX) and American Smelting and Refining (ASARCO).

Larger mine start-ups featured two long-time B.C. mining stalwarts, Granby and Placer Development. The discovery of Lornex signified the growing importance of the Highland Valley camp. *The Province* made an enthusiastic prediction: during the next five years the mining industry would create 18,000 new jobs in British Columbia – 3,000 in the mines themselves and 15,000 in ancillary developments. The provincial government estimated total mineral production of $402 million for 1968, a substantial increase over 1967 and an all-time record.

An estimate of British Columbia mineral production released by the mines ministry in 1963 showed an all-time high of $250.6 million with copper valued at $38 million, iron $19 million and oil-gas $36.6 million.

Mining activity in British Columbia and Yukon continued to increase throughout the 1960s with a considerable leap in production capacity in the province. New projects included:

- Granduc, near Stewart ($85 million capital investment);
- Wesfrob Mines, on the Queen Charlotte Islands ($25 million);
- B.C. Molybdenum Corporation, on Alice Arm ($20 million);
- Granisle Copper, on Babine Lake ($12 million);
- Western Mines, on Vancouver Island ($15 million);
- Red Mountain Mines, at Rossland ($2 million);
- Bethlehem Copper expansion ($2.5 million);
- Minoca Mines, on Vancouver Island ($1 million);
- Boss Mountain molybdenum mine (Noranda Mines), east of 100 Mile House;
- Cassiar Asbestos ($10 million) at its Clinton Creek operation in Yukon.

When claims staked in British Columbia in 1965 were finally tallied, they totalled 41,882. The pace quickened in 1966: people began to forecast that total claims could exceed 50,000 – and might even reach 75,000. Some 400 new mining companies were incorporated in Victoria during the first nine months of 1966.

When BCIT began its first mining course with only ten students, the Chamber lent a hand by producing and distributing several thousand copies of a brochure entitled *A Career for You in Mining*, which proved so popular that an additional five thousand copies were printed.

Following repeated Chamber representations, the provincial government exempted prospectors from the *Hours of Work Act* and the *Male Minimum Wage Act*, thus recognizing the irregular nature of exploration work. The Chamber also lobbied successfully for the provision of additional radio frequencies by the federal transport department for exploration crews working in remote areas of B.C., Yukon and the N.W.T.

At the request of the federal Department of Indian & Northern Affairs, the Chamber helped arrange a meeting in Vancouver between members of the department and representatives of 50 large exploration companies active in the north to discuss the planning of future access roads. Ottawa planned a network of roads through Yukon and Northwest Territories to promote mining development. Officials said Ottawa would spend $10 million a year on new roads in those northern areas. This would continue for some years.

Leduc Glacier and Granduc Mountain, 1960

Given the uncertainty of its annual revenues, and a need for better financial stability, the Chamber decided to initiate a structured fee system. Previously it had relied on voluntary or solicited donations from companies and grants from governments.

The Chamber lost one of its best friends in 1964 with the death of Frank E. Woodside, the Chamber's popular former president and manager. He passed away in his ninetieth year after a lengthy illness. He was one of the Chamber's founders and, through his many years of association with the organization, had done much to publicize the importance of British Columbia's mineral industry and to attract capital into the province. Thirty years later, the Association named the Frank Woodside Past Presidents Distinguished Service Award after him. (See Frank Woodside, page 276).

In 1966, the Chamber's lost another original directors and past president, Stanley J. Crocker. He was also the father of Fraser Crocker, a future treasurer.

Apart from the federal Carter Royal Commission report (1966) and the subsequent vigorous debate on Edgar Benson's White Paper (1969) about future federal taxation as it might affect mining, the public policy framework for mining in B.C. had yielded good results, in terms of investment in mineral exploration, commitments to mine development and production. Economic benefits were both growing and flowing through a greater number of communities in B.C.

The Chamber hired Frederick G. Higgs as the manager's administrative assistant in 1969.

Chamber's President Len G. White studies new mining areas as pointed out by Manager, Tommy Elliott

The 1970s

~ A Bump in the Road for B.C.'s Mining Industry

The fortunes of the metal mining industry and the Chamber during the 1970s were altered by an unexpected political change, and the shift toward large, surface porphyry copper and molybdenum mines rather than underground lead, zinc and silver producers. The industry had prospered during the 20-year reign of W. A. C. (Wacky) Bennett's Social Credit government, when politics were not a major issue. Rick Higgs, Chamber Manager from 1975 to 1980 and Tommy Elliott's assistant during the earlier part of the decade, describes the political challenges later in this chapter.

The Chamber's re-elected president, Len G. White, took the industry's pulse at the annual meeting in January 1970 and found it strong. During the past decade, he said, exploration expenditures had increased annually from about $5 million to an estimated high of $40 million for 1969. "Our records show that some 100 large exploration companies and about 600 smaller ones have been involved in the search for new mines in Western Canada and it appears 1970 will be equally active," White said. The Chamber had listed 39 mines in production, or close to it, in B.C. and Yukon, with a total throughput of 140,000 tons per day. Western Canada had come into its own as an important mineral producing area.

AME BC/photographer: Bob Davidson Photo

Harry Warren, who was intimately involved with the Prospecting & Mining School

The surprise election of the New Democratic Party in the August 1972 provincial election deflated the industry's optimism. The dynamism of the NDP's young leader Dave Barrett, a social worker from Metro Vancouver's East Side, was in sharp contrast to the now septuagenarian Bennett, whose political team was also getting on in years. Moreover, the NDP had a hard-working membership with extensive experience gained in the tough federal election battles of the 1960s. With almost 40 per cent of the votes, the NDP held 69 per cent of the seats in the Legislature. The Opposition was split among three parties. The standings in the new House were: NDP 38, Social Credit 10, Liberal five, and Conservative two. Perhaps the NDP election platform in 1972 had not been specific enough to set off alarm bells within the mining and exploration community. In March 1973, Premier Barrett addressed the myth

about socialism "…which we hope we can dispel in British Columbia. We want to demonstrate that reason, common sense and planning have a place in the economic structure of our society."

Though the Barrett government would last little more than three years, its mining initiatives threatened the economic future of the provincial mining industry.

The NDP policy stated, "We believe there is sufficient money lying untapped in the resources to finance the New Deal for the people. The Government of British Columbia could increase its revenue merely by demanding its **fair share** of British Columbia's resource supply." As Raymond W. Payne wrote in an SFU master's thesis, "The second major objective was the promotion of growth based on the diversification of the economy away from its reliance on the export of primary resources."

Further, as Payne saw it, "…the NDP's economic strategy envisioned a broad regulatory structure designed to protect the public interest against the detrimental effects of unrestrained resource development."

The NDP policy commitment was written against the backdrop of significant growth for mining in the 1960s when an unbroken succession of new records for annual value of mineral production was established. Copper, for example, grew by a factor approaching 20 to some 600 million pounds and its value by a factor of more than 50 to some $500 million annually, which was all for export, as was generally the case for all minerals and coal.

The W. A. C. Bennett government had earlier brought in legislation to allow the direction of up to 50 per cent of a mine's output to a smelter in the province but this was scaled back to 12. 5 per cent. However, further processing was not the straw that would break the camel's back. Nor was "a broad regulatory structure," though there was far more than enough discretion introduced by the NDP in the *Mineral Act* regarding Free Miner's Certificates, production rights, as well as assorted fees, rentals, work commitments and the like, to cause eventual suffocation.

In the years leading up to the 1972 provincial election, mining exploration and development expenditures in the province had accounted for 50 per cent of all such expenditures in Canada. Prospectors, geologists, engineers, drillers, and a wide range of service suppliers and mine developers engaged in a massive program of mineral discovery and new mine production. And, given the indicated high level of prospecting and exploration, more was anticipated.

The impact of the NDP government was evident by 1974 when the Chamber released the results of a survey of exploration spending and claim-staking activity in British Columbia-Yukon for the past two years. The survey revealed that expenditures in B.C. were down 49 per cent to $19.4 million in 1974 from $38 million in 1973, while they were up 170 per cent in Yukon. B.C. claim-staking was down 76 per cent for the first nine months of 1974 compared to the average for the same period in 1971-1972. In Yukon, claim-staking was up 194 per cent for the same period. It was anticipated that claim-staking in Yukon would exceed that in British Columbia in 1974 for the first time in modern mining history.

A severe shock was in store for this diverse mining community. It was identified in the spring of 1974 in the form of confiscatory taxation.

Premier Barrett appointed Leo Nimsick, a former Cominco tool crib manager in the East Kootenays, as Minister of Mines and Petroleum Resources. Jim Fyles, a career civil service geologist, was appointed deputy minister but was soon succeeded by John McMynn, former manager of the Bralorne-Pioneer mine. The minister's executive assistant was Hart Horn, who had managed Nimsick's election campaign.

The Barrett government believed that mining must contribute a greater share of the *new-found* wealth to the people of the province. It was not enough for producing mines to pay B.C. mining and income taxes (as well as federal income tax). Nimsick would lead the government's agenda.

The fundamental problem was that the "fair share" mentioned in the NDP mining policy was not defined until early 1974, 18 months after the government was elected and one year after the *Mineral Land Tax Act* (Bill 64) was introduced. It was not until the *Mineral Royalties Act* (Bill 31) was introduced in February 1974, along with the recently promulgated regulations under the Mineral Land Tax Act, that it became evident what a basic royalty and a "super royalty" could do to the viability of mining in the province. The industry was

facing a mineral royalty or land tax equal to five per cent of the sale price (net of smelter returns) with a "super royalty" of 50 per cent to be paid on sales prices above the discretionary basic royalty limit. These royalties were in addition to the former profit-based income taxes. The subsequent debate about mineral royalties galvanized the mining industry, which urged the public to study and understand what was at stake and join the opposition to the NDP government's initiatives.

Introduction of the Mineral Royalties Act was cited as the reason for closure of the Reeves-MacDonald mine near Salmo by majority owner Bunker Hill Mining. The B.C. government then attempted to buy the mine and mill for $100,000 plus a royalty; they were refused and it has never reopened.

Payne subsequently wrote (in 1982):

"The campaign that the mining industry waged against the NDP's mining policies was one of the most powerful, sustained and effective efforts waged by an organized interest group in the recent history of the province…"

The campaign was led by the Chamber, recognized as a democratic organization of long standing. Its large membership comprised prospectors, the largest mining companies, consulting geologists and engineers, suppliers and service firms large and small. Each member had just one unweighted vote. The Chamber had an exemplary record with long-established services to education (such as the Prospecting & Mining School), information for employment seekers, annual

publications (Mining Exploration & Development and Mines Location Map), a public library, mineral display and meeting facilities. It was proud of its excellent working relationships across industry and governments (federal, provincial and city) and a reputation for respecting confidentiality. In short, the Chamber was legitimate in every sense.

Therefore it was no surprise that the Chamber, working with the Mining Association of British Columbia, the Vancouver Mining Exploration Group, the Chamber of Mines of Eastern B.C., the Vancouver Board of Trade and Chambers of Commerce in B.C. communities, was able to mount and sustain a campaign that had almost universal support throughout the industry.

After a few weeks studying the proposed mining royalties, the Chamber organized a major meeting at the Hotel Vancouver on March 11, 1974. Mines Minister Nimsick was offered the opportunity to speak first at the meeting but declined to attend. Peter J. Mercer, Tax Manager, Price Waterhouse & Co. addressed Bill 31 in these words:

The Bill itself contains a number of technical deficiencies and anomalies. Attempting to understand it could perhaps be compared with trying to pick up jelly with your fingers. As soon as you think you have a firm grasp of it, it falls apart in your hands.

Forced to make reasonable assumptions, he described the Basic Royalty as 2.5 per cent rising to 5 per cent of "net value", being the value the mining producer received after deduction of transportation, smelting and refining costs from the "gross value" (an assumed gross sales price).

The "Super Royalty", the royalty causing the most concern, would be 50 per cent of the amount by which the gross value of the mineral exceeded 120 per cent of a predetermined "basic value." This additional royalty, laden with ministerial discretion to establish "basic value" and the ultimate total royalty burden, led Mercer to conclude: the Bill 31 "provisions hold grave implications for anyone connected with the industry in this province."

Len G. White, a Chamber past president, said:

As quickly as the Mineral Royalties Act strikes at mineral explorers, its effects will lash out to abruptly terminate the flow of new mining dollars to individuals and businesses in the related equipment-supply-service sector. I am a consulting mining engineer. If mining companies cease to spend risk capital on the search for new mines in British Columbia, I must expect to be employed elsewhere.

And the same scenario would apply to consulting geologists, geochemists, geophysicists, stakers, line cutters, surveyors, diamond drillers, assayers, technicians together with field personnel, camp cooks and office staff.

Chamber President Edgar A. Scholz, and Vice-President Exploration, Placer Development Ltd., said:

This legislation, if enacted, sounds the death knell for exploration in British Columbia. . . . In general, the presently operating mines in B.C. will have their economic life reduced by 50 per cent. . . and probably only three of the properties not now in production will warrant bringing into production. . .Stated simply, Bill 31 makes waste of 4,000,000,000 tons of ore. . .reduces direct employment by 67 per cent and direct capital investment in the industry by more than $1,000,000,000 within the next decade. . .the ultimate adverse impact on the economy of British Columbia and on Canada is tremendous.

Harry V. Warren, Professor Emeritus of Geology, University of British Columbia (another Chamber past president) reviewed the intentions of the NDP, speculated on their fumbling and suggested they "…had never read about the foolish man who killed the goose that laid the golden eggs…It is hardly necessary to point out that small syndicates and mining companies together with large numbers of individual prospectors are absolutely essential if we are to continue to find new mines. Let us not forget those men who have found mines already…Egil Lorntzsen and Lornex, Spud Huestis and Bethlehem, Bob Bechtel and Brenda, Tom McQuillan and Einar Kvale and Granduc…Let us also remember that fifteen companies walked away from Afton! And a prospector-driller, Chester Millar, found the ore!"

Warren, who was intimately involved with the Prospecting & Mining School, also mentioned Vancouver dentist Mike Warshawski, who had participated in the discovery of the Northair mine as a week-end prospector shortly after taking the course.

Meanwhile, it was a tense time for the career civil servants within the British Columbia Geological Division. The Barrett government was reluctant to listen to advice from skilled geologists on the government's own payroll and, despite long held friendships, the mining industry was often suspicious of geological division initiatives. It was no fun to be caught in the middle. Chief Geologist (1975-1984) Atholl Sutherland Brown described what it was like in an unusually candid insider's view in *British Columbia's Geological Surveys 1895-1995: A Century of Science and Dedication.*

The Barrett government, he wrote, looked on the mineral industry as a cash cow to be milked to provide an extensive social program. A brief blip of high copper price while the government was writing new mining legislation led to the creation of super royalties on metals "to cream off windfall profits".

Relationships between government and industry quickly reached a low ebb and exploration activity virtually ceased. Industry saw its very survival threatened and dialogue with government was conducted in an atmosphere of confrontation.

The Geological Division, which had fostered good relations with industry, was caught in the crossfire…

Sutherland Brown recalled that it was a period of great change and uncertainty internally. The administration of the ministry was "abnormal." The minister's assistant, Hart Horn, was soon seen to wield more power than the minister, Leo Nimsick or his deputy, John McMynn. Horn was eventually appointed assistant deputy minister in January 1975. "It was he who wrote the mining acts, proposed the super-royalty and, to a considerable extent, directed the ministry. He was an intelligent, hard-working and quick-witted man who had a major impact on the ministry and industry with which he had a minimal amount of background knowledge and little sympathy."

[As tension between government and industry grew] "…much of the industry distrusted the Division and in some cases ordered staff to restrict information exchange or even access to exploration properties. Innocent initiatives, such as the appointment of the district geologists, were commonly interpreted by industry in the worst light as the creation of industrial spies. What little co-operation remained rested solely on long-standing personal friendships," according to Sutherland Brown.

A delegation from the Chamber of Mines met with elected government members and staff in the Cabinet Room in Victoria on March 14. It was clear that the MLAs expected that the initial anger of the mining community would soon "peter out." It was not to be.

A new group of industry participants created the Mining Emergency Fund. Its flier read:

This fund has been established as a result of widespread demands, and urgent necessity, to solicit financial support to combat Bill 31 "Mineral Royalties Act," "Mineral Land Tax Act" and other adverse Provincial Government legislation now threatening the future of B.C.'s mining industry… the jobs of thousands of workers…and the Province's overall economy.

Within a few weeks nearly $100,000 was raised to help rally public opposition. The famous black on yellow bumper stickers proclaiming "MINING B.C.'s 2nd Industry" were purchased and distributed. Large ads were placed in the major newspapers and speaking trips were funded. A number of volunteers went out to Nelson, Prince George, and the northwest communities of Terrace, Smithers, Houston and Vanderhoof. Others wrote letters to editors, ministers and MLAs.

When Bill 31 came up for second reading in June 1974, opposition MLAs were armed with an abundance of information and advice from mining professionals and experienced explorers.

Donald Mustard (a former Chamber president) recalled how the protest was taken to the province's seat of government. "We had 2,000 people on the legislature lawn in Victoria, and a black coffin representing the death of the mining industry. One day, just before the election – a day with pouring rain – The Greater Vancouver Mining Women's Association and its members stood on the bridges into the city with their children with signs that read:

DON'T MAKE OUR MEN LOSE THEIR JOBS.

The NDP really didn't like that because they saw themselves as the face of labour, and jobs. But it also created respect from the NDP; they saw we were fighting the same battle."

Rick Higgs, at that time Tommy Elliott's assistant, was sent to Victoria to open a temporary field office and ensure that MLAs were briefed. Those in Opposition were the most responsive. Care was taken that information was distributed on a non-partisan basis to all MLAs. Consulting engineer Ron Stokes, a member of the Chamber's Executive Committee and key organizer of the Mining Exploration Group, joined Higgs in Victoria to maintain the flow of information.

By the 1970s, the Chamber of Mines offered a variety of services including a member library

During an encounter with Minister Nimsick in the Legislature corridor, Higgs presented him with 38 of the "MINING B.C.'s 2nd Industry" bumper stickers, one for each member of the NDP caucus. Nimsick's response was: "There must be something behind it." Higgs turned over an edge and said, "I think it's adhesive."

Later, in a discussion between the minister, deputy John McMynn and Higgs, Nimsick asked McMynn about the extent of indicated exploration spending and where was the best place to get the information. McMynn responded, "Ask Mr. Higgs. He has the numbers." From deputy minister on down, all the staff in the mines ministry remained consummately professional throughout the period of intense debate.

AME BC/photographer: Williams Bros.

Rick Higgs speaking at the Chamber AGM

As the Bill 31 debate wound down, Higgs prepared speaking notes summarizing the rapidly evolving situation that followed an announcement by the federal government that provincial royalties would no longer be deductible in calculating federal income tax. And, with Ron Stokes' assistance, three charts on large coloured cardboard were prepared. They illustrated:

1. *The distribution of mining revenue before Bill 31, assuming the price of copper at $1 a pound and production costs of 70 cents (including transportation, smelting and refining). This showed a balanced distribution of operating profit: mining company – 16 cents; federal and provincial governments – 14 cents.*

2. *The distribution of mining revenue after Bill 31, using the same copper price and production cost assumptions. The B.C. government portion was significantly increased to 23 cents, the mining company's share was cut to five cents, and the federal portion was reduced to two cents.*

3. *The distribution of mining revenue after Bill 31 and the elimination of the deduction of provincial royalties in calculating federal tax, using the same assumptions. The B.C. income tax and royalty would increase to 28.15 cents and the federal portion would be 7.5 cents. Since the production costs were 70 cents and the combined provincial and federal taxes would total 35.65 cents, the total costs to the mining company would be $1.0565 per pound. In other words, the company would lose almost six cents on every pound of copper produced. There was no incentive to produce copper – an impossible scenario.*

These notes were offered to the former Minister of Mines Frank Richter but he was unsure of the subject matter and declined to use them. However, Peace River MLA Ed Smith, with help from MLA Pat Jordan (North Okanagan), used the notes and charts to make the presentation to the House.

Minister Nimsick understood the arithmetic but not the implication. He said, "You can't get 118 out of 100" (the effective rate of taxation was 118 per cent).

Fair share was demonstrated to be anything but, and there was a complete absence of reason and common sense, as originally promised by Premier Barrett.

The campaign by the Chamber and its allies carried on with more letters, editorial material and speeches around B.C.

The NDP was defeated in the general election of December 11, 1975.

In 1976, the Chamber participated with Premier Bill Bennett's Social Credit government in rebuilding workable mining policies in British Columbia, attracting investment and individuals who had been forced to leave for employment elsewhere back to the province. Fortunately, the new Mines Minister, Tom Waterland, was a mining professional who understood the situation and what had to be changed to maintain the profitably of the mining industry.

As a postscript, during the waning stages of the 1979 general election, Barrett attempted to rid himself and his candidates of the earlier conflict over mining policies. He invited Bob Matthews, MABC and Higgs, representing the Chamber, to attend a private meeting in Vancouver's Four Seasons Hotel. Clearly, he wished to be able to emerge from the meeting to say the vigorous conflict of 1974 and 1975 was a thing of the past. Following Chamber policy, which held that there was ample time to discuss public policy between elections, Higgs did not attend. Dave Barrett and the NDP were defeated at the polls once again.

While the Chamber executive had been preoccupied with provincial political issues, the normal administrative work continued. The organization continued its educational classes, kept up its publishing program, supported earth sciences at UBC, rehabilitated its library, publicized the mining industry's role as a generator of wealth, and tried hard (but not always successfully) to get along with logging, fishing, environmental and recreational interests. At the same time, it encouraged and supported start-up associations with comparable aims, and endorsed public policy initiatives that expanded economic infrastructure. It sought to encourage sympathetic stories of mining's importance in the news media and chastised critical reporters.

During the decade, the Faro mine in Yukon, operated by Cyprus Anvil and Dynasty Exploration, was rapidly becoming the mainstay of the economy and additional discoveries in the same area emphasized the long-term importance of mining to the territory.

Regarding ongoing discussions among the Chamber, MABC, the Forestry Association and the provincial government, the executive considered key points to be impressed on government officials:

- *Substantial mineral deposits had far greater value per acre than any other basic industry.*

- *When mineral deposits are exhausted, the land reverts to the Crown and can be used for other purposes.*

- *Producing mines occupy only a small portion of British Columbia's land surface – far less than that occupied by the forestry industry and recreational or parkland. Moreover, many parks have been created without consideration of their mineral potential.*

The Chamber has always been a proponent of the "multiple-use" concept as applied to resources on Crown land and when the Interior Resource Users Association was formed, the Chamber became a member of that organization, later supplying its chairman and a vice chairman. This group was seen as an excellent example of cooperation between various resource users.

A valuable innovation was instituted in the Chamber's relationship with the federal government when Higgs became manager, replacing Elliott, who retired in January 1975. This was important because Yukon was administered federally and many Yukon mining policies were being proposed at the time. Donald Mustard recalled that "Rick had been a field organizer for the Liberal Party in B.C. and he had connections with the Liberal federal government of the day. He arranged for Bob Sheldon, who was the president, and his vice presidents, Bill Dunn, and myself, to meet MPs from B.C. in Ottawa. These were Ron Basford, Minister of Justice; Iona Campagnolo, Minister of State for Fitness and Amateur Sport; and Leonard Marchand, who would become Minister of the Environment. It started off as handshake meetings but, from then on, we would meet with the federal government to address legislation twice a year, once after the Energy & Mines Ministers Conference in the fall, and once at the time of the PDAC conference in Toronto, in March. These meetings were continued into the mid-1980s."

The decision in 1971 by U.S. President Richard Nixon to allow the price of gold to float freely invigorated the B.C. industry at a time when good news was greatly needed. In January 1974,

Chamber president Ed Scholz reported "The current high price has brought a new lease on life to existing gold mining camps. Abandoned mines are being rejuvenated and, with the rapidly increasing search, new gold mines will be found." He concluded: "…there are indications that gold may rise to $200 per ounce." The Chamber received many inquiries about placer and lode gold possibilities in Western Canada. And on January 1, 1975, American citizens were allowed to own gold for the first time in many years.

After vigorous fund raising by the Chamber and its friends, a new Geological Sciences Centre at UBC was officially opened in April 1974. Earlier in the decade, Aaro Aho, one of the discoverers of the Cyprus Anvil lead-zinc mine in Yukon, joined the university senate and headed a campaign to raise funds for the new building. Private donors gave $2.4 million while the government contributed $1.5 million.

The Prospectors classes run by the Chamber continued to be popular. In October 1974, for example, 198 students had enrolled, a number attributed to the excellent publicity the school had earned. The Chamber continued helping other organizations develop prospectors' schools, based on its own successful model, and sought provincial government support for a portable prospectors' training school to serve up-country communities. It also continued to expand, offering a Placer Mining School to follow the regular Prospecting School in 1976. Subjects covered included: placer

history, minerals, geology, methods, evaluation and law and included a field trip.

The B.C. Mining Museum at Britannia Beach (now re-named the Britannia Mine Museum) was officially opened in May 1975. Representatives of various mining organizations were among the official party that travelled along Howe Sound on the Royal Hudson steam train. The provincial and federal governments, along with the mining industry, had contributed financial support. The Chamber's president and manager were elected to the museum's board of directors. Two years later, the Chamber gave the museum a further $5,000 to help build an educational auditorium. (See Britannia, page 153).

In October 1975, Teck Corp. announced a decision to start up the Afton mine at Kamloops to produce 25,000 tons per year of copper in concentrate and also to construct a copper smelter for Afton output. NDP mines minister Gary Lauk, who replaced Nimsick, had announced a subsidy of two cents per pound for the first four years of smelter operation, totalling approximately $4.5 million. The mine opened in 1978.

A 1976 survey showed spending in British Columbia was up to $17.7 million in 1976 from $15.6 million in 1975. Yukon exploration spending was down from $15.5 million in 1975 to $14.5 million in 1976. Coal spending in British Columbia was up almost 200 per cent to $10.5 million in 1976 from $3.5 million in 1975.

British Columbia's actual mineral production value was on a significant uptrend, reaching $1.364 billion in 1975 and $1.486 billion in 1976. The gross value of British Columbia's mineral production for 1978 was estimated at $1.9 billion, up from $1.8 billion in 1977. In 1976 it was reported that Kaiser Resources Ltd. was spending $15.5 million as part of a $40 million expansion related to the Balmer Coal Seam planned for production in 1978.

On October 29, 1976, Premier Bill Bennett transferred Tom Waterland from Mines & Petroleum Resources to the Ministry of Forests. James R. Chabot was appointed the new mines minister. The Chamber' officials complimented Chabot on his appointment and offered full co-operation but expressed regret at the loss of Waterland, who had rectified much of the adverse mining legislation introduced by the NDP government.

Upon the death of one of its revered members, the Chamber renovated its library and named it the "Charles S. Ney Library" in December 1976 in recognition of Ney's many services to the industry. The library received a valuable addition in 1977 when Norman Benson of *Western Miner* donated 33 bound volumes of the magazine, including those published in 1930-1943 and 1948-1968.

First Cordilleran Geology and Exploration Roundup, 1984

The 1980s

~ Boom and Bust

At the start of the decade, long-time Chamber manager Rick Higgs resigned and was replaced by geologist Jack M. Patterson, who had 20 years of mineral exploration experience combined with, most recently, five years as a senior mining administrator in the federal government.

The Chamber enhanced its status with two significant steps during the 1980s. The inaugural issue of the quarterly *Mining Review* was published in 1981, partly because it was felt that other Canadian mining magazines, mostly Toronto-based, ignored B.C. and

Yukon. In 1984, in conjunction with government geological partners, the first Cordilleran Geology and Exploration Roundup was held.

Patterson began regular reports in the inaugural issue of *Mining Review* when he had only been in the manager's job for three months. He commented: "These days, there is an increasing awareness of the importance of government relations to any industry. Recognizing this, we will be doing our best to maintain and improve our relations with politicians and civil servants in all jurisdictions … the Chamber will be communicating on an ever increasing scale with the

B.C. government, primarily through the Ministry of Energy, Mines and Petroleum Resources; the federal government, primarily through the Department of Energy, Mines and Resources and the Department of Indian Affairs and Northern Development; and the territorial governments of both Yukon and the Northwest Territories." Patterson said he hoped to keep members up-to-date on relevant exploration matters such as claim staking, new mineral policies and mineral legislation. "As I have a particular interest in federal lands North of 60, I will try to keep up-to-date on exploration matters regarding Yukon and Northwest Territories."

Mining Review marked a new direction in the Chamber's communications; it was full of news about the industry, economic conditions and public policy. The *Mining Review's* section headed "Chamber News" served as the organization's official voice, informing members about the Chamber's proliferating activities and lobbying initiatives. Then-Chamber president Don Mustard wrote in the first issue: "There is certainly no lack of topics for the magazine to cover." This was certainly true, as subsequent issues demonstrated.

R. J. (Bob) Cathro, president 1981 to 1982; and N. C. (Nick) Carter, president 1988 to 1989, have recalled the genesis of the hugely successful Roundup, which would become a financial bulwark for the Chamber (later AME BC). From a modest attendance of 700 in the first year, it was still going strong more than a quarter of a century later, with over 7,000 delegates attending the 2011 event. (See AME BC's Roundup, page 83).

The 1980s alternated between optimism and grim pessimism. The decade began on a high note as reflected in Don Mustard's report to the Chamber's 69th annual meeting in January 1981. Optimism had returned to the industry after the turbulent decade of the 1970s, he said, and exciting times lay ahead for the country with its unlimited potential for energy development and its enormous bounty in natural resources.

"With a value of over $32 billion [in 1980], mineral output in Canada is at an all-time high. Metals were responsible for $9.7 billion of the production, an increase of nearly 22 per cent over 1979. British Columbia retained its position as the third largest producer of minerals in Canada, after Alberta and Ontario, with a value of $2.93 billion compared with $2.95 billion in 1979, and the metals and coal sectors held their own with values of $1.41 billion and $467 million respectively. In the Yukon Territory mineral values increased from $299 million to $303 million."

In prospecting and exploration, 1980 was by far the most energetic in history. In British Columbia $108 million had been spent in exploration, up from $60 million in 1979, with $81 million spent on metals and $27 million on coal exploration. The equivalent figures for Yukon were $36 million and $3 million, respectively, for a total of $39 million, against $27 million in 1979.

"So in real dollar terms, exploration effort had resumed the upward growth that had been

terminated in the early 1970s by disastrous government policies," said Mustard. Mineral claims recorded in Yukon in 1980, at 10,892, were similar to 1979, but in British Columbia the number of mineral claim units recorded rose from 55,000 in 1979 to 72,621 in 1980.

What a difference two years made! By 1983, the industry had wiped the smile off its face. Early that year Bob Cathro reported grimly: "It would be nice to be able to say that 1982, my first year as president… was a good year for our industry. It wasn't, of course. In fact, it came close to being an unmitigated disaster on both the economic and political fronts.

"On the economic front, many sectors of our industry encountered the worst business conditions experienced since the 1930s. In part, this was due to the severity of the recession. But it was also due to the fact that the business cycles of all of the industrialized areas of the world have become synchronized. This first became apparent in 1973/74 when the simultaneous booms in the industrialized world resulted in shortages and the appearance of spectacular prosperity for producers of mine products. In some cases, apparent shortages were exacerbated by production problems, fears regarding possible cartel action, inventory accumulation by consumers, and speculation.

"Inevitably, the aftermath was equally spectacular. Consumption began to decline as all major economies weakened simultaneously, and in many cases demand collapsed as customers began to live on inventories. In most cases, the result was varying degrees of price weakness, a steep drop in shipments, and a massive transfer of inventories from consumers to producers and commodity exchange warehouses. The impact on the Canadian mining industry's financial strength and profitability was, of course, profound. And in terms of the industry's basic health, it is important to recognize that inflation made a mockery of financial statements prepared in the traditional way, and that real earnings were nowhere close to the figures being reported."

Cathro then told his audience that, except for a substitution of names, what he had said so far was an exact quotation from the presidential address to the annual meeting of the Mining Association of Canada (MAC) in February 1976 by Alfred Powis, then-president of Noranda Mines Limited.

"His words," said Cathro, "are as timely today as they were then, which is a vivid example of how poorly the Canadian mining industry has fared in the intervening seven years. Aside from brief price rallies in several metals, notably gold, silver, uranium and the ferroalloys molybdenum and tungsten, this period was marked by decreasing profitability within a shrinking Canadian industry. Although 1982 was a sudden and severe shock after a relatively prosperous 1981, it generally followed a downward trend that began 10 to 15 years earlier. Viewed in this wider historical perspective, 1982 was only the worst shock yet in an ongoing series of bad tremors."

Cathro said every indicator of industry activity declined sharply during 1982, following a severe

drop in metal prices early in the year "caused by the worldwide economic recession. The effects on the capital-intensive mining industry were aggravated by double-digit inflation and unprecedented short-term interest rates. The results were disastrous, particularly for producers caught in the midst of capital projects or takeovers financed with floating-rate debt. The impact was felt especially hard by base metal producers. By mid-year, approximately half the 130,000 mine production workers in Canada were affected by some type of layoff. For the first time in decades, the future of mining communities and even mining regions has been threatened. Only the lowest cost producers or those with high precious metal content escaped the debacle. In short, the industry is drowning in red ink," said Cathro.

One of the most severely-hit mining regions was northern British Columbia and Yukon, where only the Erickson and Scottie Gold Mines and the Granduc Copper Mine were still operating (the latter at a loss). In the past year, Cyprus Anvil, United Keno Hill, Whitehorse Copper, Cassiar Resources and Canada Tungsten Mines had closed, at least temporarily; some were to remain closed permanently. As Betty O'Keefe relates in *Mines of Babine Lake*, Noranda closed Bell Copper and Granisle Mines in mid-1982 and they remained essentially closed until 1985. Granisle's population dropped from 1,500 to under 500. In 1985 the provincial government appointed Art Phillips as Critical Industry Commissioner with a mandate to negotiate terms under which closed or struggling

resource projects could become viable operations again. Bell Copper was the first mine in B.C. to reach an agreement with the commissioner to re-start operations after three years of closure.

Cathro noted that during 1982, no less than 15 multinational corporations had closed Vancouver offices and/or terminated their exploration efforts in B.C.

"This was unquestionably the worst year ever for the Vancouver exploration community. Other indicators such as the number of helicopters and drills working in the industry were also down substantially. Unemployed geologists registered with the Vancouver Manpower Office rose to 94 at the end of 1982 compared to 18 one year earlier. The level of claim staking dropped significantly in both British Columbia and Yukon."

Cathro said that, aside from the Northeast Coal Project and the expansion of the Westmin Mine, no new mines would open in 1983 and none were currently under construction.

The message wasn't much more cheerful when Chamber president Don Rotherham presented his annual review January 1985. He said the Chamber faced an estimated deficit of $15,000 for 1984. In addition, the organization has been told not to expect to receive its annual $10,000 grant for 1985 from the Department of Indian Affairs and Northern Development.

There were, however, some bright spots during 1984. Rotherham noted that a Chamber poll revealed that expenditures in the mining industry had increased the previous year. "Coal expenditures were almost double last year [than] what they had been in 1983, coming in at a total of $12 million. Majors were the biggest spenders, putting $30 million into exploration efforts, followed by the juniors, who pumped $24 million into the economy. Oil and gas concerns spent $17 million, followed by coal."

The decade ended on a note of considerable optimism. In his outlook for 1989, then-Chamber president Carter told Roundup delegates that while B.C.'s 1987 record-high levels of exploration expenditures were not matched in 1988; most indicators were well above those of preceding years.

"New discoveries, scheduled new mine openings and improved base metals prices point to a good year for the industry in '89."

Promising future projects, Carter stated, were Skyline Resources' Johnny Mountain gold mine in the Iskut River area of northwestern B.C.; the Golden Bear (North American Metals B.C.), west of Dease Lake; Snip (Cominco/Delaware) in the Iskut River area; Gold Wedge (Catear Resources) at Sulphurets Creek; Silbak Premier Big Missouri (Westmin/Pioneer/Canacord), north of Stewart; and Lawyers (Cheni Gold Mines) in the Toodoggone area. These projects were expected to increase by 50 per cent the province's 1988 gold production and add to its annual silver production. It was also a good year for Yukon, Carter pointed out, attributing the past year's increased mineral production to Curragh Resources' Faro mine, where lead-zinc production was up 80 per cent over 1987 levels. Another bright spot was placer gold production; at 1.6 million ounces, it was 17 per cent higher than 1987 and the highest since 1917.

Canadian junior companies grew in numbers and stature in the 1980s despite volatile commodity prices and stock markets, filling a void left by the withdrawal of senior producers and multinational oil companies from mineral exploration. Most of the newly listed entities were based in Vancouver, which became Canada's venture capital centre following the mid-1960s Windfall scandal.

Peter Brown, a third-generation British Columbian, likely had no inkling that his destiny would be linked to Vancouver venture capital when he started his brokerage career in Toronto and Montreal in the early 1960s. When Toronto closed its doors to this high-risk sector in the wake of Windfall, Brown returned home and, in 1967, acquired control of a small brokerage firm with partner Ted Turton.

Jack Patterson with past manager Tommy Elliott and president Nick Carter

Canarim Investment, later known as Canaccord Financial Inc., underwrote and financed thousands of juniors companies listed on the Vancouver Stock Exchange (VSE) over the years. But in contrast to the wild-and-wooly days of the past, juniors were expected to have properties of merit backed by geological reports. The pairing of technical expertise and venture capital, enhanced by the introduction of flow-through share financing, contributed to some of the VSE's greatest success stories.

Another transformative event occurred in 1980, when gold and silver hit $850 and $49.45 per ounce, respectively. Prices didn't stay at these record highs, but base metal prices were much harder hit as the economy soured in 1982 and 1983. Nimble juniors shifted their focus to gold, an industry dominated by six South African mining houses, which then accounted for 71 per cent of mined production.

In 1983, Peter Munk formed a junior company based on a view that gold mines in the Americas would be a safer investment than mines in South Africa, a nation in turmoil during the fight against apartheid. Barrick Gold became the most famous and successful junior to focus on gold in the 1980s, but it wasn't the first.

Vancouver promoter Murray Pezim triggered the first gold rush of the decade after agreeing to finance drilling of an Ontario gold project held by Nell Dragovan's International Corona Resources. The project had been drilled before with mixed results, hence Ontario prospectors Don McKinnon and John

Larche had no luck optioning the Hemlo project until Vancouver-based Corona stepped up to the plate.

Toronto-born Pezim also came to Vancouver after eastern markets clamped down on speculative junior mining investment in the post-Windfall years. Often portrayed as a flamboyant gambler, Pezim was astute enough to rely on geological talent; in this case, the advice of geologist David Bell, who saw potential for a new type of gold deposit at Hemlo. The initial drilling results in 1981 were met with industry skepticism, but Pezim kept the faith and the money flowing until Hole 76 convinced even doubters that Corona's project was a mine in the making.

Teck Corporation formed a joint venture with Corona to build the David Bell mine, and through court action, Corona gained control of an adjacent property developed into the Williams mine by Lac Minerals. A third mine, Golden Giant, was developed by Noranda, which acquired the project from two Vancouver-based juniors, Golden Sceptre and Goliath Resources founded by Frank Lang and Richard Hughes.

The Hemlo camp has produced more than 20 million ounces of gold since 1985, making it one of Canada's most prolific gold camps – despite once having been considerd an area of low potential.

Pezim claimed that "Hemlo saved Canada's mining industry" as the discovery came in the midst of a downturn that hit senior producers hard. This may be an exaggeration, but it is true that Hemlo gold helped Teck and Noranda weather these lean years

better than many of their peers. The discovery and subsequent staking rush was a boon for junior companies at a time when it was needed most.

Vancouver venture capital and geological expertise also helped pioneer the use of heap-leaching to process low-grade gold ores, which led to the creation of a new crop of junior companies. Chester Millar — already famous for his 1960s discovery of the copper-gold deposit that became the Afton mine near Kamloops — took an interest in the process in the 1970s and recommended it to the owners of a struggling California gold mine. The process worked, and as a result, the B.C.-born mining engineer became the co-owner of the first open-pit heap-leach mine in the state.

Millar saw that the process would allow juniors to become gold producers on their own, without the help of majors, and put the theory to the test. He demonstrated the success of the heap-leach process at several open-pit gold mines in the American West that became foundations of growth for Glamis Gold and later, Eldorado Gold.

Geologist Ross Beaty also used the method to good success at the American Girl mine in California, which helped establish his company Equinox Resources as a gold producer. Ross Fitzpatrick's junior, Viceroy Resource Corp. , set new standards of environmental excellence at the Castle Mountain heap-leach gold mine in California. Robert Friedland was less successful at the Summitville gold mine in Colorado, but would make an industry comeback of legendary proportions in later decades.

The 1980s were a period in which financiers and promoters formed partnerships with geologists and engineers, in much the same vein as Peter Munk's alliance with Bob Smith. The end result was a financially and technically stronger corporate entity.

Robert Dickinson and Robert Hunter — often called the "two Bobs" — were among the most productive and enduring of the Vancouver-based partnerships. Their first success in the early 1980s was the Golden Bear gold mine in northwestern B.C., followed by the Mount Milligan copper-gold project later in the decade which, after a 15-year wait, was (in 2011) poised to B.C.'s first major new metal mine. As the HDI group grew with additional principals (Ronald Thiessen and David Copeland), it was also involved in other major discoveries, such as Kemess, advancing the project to the permitting stage. The Kemess mine would ultimately become a significant producer in the 1990s and 2000s under the auspices of Northgate.

Another enduring partnership of the time was between geologist Mike Muzylowski and financier Douglas McRae, who together transformed Vancouver-based Granges Inc. into a mid-tier gold and base metal producer active primarily in Manitoba.

Some juniors focused on acquiring dormant mines closed during industry downturns in order to become producers, or developed mines on their own. Vancouver-based Aurizon Mines is just one example of a junior that successfully used this strategy to become a mid-tier gold producer in Quebec, where it continued to operate well into the 21st century.

Other juniors specialized in generative exploration, a strategy used by Murray Pezim's group of companies in the 1980s. One of those juniors, Calpine Resources, attracted attention with the Eskay Creek gold-silver discovery, a joint venture with Stikine Resources managed by geologists Lawrence Nagy and Ron Netolitzky.

Eskay Creek, as with Hemlo, had its doubters. Pezim and his geological team led by Chet Idziszek drilled 109 holes before the rich 21B zone was discovered. Eskay Creek was developed into Canada's highest-grade gold mine by Homestake Canada (later acquired by Barrick Gold), bookending a "golden decade" for junior companies.

The risky, long-term nature of mineral exploration and mine development continued to demonstrate itself. Norman B. Keevil, Jr. of Teck presented a speech in 1987 stating that 92 per cent of the metal output of the Trail smelter was derived form Canadian concentrates; however, it was then estimated that, by 1998, Trail would depend on imported concentrates for 90 per cent of their metal output. Keevil said, "The biggest danger we face is that we will run out of ore. Not that the resources are not there, but that we will not discover and develop them faster than we run out of established reserves. The challenge of today is exploration. More exploration and better exploration."

Probably just as true today!

The 1980s saw the retirement of Sanford Woodside, who had served the Chamber and the industry for 47 years. Don Mustard remarked: "Everyone who has ever visited the Chamber will remember Sanford for his cheerfulness and willingness to help with advice based on his long experience of the industry in the province. I was always particularly impressed with his encouragement for our young people who might be considering a career in mining and exploration."

Chamber President, Don Rotherham speaking at the first Roundup, 1984

Flow-Through Financing and Junior Mining Companies

Flow-through financing has been used extensively since the early 1980s by junior mining companies to raise exploration funds. This single tax incentive is largely responsible for the substantial amounts of risk capital raised for mineral exploration within Canada. Its importance to junior companies cannot be overstated and indeed, a good portion of the Chamber's government lobbying efforts was directed toward its retention and expansion.

The flow-through financing concept involves the sale of shares by a junior company to the public to finance technical surveys, surface sampling, trenching and drilling, all of which are deemed by Canada Revenue Agency to be qualified Canadian exploration expenses (CEEs). Head office and other overhead costs do not qualify as CEEs. The junior company, rather than booking the CEEs as an expense to be carried forward and deducted at some future time against potential income (an unlikely event in the history of most juniors), instead passes these benefits through to individual investors who can deduct 100 per cent of the CEEs against any income. Investors, as shareholders of the junior company, also get to enjoy the benefits of potential capital gains or losses.

Changes to the tax acts have also provided an opportunity for the provinces to enhance the attractiveness of flow-through financing. A current British Columbia example is the 15 per cent Mineral Exploration Tax Credit which, when added to the existing federal tax credit, brings the total deductibility of an investment in flow-through shares by B.C. residents to 130 per cent of their initial cost of purchasing the shares. These extra benefits are always in danger of being eliminated and remain a hot topic for discussions between AME BC and provincial and federal officials.

The flow-through concept has been around for some time. It was initially intended to encourage the exploration and development of petroleum resources in western Canada and, consequently, it was ignored by the mining industry, which assumed that it didn't qualify. In the late 1960s, the enterprising Vancouver-based firm Cordilleran Engineering Ltd asked its legal counsel, Jurgen Lau (winner of the Frank Woodside Distinguished Service Award), to determine if this method of financing could be used for mineral exploration. As recounted by Scholz Award winner Bert Reeve (one of the principals of Cordilleran, along with Huestis Award winner John Stollery), Lau advised that there was nothing in the tax act prohibiting the use of flow-through shares to finance mineral exploration.

It is believed that Cordilleran Engineering was the first mineral explorer to use that concept for its corporate clients in Canada (the Columbia Syndicate), beginning with Windermere Exploration's 1969 program near the Churchill Copper deposit in the Racing River area of northeastern B.C. Initially, the shares were not flow-through, only the expenses, with flow-through shares coming later. Other Cordilleran-managed companies that made use of flow-through financing included Castlemaine, Kapvik and Barrier Reef. The latter was responsible for the discovery of significant lead-zinc deposits at Robb Lake in northeastern B.C. and at Goz Creek in eastern Yukon, the first Mississippi Valley-type deposits found in the Canadian Cordillera. Barrier's most important discovery was the Blackdome gold mine, developed by an affiliate, Blackdome Mining Corp. It was taken over by Ventures Trident Group of Denver in 1989 and made a profit of $45 million in its 4.5-year life (1986-1991). The shareholders of Castlemaine and Kapvik also received Blackdome shares. Regional Resources, another Cordilleran-related company, used flow-through financing to discover the Logtung tungsten-molybdenum porphyry deposit near the B.C.-Yukon border in the late 1970s.

The Cordilleran family of junior companies certainly demonstrated the value of flow-through financing to the Canadian economy and paved the way for the widespread use of flow-through financing by other junior reporting companies in the 1980s. It is important to note that, unlike modern flow-through-financed projects that invariably consist of drilling programs on established mineral properties, the early ventures used flow-through to finance grassroots exploration programs. As noted by Jurgen Lau years ago, nothing in the tax act prohibited this type of exploration, which may come as bit of a surprise to today's promoters and explorers.

Roundup 1994 ("The Cordilleran Roundup hosted by the Chamber in early 1994 had a distinctly international flavor, with delegates comparing notes about their exploration projects in Chile, Mexico, Venezuela and the newest hotspot, mineral-rich Peru").

The 1990s

~ Transformation and Turmoil – Re-Kindling Interest in B.C.

The 1990s were tumultuous and transformative years for Canada's mining industry, particularly in British Columbia, where the winds of political and social change swept in the last decade of the 20th century. The environmental movement was on the rise, Aboriginal land claims were increasing in complexity, and the Social Credit Party, that had governed the province since Dave Barrett's 1975 defeat, was in freefall.

At the same time, the entire industry was struggling to recover from the October 1987 (Black Monday) market crash and reduced access to flow-through financings.

Exploration spending across Canada, which had peaked at more than a billion dollars in 1987, fell to less than half that figure by 1990. Capital investment in mining, as a share of all investment, also fell by 50 per cent from earlier years. B.C. appeared to be holding its own, with spending of $226.5 million, but this was mostly attributable to the Eskay Creek (precious metals) and Mount Milligan (copper-gold) discoveries.

Chamber manager Jack Patterson warned in early 1990 that juniors were having difficulty raising exploration capital. "Other changes are setting the stage for some unsettled times for the mining industry in the years ahead," he said.

Change came early, starting with the election of British Columbia's second NDP government in 1991. Michael Harcourt's victory sent a chill through the mining community.

The newly elected premier tried to reassure the industry that he was no Dave Barrett.

"We don't want to see mining become a sunset industry," Harcourt told a skeptical audience at an industry event in early 1992. He also promised to streamline the mine development process and make it "time-specific" and a "one-window process."

The mood soured even more after Harcourt announced that the Environment, Lands and Parks Ministry would now manage the mine development review process. He explained that allowing the Ministry of Energy, Mines and Petroleum Resources to continue in this lead role would create "…an underlying perception of bias and conflict of interest."

Industry concerns grew as Premier Harcourt and Mines Minister Anne Edwards each reaffirmed the NDP position to "double parklands" and settle Aboriginal land claims.

A commission led by Richard Schwindt, a professor at Simon Fraser University, was established to inquire into compensation for the expropriation of resource interests.

The Chamber called for compensation based on fair market value (like other expropriations and as the Supreme Court of Canada had suggested in the Tener decision) but the Schwindt report released in late 1992 instead recommended limiting compensation for expropriated claims to costs accrued for only the last five years. Mining leases would be compensated at market value, but only those with a "bankable" feasibility study.

"If the government follows through with these recommendations, it will destroy the security of mineral tenure and make valueless the mineral inventory we have accumulated for more than 150 years," Patterson stated in response to the report.

Many companies responded by shifting their exploration and mining activity to more favorable jurisdictions. With feelings running high, then mines minister Anne Edwards was tagged as the "… best mines minister CHILE ever had!" To stem the decline, industry associations set out mining's case publicly in an organized, systematic manner. They pointed out that Chile, Mexico and other nations were welcoming Canadian investment in mining, whereas B.C. was heading in the opposite direction, endangering its economic future.

The mining industry also argued that its footprint was small, relative to logging and other resource industries. Its message, however, was over-whelmed by environmental groups calling for more wilderness "protection" and stringent regulations for resource developers.

Land-use conflicts were not new in British Columbia, but the environmental movement had evolved since the first rag-tag groups formed to save old-growth forests in the 1980s. By the early 1990s, the mining industry faced new opponents: large international environmental organizations that were militant, well-funded and politically active. Their leaders were articulate, media savvy and generally impervious to reason. They claimed the

moral high ground and used a barrage of tactics to stigmatize their opponents.

Chamber president Bill Wolfe noted in his 1991 report that the top 20 environmental groups in North America had annual budgets totalling $685.8 million, staffs of 3,853 and memberships totalling 7.8 million. The Chamber then represented 1,600 corporate and individual members, with a staff of four and a $200,000 annual budget.

The environmental movement had the ear of the government and the support of many native leaders, as well as much of the general public. What they needed next was a high-profile cause, which they found at Windy Craggy, an undeveloped copper-gold-silver-cobalt deposit in a remote wilderness in the northwest corner of B.C.

The industry had a prior claim, staked decades earlier.

Geologist Jim McDougall of Frobisher Exploration (later Falconbridge) had made the first discoveries at Windy Craggy in 1958, following up targets identified by aerial prospecting and reconnaissance surveying. The area was selected as prospective because of the presence of historic copper and silver mines in the region. Subsequent exploration led to the classification of Windy Craggy as a volcanogenic massive sulphide (VMS) deposit. Such deposits typically occur in clusters in favorable mineral belts. Significantly, Windy Craggy also contains a large resource (the largest known worldwide at that time) of cobalt, an important strategic metal.

AME BC

Geologist Jim McDougall of Frobisher Exploration (later Falconbridge) had made the first discoveries at Windy Craggy in 1958.

Geddes figured that Ottawa and B.C. would receive an estimated $545 million and $720 million respectively in taxes over the mine's life.

Geddes argued that its proposed mine plan had also addressed issues such as seismic risk, acid rock drainage, as well as other environmental and social considerations.

Critics pounced on every aspect of the project during the review process.

Environmental groups claimed that a mine would destroy the wilderness qualities of the Tatshenshini River region and pose a multitude of environmental hazards. The B.C. Ministry of the Environment submitted a detailed 31-page comment. The U.S. Environmental Protection Agency, the U.S. Department of the Interior (responsible for national parks) and other American agencies also expressed concerns, particularly about acid rock drainage and potential impacts on salmon.

Geddes Resources optioned Windy Craggy in 1981, and then spent almost $50 million to exercise its option and advance it to the mine development review stage. The company proposed a 20,000-tonne-per-day mine that would extract 297 million tonnes with an average grade of 1.4 per cent copper over 20 years.

Windy Craggy was viewed as "the future of copper mining in British Columbia," as many mines were nearing the end of their lives. It had significantly higher grades than producing copper mines in the province and exceptional potential for new discoveries.

Mine construction was expected to take three years at an estimated cost of $550 million. Once in operation, Windy Craggy was projected to employ 500 people directly, create another 1,500 indirect jobs and generate economic benefits for local communities, the province and Canada.

Geddes pointed out that its deposit at Windy Craggy Mountain was 18 to 25 kilometres from the Tatshenshini River, that local fish catches were minimal, and that lime-rich rocks in the area would neutralize any acidity, which would protect water quality and fishery resources.

River rafters, tour operators, and environmentalists joined forces to stop the mine.

Tatshenshini Wild, representing 50 environmental groups from the U.S. and Canada, spearheaded a high-profile international campaign to "protect" the "endangered" river and region. Al Gore, then a U.S. Senator (later vice president), championed the cause.

As the Windy Craggy controversy intensified, the government passed the *Commissioner on Resources and the Environment Act* (CORE) and appointed a commission led by Stephen Owen to take the lead in provincial land-use planning. CORE was given powers to hold hearings and provide advice on controversial projects such as Windy Craggy.

Under this new Act, the mines minister suspended the Windy Craggy Mine Development Review Process and instructed CORE to study future land and water use for the region.

After six months of study, CORE released the Windy Craggy report, which outlined three options for the government to consider: create a protected wilderness area; allow mining only in 25 per cent of the area and protect the balance; or delay the decision.

CORE reviewed an assessment of the region by government geologists that identified a number of copper occurrences within a district-scale favorable belt of rocks. The report noted that some of these occurrences "have significant potential to equal or exceed the Windy Craggy deposit in size and grade." The report nevertheless concluded that mining activity "…would be incompatible with full preservation of

wilderness," and that the final land-use decision was "unlikely to be resolved through a consensus process."

Premier Harcourt chose to expropriate Windy Craggy, along with claims held by more than 20 companies and individuals in the region. On June 22, 1993, he announced the creation of the Tatshenshini-Alsek Park, which closed almost a million hectares of wilderness to natural resource development. The next year, the park would be added to the World Heritage List as an extension of the Kluane National Park/Wrangell-St. Elias National Park and Reserve and the Glacier Bay National Park World Heritage Site.

Harcourt's decision stunned the entire mining and international investment community.

Industry leaders, geologists, engineers, mine suppliers, and Howe Street brokers took to the streets of Vancouver in protest, wearing black arm bands. Some waved placards that read: "Super-Royalty 1974, Windy Craggy 1993 — We will never forget."

Premier Harcourt was booed and heckled by the visibly angry delegation as he promised to "fairly" compensate claim holders in the Tatshenshini region and "work with the industry" to develop other mines in the province.

Wayne Spilsbury, a geologist for Teck Corporation and vice president of the Chamber, said locking up one of the province's best deposits and one of the

best hunting grounds for new deposits "…ignored the interests of future generations." The prevailing industry view is that the Tatsenshini mineral district could very likely rival established mining camps in Eastern Canada, such as Sudbury, Thompson, Rouyn- Noranda, Thompson and Flin Flon.

Gary Livingstone, president and CEO of MABC, said the decision "…crystallizes the uncertainty that exists for our industry in this province." He accused the government of changing the rules "to reflect the demands of special interest groups" and warned that British Columbians would pay the price.

"Mining is a growth industry in the rest of the world and unfortunately for British Columbians, these investment dollars and the wealth and jobs it creates will flow to other jurisdictions who are actively seeking partnerships with mining."

Long-serving Chamber director, geologist and exploration executive David A. Barr in his 2004 autobiography *One Lucky Canuck* was scathing in his comments. He wrote: "…[the park's creation] was undoubtedly the most ill-conceived and disastrous land-use decision ever made by a B.C. government. In effect, the park remains a monument to the greed and deceit practiced by its proponents and the equally green government. The government's decision, which destroyed its credibility as a responsible steward of the province's resources, sent a negative message to potential investors in the B.C. mining sector, but was to take several years to achieve general recognition – and then only by a limited sector of the public."

After being applauded by Al Gore and environmental leaders, Harcourt was left to deal with the thorny issue of compensation. Royal Oak Mines had acquired 39 per cent of Geddes by this point, and as its controlling shareholder, threatened to sue for compensation.

Estimates of the value of the project (by government and industry sources) ranged from $15 billion (gross metal value) to $8.5 billion (after cost recoveries) over the mine's life.

The case never came to court. Royal Oak and the government negotiated a compensation plan. The Province paid $29 million directly to Royal Oak and paid another $138 million towards the development of Royal Oak's Kemess South project in B.C. The settlement was controversial as it came with government strings, including $20 million for a B.C. mining development fund (to be matched by Royal Oak) among others conditions.

ఌ

The Cordilleran Roundup hosted by the Chamber in early 1994 had a distinctly international flavor, with delegates comparing notes about their exploration projects in Chile, Mexico, Venezuela and the newest hotspot, mineral-rich Peru. The Canadian focus was almost exclusively on recent diamond discoveries in the Northwest Territories, with the discovery credited to B.C. geologists Charles (Chuck) Fipke and Stewart Blusson. Their discovery sparked a staking rush and exploration boom at a time when it was needed most.

Exploration spending in B.C. slumped to $68 million, down from $72 million in equally dismal 1992. Chamber President Mike Beley attributed the decline to five issues: security of mineral tenure; competitiveness; access to land; permitting; and Windy Craggy.

"Our government's current attitude toward development of natural resources forces us to reach out around the world to remain active in our chosen field of endeavour."

Some said it was simply too risky to do business in B.C. "You have to go where you can advance your projects without roadblocks," said Clive Johnson, then president of Bema Gold, a junior active in Chile. "I run a business, so I have to go where I can do business."

There were very real and far-reaching social costs associated with this exodus. Extended stays by field personnel in foreign countries led to family break-ups and several B.C. geologists lost their lives working in countries where safety standards and services were not as advanced as our own. (The Association of Professional Engineers and Geoscientists of British Columbia named its C. J. Westerman Award for Geoscience after one.)

Another result, many highly-trained and qualified people left the industry; the effect is seen today in a large gap of qualified personnel ready to replace retiring managers, technologists and senior mining people.

The industry downturn prompted B.C.'s mining associations to assemble under one roof at 840 West Hastings Street, in May 1994. MABC and the Mining Suppliers, Contractors and Consultants Association of B.C. continued to share "Mining House" with the Chamber for almost a decade.

The Chamber and MABC continued to take part in the Land Resource Management Plan (LRMP), which had a mandated goal to increase provincial parks to 12 per cent of B.C., as well as the CORE process. This involved criss-crossing the province to attend land use meetings, providing input into the Mineral Exploration Code, mining laws, Aboriginal land claims, safety regulations and other issues. Both organizations relied heavily on volunteers, who put in countless hours over many years.

CORE was charged with developing a land use planning system and a resource and environmental management strategy for the province at provincial, regional and local levels. The land planning system had begun with three round tables in 1992: Vancouver Island, Cariboo-Chilcotin and Kootenay-Boundary; the latter quickly split into two separate round tables, east and west. These round tables included broad public participation and representation, especially from environmental groups, and were supposed to deliver certainty to all concerned – the industry would know where it could and could not mine. The process was very time-consuming and costly; the Kootenay Boundary Land Use Plan was not approved until 1995, and its strategy impelemented only in 1997, resulting in years of uncertainty. The Chamber and MABC estimated costs for industry participation exceeded $1.5 million.

Land use planning necessitates comparisons of relative values of differing opportunities, and this requires knowledge of values and resource inventories; information that accumulates gradually through iterative research and decision-making. Mineral explorationists cannot plan discoveries; they don't know what the mineral inventory is – only that it is constantly changing.

Hence, the industry is disadvantaged in these discussions. Mineral resources are hidden, and almost by definition, discoveries cannot be planned. (See Why Is It So Hard … page xxi).

Also, the toll on volunteers is significant: In at least one instance, a self-employed industry negotiator was threatened with legal action if any of a prospector's claims were taken as a result of the process. When the negotiator expressed concern to the government representative in charge the response was: "No judge would ever let that stand in court." But there was no offer or assurance that the volunteer's legal expenses would be covered.

Some companies refused to allow their employees to participate for fear of legal implications and liabilities. Environmental groups did not face the same challenges. There was no understanding on the part of government of the untenable positions in which industry representatives were placed.

While all this was going on, government delegations from foreign countries criss-crossed Canada, inviting mining companies, big and small, to invest in their mineral sectors.

Major producers answered the call, including Falconbridge, which closed its Vancouver office to open one in Santiago, Chile, just before the Windy Craggy decision in 1993. Juniors also found it easier to raise capital for foreign projects and racked up a series of major discoveries in South America, Africa, Central Asia and Indonesia.

In 1995, the Vancouver Stock Exchange raised $1.54 billion of capital, much it for foreign mineral projects, followed by $992 million in 1996. The exodus of mining talent and capital concerned industry associations across Canada, for much of the decade. The MAC coordinated a national campaign. (See MAC, page 57).

Locally, Chamber members became deeply involved in the *Keep Mining In Canada* political lobbying initiative (subsequently re-named *Mining Works for Canada*). Political change came again in 1995, when Premier Harcourt was forced to resign because of a scandal relating to one of his cabinet ministers. To the surprise of many pundits, the new leader, Glen Clark, led the NDP to another electoral victory in 1996.

Scandal also hit the mining industry in 1997, when it was found that a purported massive gold deposit in Indonesia had been salted (placer gold was introduced into crushed drill core). Bre-X Minerals had grown from a penny stock on the Alberta Exchange into one of the top traders on the Toronto

Stock Exchange before it crash-landed, shaking the foundation of Canadian capital markets. Junior companies bore the brunt of the market meltdown, which sharply curtailed their ability to raise exploration capital. (See Bre-X, page 58).

The TSX and Ontario Securities Commission set up the Mining Standards Task Force to review the standards governing mineral exploration and the disclosure of results, and make recommendations for improving these standards to restore investor confidence. Two members, Ed Kimura and Neil Hillhouse, were from B.C.'s mining community.

The end result was National Instrument 43-101, a codified set of rules and guidelines for the

AME BC

Bill Wolfe

disclosure of information related to mineral exploration, including classifications of reserves and resources, and the concept of a "Qualified Person" to take responsibility for public information releases about mineral projects.

The Chamber of Mines supported this initiative while struggling through one of the worst industry downturns in recent history. Jack Patterson retired from his post in May of 1998, after 18 years of dedicated service. Bruce McKnight was appointed executive director.

In early 1999, the Chamber and MABC withdrew from the land-planning process. The NDP government had achieved its goal of doubling parklands to 12 per cent of the land mass, and yet continued to restrict resource development through the creation of Special Management Zones advocated by environmental groups. The decision to withdraw was not easy, but the Chamber felt it was necessary as the land-planning process had become excessively focused on the forest industry and its high-profile disputes with environmental groups. With mineral exploration and mining at

depressed levels, public concern was also largely focused on keeping the forest industry alive, as it sustained many communities in the province.

Through this period, the mining industry felt largely disenfranchised. The intention was to drive change in the process. Mining felt (rightly) that it was not being heard and that its interests and concerns were being ignored and overridden. Further, the process was expensive in terms of both time and money and prospects of reward were not forthcoming.

Another major development was the 1997 Supreme Court of Canada ruling on the Delgamuukw land claim by the Gitxsan and Wet'suwet'en people that would transform the relationship between Aboriginal and resources interests. (See Aboriginal Engagement, page 94).

B.C.'s mining industry hit rock bottom in 1999, when exploration spending fell to a mere $40 million. No new mines opened, but two mines closed (Blackdome and Gibraltar). Almost 40 per cent of the province was now either a park, protected area or a wilderness

Jack Patterson presents Don Mustard with Gold Pan Award, 1995.

management zone with significant access or resource development restrictions. The sharp downturn had left many companies, including senior producers, vulnerable to takeovers by stronger entities. Industry consolidation seemed likely, if not inevitable.

A glimmer of hope came from a public opinion survey commissioned by the Chamber, which showed that 96 per cent of those polled supported increased mining in B.C., "…provided there was an economic benefit and little adverse impact on the environment."

In 2003 the Chamber's Office was relocated to the 8th floor of 889 West Pender St.

The MAC Campaign

The Mining Association of Canada (MAC) launched a series of initiatives to reverse the country's decline of mining investment in the 1990s.

"A country's mineral potential can only be realized if it can attract the necessary mining capital," MAC President Gordon Peeling told at a London (U. K.) audience in 1998. "Unless a country's government can maintain a stable and constructive business climate, mineral investment will suffer."

Peeling cited the rapid increase in the creation of parks and other protected areas where mining was banned. He also cited the "notorious Windy Craggy decision," and unsettled native land claims as contributing factors leading to investment uncertainty.

Another problem was escalating costs and project delays resulting from newly introduced environmental [mine permitting] regulations. "These regulations were, in some cases, duplicated at the national and provincial levels of government," Peeling noted.

Peeling said polls showed that the perception of mining and its environmental performance had eroded since the 1980s, most notably in large urban centres.

MAC's response was to initiate three major programs, each with a different goal.

"The first objective was to build trust with Canadians, and the chosen field of action was environmental," Peeling explained. "The second was to build alliances, and the method was to seek accommodation with other interest groups. The third was to build momentum for policy change. The method was political mobilization at the grass roots."

The industry initiated and funded (with government) a research program on acid rock drainage, which Peeling described as "the most serious environmental problem associated with metal mining." About $20 million was spent on this worthwhile initiative.

MAC developed an Environmental Policy — the first such policy issued by any national mining body — and made its endorsement a condition of membership. This policy (updated in 1995) was positively received by industry and government.

MAC also promoted the establishment of the International Council on Metals and the Environment. As well, it worked with member companies on voluntary emission reductions, a research program on metals in the environment, and a guide to safe management of tailings facilities.

"This series of initiatives has established the members of the MAC as serious players in the environmental arena," Peeling said.

MAC also launched the Whitehorse Mining Initiative (WMI), aimed at building alliances with labour, environmental and native leaders. While positive relationships were forged, WMI was less successful than initially hoped (from an industry perspective) in achieving a breakthrough in the contentious issue of land-use planning policies.

In this period, one of MAC's most successful initiatives was a political action campaign, "Keep Mining in Canada," aimed at urging governments to help do precisely that.

"We decided to look for support primarily among those who know the industry best and are dependent on it, namely Canadians who live in mining communities," Peeling said.

The grassroots campaign was formally launched in September 1993, and was later renamed "Mining Works For Canada." The annual cost was less than $1 million.

Mining communities hit by the industry downturn backed the campaign and put pressure on governments to help the struggling sector. Industry associations, including the B.C. & Yukon Chamber of Mines, were also strong supporters of the national campaign.

Peeling said these campaigns helped promote mining as an industry with a future.

And positive changes did come, albeit incrementally over time — starting with tax relief for mine reclamation expenses, streamlined regulations and improved government policies — along with greater public acceptance of mining.

"We are proud that our strategic approach has helped to bring them about," Peeling said.

The Bre-X Scandal

The Bre-X scandal, perpetrated on the Busang property in the jungles of Kalimantan on the island of Borneo, inflicted enormous damage on mining exploration around the world.

Bre-X was listed on the Alberta, Montreal, NASDAQ Exchanges and TSX 300 Composite Index. The scandal involved a cleverly conceived drill core sample-salting scheme initially started on a small scale primarily to showcase some high-grade gold assays to promote and entice additional financing for continued drilling. As the drill programs escalated into major undertakings, the sample-salting practice became more sophisticated and drill hole after drill hole reported spectacular mineralized intersection.

The supposed motherlode was promoted as hosting 50 million ounces of gold, then 70 million, and then 100 million. One optimistic report even touted the potential of a 200 million ounce deposit. Bre-X shares rose meteorically from a penny stock in 1993 to $280 and a market cap of $6 billion in 1996 before a 10-1 stock split. Many major mining companies, noticing the exciting hype of a giant gold deposit, sought a piece of the action. Many junior exploration companies acquired properties in Kalimantan and raised millions of dollars for exploration. Numerous under-the-table deals were struck in the mad scramble to acquire properties anywhere within flying distance of Busang.

Then the bubble burst, or more appropriately, exploded. The major company that successfully won the favour from the Indonesian government to develop the Busang gold property started drilling twin holes alongside the original high-grade holes to confirm the gold grades. The results rocked the global mining and financial industry; the twin holes contained no gold of economic interest. This announcement of a huge gold swindle on March 27, 1997 caused a massive sell-off of Bre-X stock. Stock exchange computer systems crashed. Within 30 minutes Bre-X stock suffered a paper loss of $3 billion. As with every market situation, some people profit, some lose. Numerous fortunes were made by investors wise enough to get out early. Sadly, it was the later investors who lost; hundreds lost their life savings.

From the ashes of Bre-X, National Instrument 43-101 was struck. Other regulatory policies and guidelines were also imposed to reduce the risk of fraud.

Mineral exploration essentially came to a standstill. The fallout from the Bre-X scandal added to other factors to create the perfect storm that led to a 72-month bear market for mining shares and difficult project financing:

- Decline in the gold price below $300;
- The stock market's focus on the Tech Cycle;
- The B.C. NDP government 1996 through 2001; and
- B.C. juniors moved to Latin America and other off-shore jurisdictions.

Many market and mining professionals agree: new rules and regulations alone cannot prevent another Bre-X; only honest professionals, working conscientiously and ethically will prevent such dishonest activity.

Caption: Chamber past presidents with Richard Neufeld at December 15, 2003 Chamber office opening. Back row: Gerry Carlson (1994-1995), Mike Beley (1992-1993), Lindsay Bottomer (1998-1999), Shari Gardiner (2002-2003), Donald McInnes (2000-2001), Nick Carter (1988-1989), Bill Wolfe (1990-1991). Front row: Don Rotherham (1984-1985), B.C. Energy and Mines Minister Richard Neufeld, Ralph Macdonald (1967-1968), Donald Mustard (1979-1981).

The 2000s

~ B.C.'s Resurgence – Corporate Citizenship, Social Challenge

At the start of the new millennium, outgoing Chamber President Lindsay Bottomer had cheerful news for the two thousand-plus participants at the January 2000 annual Cordilleran Roundup. Bottomer noted that globalization of exploration and mining over the previous decade had given members an opportunity to work elsewhere, compare the Canadian and North American industries to those of other countries and recognize the advantages that North American jurisdictions enjoy. In particular, provinces like Quebec and Manitoba had maintained healthy levels of exploration. Both provinces had acknowledged the important role of mining in the economy, particularly, of non-urban areas; the need to facilitate exploration access to most of the provincial land base while balancing the interests of all other land users, and providing certainty for business investment.

Equitable land access was one of the key issues on which the B.C. mineral exploration and mining sector, including the Chamber, persistently lobbied the provincial government. Other issues included securities legislation, regulatory reform and the continued improvement of relations with First Nations.

A new business plan for the Chamber was developed and adopted in early 2000. As well, collaboration between the Chamber and BCIT resulted in the creation of a jointly-offered prospectors' course providing credit in the first-year geology program.

B.C. politics saw a significant change in 2001 with the election of a Liberal government led by Gordon Campbell. The Liberals won 77 of 79 seats. Premier Campbell and mines minister Richard Neufeld appointed MLA Ralph Sultan to lead a Mining Task Force, which ultimately saw significant input from the Chamber and MABC as well as from about 80 sources across the province. From this, industry submitted a "5-Point Plan for Mineral Development in British Columbia" to the new government.

The five-point plan consisted of guidance on how to address key issues, namely:

1. *Land Access and Security of Mineral Tenure.*

2. *Aboriginal Land Claims.*

3. *Taxation.*

4. *Permitting and Regulations.*

5. *Workers' Compensation Board.*

Soon, the province's business climate improved and regulations were reduced. Personal income taxes were cut by 24 per cent and corporate taxes by 18 per cent. The provincial sales tax on machinery and equipment for mining, forestry and energy industries was removed, and a staged elimination of the corporate capital tax was introduced. In addition, a new 20 per cent B.C. flow-through share tax credit was established, which provided the province with the most attractive tax credit program in Canada.

Land use concerns were accommodated by Bill 54 that incorporated the two-zone model for mineral exploration. The model recognizes that it is impossible to plan for the discovery of hidden resources. In the parks zone, mineral exploration and mining were forbidden. In the open zone, mineral exploration and development were allowed, subject to laws and regulations designed for the sector.

By 2002, mineral exploration activity in B.C. was rebounding. Exploration spending hit $39 million (up from $29 million the previous year), but it was recognized that in order to be sustainable; spending would have to rise to $100 million or more. Dan Jepsen became executive director, replacing Bruce McKnight, and Shari Gardiner was the first woman to become president of the Chamber.

The 2002 Cordilleran Roundup was very successful. All the booth spaces were sold out by the end of 2001. With a record attendance of 2,400, a change of venue was needed. Arrangements were made to hold the 2003 Roundup at the Westin Bayshore in 2003. This move accommodated increasing attendance and brought the trade show and technical sessions under one roof.

A review of the Chamber's strategic plan noted good progress since 2000, including the development of a competitive benefits package for members; updating and printing of 2000 copies of the Chamber's Safety Manual; development of environmental principles which could be adopted by members; contributing to the Environmental Excellence in Exploration (E3) initiative of PDAC; and development of a community engagement manual for explorers focusing on First Nations communities in B.C., which could also be applied worldwide.

In 2003, mineral exploration expenditures continued to recover, reaching $55 million. With Gardiner in her second year as president, the Chamber held the twentieth annual Roundup conference, attracting over 3,000 participants. In early October, the Chamber relocated to the eighth floor of 889 West Pender Street, following the sale of the Mining House at 840 West Hastings in August of 2003 for $1,750,000. The Association got a modern office and a nest egg to weather any future downturns in the industry; on the other hand, the Chamber's street-level storefront had been welcoming to thousands of entrants to the B.C. exploration and mining industry over the years.

That same year, the Chamber's 175 volunteers on 15 committees were very active for the industry, particularly on land issues for a responsive government. By far, the largest working group was the Roundup Committee with 28 members.

Two new work groups that got underway in 2003 were the Geoscience Committee and the Rocks to Riches Geoscience Program and Management Committee, both of which were government sponsored. The Chamber took a lead role in promoting the need for renewed geoscience funding in B.C. Early in the decade, B.C.'s geoscience expenditures were the lowest in Canada. Manitoba spent twice as much on geoscience as B.C. and Ontario five times more. The individual states in Australia, B.C.'s major competitors in the mining industry, annually spent up to nine times more on geoscience than B.C.

Elsewhere, the Chamber stressed, government spending on geoscience generated an immediate fivefold return in mineral exploration spending, which leads to new discoveries and mines. Increasing the British Columbia government's investment in geoscience to a minimum of $10 million annually could potentially lead to more than $1 billion in new mineral discoveries, it argued.

It was clear that new economic mineral deposits were not being discovered fast enough to maintain the province's current known reserves. For long-term sustainability of the mining industry, B.C.'s mineral explorers needed to explore new areas, which

David Caulfield, 2005 Chamber President

Michael Gray, 2004 Chamber President

required a renewed commitment by government to geoscience. The government listened – and responded to the industry's plea. The Chamber received a one-time grant of almost $1.7 million in 2003 to administer the delivery of targeted geoscience. The beginning of what was later to become Geoscience BC was now well underway.

In 2004, Michael Gray became the Chamber's new President and MLA Pat Bell became the first Minister of State for Mining. B.C. experienced a long-awaited period of revitalization in exploration investment, business certainty and government support. Increases in the price of copper (45 per cent), gold (13 per cent), zinc (24 per cent), and

silver (34 per cent), sparked by growing Chinese demand and was coupled with a business-oriented political climate. B.C. experienced a dramatic increase in mineral exploration, reaching $130 million in expenditures, the highest since 1991. Three mines opened and thirteen were in the permitting process. Annual claim staking reached a 13-year high of 46,802 hectares.

A sustained focus was anticipated on full implementation of Bill 54 and the two-zone land use model for mineral exploration and mining. The Chamber also helped to improve relations with the tourism industry and First Nations. A Memorandum of Understanding between the Chamber, the

Rob Pease, 2006–2007 AME BC chairman

Council of Tourism Associations of B.C. and the Mining Association of British Columbia (MABC) was signed on January 22, 2004. Through the support of the Ministry of Sustainable Resource Management, a first draft of the Aboriginal and Community Engagement Guidebook was completed.

The year 2005 saw a dramatic increase in mineral exploration, with expenditures reaching $220 million and gross mining revenues of $6 billion.

That year, David Caulfield became the Chamber's president and MLA Bill Bennett become the second Minister of State for Mining. Mineral Exploration Roundup 2005 attracted over 5,200 participants. Premier Campbell announced a $25 million commitment to geoscience research. Later in April, Geoscience BC was created from the grant and made its first call for proposals for new projects. A joint Chamber/BCIT Aboriginal Minerals Training Program was launched with Jim Morin as head.

December 8, 2005 was a significant date for the Chamber. The Chamber officially changed its name to the Association for Mineral Exploration British Columbia. As well, the Association changed the titles of its lead representatives, with the executive director becoming president and CEO and the president becoming the chairman of the board. A month earlier, the membership had approved resolutions to change the name and bylaws of the Association to better reflect its mandate to serve the mineral exploration and development community in B.C. Despite its 93-year history, the B.C. & Yukon Chamber of Mines was often confused with MABC. As well, Yukon had its own Chamber of Mines. By the end of 2005, AME BC had 2,824 individual and 161 corporate members.

In 2006, with Rob Pease as chairman, AME BC continued its drive to provide leadership on mineral issues, to pursue the development of working relationships and partnerships both inside and outside the sector, and be a driving force of advocacy for the mineral exploration community.

AME BC membership hit a new record of over 3,620 individuals and 190 corporations and there were 220 volunteers and 10 staff members.

Mineral Exploration Roundup 2006 attracted 5,400 participants from 28 countries, and featured the first trade show by an Aboriginal community, the Tahltan Central Council. This event marked a new era of cooperation, understanding and appreciation between Aboriginals and the B.C. mineral exploration and development sector.

In close cooperation with the MABC and the provincial government, AME BC executed a number of key initiatives focused on promoting the B.C. mineral sector, including a trade mission to Toronto to open the TSX exchange, three visits to Ottawa to focus on the need for a streamlined mine permitting process, and formal participation at China Mining 2006 in November.

Gross mining revenues in B.C. had almost tripled since 1999, growing from just over 3 billion in 1999 to over $8 billion by 2006. With $265 million spent on exploration in the province; in only five years, B.C. had moved from capturing 5.7 per cent of Canada's mineral exploration expenditures to 17.6 per cent. Also of note, B.C. had also climbed in the Fraser Institute's ranking of mineral exploration jurisdictions in its Annual Survey of Mining Companies, from 44th out of 47 jurisdictions in 2002/2003 to 23rd out of 64 jurisdictions in 2005/2006.

In 2006, the fourth edition of *Safety Guidelines for Mineral Exploration in Western Canada* was released.

Also, in conjunction with PDAC, AME BC launched a nationwide safety survey that built on its 26-year record of promoting safety awareness in British Columbia and Yukon. As well, the Association's *Mining Review* magazine was rebranded *Mineral Exploration* as a communication medium for the B.C.-based mineral exploration and development community.

In 2007, with Rob Pease into his second year as chairman and MLA Kevin Krueger now as the third Minister of State for Mining, a period of sustained growth in the mineral exploration and mining sector in B.C. occurred. It was marked by a record $416 million in exploration expenditures and almost $7 billion in gross revenues from mining. B.C. accounted for twenty-five out of the 50 mines in the permitting process in Canada. In early 2007, AME BC had 129 corporate members, 4,200 individual members and more than 260 volunteers. Attendance at Mineral Exploration Roundup grew to over 6,000 in 2007.

That same year, AME BC, together with the MABC and Geoscience BC, appeared before the B.C. Select Standing Committee on Finance and Government Services to provide recommendations for the provincial budget. These recommendations included implementation of a mineral tax credit equal to 50 per cent of pre-production costs; creation of a resource revenue sharing program providing affected First Nations with a share of government revenue collected from mines and a call for continued funding for Geoscience BC.

Alongside the many successes, the industry continued to face challenges in land access, exploration and new mine development. Amendments to Section 19 of the B.C. *Mineral Tenure Act* lowered the threshold for landowner notice provision. AME BC, together with the MABC and Geoscience BC, developed proposed amendments in a joint position paper. In the fall of 2007, a joint federal and provincial environmental assessment panel recommended against the Kemess North gold-copper project. Late in the year, the Galore Creek project was suspended, illustrating the challenge of escalating engineering and construction costs in B.C. and internationally.

Industry consolidation, which began in the late 1990s, escalated during the decade, creating a new dynamic; the number of Canadian senior companies was dramatically reduced through a series of mostly hostile takeovers. Placer Dome was acquired by Barrick Gold in 2006, ending an era for one of B.C.'s oldest companies. In the same year, Xstrata PLC acquired nickel miner Falconbridge, while Falco's former rival Inco was taken over by the Brazilian company known today as Vale. Similar industry consolidation took place in the United States, Australia, South Africa and other mining nations.

By 2008, with Dr. Robert Stevens as chairman of AME BC, over 800 (or 50 per cent) of Canadian exploration and mining companies were based in B.C.,and Vancouver had the largest concentration of exploration and mining professionals in the world. With the reduced number of majors, the industry was now dominated by junior companies, including some that had made, or were making, the transition to producer status.

B.C. alone had over 600 exploration sites, 18 major mines in operation and more than 20 new mines seeking permitting approvals from provincial and federal agencies. In April 2008, however, Minister of State for Mining Kevin Krueger announced the B.C. government was banning uranium and thorium exploration. This news sent a major shockwave across the province and the global mineral exploration and development sector. AME BC began a campaign with the goal to eventually overturn this decision and to secure fair compensation for expropriated tenures.

In May of 2008, the multi-stakeholder B.C. Mineral Exploration and Mining Labour Shortage Task Force, including representatives from AME BC, released its human resources strategy to attract 15,000 workers to the mineral exploration and mining sector in B.C. over the next ten years. Shortly thereafter in June, MLA Gordon Hogg became the fourth Minister of State for Mining. By mid-year, the early stages of the most severe global economic recession since the 1930s were readily apparent. In the fall of 2008, Gavin C. Dirom was hired as the new President & CEO of AME BC.

Using the newly-minted 2008-2012 strategic plan as a guide, the Association embarked on a quest to determine the top seven issues for the B.C. mineral exploration community. Broad challenges facing the sector, such as in areas of (1) permitting, (2) land use and access, (3) Aboriginal relations, (4) geoscience, (5) infrastructure, (6) human resources and (7) taxation were identified. AME BC also moved forward by increasing engagement with members and regional exploration groups, conducting member surveys, revitalizing committees and evaluating communication tools.

In his year-end address as chairman, Robert Stevens remarked that one thing was certain about 2008 – it was an exciting year. Early in the year, the Mineral Exploration Roundup conference attracted a record attendance of over 6,700 people from 48 countries. In contrast, the year closed with global stock markets and most metal prices down 50 per cent or more from their peaks earlier in the year. Mineral exploration expenditures in 2008 dropped to $367 million.

The year 2009, as expected, was a rollercoaster year for the mineral exploration and development sector. It opened with economic uncertainty and lower commodity prices. Venture capital was gone, projects were placed on hold, exploration budgets were slashed, and many company stock prices were at 52-week lows.

Steady and consistent advocacy work by AME BC and its partners at MABC, however, was beginning to pay off with the announcement of $130 million in federal funding for the Northwest Transmission Line along the Highway 37 corridor in northwestern B.C. The B.C. Aboriginal Mine Training Association was also formed with $4.4 million in funding from the federal government. All of which was very good news, even though provincial land use and access challenges, and political decisions, continued to hamper the sector's ability to explore and ultimately develop new mines.

Politically, many changes occurred that impacted the sector in 2009. After successfully representing the interests of mineral explorers and developers on key land use and Aboriginal relation issues, Gordon Hogg was replaced by MLA Randy Hawes in June of 2009 as Minister of State for Mining, the fifth minister since Pat Bell. Also, MLA Blair Lekstrom succeeded Richard Neufeld as the Minister of Energy, Mines and Petroleum Resources. Neufeld had been minister from 2001 to 2009.

Also in 2009, MABC and AME BC acted as joint interveners in the Supreme Court case of *Mining Watch vs. DFO/NRCan* with respect to the Red Chris mine's environmental assessment process.

The associations argued that sustainable development and effective environmental review requires governments to maximize resources through better coordination and harmonization, as was done in the case of Red Chris. The case, which was concerned specifically with the ability of the federal government to exercise discretion in the scoping of project reviews, did not contest the quality and substance of the environmental review of the project.

The Supreme Court of Canada ruled that the federal government has that right under the Act but advised that duplication of effort and resources was needless and wasteful and that the Red Chris studies/permits should stand.

Primarily due to the global recession and provincial land access and use issues, B.C.'s share of Canadian exploration expenditures dropped to dropped from 13 per cent in 2008 to 11 per cent in 2009. Nevertheless, Vancouver remained the global hub for the exploration industry with 30 per cent of exploration financing raised by B.C.-based companies. In addition, the B.C. mining industry produced gross revenues of $5.7 billion for the provincial economy in 2009.

AME BC

Dr. Robert Stevens, 2008-2009 AME BC chairman

Lena Brommeland, AME BC 2010 chair

Mona Forster, AME BC 2011 chair, at Roundup 2012

2010 to 2011

~ China's Emergence; Mining Booms

The year 2010 marked a turnaround for mineral exploration and development in B.C. and internationally.

With almost 6,000 participants attending Mineral Exploration Roundup 2010, the year began with an optimistic spirit that never let up. The reality of 2009, with its severe but relatively short economic challenges, faded into memory and tremendous opportunities beckoned. The mineral exploration and development sectors, buoyed by record commodity prices for gold (over $1,400 an ounce)

and copper (over $4 a pound) led the resurgence of the global economic recovery.

Lena Brommeland took over as the chair of AME BC in January and Bill Bennett returned to the provincial cabinet as Minister of Energy, Mines and Petroleum Resources in June after Blair Lekstrom resigned. Exploration expenditures in B.C. increased significantly to $322 million in 2010 and a modern-day gold rush was underway. And new to Roundup was the inaugural AME BC policy forum held with members to determine the Association's advocacy focus. As well, the first ever roundtable with senior government officials was held to discuss permitting, land use and access, geoscience and taxation.

For the first time in well over a decade, new major metal mines were under development in B.C. Construction was proceeding at the New Afton and Mt. Milligan projects, and the provincial government announced economic and community development agreements with local First Nations that, for the first time, included government resource revenue sharing. The Copper Mountain mine at Princeton was also well on its way to reaching a 2011 production target, and the Northwest Transmission Line along the Highway 37 corridor in Northwestern B.C. progressed through its environmental assessment process with tremendous support from local communities. There was significant optimism about the potential $10 billion in major mine developments and a move off diesel-generated power for northwestern communities.

After six months acting as interveners in the Supreme Court of Canada case between *Mining Watch* and the federal government and Imperial Metals, AME BC and MABC welcomed the court's decision on January 21, 2010 that allowed the major Red Chris mine project in northern British Columbia to proceed to permitting and construction. The associations also welcomed the court's recognition that federal and provincial environmental assessment processes can and should operate so as to minimize duplication. There were also challenges. Although the Prosperity gold-copper project in central B.C. received approval from the provincial government, it was rejected by the federal government. These differing

decisions reinforced the need for a streamlined project approval process and a coordinated effort between provincial and federal agencies.

Land-use and access issues continued to hamper exploration in B.C., highlighted by the province's decision in March 2010 to ban title registration and exploration in the Flathead Valley. The 160,000-hectare Flathead area, located in southeastern B.C., was part of the Kootenay land use plan developed in the 1990s with extensive public participation and input. The decision demonstrated that land use plans that welcomed mineral exploration and development could be overturned without consultation. This issue was of particular concern to the Association and its membership, because of the loss of an opportunity to develop mineral resources and receiving fair market compensation for mineral rights held in good standing. It was disappointing since land use plans were supposed to deliver certainty to the industry.

The latter part of 2010 was marked by sweeping political changes. Although the Association continued to strengthen relations with the Minister of State for Mining Randy Hawes, AME BC was challenged by Energy and Mines Minister Bill Bennett's decision to leave his caucus, and the resignation of Premier Campbell in November, shortly after announcing major reorganizational changes to the B.C. Cabinet and ministries.

The most significant of the latter changes was the moving of almost all of the natural resource administrative personnel, including those from the

previous Ministry of Energy, Mines and Petroleum Resources, into one agency called Natural Resource Operations led by Minister Stephen Thomson. Pat Bell became Minister of Forests, Mines and Lands, another new, but separate, ministry.

Notwithstanding the political changes, AME BC steadily advocated for the two-zone land use model in areas such as Atlin Taku and Dease-Liard; and worked to protect mineral tenures and access to the public's mineral resource endowment, enhance security and ensure fair market compensation in the event mineral tenures were expropriated or restricted (eg. the *de facto* Flathead park). As well, AME BC facilitated broader discussions with B.C.'s regional exploration groups regarding their key issues and government's proposed amendments to the Mineral Tenure Act Regulation. Strong relationships between many AME BC members and First Nations were further enhanced with the government's historic revenue-sharing announcement in 2010.

While AME BC remained supportive of the principles of corporate social responsibility, members and staff were pleased that Parliament did not pass federal private member's Bill C-300. The bill was poorly balanced and could be used, without proof or cause, to challenge the performance of mineral exploration companies abroad without examining the objectives of those who identified the purported poor behavior. This issue, however, may require further attention from the Association, given the extensive involvement of Canadians seeking mineral deposits globally.

Asian demand for commodities and metal prices remained strong in 2011 and the industry remained optimistic with Roundup 2011 setting another record with over 7,000 delegates. As Mona Forster became chair of AME BC, the work of the Association was clearly laid out in front of it. The *Vancouver Sun* pointed out in a lead editorial in January 2011, "Since 2001, the Campbell government has removed about two million hectares from potential development in what it calls 'proactive stewardship of ecological and cultural integrity.'"

The *Sun* reminded its readers that AME BC and MABC had asked governments to come up with a streamlined "one project, one process" joint federal-provincial approvals regime but there had been little evidence that politicians of either level had responded to the request in any concrete way. Moving mining projects forward efficiently should be a non-partisan issue, the newspaper asserted.

The *Sun's* editorial concluded: "Mining provides more than 12,400 jobs, and is the largest private-sector employer of Aboriginals. The provincial government estimates the number of jobs in the entire mining and mineral sector at 28,000 in more than 50 communities. Most of these are highly paid, unionized jobs that average $112,800 a year. [B.C.'s mining industry] is being held back by a sclerotic regulatory regime. Opportunities are being squandered; money is being wasted. It's an easy fix. All that's needed is government cooperation and a green light."

AME BC President and CEO Gavin Dirom further stressed the need for change in an opinion piece in the *Vancouver Sun* on January 14, 2011. He noted that a modern "gold" rush was underway in the province, led by copper, gold and steel-making coal developments and he reminded readers:

"…While explorers require large areas to search for elusive new deposits, actual mining has used less than one percent of the provincial land base over the last 150 years. Total payments to government by the B.C. mineral industry had increased to an average of about $565 million for 2005-2009, from an average of $340 million for 2000-2004. Further, government incentives for B.C.'s minerals sector yielded amazing returns. In 2009, every tax dollar invested provided a return of $289, compared with an $8 return for every tax dollar invested in forestry."

A natural business cluster existed with approximately 60 per cent of Canadian mineral exploration companies based in B.C. The supporting legal, technical and financial specialists made the province and especially Vancouver a world centre of mineral exploration and mining excellence. The B.C. industry paid some of the highest salaries in Canada and was expected to create 15,000 new jobs within the next decade.

"Responsible mineral explorers understand that there will always be impacts when developing rare and valuable deposits, and agree that these need to be soundly assessed and properly mitigated. We look forward to ensuring B.C.'s mining proposals are evaluated fairly, thoroughly, and efficiently. If we get it right, and I'm optimistic we will, the social

and economic benefits from responsible mineral development to all of us could be demonstrated and showcased through strong environmental standards, local poverty reduction, construction of affordable homes and improved education and health care," wrote Dirom.

By the spring of 2011, Christy Clark became the leader of the governing B.C. Liberal Party, and subsequently premier. With a vision to be an agent of change and to create an economy to support families and their communities, she re-organized several ministries. MLA Rich Coleman became the Minister of Energy and Mines and MLA Stephen Thomson became Minister of Forests, Lands and Natural Resource Operations. Randy Hawes became Parliamentary Secretary to Minister Thomson.

In May 2011, after two years of consistent lobbying, Minister Steve Thomson announced $12 million for funding of Geoscience BC over two years. In a news release on May 10, AME BC said:

"Geoscience BC has shown great leadership in demonstrating how industry can partner with governments and academic institutions to deliver world-class data that leads to new exploration and ultimately benefits communities throughout the province," said AME BC chair Mona Forster. "It is fitting that this announcement comes during B.C. Mining Week, a time to celebrate how our industry has grown and changed and perhaps more importantly, a time to highlight how mining contributes to the B.C. economy and society, now and into the future."

Mineral Exploration & Mining – Background and Basics

Bralorne Pioneer mining camp, 1939
AME BC

A necessary tool –
a geological rock hammer

Britannia Mine

Merry Widow exploration
camp, 1957

Students stake claim at Chamber prospectors' school, c. 1970s.

B.C. ~ A Centre of Excellence for the Mineral Industry

Western Canada's mining industry was transformed by technical innovation during the past century as visionary leaders pursued better ways to discover, mine, process and market valuable resources. Some breakthroughs transformed the economy and society as well, often in ways once never imagined.

An early example of ingenuity and innovation was the development of tramway systems for transporting ore from mines in the Kootenays. It had lasting impact.

A Mr. Byron C. ("BC") Riblet, of Spokane, Washington, was approached in 1896 to build a tramway at the Noble Five mine in Sandon to move ore from the top of Reco Mountain to the mill in the valley below. (Folklore has it he thought he was going to Sandon to build a streetcar line!)

Aquatic life sampling in northwestern B.C. – an example of B.C.'s mineral exploration industry and its suppliers collaborating with local First Nations

Over the next decade Riblet built thirty tramways before returning to Spokane to found the Riblet Tramway Company which specialized in building mining tramways in Alaska, Canada, the western United States and South America. Riblet built its first chairlift in 1938 at Mount Hood, Oregon and the company went on to become a major supplier of chairlifts to ski resorts, installing over 400 systems as the sport gained popularity. The firm remained in business until 2003.

Skiing – and the tourist industry it supports – has been a major beneficiary of technology first developed for the mining industry!

Pioneer-era miners may have imagined that pack trails to the Fraser River and Cariboo goldfields

would later become highways opening up a new province, as an example. But they likely never foresaw that skills acquired by building roads through mountainous terrain would lead to advancements in open-pit mining and geotechnical engineering on a global scale. Carroll Brawner made this leap after ten years of experience as a civil engineer with B.C.'s gung-ho Department of Highways in the 1950s and 1960s. In 1963, he co-founded Golder Brawner and Associates (later Golder Associates), which provided technical guidance for the design and construction of hundreds of large-scale open-pit mines, including coal operations and tailings dams, around the world.

In 1978, Brawner joined UBC's Department of Mining Engineering (now the Norman B. Keevil Institute of

Mining Engineering), where his courses on tailings dams and slope stability and mine design inspired hundreds of students. In 2008, he was inducted into the Canadian Mining Hall of Fame for his many contributions to engineering excellence.

Another gold-rush-era development, the construction of the White Pass & Yukon Route from the Alaskan port of Skagway through the rocky coastal mountains to Whitehorse, Yukon, benefited northern economies and helped revolutionize global trade and cargo-handling as well. The $10-million narrow-gauge railroad was completed in only 26 months, driven by bullish backers who bragged that given enough "dynamite and snoose" (snuff), they could "build a railroad to Hell."

Completed in 1900, the 110-mile "railway built of gold" became an International Historic Civil Engineering Landmark, a designation shared with the Panama Canal, Eiffel Tower and Statue of Liberty. But as the Klondike stampede lost steam, the line was never extended to Dawson, as initially hoped. Most mines in northern Yukon still had to rely on sternwheeler steamboats in summer and horse-drawn sleds in winter for transport, as was the case with the Keno Hill camp near Mayo in the early 1900s.

The rich silver mines at Keno Hill produced 44 million ounces of silver and 96 million pounds of lead from 1920 until 1941, when rising costs forced their closure. Visionary mine-finder Thayer Lindsley, of Ventures Limited, and intrepid mine-maker Fred Connell, of Conwest Exploration, saw an opportunity to revive the camp following the construction of the Alaska Highway in the late 1940s. They formed United Keno Hill Mines as a partnership to operate the project, and in 1950, they built a 230-mile road connecting the Keno Hill Camp to the Alaska Highway and Whitehorse, terminus of the White Pass & Yukon Route.

The link to rail and coastal ports contributed greatly to the success of United Keno Hill Mines, which ultimately became Canada's largest silver producer (silver production in the district ultimately reached 217 million ounces). In the early 1950s, White Pass & Yukon Route and United Keno pioneered the "Container Route," the inter-modal movement of containers by truck, train and ship. Custom-designed rail cars were built to transport the eight-cubic-foot containers, originally known as "Unitized Freight Transportation."

White Pass & Yukon Route commissioned the world's first dedicated container ship, the *Clifford J. Rogers*, to transport concentrates from Keno Hill and later asbestos fibre from Conwest's Cassiar mine in northern B.C. to coastal seaports, including Vancouver. The system also allowed for low-cost back-hauling of heavy equipment, fuel and supplies to the mine sites. Other industries recognized the cost and time advantages of reduced handling, paperwork and inspections, and better protection of transported items from pilferage and the elements, resulting in an explosion of container traffic worldwide.

The railway stopped operations in 1982, as mines closed due to low metal prices. Activity resumed in 1988 as a seasonal tourist operation that attracts thousands of visitors.

Failure plagued a pioneer-era smelter spree in B.C., in which 75 per cent of 24 smelters built between 1868 and 1915 wouldn't return a dime of their investment. Historical accounts attribute the failures to "…managerial incompetence and technological ignorance." But five smelters that did enjoy some success left a lasting legacy, notes Jay Morrison in *Pioneer Smelters of British Columbia*. "They were responsible for the building of railroads that opened up the entire southern part of B.C. to settlement and development. Because smelters needed coke, coal mining in the Crow's Nest Pass prospered." They also "…gave momentum to the mining industry that has made it the giant that it is today."

The most successful smelter of all — built in Trail by a predecessor of Cominco (now Teck) in 1896 — also created a global giant in mining and metallurgy. The smelter struggled in its early years along with its competitors but ultimately succeeded because of technical innovation guided by two brilliant metallurgists, Selwyn Blaylock (1879-1945) and Randolph Diamond (1891-1978). Blaylock recommended the purchase of the Sullivan mine near Cranbrook, despite challenges related to its complex silver-lead-zinc ores. Diamond led an in-house research team that developed a new process for ore separation known as differential froth flotation. This process unlocked the value of

the Sullivan deposit and dramatically boosted metal production at the Trail smelter.

"Since that time, the [Sullivan] mine has produced ore containing some 17 million tonnes of zinc and lead metal and more than 285 million ounces of silver for a total value, to the British Columbia economy, of more than $20 billion in today's prices," stated Douglas Horswill of Teck Cominco in a 2001 editorial in *The Northern Miner*.

Placer Development (later Placer Dome) was at the forefront of technical advances that contributed to the success of a new generation of B.C. mines. The company was the first to introduce trackless mining at the Jersey-Emerald underground mines (tungsten, lead and zinc) in the Salmo region. The tracked ore-car system used for decades at underground mines became a relic of the past, replaced by automated load-haul-dump fleets that offer lower costs, higher productivity and greater mine-plan flexibility.

Placer had several visionary leaders in the post-war years, notably John Simpson (1901-1988) and Edgar Scholz (1915-1980). They were pioneers in applying large-scale, low-cost open-pit mining methods to low-grade copper, molybdenum and gold deposits. Their shared B.C. successes include the Craigmont Mine — the first large, integrated open-pit mine in Western Canada, and the first Canadian operation to introduce sub-level caving as a bulk-mining method — and the Gibraltar and Endako mines among others.

Scholz also transformed Placer's exploration strategy while rising up the ranks to vice-president of exploration in 1965. He insisted that Placer examine exploration projects as future mineral inventory, a departure from the common practice of holding only a few core projects that met development criteria of the time. Placer was one of the first companies to assemble a pipeline of projects at various stages around the world, which in turn provided for growth, diversification and greater flexibility to respond to cyclical metal markets. As an example, Scholz believed even in the 1950s that gold prices would ultimately rise and began assembling early-stage gold properties in the American West, Australia, and Papua New Guinea. Many of these projects, including Cortez in Nevada, were developed into world-class gold mines during the next twenty years. Scholz was also a pioneer in the use of heap-leaching processing to exploit low-grade gold deposits.

Exploration methods have evolved greatly over time. Pioneer-era prospectors would be astounded at the variety and capabilities of geophysical techniques — many developed in Canada, and now used worldwide — including deep-penetrating airborne systems used to detect potential mineralized bodies buried at great depths. Geophysical surveys allow for low-cost early-stage exploration of large areas with minimal impact on the environment.

A transformative step in mineral exploration was the introduction of remote sensing, which initially involved the use of aerial photographs to identify surface features that might indicate favorable sub-surface geology. Remote sensing evolved as satellite images and Geographic Information Systems (GIS) technology became available in recent decades. Multi-spectral imaging and thematic mapping allow large areas to be geologically mapped remotely at a level of detail not possible in the days of aerial photo interpretation.

Remote sensing today provides an arsenal of tools for geologists, which is a boon for exploration as most deposits exposed at or lying near surface have already been found. Spectra used for remote sensing can collect data such as the weathering and alteration products of mineral deposits, which pinpoint areas of interest for surface exploration. The cost and time-savings advantages over methods used decades ago are incalculable.

Internet technology has revolutionized almost every aspect of the mining and mineral exploration process, including safer and more accurate drilling and blasting. As an example, Smithers-based Hy-Tech Drilling Ltd. designed and developed an in-house online data management system that allows clients to track job progress and costs. And the company benefits too, through instant access to job-site data, reduced downtime and more efficient ordering of parts and equipment.

Harvey Tremblay founded Hy-Tech with one drill in 1991, and has since expanded to a fleet of more than two dozen drills operating in western Canada and abroad. In 2010, he received AME BC's David Barr Award in recognition of his long-time advocacy of high safety standards in difficult environments. Among his contributions was a partnership with Northwest Community College for a program that helps new drillers gain the skills needed to work safely in challenging terrain.

Drilling techniques have evolved greatly over the years, in efficiency as well as safety. The Galore Creek copper-gold project in rugged northwestern B.C. was the site of a drilling breakthrough in the 1960s, according to Barr, then a senior geologist with Kenneco Explorations. Contractor Midwest Drilling decided to experiment with a wireline drill, then in the development stage and considered problem-plagued.

"The wireline method revolutionized diamond drilling performance," Barr said in his autobiography, *One Lucky Canuck*.

The big advantage was a dramatic reduction of rod-pulling to retrieve the core barrel as was required by

Harvey Tremblay, winner of AME BC's David Barr Safety Award, 2010

previous drilling practice. Because of Galore Creek's fragmented ground, Barr said it could take three days to drill and recover a 25-foot interval of a hole.

"In 1991, progress with wireline drills averaged 230 feet per 24-hour machine day based on 44,900 feet of drilling completed in 48 holes with an average of three drills."

Kennco was also a pioneer in the introduction of geochemical surveys in early-stage mineral exploration, which resulted in a string of discoveries in Western Canada, including gold deposits in the Toodoggone and Galore Creek, a large copper-gold-silver deposit. Kennco also explored many deposits later developed (by others) into mines, such as Brenda, Endako, Lornex, Equity Silver (Sam Goosly), Huckleberry and Kemess, all in B.C.

Many recent advances in B.C.'s minerals industry were outside the traditional realms of mining, milling and exploration. Mine-site reclamation and environmental management were not priorities in the pioneer era, but are essential to success today.

Clem Pelletier recognized a growing need for experienced environmental planners when he founded Rescan, an environmental consulting firm, 30 years ago. Trained as a process chemist and metallurgist, he had previously spent 14 years with the Island Copper Mine on Vancouver Island. The mining industry endured some lean years in the late-1980s and early-1990s, but two major discoveries subsequently developed into mines gave Rescan a high-profile start. The firm won contracts for the Ekati diamond mine, in the Northwest Territories, and the Voisey's Bay nickel-copper-cobalt project, in Labrador, and grew from there into an internationally recognized, full-service environmental consulting firm.

Vancouver-based Rescan has won many awards for its environmental contributions in Canada and around the world and is also known for its progressive joint ventures with Aboriginal groups. The firm celebrated its 30th anniversary in 2011.

The minerals industry has also progressed in other areas that were given short shrift a century ago, notably corporate social responsibility (CSR) and Aboriginal engagement. Economic objectives trumped social and environmental values in the pioneer era, but times have changed, along with the industry. Companies now routinely consult with local communities, including Aboriginal leaders, before starting exploration programs. Mine proposals must go through a rigorous permitting process to ensure that the environment is protected and the site is restored as close as possible to its natural state after mining.

AME BC has developed tools and guidebooks to help resource companies implement CSR policies, as well as consultation and engagement with Aboriginal communities.

Another vital objective for AME BC involves something much more valuable than gold and diamonds, production and profits. A century ago, safety was often secondary to construction and production targets at mines, railways and other industrial work sites, resulting in widespread strikes and labor unrest. The first coal mines were notorious, with poorly paid new immigrants suffering the brunt of fatalities and injuries.

Safety is now paramount, as AME BC President Gavin Dirom pointed out in a letter published in a letter to Victoria's *Times Colonist* in mid-2011. "Over the past forty years, the B.C. mining industry, organized labour, and non-governmental organizations have successfully collaborated on developing effective regulation such as the Health, Safety and Reclamation Code for Mines in British Columbia, resulting in a world-leading safety record three times better than the average for all sectors in B.C. This is a well-deserved result that all citizens should know about and something that we can all take pride in."

Dirom emphasized that "…changing unsafe workplace behaviors through collaboration, training and leadership are the keys to achieving a culture of safety."

Since 1980, AME BC's Health & Safety Committee has provided strong leadership in providing tools and guidelines, including the booklet *Safety Guidelines for Mineral Exploration*, for a safe day, every day.

As Dirom often says, "The most important thing to come out of a mine is a miner."

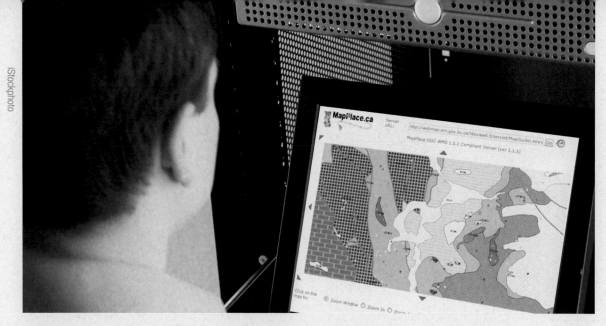

MapPlace, an example of B.C. software development expertise

MapPlace and Mineral Titles Online

B.C.'s strength in software development also has extended into the mineral exploration industry.

MapPlace was the product of government geoscientists and IT professionals with the B.C. Geological Survey led by Ward Kilby.

With the internet taking off in the 1990s, the geological survey was looking for a way to expose geological information to the internet and the global mineral exploration community. MapPlace quickly became the benchmark for serving up geological information to meet the research-heavy needs of the mining industry, to governments and to the public.

On the theory that every dollar invested will return at least four dollars and create a revenue stream for local and regional economies, MapPlace had the support of the Ministry – and the industry loved it.

MapPlace evolved to provide a number of tools and online prospecting applications that allowed the exploration community to become more efficient in gathering historical information and projecting geological models to ground held.

Another world-leading innovation was Mineral Titles Online (MTO), which was implemented by the B.C. Ministry of Energy, Mines and Petroleum Resources in January 2005 – yet another example of the high tech nature of B.C.'s mineral exploration sector. It introduced a modern, e-commerce approach to the way mineral tenure is acquired, managed and maintained in the province.

MTO was one of the most significant changes to the way the mining and exploration industry does business with the province in some 150 years of activity. A key objective was the focus to shift tenure management-related dollars into investments in ground exploration. In the years that followed MTO's launch, ground held in B.C. moved from an average of 4.5 million hectares to over 15 million hectares and exploration moved from lows of $25 million to over $400 million, and government retained the capacity to handle the increase in volume with a reduced workforce.

MTO has won numerous awards and recognition for its cutting edge approach to real-time mapping, tenure acquisition and management.

In addition to becoming established as industry standards for geological exploration research and property management, MapPlace and MTO have been acknowledged as being important for youth recruitment to the mining industry, providing young entrants with tools they can relate appreciate.

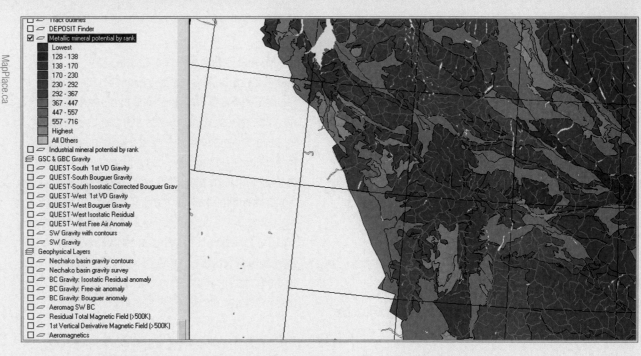

MapPlace.ca

Metallic mineral potential as viewed on MapPlace

Mineral Potential Assessment

During the 1990s, British Columbia became the first province or state to complete a comprehensive mineral potential assessment of its jurisdiction, an area of 948,596 square kilometres. The Mineral Potential project was initiated in 1992 by the B.C. Geological Survey to meet the need for current regional mineral potential information in support of regional and sub-regional land use planning.

These planning processes had the responsibility to make recommendations on protected areas, as described in the provincial Protected Areas Strategy. As mineral exploration and mining are proscribed in protected areas, it was important that participants in the planning process be provided with the best possible information, a semi-quantitative assessment of the mineral resource potential of areas under consideration for protection.

Project objectives were threefold:

- Rank the land base of the province by its ability to support economic activity through mineral exploration and extraction.

- Produce results that are credible and understandable by all user groups, to assure the results of the analysis are used in the land use planning process.

- Incorporate the expertise of the mining and exploration communities.

The study took five years to complete and involved over 30 person-years of staff time. It relied on a variety of government databases, including mineral occurrences, bedrock geology, regional geochemical survey, aeromagnetic survey and assessment reports. One of the major inputs to the project was an updated digital geological map of the province that drew on the collective expertise of many of the British Columbia Geological Survey staff. It also incorporated new geological mapping by the Geological Survey of Canada.

In addition a suite of deposit models were compiled and created to characterize the types of mineral deposits found in B.C. All the mapping products from the mineral potential project and much of the related data were posted to the web to allow users access to the information. It was this effort to communicate the results of the assessments in a timely manner that led to the creation of MapPlace.

The Mineral Potential Project developed a methodology that was largely based on the United States Geological Survey (USGS) three-part mineral resource assessment process that had been in use for several years on a variety of assessments around the world. While the basic assumptions were similar to those made by the USGS, there were several significant differences in the B.C. project including the scope of the project, the use of industry experts and the inclusion of industrial mineral deposits. The assessment process included not only estimates of the undiscovered resources but also included discovered resources for all known deposit types.

Estimation workshops were held for each of nine study areas in the province, at which industry experts and government staff could make estimates based on the probability of expected numbers of undiscovered deposits. To maintain the scientific integrity of the process, the expert estimates were made in confidence, following a group discussion of the available information, to avoid the psychometric issues surrounding group decision dynamics that commonly lead to an unscientific 'consensus' result. The result of an estimator's input was a probability distribution of the likelihood of a specific deposit type existing in a specific tract. Typically there would be three to five estimators making estimates for each deposit type in each tract. The province was divided into 794 tracts based on geological characteristics. Estimates were made assuming a median deposit size for the deposit type being estimated.

The results of the estimation process were probabilities of various numbers of each deposit type existing in each tract. A Monte Carlo simulator, Mark3B, provided by the USGS was used to combine the estimated number of deposits in each tract with the probability distributions of the grade and tonnage of each deposit type to determine the probability distribution of commodity volumes associated with each deposit type in each tract. The result was the ability to specify the volume of each commodity for each deposit at any desired confidence level. The Monte Carlo simulator creates these results by randomly sampling and combining the grade and tonnage of the known deposits that are included in the deposit model with the estimation probabilities. The results from all the deposits within a given tract are combined by commodity to give the total probability distribution for each commodity within each tract. The relative value of each commodity is based on their dollar value over a ten year period.

The objective of the mineral potential process in B.C. was to provide a relative ranking of the land base that could be considered along with many other land values in the land use planning process. To obtain the relative ranking, the median gross in-place value of all the commodities in each tract, normalized by the tract area, was used. These ranking were usually displayed with a ten class colour scheme where each class contained approximated 10 per cent of the assessment area. This very simple display scheme only conveyed a fraction of the information generated by the assessment. Some of the additional information has been included in MapPlace tools such as the Discovery Potential tool within the Exploration Assistant which maps out the areas most likely to host each of the deposit types include in the assessment. The estimates were often based on over 100 years of combined exploration experience of the expert estimators. Additional analyses have been conducted using the deposit types and their distributions to predict the style of potential mines and their associated employment and other economic impacts.

The assessment aimed to provide a scientifically sound evaluation of the relative mineral potential of the province based on estimations of undiscovered and discovered mineral resources. This information was then used in the planning process to recommend land use management plans based on the societal values represented by the participants in the planning process. The quality of the mineral potential assessment cannot be evaluated by the outcome of such a planning process other than by the fact that the information was used. A more telling evaluation was the concern expressed by professionals involved in the mineral industry that by identifying the most prospective areas they would become targets for alienation by anti-development segments of the planning processes. Fact or fiction, this concern signified an understanding and trust in the results of the assessment by those most qualified to judge.

Scott Heffernan

Mineral resource assessment starts in the field. Will Lepore collecting samples on the Tide property, northwestern B.C.

A claim tag – vital proof of mineral title in B.C. up to 2005, when Mineral Titles Online was launched.

Claims Staking in British Columbia

The history of claims staking in B.C. is a remarkable story of adaptation to need as the province evolved from its colonial beginnings.

Only limited historical information is available on the allocation of mineral rights during ancient times, except that the monarch or overlord owned them. During the Middle Ages in Europe, royal charters were granted to miners who paid tribute to the Crown. In the 17th century, miners in England bounded the

ground they wished to mine with stakes. About that time it became customary for a miner to work the claim continuously in order to retain his rights.

How much, if anything, Governor James Douglas knew about mining laws when gold was discovered on the Queen Charlotte Islands, we do not know. However, he was a man of action and took possession of the gold by issuing a proclamation on March 26, 1853 stating that only those with a mining licence issued by the commissioner in Victoria could mine gold within a described area.

When gold was discovered in the Fraser-Thompson Rivers country in 1857, Douglas issued a similar proclamation to regulate the flow of miners arriving from worked-out gold fields of California. Governor Douglas's actions not only reserved mineral rights to the Crown, but established British rights to the colony in-so-doing.

In 1858, Colonial Secretary Sir Edward Bulwer-Lytton suggested that Douglas establish regulations governing mining and sent him a copy of regulations used to manage recent gold rushes in Australia. Douglas proclaimed the Gold Fields Act in 1859.

This referred almost exclusively to placer but quartz claims, as hard rock mineral claims were known at the time, were also recognized. The Act provided for district gold commissioners and rules for locating and recording claims. It also defined a "free miner" as a person over 18 years of age with a Free Miner's Certificate. The certificate cost one pound sterling per year and authorized the holder to enter Crown and private land to search and dig for gold.

The Gold Fields Act allowed local mining boards to form when at least 101 free miners successfully petitioned the gold commissioner. American miners preferred being governed by mining boards that consisted of up to 12 free miners who made rules to adjust staking practices to suit local circumstances. For example, when Henry Davis, a 49er over-staked several existing claims, the board sanctioned a 12-foot fraction between the claims which yielded him $12,000 in gold and the nickname of "12-foot Davis."

From the beginning, miners were required to work their claims continuously. If absent more than 72 hours the claim was forfeited, unless the gold commissioner granted leave due to illness or permission to layover until spring, when the successful gold miners headed south to spend their new-found wealth. The continuous work requirement ended in 1883 with a provision to do $100 worth of work within three months of recording a claim. After 1891, work could be performed anytime during the year and recorded with the Gold Commissioner before the anniversary date in order to renew the claim for another year.

Following the Cariboo gold rush, claim staking rules gradually moved toward those we recognize today. In 1892, quartz claim allotments grew from the initial 100 feet square to 1,500 feet square. Also, the medieval provision called Apex rights (or extra-lateral rights), that allowed miners to claim ore-bearing veins that extended outside a claim boundary, came to an end. Henceforth mining rights stopped vertically downward from a claim boundary.

This is when two-post claims came into existence. A prospector staked his claim by cutting an initial post to specified dimension, marking out a location line along the terrain until he reached an estimated 1,500 feet from the initial post and placed a final post to complete his claim location. Two-post staking offered a prospector the convenience of projecting claim boundaries laterally without walking over rough terrain. Thus the lateral boundary would simply be described as lying 1,500 feet left or right of the location line. It could also be described as lying 750 feet left and right, or any combination, provided it totalled no more than 1,500 feet. The requirement that a discovery post be placed along the location line on top of a mineralized outcrop was dropped in 1938.

Early placer claim types were either creek, bar or dry diggings, rectangular in shape, and staked using four corner posts. Allowable claim dimensions gradually grew from 25 to 100 feet as the rush progressed and individuals required larger parcels to survive. A separate statute dealing with hard-rock minerals was enacted in 1877 but

placer claim staking remained under the old rules until 1891 when a separate statute was created for placer minerals. This allowed placer miners to stake a placer lease application using two posts to locate a rectangular area ½ by ¼ mile. The gold commissioner would then issue a 25-year lease that the miner would hold by performing at least $250 of assessment work each year in addition to paying an annual rent.

Throughout colonial and provincial history there existed provision for a claim holder to have his claim Crown granted. In the 1860s, a number of placer claims were legally surveyed and granted in the Barkerville area. Some of these titles still exist today and possess a unique combination of surface and complete sub-surface rights. Claim holders, who performed a prescribed amount of work, had their claim surveyed and were granted leases over their claims. Over 20,000 claims were Crown granted, many of which have now lapsed. The system of Crown granting claims was replaced in 1957 by the issue of a mining lease.

Specified subsurface rights were granted to land owners as early as the 1870s. Subsurface rights were also attached to the railway land grant lands. Determining the exact nature of these rights is a job for a land title expert who examines the original grant documents in the Land Title Office.

Early Development

The colonial period established the initial rules for claim staking and title maintenance; it also established the importance of the gold commissioner in managing mineral titles effectively.

Prospectors typically operated in specific regions and travelled to the nearest mining recorder to record their claims. The mining recorder would swear the affidavit, accept the fee and forward it to the gold commissioner for the appropriate mining division. The Department of Mines maintained gold commissioner offices in Victoria and Vancouver, but most gold commissioners were government agents, appointed to manage mining divisions in Kamloops, Cranbrook, Nelson, Smithers and other centres. Collectively they administered over 40 mining divisions in the 1920s. This number was reduced to 24 divisions in 1940 as a result of consolidating such small areas such as Bella Coola and Portland Canal with the Skeena division managed by the government agent in Smithers.

Prospectors developed a strong trust relationship with gold commissioner staff during this time. Staff would often take the time to fill out the necessary forms for uncertain applicants and explain changes in staking rules. In 1934 gold commissioners were authorized to buy a certain amount of placer gold from miners to help them survive during the Depression. The following year the ministry of mines established four placer training camps in the interior which helped hundreds of unemployed develop a prospecting trade. When claim tags were first introduced in 1934, staff worked hard to persuade prospectors to nail tags onto their claim posts instead of carrying them around on a wire loop for safekeeping.

Each gold commissioner office operated independently for many years and performed such duties as resolving staking disputes, negotiating access agreements onto private land and undertaking enforcement action when necessary. They met with landowners and claim holders to resolve access issues. Gold commissioners also maintained a map of recently-staked claims for prospectors to examine before setting out. One mining clerk recalled seeing a prospector lift his arms after leaning over the counter map and noticed the map was now blank. All the work she had done that morning had been eliminated. Instead, she saw a perfect imprint of the map on the prospector's forearms, presumably lifted from the paper by the corrosive effect of mosquito repellent on his skin.

In time, each statute governing claim staking included a leniency clause designed to forgive the well-meaning prospector. If a claim is officially challenged and it was shown in appeal court that a staker failed to comply with the staking requirements but that the failure was not intended to mislead others, a judge could dismiss challenges to the claim.

Some improvements to the staking system stemmed from legal precedents set during litigation, or from representations for change made by prospectors to government. In 1891 changes were made to allow prospectors to locate inaccessible ground by a witness post. Following litigation, a location line of a two post claim was to be measured horizontally and not along sloping terrain. The change also specified that, should a final post be found to be more than 1,500 feet from the initial post, it does not invalidate the claim. But, upon legal survey, a new final post would be placed at the correct distance from the initial post. The gap created by the over-extended location line could be covered by a fractional claim. Each change helped reduce uncertainty that might erode the security of staked claims when legally surveyed.

Modern Times

In 1942 the ministry of mines decided to create a duplicate record of each mining claim in the Victoria and Vancouver gold commissioner offices.

This meant that gold commissioner offices in the interior of the province would periodically send copies of every title transaction made in that office. The Victoria office undertook to prepare mineral titles reference maps to show the status of all claims staked in the province. This change provided title status information centrally. Over time, however, the department could not keep up with the volume of work involved. Also the pressure to reduce the size of government administration led to the search for another solution to maintain accurate and timely mineral title records. This situation set in motion a search for a solution over the ensuing 50 years.

The two-post staking system served prospectors well when it came to covering small areas in rugged terrain. However, as mineral exploration expanded, its geological target moved from vein structures to large porphyry deposits and two-post claims were used to cover larger areas. Thus, as more mining properties reached advanced exploration, requisite legal surveys conducted by mining companies discovered gaps and fractions not shown on the map. This led to significant delay as parties challenged each other to resolve ownership as the property became more valuable. It often led to disaster for the initial stakers if their claims were overstaked by another party, challenged and cancelled after investigation for being incorrectly staked.

In 1974 a new staking method called the Modified Grid System (MGS) was introduced as a hopeful solution to the two-post claim problem. The MGS claim used a Legal Corner Post (LCP) and three corner posts to define claim boundaries. Claim size could vary from one 500 metre grid unit up to 20 units. The prospector was required to place the LCP and cut a boundary line on all four sides of the claim, place identification posts every 500 metres along the boundary, place three corner posts with tags and return to the LCP to insert the completion time of the staking on the LCP tag. The prospector was required to accurately position the LCP on the Titles Reference Map.

From this point on, staking of two-post claims was forbidden. However, after prospectors made a representation to the minister, two-post claim staking was restored, allowing a prospector to stake only eight claims per year. Years later, two-post staking was restored without restriction. The combination of two-post staking and MGS created a new dynamic in acquired mineral claims in the province. An MGS claim required significant effort and time to locate the entire claim boundary, while two-post claims required less effort and the location line path could be selected to follow easier terrain.

In the early 1970s the ministry hired claims inspectors to verify the location of the Legal Corner Post in the field and correct the Mineral Titles Reference Maps as needed. Verification of two-post claims took more time and often resulted in exposing gaps and fractions which invited overstaking. The inspectors also investigated claim staking disputes and provided the chief gold commissioner with a report and recommendation as to whether the disputed claim should be cancelled, or the complaint dismissed.

AME BC

Staking a claim, 1978.

In Victoria, it became apparent that staff could not maintain up-to-date mineral title records and maps in each gold commissioner's office as well as in the Vancouver and Victoria offices. In the early 1980s the first attempt at automating mineral title records and maps was made. An electronic copy of over 100,000 claim records was entered into the computer system and a project to convert over 2,000 claim maps to digital form was initiated. Progress was slow and expensive, but staff and prospectors began to enjoy the benefits of having up-to-date printouts of claim records appear in their local gold commissioner office. Up-to-date computerized claim maps also began to appear but unfortunately, they were few and covered limited areas. Staff struggled to keep the majority of the manual mineral title reference maps up to date.

In the 1980s, government began to embrace computerization more seriously. Computerization of base maps became a corporate initiative funded by a number of ministries. Computerized record keeping also improved and methods were developed to link each claim record to its corresponding claim plotted on a computerized map. A communications network for computers was established to the gold commissioner offices, allowing each office to view claim records in real time. The Internet offered the opportunity for clients to access reasonably current claim records online. During this time, gold commissioner offices and staff were downsized and consolidated as the labour needed to update paper records and maps was no longer needed

Meanwhile, claim staking continued to increase due to high commodity prices in the 1990s. Advanced exploration properties typically struggled with claim staking disputes. The claims inspectors were kept busy investigating complaints and preparing reports for decision. The Eskay Creek camp was an extreme example where the original MGS or four post claims staked over the property were overstaked by six more layers of claims. It took months to inspect the claims and resolve each dispute. Some of these decisions were appealed to provincial and federal courts which took even more time and expense before ownership of the rich orebody was established.

This event and many others illustrated the vulnerability of ground staking. It was particularly evident that staking four post claims attracted challenges because it proved difficult, if not impossible, for anyone to stake four post claims flawlessly during a staking rush in rugged terrain. As a result, it became routine for prospectors to overstake and challenge four post claims whenever the value of the property was high enough to justify the expense.

In 1995 the definition of mineral was modified to include dimension stone which had been legally part of private land ownership since colonial times. Decorative stone was an emerging market at that time — suitable stone mostly came from Europe and Eastern Canada; local supply was limited by ownership entanglements in the province. The inclusion of dimension stone as a mineral had a profound impact on the province's stone industry, which still flourishes.

In 2005, government launched Mineral Titles Online (MTO), which completely transformed mineral title administration in the province. Clients received the ability to conduct all mineral title transactions online. The province was divided into grid cells, which free miners could select online, create a record of title and pay the recording fee, all within a few minutes, all through the Internet.

During the years leading to MTO, claim holders were urged to correct the location of their claims on the map. This became important because soon after implementation of MTO, all original or legacy claims were deemed to be correct on the map regardless of where their posts were located on the ground. This signalled a major shift in how mineral titles are managed, as the location of a claim on the ground had always been paramount.

British Columbia was the first jurisdiction to design and implement a real-time, full-service online staking system which has dramatically reduced the time and cost for claim-staking, and has streamlined the filing and record-keeping procedures.

Honourable Life Members receive gold pans at the first Roundup

AME BC's Roundup

Mineral Exploration Roundup, or Roundup as it is fondly known, is the cornerpost of AME BC.

Since its debut in 1984, through the peaks and pits of the exploration cycles, Roundup has consistently provided a valuable venue for the exploration community to meet, discuss, learn and play. What began as a discussion on a ferry in February 1982 has become the world's premier technical mineral exploration conference.

The nub of the ferry-born discussion was how to tackle the declining membership, declining attendance at the annual general meeting and ensuing declining revenues of the B.C. & Yukon Chamber of Mines. The annual general meeting's format of a daylong meeting followed by a dinner and dance was getting old and the members' apathy was apparent by their absence. The exploration sector was struggling at the time, and the Association's executive members recognized the need for a nucleus to pull together all those who had a vested interest in the survival of mineral exploration in B.C., hence the huddle on the ferry

among managing director Jack Patterson, president Bob Cathro, and soon-to-become second vice-president, Nick Carter. These three, along with Don Mustard, Don Rotherham, Charlie Aird and Terry Macauley, who masterminded the technical program, were the architects behind the concept of building a conference around the AGM.

The B.C. Geological Survey branch of the Ministry of Energy, Mines and Petroleum Resources was approached with the concept of combining its open house with the AGM. The open houses, put on by the geological divisions of the federal, provincial and territorial governments, lacked verve and did little to stimulate exploration investment. The geological survey leapt at the opportunity to move its open house to Vancouver from Victoria and run it as part of the bigger program envisioned by the Association. Carter recalled there being some discussion as to whether or not the date of late January was feasible for the survey to have its field data ready for presentation. He successfully argued the point that it was invaluable to the exploration community to have the data available early in the year. The traditional release of field data is one of the many reasons Roundup kick-starts the year for B.C.'s exploration sector. Eventually everyone came on board and the conference was billed as a "joint venture of the British Columbia Ministry of Energy, Mines and Petroleum Resources; Geological Survey of Canada; Indian and Northern Affairs Canada (Yukon branch) and the Chamber."

Roundup Then

Jack Patterson coined the name "The Cordilleran Geology and Exploration Roundup," which summed up the focus of the conference in that era. Since then, the name has changed somewhat to better reflect the conference's growing global reputation.

The executive, staff and a handful of volunteers threw themselves into building a three-day conference from scratch. In 1984, the first Roundup was held at the Holiday Inn Harbourside. It was a resounding success with more than 700 registrants from government, industry and the supply and service sector. Looking back, Bob Cathro said, "I recall being delighted that our idea proved correct – that the poorly-attended geological survey open houses and AME BC's poorly-attended AGM could be improved for the benefit of the members. We were trying to improve the format of the AGM so that it wouldn't lose so much money. We certainly had no idea it would grow into a small industry of its own that would guarantee the financial viability of the Association."

The Core Shack also made its debut in 1984, marking the first time in North America that such a varied assortment of drill core was displayed at a major geological conference. The previous year, at the annual convention of PDAC, core from the Hemlo deposit was on display in Noranda's hospitality suite. For many, it was the first opportunity to view core from that camp and the novelty of the experience caught the imagination of Jeff Franzen. He became the driving force behind the initial Core Shack – the model of which is still followed today. Franzen arranged for Noranda, Golden Sceptre and Goliath to bring core to Vancouver. He also assembled an impressive array of core from deposits around B.C.

It's interesting to note that in 1983, the AGM, traditionally held at Hotel Vancouver, was moved to the more modest Holiday Inn as a cost-saving measure. The first Roundup was also held at the Holiday Inn, but Patterson, seeing the potential for substantial growth, quickly booked the 1985 Roundup at Hotel Vancouver to allow for the inclusion of exhibitor booths. One remarkable feature about Roundup is that never, in its 29-year history, has it had to market the sale of booths – even when the industry was in a slump. The conference has always had a solid core of reliable, loyal companies who purchased booth space every year. Today, there is such demand that booth space is generally booked up a year in advance, with priority given to the previous year's exhibitors. A waiting list of hopefuls is begun shortly after the conference closes.

In 1998, AME BC teamed up with the Society of Economic Geologists to jointly host Pathways '98, thereby marking a turning point in the stature of the conference. Whereas the previous conferences had been run by Association staff and a few volunteers, the magnitude of preparing for the much larger 1998 conference demanded a more targeted approach. A Roundup Committee was formed and from that hub, along with a vast number of volunteers, Pathways '98 was a record-smashing success. In fact, the conference was so large it had to straddle both the Hotel Vancouver (booths and entertainment) and Hyatt Regency (talks and presentations). Roundup stayed with that format until 2003, when the conference moved to the more commodious Westin Bayshore, thus amalgamating the whole conference under one roof. There was some grumbling within the membership that the Westin was too far away from the nucleus of offices in the heart of Vancouver, but a complimentary shuttle bus service dissolved the dissent. Concern was also voiced that the conference might never grow to fill the space at the Westin Bayshore, but that fear certainly was unfounded. The first year there was an unqualified success and, since that time, the hotel has been very creative in expanding the available space, using marquis tents for the core shack and prospector's tent exhibits.

The timing of Roundup has always been in its favour, set as it is just after the post-Christmas trough, when everyone is back from holidays but before the winter drill programs begin. It is the first conference of the year, so everyone is eager to network and reconnect with peers and friends. The energy in the air is almost palpable.

Roundup Now

Roundup has become, to AME BC, almost an industry unto itself.

An entire team of staff members is now dedicated to planning the event and overseeing the vast minutiae of details during the conference. A former Roundup chair, Randy Turner, says the event's unwavering success is due to the energy and commitment of AME BC staff and the army of volunteers. It is one thing to attract volunteers when the sector is flatlining, but it is quite another to do the same when it is enjoying feverish activity. B.C.'s exploration community is proud of its conference, and that pride is reflected in ensuring that Roundup is better every year.

In terms of attendance the annual conference continued on an exponential uptrend to 2008, reaching 6,700 participants. That year began a difficult time for the industry and the global economy and, as a result, the number of participants dropped to 5,800 in both 2009 and 2010. But Roundup rebounded to record attendance in 2011 of 7,000 – and then 8,300 in 2012. Each year has brought an expanded program, new side events at which to mingle and exchange ideas and business cards and new opportunities for improving the explorer's tool kit through short courses, workshops and presentations.

The exploration community is large, stretching to the far corners of the world. Nowhere is that sense of community more apparent than in the hallways and corners of the Westin Bayshore during the last week of January.

AME BC

Roundup "Then" – Mines minister Stephen Rogers presents the E.A. Scholz Award to Bob Hallbauer, 1984

AME BC

Roundup "Now" - Dr. Norman B. Keevil, Jr. addresses the audience at Roundup 2012

A Safe Day, Everyday

"Safety is prevention of injury when exposed to danger. Promotion of safe working practices is the responsibility of all workers in the mineral exploration industry."

The above words appear in the opening text of the original Safety Manual: Mineral Exploration in Western Canada, issued by the Safety Committee of the Chamber on April 20, 1981. These words have rung true for the past 30 years but, more recently, AME BC and the Prospectors & Developers

Association of Canada (PDAC) have pared them down to a few words: "Have a safe day, everyday."

The original safety manual had a life its own. It evolved into AME BC's current Safety Guidelines for Mineral Exploration in Western Canada and was a cornerstone of PDAC's Health and Safety in Exploration toolkit. It is now a guiding document for preventing incidents in any mineral exploration setting. The safety manual and other programs AME BC offers had tragic beginnings.

The year 1980 stands out in the annals of exploration history as particularly tragic in Western Canada. Nine

individuals lost their lives that year. David Barr, then VP Exploration, DuPont Canada Exploration Ltd. was involved in the aftermath of a horrific helicopter crash. Four DuPont employees and their pilot were killed. Those whose task it was to visit the crash site, recover the bodies and inform the victims' families, were profoundly affected.

Barr dealt with his grief by vowing to do something constructive for safety in the exploration industry. That fall he launched an initiative that would become his personal mission for the next 22 years. He proposed to the Chamber, where he was a director, that a formal safety working group be created to educate and keep track of the safety record in Western Canada. Barr chaired the safety committee until 2002. The initial objective was the production of 5,000 copies of a safety manual, which was issued in draft form in 1981, and re-issued in 1982, 1989, and 2006, with over 26,000 copies distributed as this went to press.

Safety Survey

The safety committee also produced a safety survey for annual circulation to all exploration companies active in B.C. and Yukon, starting in 1982.

By 2004, surveys were sent to 150 companies, half of whom replied. Given the lack of a Canada-wide safety program, AME BC and PDAC teamed up to make the survey national, resulting in the *Canadian Mineral Exploration Health & Safety Survey*.

In order for the safety committee to track types of accidents and provide training to heighten awareness of potential hazards, all companies, regardless of size, are encouraged to respond to the questionnaire. The survey distinguishes between surface exploration, which covers geochemical, geological and geophysical work and line cutting; and diamond drilling and underground exploration. By sending out the survey and

following up with a reminder phone call, AME BC and PDAC encourage companies to think about safety and how to prepare employees for the coming field season. The Safe Day Everyday Award recognizes all companies who report a lost-time free year, and the Safe Day Everyday Gold Award is presented to the organization that reports the most lost workday-free hours in a calendar year. FNX Mining Company Inc., now incorporated within Quadra FNX Mining Ltd., received the inaugural nationwide award for 2005, and again was presented the honour for 2009 and 2010.

Workshops and Awareness

Since 1984, the Health & Safety Committee has hosted workshops about issues ranging from behavioural safety through hypothermia to safety around drills.

For the first year in 2011, this group hosted two separate workshops: *Introduction to Exploration Safety* and *Exploration Safety for Project Managers*. Over 90 people took advantage of this training with presentations from industry experts prior to the field season.

In the past, companies often questioned the need for safety awareness. As late as 2005, then Health & Safety group chair, Ian Paterson, said, "Safety

awareness is not considered a very macho attribute in this macho industry, an attitude that needs to change. The industry attracts a certain type of self-reliant adventurous person and those are the characteristics needed to do the work." AME BC's initiatives were aimed at getting "…exploration companies, especially the juniors, to realize that an improvement in safety is an improvement in efficiency that can significantly affect the bottom line." Awareness has spread, and through the leadership of Barr, Paterson and Rob Pease, AME BC's initiatives have been adopted or adapted by PDAC, Yukon Mine Training Association, Saskatchewan Mining Association, Northwest Community College School of Exploration and Mining, and companies operating around the world.

The Legacy

In 2005, the Health & Safety Committee inaugurated the David Barr Award to recognize leadership and innovation in mineral exploration health and safety. This award recognizes companies and individuals whose passion for and achievement in health and safety are reflected in the mineral exploration sector as a whole. AME BC has honoured Imperial Metals Corporation, Ian Paterson, Bill Mercer, Doug Flynn, Harvey Tremblay and Michael Gunning with the award.

Women in Mining booth at Roundup 2010.

Women in Mining:
From Bush to Boardroom

Canada's fledgling mining industry and related associations were unabashed male bastions for many decades before the first women appeared in administrative roles. But that hasn't deterred some pioneering women from achieving success in a "man's world" on their own steam, inspiring younger generations of women to follow in their footsteps.

Delina Noel personified that pioneering spirit and is still remembered in the Lillooet and Bridge River mining communities for her leadership role in building British Columbia's gold-mining industry. The trailblazing miner, metallurgist and entrepreneur was presented the Governor General's Centennial Medal for her contributions to the province in 1958. The 78-year-old then returned to the bush, near her beloved Bridge River district, where she was developing a mining project.

Born in Lillooet in 1880, Noel came to the mining industry by circumstance rather than design. At age 19, she married local prospector Arthur Noel and

travelled by pack train over McGillivray Pass to the Bridge River Valley, where her husband had mining claims. She was eager to learn the business in the field, much to the dismay of her husband's crew, who believed women were "bad luck" at mines and threatened to quit if she continued her visits. Arthur Noel responded by giving his wife authority to inspect the working faces. The miners stayed and so did Delina, who became superintendent of the Bend'Or 10-stamp mill in 1902, and later operated a five-stamp mill at the Lorne mine.

Her leadership abilities came to the fore as her responsibilities increased to include shaft-sinking, hiring miners, transporting gold bars and supplies; and finding and developing mineral properties. She was an accomplished trapper, hunter and outdoor enthusiast. Her mink coat was made entirely of pelts that she trapped herself.

Delina and Arthur Noel recovered an estimated $160,000 worth of gold from mines they operated between 1916 and 1928, a fortune at the time. They made another fortune by acquiring and selling mining properties, including the Pioneer mine, which became one of Canada's deepest and most prolific gold producers. The couple separated in 1929, but Delina remained in the Bridge River Valley, where she successfully worked her own projects and became a local icon. She was a strong supporter of the Girl Guides of Canada, opening up her custom-built log home for their activities for many years.

Viola MacMillan, known in her day as the "Queen Bee" of Canadian mining, was also introduced to the industry through marriage to a prospector. The Ontario-born dynamo was equally at home in the bush — where she explored claims and developed mines across Canada (including B.C.) — and in the boardroom, thanks to her business savvy and experience as a legal secretary.

She was best known for her leadership role in building PDAC into a vibrant industry association. But her legacy was tarnished by a wash-trading conviction (for which she was later pardoned) stemming from the 1960s Windfall scandal. Still, she was later appointed to the Order of Canada.

The Viola MacMillan gallery in the Canadian Museum of Nature now houses the world famous Pinch Mineral Collection (she donated one quarter of its purchase price) and she remains the only woman elevated to the Canadian Mining Hall of Fame. (See The 1960s, page 31 and Viola MacMillan, page 197).

Many talented women supported Canada's mining industry indirectly during the past century, including wives and "grass widows" who often pulled up roots to move from one mining town to the next. Mining camps across the nation were much improved by their collective dedication to community, charitable and industry causes.

Some women who began but left industry careers for family life remained engaged in the mining community, as Marilyn Mullan did after moving West in the 1970s. She landed her first "female geologist" position with the National Research Council in Nova Scotia, where she met and married Ash Mullan. In B.C., Marilyn became a tireless supporter of the Britannia Beach Historical Society, which was striving to raise funds to preserve the struggling B.C. Museum of Mining. In 2003, she received AME BC's Frank Woodside Past Presidents' Award for her many years of dedicated effort in support of the museum.

A year earlier, Sheila Holmes received the same award for distinguished service after more than 20 years as Office Administrator with the BC & Yukon Chamber of Mines.

"Sheila helped many prospectors and job-seekers who came through the doors over the years," says Don Mustard, past president of the Chamber. And so did May Martin, who also worked in administrative capacity for more than a decade before retiring in 1975.

Later, in the early 1990s, Maureen Lipkewich pioneered the introduction of geoscience education to public schools as a partnership between teachers and B.C.'s minerals industry. The widely emulated Mineral Resources Education Program is now considered the best of its kind in the world.

Mining companies began recruiting more women in the post-war boom years, initially in administrative and clerical roles. One of the first women to break into the boardroom was Irene Wilson, who began her career working with geological engineer William Sirola in 1963. She then joined prospector Al Kulan's Spartan Explorations and Welcome North Mines, as a corporate secretary. Kulan was a Yukon legend in the mid-1960s for his role in a lead-zinc discovery near Ross River later developed into the Faro mine. Irene Wilson went on to senior management and board roles with several juniors in subsequent years, notably managing Esperanza Explorations and as founding president of Aquiline Resources. She also worked on Chamber initiatives, including a campaign to increase awareness of the VSE's role in mineral discovery. (Welcome North Mines ultimately became the public vehicle for Frank Giustra's Endeavour Financial.)

Female geologists, engineers and entrepreneurs began to appear in greater numbers in the 1980s and 1990s, in tandem with the growth of Vancouver's vibrant junior mining sector.

Among the pioneers of that era was Nell Dragovan, who acquired rights to an Ontario gold property while at the helm of Corona Resources in the early 1980s. She teamed up with Murray Pezim to finance a drilling program that, after 76 holes, confirmed the presence of rich gold deposits later developed into the Hemlo gold mines. And she didn't stop there. Along with geologist husband Chet Idziszek (who led the discovery team at the Eskay Creek gold-silver project in northwestern B.C.), Dragovan continued to serve as an officer and director of several juniors that made significant mineral discoveries, notably the Oromin Joint Venture Gold Project in Senegal (Oromin Explorations Ltd.)

Dragovan, an avid gardener in her spare time, never sought the limelight or media attention that often focused on successful women in a male-dominated industry.

Metallurgist Peggy Witte, known today as Margaret Kent, became a celebrity in the late 1980s when she assembled underperforming gold mines and successfully restored them to production. But her flagship Royal Oak Mines later floundered for a variety of reasons, including a bitter labour dispute at the Giant gold mine in Yellowknife, in which nine replacement workers lost their lives to an explosion set by a disgruntled union miner. This tragic event overshadowed many of Witte's later career accomplishments, including placing the Kemess copper-gold mine into production in north-central B.C. Royal Oak had previously acquired control of Geddes Resources and its Windy Craggy copper-cobalt project in northwestern B.C. After the government terminated the project by including it in a new park in 1993, Witte negotiated a compensation plan that included funds to advance the Kemess mine and related infrastructure. She subsequently lost control of the mine to Northgate Minerals Corporation during an industry downturn.

Linda Thorstad worked as a field geologist in Nevada and other mining camps in the 1980s before advancing to the executive boardroom with various junior companies in the 1990s. She served as an associate of the B.C. Commission on Resources and Environment (CORE) during a period of contentious land use debates and was appointed President of the Association of Professional Engineers and Geoscientists of B.C. in 1995-1996. She was also a volunteer and former vice president of the B.C. & Yukon Chamber of Mines, as well as a recipient of its Past Presidents' Award for Distinguished Service in 2004.

Two of the Canada's best known female mining executives — Eira Thomas and Catherine McLeod-Seltzer — came from mining families where dinner conversation focused on "rocks and stocks" and the menu varied from fine to plain fare depending on market conditions. And both paid their dues in the trenches before finding success.

In the early 1990s, Thomas worked as a field geologist for Aber Resources Ltd., a junior founded a decade earlier by her father, mining engineer Grenville Thomas. Their goal was to find diamond deposits of economic interest in the Barren Lands of the Northwest Territories, similar to those found in the Lac de Gras region by Chuck Fipke's Dia Met Resources Ltd. and partner BHP Minerals. But initial discoveries proved disappointing, putting at risk Aber's joint venture with Kennecott, a unit of global giant, Rio Tinto.

Thomas, then leading the Aber field team, and co-worker Robin Hopkins decided to drill an untested target under a lake, spotting the original drill holes in 1994. A clear two-carat diamond was found embedded in a piece of drill core, a rare event in diamond exploration. Subsequent drilling confirmed the presence of high-grade diamondiferous kimberlites that were later developed into the successful Diavik diamond mine.

Thomas, dubbed by media as the "Queen of Diamonds," participated in the Diavik discovery just four years after graduating from the University of Toronto with a B.Sc. in geology in 1990. And she's been at the forefront of the hunt for new diamond deposits ever since with various junior companies, notably Stornoway Diamond Corporation.

Thomas was a recipient of the prestigious Caldwell Partners and Report on Business Canada's prestigious Canada's Top 40 Under 40 Award in 2004, and was named one of Canada's Most

Powerful Women by the Women's Executive Network in 2007. In 2008, she was named a Young Global Leader by the World Economic Forum. And she also became a mother, juggling career and family responsibilities along with other women in mining, including long-time friend and Stornoway colleague, Catherine McLeod-Seltzer.

McLeod-Seltzer, daughter of renowned mine-maker Don McLeod, got her start in the tough-as-nails brokerage business before teaming up with geologist David Lowell to form Arequipa Resources in the early 1990s. The partners discovered a world-class gold deposit in Peru, later acquired by Barrick Gold for $1.1 billion.

Female mining executives were as rare as hen's teeth in the last century, and not much had changed well into the 21st century, despite the increased presence of female geologists, engineers and other professionals in the bush and the boardroom. In 2011, at 14.4 per cent, the representation of women in mineral exploration and mining was the lowest among primary industries in Canada, well below the labour force average of 47.4 per cent.

Ramp-UP: A Study on the Status of Women in Canada's Mining and Exploration Sector was conducted by the Women in Mining Canada and Mining Industry Human Resources Council (MIHR) in 2009. The goals were to examine barriers faced by women in mining and mineral exploration and then gather recommendations on how best to attract more women to the industry.

The main barriers and challenges identified were: insufficient flexibility in the work environment, making it difficult to balance family and work life; a lack of female mentors and role models; the cyclical nature of the industry; an unequal balance between men and women at the senior levels; and a generally male-dominated and male-oriented culture, among others factors.

Shari Gardiner, Executive Vice President Corporate Communications for Vancouver-based Hunter Dickinson Inc. (HDI) and the first woman to become president of AME BC, admits she was surprised and shocked by the low participation rates cited in the study.

"I thought it would be a higher percentage of women, because there are many women at HDI, and a number of them in management and the professions, although no CEOs."

Gardiner says there is better workplace flexibility now than was the case in her early career, when she was a young mother. She worked as a field geologist from 1979 to 1990, relying on a supportive husband (also a geologist) to help sustain her career.

"It was a tough time for the industry and hard to get good employment or mentorship."

But Gardiner didn't see the male-dominated environment as a barrier, as she never intended to pursue a "traditional" female career. "I really like the people and the culture of the industry, so

I disagree with that one." On the other hand, she notes that "…perhaps [some] women do not assume that they have to have the top job and instead focus on gaining a role with influence balanced with a variety of other goals."

The *Ramp-UP* study identified a "winning attitude" and being proactive in career development, learning and networking as success factors of women in mining and exploration. Volunteering with industry associations was also identified as helpful.

Gardiner became interested in AME BC after attending the first Roundup. She was later asked by Ed Kimura (her boss at Placer at the time) to attend meetings in his absence and report back on various matters. This led to her becoming involved in the Cariboo Chilcotin land-use plan, where Placer had the Gibraltar mine at the time, which in turn led to her being asked to head up the Land Use Committee for much of the tumultuous 1990s. Next, she was asked to stand for the board and become a member of the executive.

Since Gardiner was appointed the Association's first female president (2002-2003), AME BC has benefited from increased female representation at the board level and on many of its committees. Susan Craig and Lena Brommeland are just two of the many female stalwarts who have served on the Roundup Committee in recent years. Craig was on the board of directors for several years and also co-chaired (with Brommeland) the sponsorship committee, which raises funds for many AME BC events. Brommeland also served in other capacities, in addition to being a past chair and a past director.

One recommendation of the *Ramp-UP* study calls for mining employers to focus on professional development for women, particularly in view of anticipated skills shortages in the years ahead. Other recommendations were to highlight female role models through mentorship programs and encourage informal networks of support for women.

Progress is being made on these fronts. Women are now supporting and mentoring each other through organizations such as Women in Mining (WIM). Today there are WIM branches all over the world, with thousands of members.

WIM got its start in Ontario — a slow informal start — after Nean Allman, the first female reporter at *The Northern Miner* was assigned to do a story on women in mining, who were few and far between at the time in 1969. Allman says the editor liked the story so much that he suggested she take the group of four interviewed women to lunch.

(Allman was also the first female president of the Geological Association of Canada in 1981-82. She later established her own corporate communications company "to help mining companies tell their story" and was also involved in event management and the development of a new exhibit for the Canadian Mining Hall of Fame.)

The women met again for informal lunches, with the group growing in numbers as more women attended the social gatherings, which they organized on a volunteer basis. Today, the Toronto chapter of Women in Mining is a powerful networking organization, with its membership consisting of more than 250 well-connected women working in all aspects of the mining sector

Meanwhile, in Vancouver, WIM had a somewhat similar origin: it began with a lunch. Barbara Caelles, with more than 30 years' experience in the industry, was at a Vancouver Mining Exploration Group (MEG) luncheon back in 2002, and struck up a casual conversation with another MEG member, Diane Gregory. The talk got more and more specific and before long the two women were discussing the notion of a Vancouver-based organization for women in mining.

They meet every month, where, for example, presentations are given on various topics such as research being done by the Mining Industry Human Resources Council about women in the mining industry and resources available to them. "We keep it simple," Caelles said, "…lunches, a speaker. We don't lobby, just network." They began with about 20 email contacts in 2002. That grew quickly to 40, then 60, and at last count (in October 2011) was about 600. "It's word-of-mouth that keeps it going and growing."

Caelles' interest in the field began when she was a young girl who happened to love hiking. In the 1960s she was hiking in the Tantalus Range, parallel to the Sea to Sky Highway to Whistler, with

a group one of whom was a geophysicist, "I had a Eureka moment," she said. "I can get *paid* for doing what I like!" But after getting a summer job doing geophysics with AMAX, she switched to geology and graduated from UBC with a B.Sc.

In 1974, the GAC Status of Women Geoscientists committee was set up with Nean Allman as the head and later Barbara took over from Nean. The findings of the Status of Women Committee were published in *GAC Information Circular No.2 in 1976*. It brought about an awareness of women working in the geoscience profession. It was the first such study conducted.

In 2011 the B.C. Mineral Exploration and Mining Labour Shortage Task Force, issued a Report: *"Women: An Unmined Resource: A report on female participation within B.C.'s Mineral Exploration and Mining industry."*

The report is based on extensive surveying of three primary B.C.-based populations:

1. *Women working in the B.C. mineral exploration and mining industry;*

2. *Human resources decision makers in the B.C. mineral exploration and mining industry; and*

3. *Student Career Advisors from secondary and post-secondary institutions across B.C.*

Like the previous reports it had similar findings, but this time was generated from responses within B.C.

One of the quirks of the mineral exploration community is that it is remarkably small and attracts some very gifted talents. One such talent is 'Lyn Anglin. She is a scientist and a leader, an active professional citizen and a mentor.

Her research expertise is in mineral deposit geology and radiogenic isotope geochemistry. She has a B.Sc. from Queen's University in Kingston, a M.Sc. from Memorial University in Newfoundland, and a PhD from Carleton University in Ottawa. She is registered as a Professional Geologist with the Association of Professional Engineers and Geoscientists of B.C.

She was appointed President and CEO of Geoscience BC (GBC) in 2006. Prior to joining GBC, she was the acting Director of the Pacific Division of the Geological Survey of Canada (GSC). She has spent over 20 years managing exploration geoscience research projects in various areas across Canada.

Anglin is an active member of the Vancouver mineral exploration community. With extensive experience in program management, policy development, public consultation and community engagement, she is active on the boards of Geoscience BC, the Resources North Association, and the Association for Mineral Exploration BC and also a member of the Steering Committee of the School of Exploration Mining at Northwest

Community College in Smithers, serves on committees of PDAC and the Society of Economic Geologists and is a former president of the Geological Association of Canada.

She is a sponsor and promoter of education of young people. Interested in Science World, she has done a lot of outreach to grade- and high-schoolers to promote geoscience, and science in general, and feels that all young people can and should be turned onto science.

'Lyn Anglin

Mrs. McNee, Yukon prospector c. 1940s

Greg Dawson

Sampling at Oweekeno, 2003

Aboriginal Engagement

A History of Exclusion

Long before British Columbia became a Crown Colony, it was populated by Aboriginal tribes deeply attached to the lands they had occupied for thousands of years. Today, in contrast to other parts of Canada, almost two-thirds of B.C.'s Aboriginal population is still negotiating treaties for lands and resources within their traditional territories.

How British Columbia came to be an anomaly in the Canadian landscape is deeply rooted in its polarized past.

Governor James Douglas, the "Father of British Columbia," negotiated 14 treaties with First Nations on Vancouver Island between 1851 and 1854 in the same manner used for settlement in Canada and other British colonies. This policy was based on a 1763 Royal Proclamation which recognized Aboriginal tribes as sovereign nations that owned the lands they occupied. Treaties were viewed as a lawful way to extinguish Aboriginal title so ownership could pass to the Crown or other parties.

Douglas, also a senior officer of the Hudson's Bay Company (HBC) at the time, used the treaty process to secure resources on HBC's behalf, including coal beds

identified by First Nations near Nanaimo on Vancouver Island. But he wasn't always successful. When reports surfaced that a Haida woman from the Queen Charlotte Islands (now Haida Gwaii) had brought in a large gold nugget to a HBC post for trade, Douglas organized an expedition to the coastal islands. It was repulsed by "hostile natives," as was another attempt to examine rumored coal deposits there.

HBC then put out the word to coastal and mainland tribes that any yellow nuggets found in streams and rivers could be traded for goods. Enough gold was found for HBC to send its first shipment to the U.S. Mint in San Francisco by April 1858.

The news triggered a gold rush. An estimated 30,000 miners and fortune-seekers, mostly from California, streamed up the Fraser and Thompson Rivers.

Douglas put on his "government hat" to assert British sovereignty and law-and-order in the wake of the largely American invasion. He proclaimed the Crown's control of mineral rights and a system of miner's licenses. In late 1858, the Colony of British Columbia (formerly New Caledonia) was established with Douglas as its first Governor (he resigned his HBC post at this time).

The gold rush pushed Aboriginal miners from the most productive areas and off their lands in some cases. Tensions escalated as road construction, hydraulic mining and deforestation devastated salmon habitat. Diseases and social ills also took their toll.

The British Empire, then focused on expansion in resource-rich India, balked at providing financial resources to a remote new colony for treaty negotiations. Douglas shifted to a system of reserves and allowed tribes to help select the sites. He also gave natives rights to acquire land through the same system used by settlers. He was sympathetic to their plight, perhaps because he was of mixed blood and his wife's mother was Cree. But many settlers felt he was too generous.

Joseph Trutch, a British-born surveyor and civil engineer who came to B.C. from California, made no secret of his disdain for B.C.'s First Nations.

He was highly influential after making his fortune building bridges and roads to B.C. gold fields. When Douglas retired in 1864, Trutch was appointed Chief Commissioner of Lands and Works.

Trutch dismissed the Douglas treaties as "…made for the purpose of securing friendly relations…" between natives and early settlers. His new Indian Land Policy explicitly denied Aboriginal title; many reserves were reduced in size. Aboriginal people could no longer acquire land through the pre-emption settlement process.

Under the new policy, reserves in the Fraser Valley and Central Interior were the first of many to be downsized. Chiefs of the Coast Salish tribes protested in front of the Land Registry office in New Westminster, among other protests, all to no avail.

Hopes for a resolution were raised when B.C. joined the Canadian Confederation in 1871. The Dominion Government promised to assume "…charge of the Indians, and the trusteeship and management of the lands reserved for their use and benefit."

Historical accounts show Ottawa was aware that B.C.'s Indian Policy was contrary to the treaty process. But Trutch argued that a treaty system would not work in the province and would undo "…all that has been done here for 30 years past." His views resonated with settlers who wanted the best farming and grazing lands and access to resources to help establish the fledgling mining, forestry and fishing industries.

Trutch became B.C.'s first Lieutenant Governor and appointed the province's first premier, who shared his views. These views were also shared by other premiers who followed in quick succession (B.C. had 14 designated or elected premiers by late 1900, including one who served twice).

Aboriginal leaders sent petitions to Victoria and Ottawa. The Governor General of Canada, the Earl of Dufferin, toured B.C. in 1876 and noted in his parting address that the Trutch policies were implemented so as to "…greatly restrict or interfere with the prescriptive rights of the Queen's Indian subjects." As a consequence, he added, "there has come to exist an unsatisfactory feeling amongst the Indian populations."

A joint commission to investigate these concerns recommended that B.C. pursue the treaty process but the advice was ignored.

In 1880, Peter O'Reilly, Trutch's like-minded brother-in-law, became Indian Reserve Commissioner, a post he held for the next decade. He continued to reduce the size of reserves, creating yet another round of Aboriginal protests. The Nisga'a and other tribes in northwestern B.C. refused to allow provincial land surveyors on their lands.

The government used repressive tactics to stifle native unrest, including banning the cultural tradition of potlatch.

In 1899, Alberta's Treaty 8 was extended to B.C.'s Peace River Country to resolve an Aboriginal blockade threatening access to the Klondike. It was the last treaty signed that century. While not a single treaty was signed in the century that followed, breakthroughs did occur that ultimately led to a new era of Aboriginal engagement.

Stepping Stones to Inclusion

When AME BC's predecessor was formed in 1912, the issue of Aboriginal title was still simmering.

Prime Minister Wilfred Laurier urged B.C. to recognize Aboriginal land rights and in response, a Royal Commission on Indian Affairs was established in 1912. It reviewed the size of reserves, added new ones and reduced others, but achieved little else.

In 1913, Duncan Scott took the helm of the federal Department of Indian Affairs and adopted a policy of assimilation, which continued until his retirement in 1932. He also made it mandatory for all Aboriginal children to attend residential schools.

During this period, B.C.'s Aboriginal population fell to roughly 25,000, compared with an estimated 100,000 in the colonial era. They had no political voice or vote until 1949 provincially, and 1960 federally. A 1927 law making it illegal to raise money to pursue native land claims through the courts remained in effect until 1951.

The Nisga'a revived their longstanding claim, which led to the first transformative Aboriginal victory in

the courts in 1973. Their action, *Calder v. Attorney-General of British Columbia*, made its way to the Supreme Court of Canada, which ruled that Canadian law did recognize Aboriginal rights to land based on historic occupation. But whether such rights could be extinguished by law was left undecided.

In 1984, the Gitksan and Wet'suwet'en hereditary chiefs launched an action for rights related to their traditional territories in the Skeena watershed. *Delgamuukw v. British Columbia* was a long and complex case involving oral histories. In 1991, trial judge Allan McEachern found that the plaintiffs had some "subsistence" Aboriginal rights in these territories, but not ownership or jurisdiction. He also ruled that such rights were "extinguished" by colonization and pre-colonial legislation.

Bill Wolfe, then President of the B.C. & Yukon Chamber of Mines, said the ruling reflected the government's prevailing view at the time. But attitudes were starting to change, he added, notably after Bill Vander Zalm was elected premier in 1986.

"It was actually under him that this policy of non-recognition of Indian rights was canned, and it was decided that they did have a point to make."

As land use planning got under way the province took great pains in these meetings to assure First Nations that nothing decided in the discussions would prejudice their interests, which would be resolved in subsequent Government to Government (G2G) negotiations – introducing another substantial

Exploring in the Finlayson district, Yukon

source of uncertainty for industry. The new NDP government changed the legal team from the one that had won the original ruling. By 1992-93, the province was already referring to negotiations/ discussions with First Nations as G2G, reflecting a major policy and philosophical shift in approach.

The Chamber took part in a Treaty Negotiations Advisory Committee in the 1990s, but as Wolfe recalled, little was achieved by the "bickering" government negotiators.

The hereditary chiefs appealed the Delgamuukw ruling. In 1993, the B.C. Court of Appeal found that they had some "…unextinguished, non-exclusive Aboriginal rights…," but dismissed their claim to title. The following year, they were given leave to appeal by the Supreme Court of Canada.

The Supreme Court's landmark Delgamuukw decision of 1997 did not rule on the land claim, but did determine for the first time that "Aboriginal rights are not dependent on any legislative or executive instrument for their existence." It affirmed their protection under the 1982 Constitution Act and upheld oral histories as proof of historical facts.

The ruling was slammed by some, praised by others and confused most people.

The Fraser Institute called it a "…death by a thousand courts…" and a decision that "…practically gives control of 95% of the B.C. land mass to 4.9% of the population."

Some activists called the ruling "paternalistic" as it set limitations to Aboriginal title, which can only be held communally. Lands under such title could not be used "…in a manner that is irreconcilable with the nature of the claimant's attachment to those lands," unless they were first surrendered and converted into non-title lands.

Bruce McKnight, appointed Executive Director of the B.C. & Yukon Chamber of Mines in 1998, saw a silver lining in the clouds of confusion after studying the decision's implications on the mineral exploration and mining industry. The prevailing view was that land-claims uncertainty would lead to reduced investment. McKnight felt this could improve once more treaties

were completed as Aboriginal governments "…are likely to be more pre-disposed to mining as a means of economic development than some of the provincial or federal regimes."

In yet another breakthrough, the Nisga'a Nation signed the first modern-day treaty with the federal and provincial governments in 2000, culminating a century-long quest that began when they formed their first Land Committee in 1890.

By this point, AME BC shifted its strategy from monitoring Aboriginal issues to engaging First Nations directly, but resources were scarce as the industry was in one of its worst downturns and still engaged in a complex land-use planning process.

"We set up a committee and resolved to produce a guidebook to help companies, especially juniors, deal with Aboriginal issues and try to avoid problems," McKnight said, "We felt the majors like Teck had a good feeling for what was needed but were concerned about some of the juniors with 'cowboy' mentalities."

Bob Joseph, a status Indian and the founder of Indigenous Corporate Training, was invited to help the industry better understand Aboriginal issues and culture. "He was a big hit and did a great job in a number of one-day workshops," McKnight said.

By this point, Dan Jepsen had joined the Chamber as Executive Director, bringing his extensive experience as a manager of Aboriginal affairs and environment for Western Forest Products. He

believed the root of most of problems between Aboriginals and resource developers was a "lack of trust and respect" in early encounters.

"It was generally accepted [then] that First Nations were a major…problem…deterring access and confidence in investment," Jepsen said of his early years at AME BC.

Jepsen advocated a more progressive approach. He believed land claims would take years to settle, but said this didn't preclude the industry from forging relationships outside the treaty process. Throughout this whole process the Chamber was actively involved, facilitating and intervening on behalf of the mining industry.

"We are interested in exploring for new mineral deposits now," Jepsen told the *Canadian Mining Journal*, "therefore we must seek opportunities to engage with First Nations communities in a meaningful way."

The advice was timely as the Supreme Court of Canada in 2004 released anticipated decisions in two cases heard concurrently — *Haida Nation v. British Columbia* and *Taku River Tlingit First Nation v. British Columbia* — addressing the duty to consult with and accommodate Aboriginal peoples whose claims remain unresolved.

The Supreme Court ruled that governments had a duty to consult Aboriginal peoples and accommodate their interests in good faith, but third parties did not. However, because new mines required government approvals to proceed, companies must ensure that proper consultation took place, or risk rejection of their proposals.

As Jepsen told *Reuters* at the time, "…the miners' best option…" was to work closely with Aboriginal communities, even if there is no explicit legal duty to do so.

In 2005, the Fraser Institute ranked B.C. in 44th place out of 64 jurisdictions in the world, citing "…unresolved native land claims" as one of reasons for the low ranking. Jepsen countered by saying the "…true measure of investor confidence was exploration dollars flowing in the province," which had more than doubled in 2005 from 2001. As AME BC President David Caulfield pointed out at the time, companies were exploring projects with Aboriginal consent, despite unresolved land claims.

At Roundup 2005, the first issue of the Aboriginal Engagement Guidebook was released. Jepsen, Bruce McKnight and Bob Joseph were key contributors, with Bill McIntosh providing much of legal research and editing.

Jepsen said the Guidebook was reviewed and supported by 32 First Nations bands, as well as the B.C. and federal governments and more than 30 organizations.

"The Guidebook became a Canadian Best Seller," he added. An Aboriginal Engagement Toolkit was released a few years later, designed as a practical complement to the Guidebook. Laureen Whyte and Kristy Emery were co-authors of the Toolkit. As issues evolved over the years, the Toolkit largely replaced the Guidebook. (The Toolkit is now available online at www.amebc.ca.)

It is now standard industry practice for companies to consult with Aboriginal and other stakeholders in the exploration stage. In the development stage, companies typically negotiate Impact Benefit Agreements (IBAs) or other agreements to help jobs, training and business opportunities flow to local Aboriginal communities.

B.C. is now unique in the Canadian landscape for positive reasons. It was the first to adopt a revenue-sharing policy, in which a portion of the taxes paid to government by new mines and resource projects will be directed to local Aboriginal groups.

Much has changed since the old days of exclusion. AME BC's annual Mineral Exploration Roundup is attended by Aboriginal mining professionals and leaders from across B.C. and Canada. Sessions on First Nations' issues are common since the first afternoon session of this type was held at Roundup in January 2003.

Local First Nations are now invited to give the opening address at Roundup.

Douglas would no doubt approve. Trutch would likely be struck dumb.

Isaac Brown, Arnold Peters, Anthony Moore focus on their GPS

The exploration stage: camp at New Gold's Blackwater
project in north-central British Columbia.

Mineral Project Life Cycle

*A mineral project's life cycle is long
and complex. From discovery to
commissioning can take ten years
or more. Many prospectors and
geologists work their whole careers
without ever discovering a viable
mineral project.*

*The following describes the main
areas of work in bringing a mine
to fruition.*

Land Access

The search for minerals can occur on Crown land or
private land. Having access to as much of the land
base as possible is critical as most new mineral
deposits are hidden and will have to be found by
scientific exploration. Improving the likelihood of
finding mineral deposits is directly related to the
amount of land available for exploration. Deposits
that are large and/or valuable enough to be
developed are rare. Up to the end of 2010, mining
activities had disturbed less than 0.045 per cent of
B.C.'s land base.

Prospecting

Prospectors and geologists hope to find minerals that provide clues to where elements such as gold and copper may be hidden. Prospecting is usually carried out on foot and involves traversing wide areas, taking rock samples, conducting basic rock mapping, and investigating outcrops. If a mineral is found, the prospector or geologist may use hand tools or small machinery to examine the rock more closely.

Geoscience

Exploration for mineral deposits is the first step in the mine cycle. At the preliminary exploration stage, prospectors and geologists often evaluate large areas by airborne or ground-based mapping or sampling surveys of the earth's surface. Using maps and existing data produced from the preliminary stage, specific areas are singled out for more detailed studies.

Staking and Permits

If valuable mineral potential is indicated in a particular area, a mineral claim may be placed on that area by way of an on-line computer based application system. Work that includes mechanical disturbance requires a specific permit, mineral claims only allow work that involves non-mechanical surface disturbance; they do not provide ownership of the surface or permission for mechanized surface disturbance.

Getting the Word Out

Mineral exploration companies require financing to carry out their work, which is usually acquired by selling shares in a company on the stock market. Some companies also use revenue from mine production to finance the search for a new deposit. Exploration and mining companies communicate the results of their work through highly-regulated communications to the investing public.

Investors can be private individuals, venture capitalists or other mining companies. They monitor political activities in the jurisdiction where they are considering investing to ensure that the climate is conducive to a fair return on their investment.

Drilling

Drilling is boring into the earth to extract samples of rock deep in the ground. Drills take either cylindrical core or chip samples out of the ground. In the case of drill core, the samples are laid out so that geologists can see what the rock looks like at depth. Depending on the type of drill used, drills can bore holes from five to more than1000 metres in depth. Quite often gold and other metals are visible in the drill samples. If many holes are drilled over a large area, geologists can look for patterns in the rock and metal content to provide hints on the ore's depth; the orebody's width, length, and even an estimate of the dollar value of the minerals underground.

Studies

Assessment and approval form the second phase of the mining cycle. Deposit details, including metallurgy, along with environmental and socio-economic information are used to plan and design the mine. This planning includes assessing the potential value of a mineral deposit, and determining if it can be mined economically in a responsible manner.

In order to build a mine, the mineral deposit must be valuable enough to pay for the costs of design and construction (capital costs), mine operation (operating costs), and mine closure and reclamation.

In general, it takes two to three years for test work and data collection to complete environmental baseline studies. Work on feasibility studies begins as soon as a deposit discovery is made.

Environmental Assessment

Consultations with government agencies and local communities are intensive during this phase of the mine cycle. Financial, socio-economic, and environmental impacts are evaluated; nearby residents, communities and Aboriginal bands who might be affected are consulted regarding possible impact and their input is sought and used to ensure their needs and requirements are addressed.

In order to obtain environmental assessment (EA) approval, the EA of the mine must quantify the mine project impacts to the biophysical and social environment, and outline how it will address any potential effects. The EA will show how the mine project can bring social and economic benefits to the mining company, local communities and the province.

The environmental assessment phase of a mine project can typically range from one to three years for completion.

Consultation

During the exploration and mine building phases, companies consult with many different groups. These include: First Nations, local and regional communities, and provincial government agencies. A formal agreement may be made along with mine development, which usually happens during the final approval of a mine site.

Planning for reclamation and closure is a required component of the environmental assessment process. The cost of these programs is assessed and a financial assurance is put in place to cover these costs prior to the onset of construction.

Construction

Once a mine has been approved for construction, development can take anywhere from five to ten years. Construction of a mine includes necessary infrastructure such as associated buildings, roads, bridges, and airports. The timeframe depends on the location, the size and complexity of the project, the complexity of the development (including infrastructure needs and availability), and the complexity of regulations and review processes.

Operation

Mine production involves the extraction of rock, separation of ore from non-economic material, disposal of waste, and shipment of the concentrated metals or minerals for further treatment or fabrication. On-going exploration may reveal other mineralization that may lead to the expansion of the operation or an extended mine life. Project expansions involve the full cycle of studies, evaluations and permitting processes required for a new mine development.

In preparation for mine operations, recruitment, hiring and training for a wide range of personnel are required.

Closure

Mine closure and rehabilitation form the last phase of the mining cycle. However, the rehabilitation of a mine site is a multi-stage process and occurs throughout the life of the mine.

Shutdown and decommissioning involve the removal of equipment, the dismantling of facilities and the safe closure of all mine workings.

Rehabilitation

Reclamation is carried out through all stages of the mine life cycle. Following closure, it involves earthwork and full site restoration including re-vegetation of waste rock disposal areas.

The final stage is monitoring and operation of long-term water treatment facilities. During this stage, environmental testing and structural assessments can commonly continue long after a mine's closure.

Mining is a temporary land use, in most cases, measured in decades. Modern management principles and technologies now available mean that reclamation can restore a minesite to a healthy and natural habitat for fish, wildlife and communities.

SRK Consulting

Geotechnical and hydrological studies at the Galore Creek project.

The lighter side of mineral exploration in Highland Valley
– the Bethlehem Express parked outside Iona portal, circa 1956-57

Porphyry Deposits in British Columbia and Yukon

In 1899, The Engineering and Mining Journal *was a well-respected technical magazine, published weekly in New York and read around the world.*

It was as essential to the mining industry then as the Internet is today. In the May 27 issue, the editor publicly criticized the judgement of Thomas Weir, a mining engineer who managed one of the first companies exploring part of the Bingham Canyon deposit southwest of Salt Lake City, Utah. Weir had stated, in a report being used to raise development capital in London, that his property had "…an average grade of between 0.75 and 2.5 per cent Cu and contained about 291.7 million tons of copper…" The editor claimed that "…it would be impossible to mine and treat ores carrying 2 per cent or less of copper under existing conditions in Utah … Moreover, it is not probable that the price of copper is going to stay permanently (as high as) 17 or 18 cents… Therefore, the more ore it has of the kind it claims, the poorer it is."

At the time, most mining engineers would probably have agreed that this "low-grade" mineralization was simply waste rock. In fact, another owner of claims that covered part of the deposit, Colonel Enos A. Wall, is remembered because his mineralization was described derisively as "wall-rock."

Only ten years later, the claims of Weir and Wall were part of the world's first porphyry copper mine, which was still in operation in 2011 and was planning to go underground. History has given the lion's share of the credit to another engineer, Daniel Jackling, who built it, and to Guggenheim Exploration Co. and its mining arm, American Smelting and Refining (ASARCO), which financed it.

Jackling, who trained at the Missouri School of Mines, realized the "low-grade" ore (about two per cent copper) could be profitable if mined by open-pit methods using the type of steam shovels that would soon dig the Panama Canal and utilizing the new floatation process. He organized the Utah Copper Company but ran short of money. In 1905, he approached Guggenheim Exploration, which underwrote a $3-million bond. ASARCO bought a 25 per cent interest and negotiated a 20-year contract to process the mine's output.

The Guggenheim family eventually owned so many large interests in successful copper companies that they amalgamated all of them, except ASARCO, into Kennecott Copper in 1915.

Although it had its modern discovery at Bingham Canyon, porphyry mining first occurred in the sixteenth century at the Altenberg tin mine, in the Erzgebirge mining district on the German side of what is now, the Czech Republic. It isn't surprising that twentieth century geologists didn't know about Altenberg; the best reference was published in Latin by Agricola in 1556 and wasn't translated into English until 1912. By that time, American mining engineers had already achieved profitable copper production at Bingham Canyon. But it wasn't easy!

The geological setting of the porphyry districts in the Canadian Cordillera — the mountain belt running through British Columbia and Yukon — is generally similar to those in the southwest U.S. and elsewhere in the world.

British Columbia is home to a unique family of porphyry copper deposits that are only commercial here and in one other location, New South Wales, Australia. Known as the copper-gold porphyry subtype, or as the alkalic, alkaline or volcanic subclass, this family of deposits has become increasingly attractive during the last decade because of its relatively higher gold content. These deposits differ from common porphyry copper deposits in the composition (enriched in silica and potassium) and age (Upper Triassic and Lower Jurassic) of the host intrusions, which were volcanic centres that produced most of the nearby volcanic material. Most porphyry deposits in the world are younger, commonly ranging in age from Cretaceous through Tertiary.

Mineral exploration and metal mining in the Canadian Cordillera underwent a momentous transformation between the mid-1950s and the mid-1970s. It resulted from the recognition and development of porphyry-type deposits of copper and molybdenum and was accompanied by: huge increases in annual exploration expenditures and personnel; an influx of foreign exploration companies (mainly American); a rapid increase in junior mining company listings on the Vancouver Stock Exchange; the establishment of new, world-class, geochemical assay laboratories in Vancouver; a remarkable expansion of copper and molybdenum production; and, last but not least, a much bigger role for the B.C. & Yukon Chamber of Mines.

Prior to the mid-1950s, most B.C. copper production came from relatively large deposits (by provincial, not world standards) that were called "massive sulphide" for lack of a better understanding of their origin.

Until that time, only minor quantities of molybdenum had been produced in B.C. The province had been home to four main copper deposits, including the Britannia mine, near Squamish. The other three had all been operated by Granby: Phoenix, near Grand Forks; Anyox, on the coast, near Alaska; and Copper Mountain, near Princeton. These mines had all been underground operations, requiring large workforces, which resulted in high costs and low productivities. To be profitable, copper grades in the range of 2.5 per cent or higher plus small gold and silver credits were needed in the early years.

Since the first decade of the twentieth century, the bulk of the world production of copper and molybdenum has come from porphyry deposits.

Initially, most of those were located primarily in the warm, arid areas of the U.S. southwest (Arizona, Nevada, Utah and New Mexico), Mexico, Peru and Chile. Now that porphyry exploration and mining has spread worldwide and been studied in detail, the amount of published information available would fill a sizable library. Because copper is critically important for electrical transmission (essential in our industrialized world), and porphyry deposits supply the major part of world copper supply and constitute the bulk of world reserves, it is hard to believe that porphyry mining was a concept that didn't exist a little more than a century ago.

In many extensive vein systems, particularly those enriched in copper and molybdenum, the most spectacular and best mineralized veins are often surrounded and encompassed by mineralization that occurs in countless thinner veins and narrow fractures that are too low-grade to be individually mineable, as well as in disseminated grains between the fractures. In the southwest U.S. during the nineteenth century, the richest veins in many deposits were usually mined by underground methods before the economic potential of these lower-grade portions had been recognized. As a result, many extensive porphyry deposits were routinely abandoned and the miners moved on with any equipment that was salvageable. As a result, many copper camps became ghost towns, only to be reborn later as huge porphyry copper mines.

A few mining engineers and financiers with remarkable vision recognized that these overlooked, low-grade, mineralized zones were often many orders of magnitude larger than the boundaries of the historic copper camp. They reasoned that these huge, lower-grade areas could be considered as valuable mineral deposits in their own right if a way could be found to mine them on surface at a very large scale, just like an iron or coal mine, or a gravel pit. In other words, the economics of scale might make them profitable to develop. It was this theory that was first tested and proven feasible, to the astonishment and chagrin of the sceptics, at Bingham Canyon. It was an achievement of such significance that it dwarfed all previous mining advances and revolutionized the economics of mining, not only lowering the production costs of copper and other metals, such as molybdenum, silver and gold, but ensuring that the world would have abundant supplies far into the future.

The birth of the Bingham Canyon copper mine, a huge open-pit operation using steam shovels and a private railway to transport the ore from a narrow mountain canyon to a level area with enough space to construct a gigantic mill, smelter and refinery, was one of those eureka moments when vision and courage and investment capital combined to invent a new technology and prove all the experts wrong.

By 1933, porphyry copper mines were contributing 35 per cent of the world's copper and had reduced the price of the metal enough to enable the start of modern electrification. The amount of rock moved at Bingham Canyon was almost equal to that excavated in the construction of the 80 kilometre-long Panama Canal.

Porphyry deposits didn't make a significant contribution to Canada's mineral production until the early-1970s. In 2000, production of copper from Canadian porphyry deposits amounted to 267,000 tonnes, or about two per cent of total world production and approximately 43 per cent of total Canadian production. About 60 per cent of Canadian copper reserves and most of its molybdenum reserves are in porphyry deposits, largely in the Canadian Cordillera.

Porphyry deposits now account for about 60 to 70 per cent of world copper production and more than 95 per cent of world molybdenum production. They are also major sources of gold, silver and tin, and significant producers of byproduct rhenium, tungsten, indium, platinum, palladium, and selenium. In Canada, they account for more than 40 per cent of copper production, virtually all molybdenum production, and about 10 per cent of gold production.

Among the many mining axioms that have been handed down from generation to generation, the miner's favourite is certainly "Mines are made, not found." In other words, prospectors and geologists find mineralization but it requires a miner or mining engineer to turn that shiny or heavy rock into an economic enterprise. Although geologists and prospectors take the credit for discovering the porphyry deposits, they probably agree that this axiom is certainly appropriate for porphyry mines, which were low-grade, uneconomic mineral deposits that they had unwittingly walked over for decades, or perhaps centuries.

The word "porphyry," which means nothing to most people, was applied to this type of mineralization during the earliest phases of exploration. It is a geological term that refers to a granitic texture that consists of conspicuous larger crystals (phenocrysts) in a fine-grained (aphanitic) groundmass. The first four mines of this type to be developed: Bingham Canyon, Utah; Morenci, Arizona; Ruth (Robinson/Ely), Nevada; and Braden (El Teniente), Chile; were all associated with porphyritic rocks.

The next three porphyry mines developed, in Arizona, were also included in the definition even though most of the ore occurred in the schistose, metamorphic wallrocks adjacent to the intrusion. By the time geologists realized that porphyritic rocks were not an essential criterion, the name had already stuck.

It became accepted wisdom by the 1930s that a deposit had to have the following characteristics to be considered a porphyry-type:

1. *Of such magnitude and shape that it could be mined advantageously by large-scale methods, either with underground caving or in open pits.*

2. *Most of the ore minerals were disseminated or coated the walls of cracks and minute fractures.*

3. *The distribution of minerals was so general and uniform that "bulk" methods of mining were more profitable than selective methods.*

Bethlehem first concentrate
leaving Highland Valley 1963

4. An intrusion of porphyry or closely related igneous rocks had played a vital role in the genesis of the ore.

5. Richer layers of secondary (supergene) enrichment occurred close to surface because of surface oxidation, leaching and downward migration of the primary copper minerals.

The supergene criterion was dropped after recognition that it was caused by regional climatic factors, and that similar deposits occurred in colder and glaciated locations without supergene enrichment. As mining methods became more productive, miners realized that the limits of the orebody were usually determined by economic and topographic factors rather than the composition of the bedrock. Thus, when metal prices dropped or mining costs increased, the average value of the ore and the mineable limits of the deposit changed accordingly.

The earliest porphyry mines were generally copper-rich and contained some molybdenum, silver and gold.

As exploration spread, it became clear that porphyry deposits could display many variations, including different metal ratios. At least ten subtypes have been identified based on the principal metals (copper, molybdenum, gold, tungsten, tin and silver) that contribute the most value. Common porphyry deposit byproducts are rhenium, platinum group metals, bismuth, zinc, lead, and indium.

The principal ore minerals of the main porphyry deposit subtypes are:

1. **Porphyry Copper** – *chalcopyrite, bornite, chalcocite, tennantite, enargite, sulphosalts, molybdenite and electrum.*

2. **Porphyry Molybdenum** – *molybdenite, scheelite, wolframite, cassiterite, bismuthinite and native bismuth.*

Economic porphyry deposits typically contain hundreds of millions of tonnes of ore but can range in size from tens of millions to billions. Grades for the different metals vary considerably but generally average less than one per cent. In British Columbia and Yukon, new porphyry copper mines require grades ranging from 0.2 per cent to more than 1 per cent copper; new porphyry molybdenum deposits need grades of greater than 0.07 per cent molybdenum. In new porphyry gold and copper-gold deposits, gold grades range from 0.2 to 2 g/t gold.

Prior to 1940, prospectors had discovered and staked claims on numerous small prospects associated with copper and molybdenum porphyry deposits. However, none of those early mineral discoveries attracted interest from mining companies familiar with porphyry deposits.

Most of the early claims were abandoned because the richest exposed mineral showings were too small and low in grade to have economic potential at the time. Examples of the earliest staking on important porphyry deposits include:

- *Pre-1910 – Highland Valley, Copper Mountain, and Afton mines, as well as the undeveloped Catface deposit and Adanac molybdenum deposit;*

- *1910-19 – Gibraltar, Granisle and Boss Mountain mines, and the undeveloped Casino (Yukon), Lorraine and Lime Creek (Alice Arm) deposits;*

- *1920s – Island Copper and Endako mines and the undeveloped Berg deposit;*

- *1930s – Brenda mine and the undeveloped Fish Lake (Prosperity) deposit.*

In the years between the two world wars (1919 to 1939), the copper industry in the Americas had consolidated into six vertically-integrated, giant American companies. The Big Six comprised Phelps

Dodge, Newmont, Kennecott, Anaconda, ASARCO, and American Metal (AMCO). AMCO was closely associated with Climax Molybdenum, which had a virtual monopoly over molybdenum production, and the two merged in 1957 to form American Metals Climax (AMAX). With enormous reserves of high-grade copper and molybdenum ore, these companies had little incentive to explore areas of the world that had not demonstrated better potential than their own undeveloped deposits.

The first porphyry exploration in British Columbia may have taken place in 1929, when Cominco drilled five holes at what was to become the Granisle deposit, which indicated seven million tonnes grading about 0.8 per cent copper. The first targeted exploration by porphyry experts probably occurred in 1948-49 when Kennco Explorations (Western), a subsidiary of Kennecott, drilled the Lorraine copper prospect on Duckling Creek, west of Germansen Landing, with disappointing results.

The beginning of porphyry mining in Canada is generally credited to a routine exploration program started in 1955 in the Highland Valley area, between Merritt and Ashcroft and about 55 kilomtres southwest of Kamloops. The Huestis-Reynolds-McLallen Syndicate was formed by prospector Herman "Spud" Huestis, and financial partners Patrick Reynolds and Jack McLallen, to conduct an exploration program on claims staked at the end of the previous year.

Huestis had developed a taste for prospecting as a teenager, then explored in many parts of the U.S. and Canada, including the Highland Valley, before moving to the Zambian Copper Belt. In 1954, he returned to the Highland Valley to revisit copper showings he had seen in 1926. They had been staked as early as 1896 and first explored between 1907 and 1915. The Snowshoe vein was diamond drilled in 1919 by the British Columbia Department of Mines (1662 metres in 8 holes). From 1919 to 1921, a large area of disseminated mineralization had been explored with several surface pits and an 85-metre adit. No further work was performed until 1942, when the property was under option to Ventures Limited, a predecessor of Falconbridge. It drilled 730 metres (4 holes) beneath the Iona showing and one 125-metre hole beneath the Moly shaft on the Jersey claim. ASARCO then optioned the claims briefly in 1948 but did not perform any exploration. The most recent work had been trenching by Newmont in 1952 on the Iona and Jersey claims.

The syndicate formed a new junior company, Bethlehem Copper Corporation, and three geology professors from UBC, William White, Robert Thompson and Kenneth McTaggart, planned and supervised an ambitious mapping, trenching and bulk sampling program during the spring and summer of 1955. Based on encouraging assays, ASARCO's Resident Engineer Gavin A. Dirom (who served as president of the Chamber of Mines in 1963 and 1964), negotiated an option agreement in September and took over the exploration, assisted by C.J. Coveney. By the end of the year, large zones averaging about 0.49 per cent and 1.0 per cent copper had been indicated at the Iona and Jersey targets, respectively.

Although the program continued to expand the reserves, and Dirom strongly recommended that the program should be expanded, ASARCO's head office decided for some reason to drop the option in May 1958, perhaps because it felt that the deposit was too small and/or low-grade to meet its objectives. In some ironic ways, the early history of the Bethlehem property was frustrated by the same false starts and lack of faith that had delayed the initial success of porphyry mining in the southwest U.S. 50 years earlier.

Bethlehem refused to give up and began an underground program to check the surface drilling results. A decisive moment in the history of the Highland Valley and, arguably, the British Columbia mining industry, occurred in 1960, when a Japanese company, Sumitomo Metal Mining, agreed to purchase the entire copper production from a 2700 ton-per-day mill for a period of ten years. Japanese mining companies had become comfortable investing in British Columbia during the 1950s when they purchased iron ore concentrates from small mines located along the B.C. coast. (See Iron Ore, page 116).

Sumitomo's primary objective was to obtain copper concentrates to supply the growing needs of its smelting and manufacturing plants. Instead of demanding equity in Bethlehem in return for loans, it was content to provide purchase guarantees that enabled Bethlehem to raise equity and debt financing; existing shareholders maintained control. Construction of the Bethlehem plant began in the fall of 1961 and production began at the end of 1962. More exploration revealed that four separate deposits were present and that the mine was much larger than first thought. As the operation became more efficient, the plant was expanded five times to over 15,000 tons/day by 1975. A fifth deposit, the JA, was discovered in 1971 but remained uneconomic into the present century, mainly because it is covered by at least 240 metres of overburden.

Regional geological mapping and exploration by other junior companies on other old copper prospects nearby revealed that the Bethlehem mine, as big as it was relative to previous underground British Columbia copper mines, was just one of a cluster of similar but larger deposits that occur within a 15-square-kilometre area. From north to south (with the operating companies in brackets), they were named Bethlehem, Valley Copper (Cominco), Lornex (Rio Algom), and Highmont (Torwest, Highmont, and Teck). Intensive exploration of those three began between 1962 and 1966. The 1964 discovery of the large Lornex deposit on claims previously optioned by Noranda and Kennco was another important milestone in the history of the Highland Valley. The discovery was made by Egil Lorntzsen and was explored by Riocanex, its parent Rio Algom, and Yukon Consolidated Gold. The Lornex mine began production in 1972. Another important achievement was Cominco's 1968 discovery of the Valley Copper deposit, one of the largest in British Columbia. By the time a feasibility study had been completed, however, the economic climate for opening new mines was deteriorating in British Columbia and production had to be

delayed until 1983, a few years after Cominco had taken over Bethlehem. Following many years of exploration that showed that the deposits partially overlapped property boundaries, all four operating companies amalgamated their properties as the Highland Valley Copper Partnership in 1986, with Cominco as the operator of the Valley Copper mine. Teck now holds a 97.5 per cent interest.

Bethlehem's success in achieving profitable production without giving up control of the project was a tremendous incentive for prospectors and geologists to become familiar with the geology of porphyry deposits, to revisit all the old copper occurrences, and to search for new ones. It also gave a major impetus to financiers and promoters to provide grubstakes and to form new exploration syndicates and junior companies. New discoveries were announced regularly and the porphyry boom was on, considerably assisted by the recent availability of small piston-engine helicopters, more efficient wire-line diamond drilling, and additional concentrate purchase agreements from Japanese companies.

The next phase, called the Boom Years (1962-72), saw a steep increase in activity and competition. The first major success was the Endako molybdenum porphyry, situated midway between Smithers and Prince George and named for the nearby community. Encouraging diamond drill results obtained in 1962 by R and P metals, a junior company, encouraged Canex Placer (Placer Development) to outbid AMAX for the right to option the claims. Subsequent exploration and

development resulted in production in 1965. Noranda opened a much smaller molybdenum mine, Boss Mountain, a few months later.

The most aggressive U.S. companies in British Columbia in the early years, until Bethlehem began production, had been ASARCO, AMAX and Kennco/Kennecott. The latter focused on geochemical exploration and had an enviable discovery record that included the Galore Creek, Kitsault (Lime Creek) molybdenum, Huckleberry, Berg, Kemess North and Pine deposits. AMAX examined virtually every molybdenum occurrence in B.C. and optioned the Yorke Hardy (Davidson) deposit near Smithers. First discovered in 1944, it lay 300 to 450 metres below surface and is the largest undeveloped molybdenum deposit in Canada.

Granby was one of the early Canadian participants in porphyry deposit exploration, conducting exploration at Babine Lake that resulted in production from the Granisle mine in 1966. Meanwhile, a Canadian syndicate composed of McIntyre Porcupine, Kerr Addison and Silver Standard staked claims at the large Schaft Creek deposit, southwest of Dease Lake, which, in 2011, remained undeveloped because of its remote location.

Four years after placing Endako into production, Canex Placer, in partnership with an American company, Duval Corp., consolidated the ownership of older claims covering the Gibraltar copper porphyry, at Williams Lake, that were mostly held by a junior company, Gibraltar Mines. An intensive program of exploration resulted in another new mine in 1972.

Utah Mines discovered the Island Copper porphyry deposit near Port Hardy on Vancouver Island in 1966 while exploring for iron deposits. It reached production in 1971.

The Brenda copper-molybdenum porphyry mine, near Kelowna, which began production in 1970, was a particularly important success story. It was noteworthy because it had a far lower average grade (0.183 per cent copper and 0.082 per cent molybdenum at start-up) than any deposit mined previously, anywhere. It was operated by a junior company, Brenda Mines, in which Noranda and Nippon Mining became large shareholders. With significant molybdenum production from Brenda added to the major production from Endako and lesser amounts from Kitsault and Boss Mountain, British Columbia became the second largest producer of molybdenum (20 per cent) in the world in 1977, behind the U.S.

Noranda was also successful at Babine Lake, where exploration led to the discovery of the Bell Copper (copper-gold) porphyry deposit in 1963 and production in 1972, as well as the nearby Morrison deposit, which was extensively drilled between 1963 and 1973.

Ingerbelle, a member of the copper-gold family of porphyry deposits, was the fourth new porphyry mine, in addition to Lornex, Noranda's Bell, and Gibraltar, that started production in 1972, the peak year of the porphyry boom. It was built adjacent to the site of Granby's former Copper Mountain underground mine after the complicated claim ownership, dating back to 1895, had been consolidated and sold to Newmont in 1966. The flurry of new mines in 1972 was partly driven by the end of an important federal tax incentive that terminated at the end of that year. It provided for a three-year tax-free period on the production from new mines anywhere in Canada.

A sharp drop in exploration occurred in British Columbia from 1972 to 1975, partly due to the end of the eligibility for the tax-free treatment, but mainly because of the election of an NDP government unfriendly to the mining industry. (See The 1970s, page 35). Exploration gradually resumed when the NDP government was defeated.

This initial robust period of porphyry exploration, discovery and production was followed by a slower, more cyclical pace. Several periods of weak activity in the mid-1980s and late-1990s, related to sharp declines in the copper price, were interspersed with short recoveries. Imperial Metals, a junior company, built two new producers in 1997: Mount Polley (Cariboo Bell) and Huckleberry (See Imperial Metals, page 228).

Other discoveries from the 1960s and 70s were too low grade, lacked infrastructure or were otherwise not viable candidates for development. Many of the projects that were not economically feasible at that time were renewed in the second decade of the 21st century with the support of stronger metal markets, enhanced infrastructure and/or improved technology. To name a few, examples are:

- Imperial Metals – Red Chris
- Thompson Creek Metals – Mount Milligan copper-gold
- Copper Fox Metals – Schaft Creek copper-gold-molybdenum-silver
- NovaGold / Teck – Galore Creek
- Yellowhead Mining – Harper Creek copper-gold
- Taseko Mines – Prosperity copper-gold
- Avanti Mining – Kitsault molybdenum

Significant changes in metal prices, particularly gold and copper, have had a major impact on the value of the copper-gold porphyries and made them a high-priority exploration target. In August 2011, a gram of gold sold for almost $59, compared to about $1.12 in 1972 – an increase of over 50 times. By comparison, the increases in copper and molybdenum prices during that period are only about six times, and three to four times, respectively.

Nick Carter has compared the approximate gross recovered grades of copper and gold to date from the two types of copper porphyry mines in British Columbia. His calculations showed that copper-molybdenum deposits had average recovered grades of 0.34 per cent copper and 0.05 g/t (0.002 oz/ton) gold, whereas copper-gold deposits had average recovered grades of 0.46 per cent copper and 0.21 g/t (0.006 oz/ton) gold. At 2011 prices of about $3.00/lb for copper and $1500/oz for gold, and ignoring the value of the molybdenum credits, copper-molybdenum porphyry ore has an average recovered value of $50.40/ton, compared to a value of $117.60/ton for copper-gold ore.

While this analysis is admittedly crude and preliminary, it is useful for demonstrating why copper-gold deposits have become such an important target. Gavin E. Dirom has shown that the Babine Lake deposits (Granisle, Bell and Newman), which have significant molybdenum contents, have average resource grades for copper and gold that are almost the same as those of the copper-gold family.

Most of the copper-gold porphyry deposits and related intrusions in British Columbia occur in a narrow belt of volcanic rocks that extends northwest from the U.S. border, near Princeton, through the Kamloops and Prince George areas to Dease Lake, where it meets a similar belt that trends northeasterly from the Stikine River district. The Princeton to Dease Lake belt has been dubbed the Quesnel Trough and the host rocks are referred to as the Quesnellia geological terrane. Copper-gold mines that are presently in production include Mount Polley and Copper Mountain.

A large portion of British Columbian and Canadian reserves of copper and gold are contained in the following deposits that occur in Quesnellia and the Stikine belt, some of which are nearing production or are in advanced stages of exploration: New Afton, Ajax, Mount Milligan, Lorraine, Red Chris, and Galore Creek.

Galore Creek is a cluster of several deposits with enormous reserves of 1.3 billion tonnes averaging 0. 45 per cent copper and 0.29 g/t gold. However, most copper-gold porphyry deposits tend to have a much smaller footprint and tonnage than the average copper-molybdenum variety, which makes them harder to find. To make the search even more difficult, a long stretch of Quesnellia centered on Prince George is covered by relatively thick glacial till or a thin cover of younger volcanic rocks. That was what convinced Geoscience BC that the principal current mineral exploration challenge in British Columbia is unlocking the potential of Quesnellia by locating the volcanic centres associated with copper-gold deposits. Its QUEST program, launched in 2007, included the largest combined program of airborne gravity, electromagnetic and magnetic surveys ever conducted in the province, plus significant amounts of geochemical sampling and re-analysis.

The Vancouver mineral exploration community is, arguably, as competitive as any group of geologists and mineral explorers anywhere in the world but they have also developed a reputation for supporting initiatives and legislation that improve the common good. There is probably no better example of its cooperative strength than the remarkable technical collaboration that began in early 1974. An ad hoc group of senior leaders representing mining exploration companies and the provincial government proposed that the technical insights gained from twenty years of remarkably successful exploration for porphyry deposits should be collected and published.

The timing was perfect and those who had participated supported the idea enthusiastically. Memories had not been dimmed by the passage of time, the principals were proud of what had been accomplished and had not yet scattered around the world.

The result was a volume containing 48 technical papers summarizing the geology of all of the most advanced porphyry deposits in the Canadian Cordillera. With investment in porphyry deposits facing another serious slowdown because of low metal prices and regulatory problems, another team of 14 geologists was formed to begin work on a sequel. This was a more ambitious book that included deposits in Alaska and Washington and consisted of an additional 69 papers. These two CIM Special Volumes comprise a collective work of some 1,400 pages penned by some of the best geological minds of the time; an exhaustive public resource that serves as a record of the mineral endowment that was discovered during this remarkable period.

A paper by Newell et al. in the 1995 Special Volume identified several of the reasons why American companies, which had the advantage of arriving in the Canadian Cordillera early in the porphyry search with teams of experienced geologists and the best exploration technology, didn't achieve better results. Although they had an enviable discovery record, they were often unwilling to participate in the development stage.

An area for much discussion and disagreement amongst investors, pundits and mining professionals is why a company decides to drop or sell a particular mineral property. It is easy to be critical in hindsight but, in many cases, the negative decision may have been the correct one because the company owned better projects elsewhere or perhaps corporate priorities changed in the face of a market downturn or a chance to invest in a more attractive property.

Like any other endeavour, mineral exploration is subject to whims of fashion; theories and approaches to problems are often rigidly adhered to, to the exclusion of new ideas and innovative thinking, which can lead to bad decision-making. Large porphyry deposits can have very long lives; geologists who work within a corporate culture centred on their own deposits face the risk of becoming too rigid and cautious when they consider investments in deposits with different characteristics.

There are been many examples where field personnel have presented promising projects or negotiated attractive option agreements to their head offices only to have them rejected because the exploration staff's recommendations do not fit accepted models. In many cases, poor decisions are made through timidity or unfamiliarity with local geology, allowing later investors to obtain the benefits of previous work.

The 1960s and 1970s saw considerable growth in the number of mining companies and geologists headquartered in Vancouver. In CIM Special Volume No. 15, Don Mustard tabulated the growth and diversification of permanent exploration geologists in Vancouver between 1960 and 1973 as follows:

Employer	1960 – 1961		1972 – 1973	
	Company	Geologists	Company	Geologists
Major mining companies	14	33	30	191
Junior mining companies	16	23	38	79
Petroleum Companies	–	–	12	56
Independent geologists	–	23	–	141
Total:	**30**	**79**	**80**	**467**
Canadian	21	37	39	158
American	7	16	26	123
Japanese	–	–	8	19
European	2	3	7	26
Total:	**30**	**56***	**80**	**326***

(* does not include geologists based outside Vancouver)

A problem unique to American companies was that they were constrained by U.S. anti-trust and tax legislation from acquiring promising properties except by grassroots discovery or traditional option to purchase. It was difficult, if not impossible, for them to enter into exploration agreements involving the takeover of a junior company on the instalment plan. This approach, which was innovative in the 1960s but later became commonplace, was attractive to shareholders of junior companies. Major mining companies from Canada and other foreign countries did not face these constraints and used this type of deal to gain control of juniors owning the deposits. Examples include Placer Development, at Endako and Gibraltar; Rio Algom, financed by the English company Rio Tinto, at Lornex (now part of Valley Copper); and Teck at Afton.

The growth and diversification of the Vancouver-based mineral exploration sector continued through the 1970s, 1980s, and 1990s. By the 1990s, it was estimated that 850 companies called Vancouver home, a number that has remained constant to this day.

Porphyry deposits in the Canadian Cordillera presented much different exploration challenges than other types of deposits that local prospectors and geologists were more familiar with. They soon realized that it was far more important to concentrate on size, rather than on small pockets of high-grade. In addition, location was of paramount importance because the unit value of the ore was too low to cover high transportation and energy costs to remote deposits.

Although the geological setting of British Columbia and Yukon is reasonably similar to that faced by geologists working in warm, arid climates in the porphyry districts in the U.S., Mexico and the South American Andes, many newcomers found the exploration challenges presented by extensive vegetation and glacial drift cover, and colder winters, quite daunting. Moreover, since glacial scouring had removed most of the higher grades associated with supergene enrichment, the potential grade of porphyry deposits in the Canadian Cordillera was lower than what had been encountered in the early years in other porphyry mining regions. On the other hand, most of the richest parts of the deposits in the older districts had already been mined and their average grades were steadily declining.

The most important step in locating the best part of a porphyry target is careful geological mapping. All porphyry deposits exhibit a predictable, concentric zoning pattern around a central core, which is not always the best-mineralized part. Therefore, porphyry exploration depends on accurate recognition of the alteration effects that have been superimposed on the various varieties of granitic, volcanic and sedimentary rocks that may be present, and measuring and relating the metal content to the different alteration zones. Collecting this much data over an area of many tens or even hundreds of hectares, often mountainous and obscured beneath thick forest and overburden cover, explains why the investigation often takes many years and is very costly.

Geochemistry proved to be the most effective and efficient exploration tool for measuring the distribution of the principal metals, usually copper and molybdenum, but often including lead, zinc, silver and gold. When the porphyry search began in the Canadian Cordillera, conventional assaying was quite expensive and detection limits were so high that it was used only to measure the grade of fairly obvious mineral showings. Because the prices of gold and silver didn't begin to increase much above mid-1930s levels until after 1972, very few samples were even assayed for those metals at the exploration stage. Geochemical assaying lowered the detection limits down to the parts per million (ppm) range for most metals and down to the parts per billion (ppb) range for precious metals, and the cost per sample was lowered significantly.

Geochemical samples consist of a handful of soil, or stream sediment (silt), and are ideally collected from between the black organic layer at surface and the rocky layer close to bedrock. Much to the chagrin of geochemists, the process of collecting these samples is called "dirt-bagging" and is a common entry-level position in field exploration. The huge volume of samples that were collected was the reason that world-class geochemical labs developed in Vancouver, with sample prep offices (where samples are crushed and screened to reduce air freight charges) located in the main regional exploration centres.

Geochemical sampling became an invaluable tool used for identifying the highest priority targets for drill testing.

Since the amount of total sulphide present was far lower than in most sulphide deposits and was often disseminated, electromagnetic surveys – a standby in the search for massive sulphide mineralization in Canada and elsewhere – were generally ineffective, except in cases where intense sulphide fractures or stockworks were present (e.g. Bell Copper).

The induced polarization (IP) method was found to be a more effective geophysical method for detecting disseminated mineralization. Other geophysical techniques, such as magnetic, resistivity, self potential, electromagnetic, radiometric and gravity, were usually used to assist with geological interpretation.

Magnetic, electromagnetic, resistivity and gravity surveys can also be carried out using airborne survey techniques where the geophysical instrumentation is flown in a helicopter or fixed wing aircraft. Global positioning system (GPS) capabilities and the nearly exponential growth in computer hardware and software have made such surveys far more reliable and accurate than in the early stage of the porphyry search, which relied on visual tracking of flight lines on air photographs. GPS was developed in 1973 and became fully operational in 1994.

Some areas of mineral exploration are very high tech, calling upon the latest computer applications and space-age technologies. Remote-sensing – using satellites and discrete bands of the electromagnetic spectrum, such as radar, thermal, infrared, near-visible and visible – is also used to collect digital data that can be used in the search for porphyry deposits and their environments based on the spectral variations within rock types, alteration minerals, vegetation and the like.

Increased computing power has enabled geoscientists and mining engineers to access and manipulate vast amounts of data in the search for and development of porphyry deposits. This is becoming increasingly essential as near-surface porphyry environments are fully explored and the search extends to deeper targets. The challenges to develop deep mines economically and safely can only be met using the most advanced technologies and highly skilled and dedicated people.

One of the most surprising results of the porphyry rush was that members of the Big Six – which dominated world production of copper and molybdenum when the porphyry search began in the Canadian Cordillera – developed and controlled only three of the first 15 porphyry mines. Those were Ingerbelle/Copper Mountain, by Newmont; Island Copper, by Utah; and Kitsault (BC Molybdenum), by Kennecott (and later AMAX).

Another big surprise is what subsequently happened to the members of the Big Six. AMAX (which had previously been swallowed by Cyprus) and Phelps Dodge were taken over by Arizona-based Freeport McMoRan Copper & Gold, the world's largest publicly-traded copper company. Newmont is now the world's second largest gold producer. ASARCO is now a subsidiary of Grupo Mexico, which operates copper mines in Arizona, Mexico and Peru. Kennecott remained true to its roots as operator of the world's largest copper mine at Bingham Canyon, but it is now only the Utah division of the English mining giant Rio Tinto. As for Anaconda, it now exists only as an environmental liability for British Petroleum.

Granby (Granisle and Phoenix), Noranda (Bell Copper, Brenda and Boss Mountain), Placer (Endako and Gibraltar), and Cominco (Valley Copper), were all Canadian mining companies that successfully developed porphyry mines in British Columbia. None of these exist today.

The size and importance of porphyry mines is perhaps demonstrated best by comparing their productivity with that of British Columbia's four largest underground copper producers. Approximately 1.25 million tonnes of copper metal were produced during the 145 combined years that the Phoenix, Britannia, Anyox, and Copper Mountain mines were in production between 1900 and 1974. The same amount of copper was produced every five years by porphyry mines between the early 1970s and the mid 1990s, and is currently produced in approximately seven years by the Valley Copper mine, the largest in British Columbia. The modern workforce, which enjoys high wages, comfort and safety, and mostly lives at home, is only a small fraction of the former underground workforce.

B.C. Geological Survey geologist Andrew Legun
at the Northeast Coal Workshop, 2009

Coal and Metallurgical Coke

Coal, black or brownish rock-like organic material is formed from the remains of decayed vegetation compacted into a solid through millions of years of chemical changes under pressure and heat.

It comprises primarily carbon and an assortment of other elements such as oxygen, hydrogen and sulphur. It is used widely as an energy source, especially to generate electricity (thermal coal.) Some types of high-carbon coal can also be transformed into coke and fed with iron ore into blast furnaces for iron and steel production (metallurgical or coking coal.)

Coal from one deposit may differ greatly from that of another because it consists of a complex range of materials. These differences result from the varying types of vegetation from which the coal originated; the depths of burial and the temperatures and pressures at those depths; as well as the length of time the coal has been forming in the deposit. The varying amount of mineral matter in a coal deposit may also have a significant effect on its properties and classification.

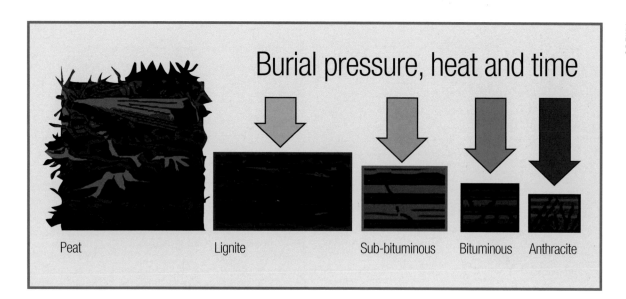

Burial pressure, heat and time

Peat   Lignite   Sub-bituminous   Bituminous   Anthracite

(Figure courtesy of Kentucky Geological Survey and University of Kentucky)

Miners and boy at entrance to coal mine near Port Alberni

The kinds of coal, in increasing order of alteration, are lignite (brown coal – immature), sub-bituminous, bituminous, and anthracite (mature).

Coal starts off as peat. After a considerable length of time, heat and burial pressure, it is metamorphosed from peat to lignite. Lignite is considered to be "immature" coal at this stage of development because it is still somewhat light in colour and it remains soft. As time passes, lignite increases in maturity by becoming darker and harder and is then classified as sub-bituminous coal. As this process of burial and alteration continues, more chemical and physical changes occur and the more-altered coal is called bituminous. At this point the coal is dark and hard. Anthracite is the last of the classifications and this terminology is used when the coal is very hard and shiny, almost pure carbon.

The degree of alteration (or coalification) that occurs as a coal matures from peat to anthracite is referred to as the rank of the coal. Coal rank is usually assessed by a series of tests, which determine the fixed carbon, volatile matter and moisture contents; heating value and agglomerating (or caking) properties.

Low-rank coals, which include lignite and sub-bituminous coals, have lower energy content because they contain less carbon. They are lighter (earthier) and have higher moisture levels. As time, heat, and burial pressure all increase, the rank does as well. Higher-rank bituminous and anthracite coals contain more carbon, which results in a much higher energy content; they have a more vitreous (shiney) appearance and lower moisture content then lower-rank coals.

High-ranked anthracite is found almost exclusively in remote regions of northern B.C. and Yukon. Anthracite is not mined in Canada at present.

Bituminous coal is found in Alberta, B.C. and the Maritimes. Bituminous coal can be used to produce coke for metal smelting, where it is referred to as metallurgical coal or for generating steam for electrical generation, where it is called thermal or energy coal. Thermal coal is also used to burn, or slake, lime to produce Portland Cement, which is used to create concrete, for construction.

The distinction between thermal coal and metallurgical coal is not absolute. Generally, thermal coal contains more ash (material that will not burn) and does not coke well (when exposed to the coking process (see below) does not yield a strong, porous, high carbon product suitable for charging into a blast furnace).

Metallurgical coal is coked by baking it in an oven at temperatures as high as 1,000°C (1,832°F). The coking process drives off volatile matter and fuses the residual or fixed carbon and ash to create a very porous, strong product with a high carbon content (metallurgical coke).

Coke is primarily used to smelt iron ore to pig iron, which is further processed to yield steel. Coking coal and the coke made from it should be low in sulphur and phosphorus so that, during the smelting process, sulphur and/or phosphorus do not carry through into the resultant steel, embrittling and weakening it.

Coke is important in steel smelting, providing both heat and a strong supporting base for the iron ore in the blast furnace. If the coke does not provide this structural support, the contents of the furnace would slump to the bottom of the melting chamber, causing the burning coke to smother and blocking the flow of the molten iron through the base of the hearth, where it is cast into pig iron.

The pig or cast iron is rich in dissolved carbon and must be further treated to reduce carbon levels to create raw steel.

Sub-bituminous coal is softer than bituminous and contains more moisture, making it less economic to transport long distances. Alberta is the only province where sub-bituminous coal is mined.

Lignite is a soft, brown or black coal found in southern Saskatchewan, southeastern Alberta and southwestern Manitoba. Only the Saskatchewan deposits are currently being mined, to generate electricity.

Coal in British Columbia, which is Jurassic or younger in age, varies in rank from lignite to anthracite and is distributed throughout the province. There is estimated to be an ultimate coal resource available for surface or shallow underground mining of over 20 billion tonnes in the province.

An estimated 250 billion tonnes, to a depth of 2000 metres, is of interest for coalbed methane (CBM) exploration.

The major coalfields in B.C. follow the northwest trending belt of Jurassic-Cretaceous rocks, which parallel the Rocky Mountain foothills in the northeast and southeast of the province. The geology is characterized by folds and thrusts, which can make underground mining difficult; but combinations of topography and dipping coal measures often produce attractive open pit mining potential. The Kootenay coalfields, in the southeast, host five coal mines with proven in-place reserves of over 1. 3 billion tonnes.

The Kootenay coals are generally medium-volatile bituminous but vary from high-volatile bituminous to low-volatile bituminous. The Peace River coalfield, in northeastern B.C., has in-place mineable resources of over one billion tonnes of mainly medium-volatile bituminous coal, though high-volatile and low-volatile bituminous resources also occur. The Peace River region hosts two coal mines and there is active exploration being undertaken in the area, as well.

Most of the coal exported from British Columbia is a medium-volatile coking coal from the Kootenay and Peace River coalfields, similar in quality to many Permian coals exported from Australia.

B.C.'s metallurgical coals are valued for improving both hot and cold coke strength and decrease coke oven pressure.

The Quinsam Mine exports thermal coal and the Willow Creek mine a high rank thermal coal, is sometimes used for Pulverised Coal Injection (PCI coal) to increase energy and reduce coke consumption in steel smelting. About half of B.C.'s export coal is destined for Japan and most of the rest to Europe, Korea and South America. The province uses very little coal internally, most of its electricity being generated by hydro power.

Tramway at the Merry Widow mine, 1957

Iron Ore Mining: 1951 to 1984

The big news for mining in British Columbia in the 1950s was the development of a number of iron ore deposits in response to the needs of Japanese steel mills.

As with most new mines, timing was everything. In this case it was the right commodity in the right place (the B.C. Coast) and at the right time, just before the discovery and development of large, high-grade iron ore deposits in Brazil and Western Australia that would come to dominate the Chinese and Japanese markets.

This opportunity was almost lost. While W.A.C. Bennett's Social Credit government (1952-1972) was generally friendly to mining, it supported the previous Coalition government's policy of discouraging development of iron ore deposits for export markets. Senior levels in the Department of Mines also supported restricting development of iron ore resources to ensure feed for a domestic iron and steel industry.

More than 50 iron skarn deposits along the B.C. Coast had been identified and explored early in the 20th century and the general consensus (later proved correct) was that most of these deposits were of limited size.

Mine	Location	Years of Operation	Operator	Mining Method	Tonnes (millions) Processed	Tonnes (millions) Iron in concentrates	By-Products
Tasu	Moresby Is. , QCI	1967–1984	Falconbridge	Open Pit	22.7	12.4	Copper, Silver, Gold
Texada	Texada Island	1952–1976	Texada	Open Pit, UG	21.0	9.3	Copper, Silver, Gold
Brynnor	Vancouver Island	1962–1968	Noranda	Open Pit	4.5	3.0	
Jedway	Moresby Is. , QCI	1962–1968	Granby	Open Pit, UG	3.9	2.1	
Argonaut	Vancouver Island	1951–1957	Utah	Open Pit	4.0	2.0	
Merry Widow	Vancouver Island	1957–1967	Empire Dev	Open Pit	3.4	1.7	
Coast Copper	Vancouver Island	1962–1973	Cominco	UG	2.6	1.5	Copper, Silver, Gold
Nimpkish	Vancouver Island	1959–1963	Nimpkish	Open Pit	2.2	1.3	
Zeballos	Vancouver Island	1962–1969	Falconbridge	Open Pit, UG	1.8	1.3	
Head Bay	Vancouver Island	1959	Hualpi Ent.	Open Pit	0.6	0.2	
Iron Mike	Vancouver Island	1966	Orecan	Open Pit	0.1	0.1	
				Totals	66. 8	34. 9	

The *Iron and Steel Bounties Act*, designed to promote the production of pig iron by way of a subsidy, had been in effect for a number of years. *The Iron Ore Supply Act* placed a reservation on iron ore, thus prohibiting its export from any mineral claims acquired after approval of the enabling order-in-council in early 1951. A royalty on any production of iron ore for export from Crown-granted mineral claims was also proposed several years later by the Social Credit government.

These initiatives were strongly opposed by industry and, most notably, by the Chamber. After some of the legislation was disallowed by the B.C. Supreme Court in 1958, the W.A.C. Bennett government rescinded the reservation on iron ore on mineral claims located after 1951 in all coastal mining divisions.

This policy change opened the door for rapid exploration and development of a number of known iron prospects on Vancouver Island, the southern mainland coast and islands and the Queen Charlottes. These prospects were skarn deposits consisting of pods and lenses of iron ore in the form of magnetite developed in limey sedimentary rocks at the margins of granitic intrusions. Some of these iron deposits included byproduct copper and precious metals mineralization.

Eleven of the more than 50 known iron skarn occurrences and deposits along the coast became producers of iron ore for the Japanese market. In total, 67 million tonnes of ore were mined and upgraded, resulting in the production of 35 million tonnes of iron concentrates. More than 70 per cent of this production came from two mines: Tasu (Wesfrob) on the Queen Charlotte Islands and Texada on the island of the same name, between the southern mainland and Vancouver Island. Tasu operated for 18 years and Texada for 24 years; both produced significant by-product copper, silver and gold.

Most of the remaining production came from seven smaller deposits, mainly on Vancouver Island, which each produced between 1.3 and 3 million tonnes of iron in concentrates over mine lives of between four and 10 years. Unlike most of the producers, one of the smaller deposits, Brynnor, was a new discovery found near Long Beach on Vancouver Island, which was developed by Noranda interests. Two much smaller deposits, Head Bay and Orecan on northern Vancouver Island, produced only 110,000 and 200,000 tonnes of iron concentrates respectively, and were in production for less than a year.

Also of note, from 1982 and onwards, the Craigmont copper mine, near Merritt, recovered magnetite concentrate from tailings for sale to B.C. and Alberta's coal producers to use in the dense medium separation circuits of their coal washeries.

There is a specific set of circumstances that allow for the economic development of a project. Not only must technological, environmental and social factors weigh in favour of the project, market prices must support profitable production, which was the case when B.C.'s iron mines were in operation. Although most of these former iron ore producers were profitable in their day, it is doubtful that any of these projects would be targets for development today. To put this into perspective, the 35 million tonnes of iron concentrates produced between 1951 and 1984 are about the same as Rio Tinto, the world's largest iron ore company, currently produces every three months.

The B.C. iron producers were products of their time and were critically important for attracting the first Japanese investment in provincial mining projects, thus paving the way for significant investments in B.C. copper mines a decade later. Also of note is the fact that the first airborne geophysical (magnetic) surveys flown in B.C. over prospective iron ore districts in selected parts of the coast in the late 1950s were conducted because of a B.C. government initiative.

The sole beneficiary of the government's policy was the Consolidated Mining and Smelting Company, which received a little over $1 million for the production of pig iron from iron sulphides at a short-lived steel plant adjacent to the Sullivan lead-zinc mine. The Barrett NDP government repealed the Iron Ore Supply Act in 1974.

Kivalliq Energy Corp.

Lac Cinquante, Nunavut: by 2009, uranium
exploration was still going strong outside B.C.

Uranium Exploration Policy in B.C.

*Uranium exploration showed
early promise in British Columbia,
spurred by surging spot prices
during the global energy crisis
of the 1970s.*

Yet in 1980, the government imposed a seven-year
moratorium on uranium exploration and development
just as this effort was about to achieve its first successes
in the province. And it was déjà vu in 2008, when the
B.C. government abruptly imposed a ban on uranium
exploration, development and mining — this time
without an expiry date.

The Vancouver Sun described the government's
uranium policy as "irrational and economically
irresponsible," and noted that "…uranium mining
is no more dangerous than other forms of mining,
which happens to be among the safest of all
heavy industries." The May 2008 editorial also
commented that Saskatchewan, "…the nucleus of
Canada's uranium industry, proves every day that
uranium can be mined safely and responsibly."

AME BC continues to advocate for changes to
B.C.'s uranium policy, which is in contrast to many
jurisdictions that welcome uranium exploration
as part of the quest for alternatives to fossil fuels.

And exploration continues to generate discoveries in Saskatchewan — the world's largest uranium producer after Kazakhstan — and in other prospective areas of Canada and the world. B.C. has seen only limited uranium exploration in three notable intervals since World War II, yet these intermittent efforts were successful in discovering at least two deposits of economic interest and a number of intriguing prospects.

The Birch Island (Rexspar) deposit near Clearwater was found during exploration for fluorite in the late 1940s. Both the uranium minerals and fluorite at Rexspar occur as replacements in volcanic rocks. Uranium associated with polymetallic vein deposits was also investigated in the Hazelton and Bridge River districts during this period.

In the mid-1950s uranium mineralization at Rexspar was further tested by drilling, radioactive occurrences were investigated near Lytton, and concentrates containing anomalous niobium, uranium and thorium values were recovered from pegmatite minerals in gravels near Radium Hot Springs. While spotty uranium mineralization in gneisses and pegmatites was identified near Castlegar and Grand Forks in the late-1960s, the game changer — although not immediately recognized as such — was the 1968 discovery of the Fuki deposit in the Okanagan highlands, southeast of Kelowna, by Power Reactor and Nuclear Fuel Development Corporation (PNC) of Japan.

The PNC geologists were attracted to south-central B.C. by the widespread distribution of Tertiary volcanic and sedimentary rocks, a geological setting similar to uranium-bearing environments in Japan. Exploration in the Kamloops area was not successful and the project was in danger of being abandoned before a decision was made to carry out reconnaissance work southeast of Kelowna. While driving up a new forest road east of Beaverdell, the Japanese geologists observed that the scintillometer in their vehicle had detected anomalous levels of radioactivity. Since there was no bedrock exposure to explain the high readings, the Japanese geologists decided to employ what they referred to as a "time-honoured Canadian exploration method." This consisted of offering two bottles of scotch for the road-crew bulldozer operator who kindly opened up the discovery exposure for the Fuki deposit, obscured by only a few meters of overburden.

PNC's discovery was the first recognition in B.C. of basal or paleo-stream channel deposits in which secondary uranium minerals are contained in young (Tertiary age), poorly consolidated, carbonaceous-rich sands and gravels that were protected from subsequent glaciation beneath slightly younger volcanic rocks. The origin of these uranium deposits, similar to deposits in much older (Mesozoic) rocks in Utah and Colorado, involves erosional processes and the leaching of uranium and thorium from older granitic or volcanic rocks, transportation of these elements in ancient streams and the precipitation of both in a reducing environment caused by the presence of carbonaceous material sometimes in the form of low-grade coal measures.

Prior to these events, B.C. was not considered particularly prospective for uranium discoveries. This view changed as exploration accelerated in the 1970s, spurred by a Canada-wide exploration boom following high-grade uranium discoveries in Saskatchewan's Athabasca Basin. Another catalyst was world spot prices averaging $40-45 per pound between 1976 and 1980, up from $10 per pound in 1974.

The recognition of basal uranium deposits in the southern Okanagan provided an obvious exploration target as higher prices made uranium an attractive commodity. Similar occurrences, within a 30-kilometre radius of the Fuki deposit, were identified at Hydraulic Lake and Lassie Lake by Tyee Lake Resources and Lacana Mining Corporation, respectively.

Initial drilling showed Lacana's Blizzard Lassie Lake deposit held particular promise. A consortium was formed to advance the property. It was headed by Lacana and Norcen Energy and included Campbell Chibougamau Mines, E&B Resources and Ontario Hydro. Drilling through 1978 outlined a resource of 2.1 million tonnes grading 0.226 per cent uranium oxide or about 4.5 pounds uranium per short ton. Resources identified on several of PNC's properties, including Fuki, totaled four million tonnes averaging 0.04 per cent uranium oxide. Joint venture partners Noranda and Kerr Addison outlined 1.7 million tonnes grading 0.037 per cent uranium oxide on Tyee Lake's Hydraulic Lake property.

Similar geological settings in the central and southern interior were also explored for basal-type uranium mineralization. Government regional geochemical surveys identified a number of granitic bodies with anomalous uranium values in southeastern and northwestern B.C., which were thought to be potential source rocks for basal type deposits, as well as being hosts for primary deposits. The sources of some of the anomalous uranium values in stream sediments in the South Okanagan Lake region were later found to be concentrations of very young uranium mineralization occurring extensively in surface soils, (examples of presently-forming mineral deposits).

By late 1978, an estimated 60 per cent of mineral claims recorded that year had been staked for uranium. By the end of the decade, such claims covered 461,400 hectares, or more than one million acres, mostly covering lands in the southern part of the province between Okanagan and Lower Arrow Lakes. Other areas of uranium-related staking were in the southern Cariboo, west of Prince George, and east of Atlin in northwestern B.C.

At the time, at least two advanced projects appeared to have good potential to become producers — the Blizzard deposit and Rexspar, where definition drilling by Denison Mines had outlined a resource of a little over one million tonnes grading 0.077 per cent uranium oxide. But the possibility of uranium mining in B.C. generated concerns among residents of the North Thompson River region, near Rexspar, and in the southern Okanagan, where the Blizzard property was situated and where most uranium exploration was focused.

Protests outside then Premier Bill Bennett's constituency office in Kelowna led to the Social Credit government's decision to establish a Royal Commission of Inquiry into Uranium Mining in January 1979. The commission was led by Dr. David Bates, former dean of the faculty of medicine at the University of British Columbia (UBC), assisted by fellow commissioners Jim Murray, professor of geology at UBC, and Valter Raudsepp, former chairman of the Pollution Control Board of B.C.

The commission was asked to examine and to receive public input on the adequacy of standards pertaining to the health and safety of workers involved in uranium exploration, mining and processing, and to assess the requirements for protection of the environment.

The Chamber, in a formal submission to the commission in late 1979, estimated that most of the $6.5 million spent on uranium exploration in B.C. in 1978 had been incurred by major companies. These included mining companies that had been active in the province for years — Noranda, Placer Development, Kerr Addison, Falconbridge — and numerous energy companies, including the mineral units of Canadian and multinational oil-and-gas companies.

Public meetings were held in Vancouver, Kelowna, and ten other communities. The commission also visited major uranium exploration sites in the province and uranium mining areas in Ontario, Saskatchewan, and Washington State.

In August of 1979, the Bates Commission submitted an interim report that recommended against a ban or moratorium on uranium exploration. Instead, the commission proposed that the province initiate a licensing procedure for uranium exploration, conduct more detailed surveillance of exploration activity, improve safety standards for the protection of exploration workers, establish and maintain records of the levels of radioactivity in bedrock exposures and drill-core storage areas, and prohibit underground investigation of known uranium resources pending further studies.

Technical hearings to identify the technical, environmental and health problems related to uranium exploration, mining and milling began in September in Vancouver. They were intended to solicit the views of government agencies, companies active in uranium exploration and development, and various non-governmental organizations including the Chamber. The hearings continued until mid-February1980.

Not surprisingly, the creation of the commission resulted in a dramatic drop in uranium-related exploration and development activity in B.C. as most claim-owners adopted a wait-and-see strategy pending the release of the final report in late 1980 or early 1981.

The wait ended sooner than expected, on February 27, 1980, when the provincial cabinet announced that locating and recording new mineral claims for the purpose of uranium exploration would not be permitted for seven years. The moratorium also

Modern day uranium prospecting with a scintillometer

applied to the exploration and development of uranium deposits on existing claims.

The industry reaction ranged from shock and anger to bitter disappointment that a mining-friendly government had cut short the commission's work and made a knee-jerk decision for all the wrong reasons. The response from the Chamber to the cabinet by President Don Mustard and Manager Rick Higgs was swift and critical. The moratorium also came as a surprise to senior levels of the public service and led to questions as to whether mineral claims would be protected from expiry, as work would no longer be allowed. It was later announced that these claims would be protected.

Not generally known at the time was the fact that Norcen Energy and partners had negotiated an agreement with Korea Electric — with the assistance of the federal and provincial governments, including

Premier Bill Bennett — for the sale of all production from the Blizzard deposit at a contract price of over $40 per pound of uranium oxide. Initially, it seemed possible that this contractual arrangement meant these companies would have to make up this production from other sources, but with the rapid decline in uranium prices, Korea Electric agreed a month or so later to terminate the agreement.

An order-in-council ending the deliberations of the Bates Royal Commission was issued by the cabinet on the same day as the moratorium announcement. The commission was given three months to submit its findings and recommendations. This deadline was challenged, with a revised timeline calling for a final report by October 30, 1980.

In the foreword of the final report, the commissioners stated that, although their work was prematurely terminated, "We do not take the position that there is

any ethical or moral basis, regardless of improvements in these matters (treatment of uranium tailings and worker health and safety) which may well occur in the future, which would absolutely forbid the development of uranium mining" and, "in the intervening period, provided that proper controls of such activity are structured and implemented, and provided that it is considered prudent to determine for the future what uranium resources may exist in the Province of British Columbia, we see no reason to prohibit uranium exploration from the point of view of environmental protection or protection of public health."

Hopes that the government would consider and possibly act on the recommendations during the seven-year moratorium were soon dashed. Some companies withdrew from the province. Others re-focused their exploration efforts on precious and base metals, mainly gold, which was at record high prices. Uranium prices fell to roughly $30 per pound in mid-1980, and then below $20 by 1986. By the time the seven-year uranium moratorium expired in early 1987, there was little or no interest in the metal. Most companies didn't realize that the expired moratorium had been extended indefinitely by way of the Health, Safety and Reclamation Code. A section on uranium and thorium exploration detailed requirements that made it impossible to explore for these commodities without the permission of the chief inspector of mines.

Uranium prices fell to the $10 to $15 per-pound-level and remained low for most of the 1990s and into the new century. There was little reaction when the newly-elected Liberal government of Gordon Campbell took steps to eliminate a number of "unnecessary" regulations in the Health, Safety and Reclamation Code, which inadvertently included restrictions pertaining to uranium exploration. These changes were effected by a March 2003 order-in-council that coincided with rising uranium spot prices, which topped $120 per pound in 2006.

Uranium was back on explorationists' radar, even in B.C. Claims covering the Blizzard deposit had been re-staked in 1998 (when it was possible to stake claims but impossible to explore them). By 2005, a few years after the elimination of restrictions on uranium exploration, these claims were of interest to Vancouver-based junior Boss Power Inc., which undertook preliminary investigative work. But citizens opposed to uranium exploration and development again mobilized to stop all such efforts in the province, which made it difficult to secure approvals for proposed programs.

The government bowed to political pressures and removed uranium and thorium from rights for mineral claims issued under the Mineral Tenure Act after April 24, 2008. Minister of State for Mining Kevin Krueger claimed that the decision should have come as "no surprise" as government had consulted with industry groups the previous year about its intentions. Dan Jepsen, then AME BC president, countered by saying: "We were totally caught off guard." He noted that the decision "…ends all opportunities for development."

As the 2008 regulation did not apply to the Blizzard mineral claims, the provincial cabinet issued an order-in-council in March of 2009, prohibiting the chief inspector of mines from issuing necessary permits to explore for uranium and from exempting a person from requiring such permits. Again, a perceived mining-friendly government had essentially declared a second uranium moratorium, this time with no end-date. There is no evidence that the government consulted the three-volume Bates Royal Commission Report prior to making these decisions, or was even aware of its existence.

If the 1980 uranium moratorium was an example of failed public policy and recent government decisions put taxpayers on the hook for compensation of the expropriated mineral claims. Boss Power Inc. filed a statement of claim against the government in late 2008. The case never went to trial; the government agreed to a $30-million out-of-court settlement to Boss Power in late October of 2011.

Kennco's groundbreaking exploration program at Galore Creek, 1963.

The Role of Global Miners, Oil Giants and Consulting Firms

The B.C. & Yukon Chamber of Mines benefited from an influx of international mining companies in the boom years following the Second World War, including large producers with deep pockets and the ability to recruit talent from around the world.

Many technical advances occurred during this period, which led to the formation of new consulting firms providing exploration, engineering and other specialized services.

The Chamber served unofficially as an employment office in the post-war era and was often a first stop for many of the mineral units spun-out by large oil companies. Chevron Minerals of Canada, BP Minerals Canada, Esso Minerals Canada, AGIP Mining and others contributed greatly to B.C. exploration and mine development. Some of their executives supported the Chamber as well, notably Donald Mustard (BP Minerals), who served as

president from 1979 to 1981, and Charlie Aird (Esso Minerals), president from 1986 to 1987.

Kennco Explorations, a unit of global giant Kennecott Copper Corporation, focused its initial Canadian exploration efforts in Quebec and the Labrador Trough. The West Coast was a logical next step, as parent Kennecott got its start in the early 1900s mining a highly profitable, high-grade copper deposit in the Alaska Panhandle.

Kennco focused its West Coast efforts on the search for large porphyry copper deposits similar to those found in Utah (Bingham Canyon), Arizona, Chile, and

B.C.'s Highland Valley district. The company recruited talent far and wide to help with this effort, including Johannes J. (Joe) Brummer, a South African geologist whose breakthrough theories led to new discoveries in Africa's Copper Belt.

David Barr, a newly graduated geologist from the University of Toronto, was recruited in 1951. Gerald Rayner, a Vancouver-based mining engineer, joined Kennco as a summer student in 1958 and later became a fulltime employee.

"The [Kennco] team was very close-knit, very dedicated and loyal, and very smart with a good approach," Rayner says." We were almost exclusively focused on porphyry deposits and regional geochemistry was the backbone of those efforts."

Brummer, inducted into the Canadian Mining Hall of Fame in 2008, is credited with introducing stream sediment geochemistry to Canada, which led to many discoveries.

Rayner says the Kennco "intellectual trust" continued after Jack Gower took the helm and brought together a group of "breakthrough thinkers" who helped identify and explore many of B.C.'s foremost porphyry copper and copper-gold deposits. Among them was Charles Ney, a long-time Chamber volunteer and lecturer at its Prospecting and Mining School. (The AME BC library is named in Ney's honour. Gower also contributed to the Chamber, serving as president from 1965 to 1966.)

Rayner spent three years at Galore Creek in northwestern B.C., where he worked with Barr to advance a large porphyry copper-gold project. It was later found to be uneconomic, mostly because of its remote location and lack of infrastructure. Rayner left shortly after, but Barr stayed on and became vice-president and general manager in the early 1970s.

Barr spent 22 years with Kennco, which by this point had explored many projects in B.C., including Brenda, Endako, Lornex, Huckleberry and Kemess. Yet as Barr notes in his autobiography, *One Lucky Canuck*, others developed them into profitable mines. In contrast, Kennco developed only one mine in B.C., a short-lived molybdenum project.

The reason, Barr explained, was that projects had to meet rigorous parameters for capital investment, "… which included a minimum five-year payback, 10 per cent annual contribution to parents' earnings and a minimum 20-year life." Notwithstanding, he aptly describes Kennco's commitment to Canada as "…one of the largest, if not the largest of foreign-based corporations." But he also saw cutbacks coming and, in 1974, accepted an offer to join the Canadian arm of yet another international company, DuPont of Canada Exploration (DOX). DOX was a unit of DuPont USA, an established and highly-profitable chemical company with an explosives unit serving the mining industry.

Barr focused on acquiring projects for DOX, notably Great Slave Reef (lead-zinc) in the Northwest Territories, a gold-silver deposit which later became

the Baker Mine in the Toodoggone region of B.C., and the Bell Creek gold mine in Ontario.

Barr understood the challenges of operating in mountainous B.C., but nothing could have prepared him for the devastating news that four members of his team and their pilot had perished in a helicopter accident in the rugged Iskut River region on July 3, 1980. He personally notified each of the families of their loss, a painful duty that left its mark. This tragic event led the Chamber to form a safety committee that fall, with Barr as a driving force. (See A Safe Day, page 86).

R. J. (Bob) Cathro, co-founder of Archer Cathro & Associates Ltd., contributed to the creation of the Chamber's safety manual, as well as many other Chamber initiatives. He shared Barr's commitment to safety as his Yukon-based firm had also lost an employee in a helicopter accident.

"There was no GPS, very limited radio reception, only limited topographical map coverage and no geological maps for parts of the Yukon in the early days," Cathro said. "You had to rely on your wits and good luck."

Cathro and partner Alan Archer formed their engineering consulting firm in 1965, with a head office in Whitehorse. They grew up in the same town, graduated from the University of British Columbia with B. Sc. degrees in geological engineering two years apart (1959 and 1957, respectively), and spent most of their early careers in the North.

"We finally met in the Yukon and found we had all these past connections," Cathro said.

Yukon was booming at the time, thanks to a staking rush triggered by a lead-zinc discovery later developed into a mine in the Faro region by Cyprus Anvil Mining Corp.

Archer and Cathro became the "go-to" team in the territory, with a hand in a wide range of deposits and prospects, ranging from precious and base metals to coal, tungsten and uranium. Their property database, regarded as the best in the business, was later acquired by the Yukon government. The firm also opened an office in Vancouver and became prominent in northern-B.C. exploration as well. The firm's Yukon expertise was in strong demand in the 1970s, when mineral exploration in B.C. came to a sudden halt due to the Barrett government policies.

The industry outlook improved with the election of a new government in 1975. By the late 1970s, B.C. was enjoying a staking rush and exploration boom for molybdenum, triggered by a spike in molybdenum prices and a regional geochemical survey by government geologists showing new prospective areas. By 1981, however, molybdenum prices had fallen to $5 per pound from a high of $30, bringing the boom to an abrupt end. But it did establish B.C. as a prime hunting ground for the metal and attracted molybdenum talent to the province, including from AMAX Inc. (later Cyprus AMAX), owner of the Climax molybdenum mine in Colorado.

B.C. ultimately became a major molybdenum producer. Placer Development's Endako Mines and Noranda Mines' Boss Mountain Mine both began producing in 1965. Production of molybdenum from these mines and at a later date, BC Moly, subsequently Kitsault, was complemented with significant by-product production from large copper porphyry mines such as Lornex, Valley Copper, Brenda, Gibraltar and Island Copper mines.

Cathro served as Chamber president from 1982 to 1983, which were tough years for the industry because of weak metal prices, high inflation and soaring short-term interest rates. In 1982, he noted that "…no less than 15 multinational corporations closed Vancouver offices and/or terminated their exploration efforts in the region."

The 1980s saw a revival in gold exploration, spurred by discoveries made by Vancouver-based juniors that were ultimately developed into mines in the Hemlo region of Ontario and later in the decade, the Eskay Creek gold-silver mine in the Iskut region of B.C. and by record high gold prices early in the decade.

The 1987 market crash, combined with weak metal prices and land-use battles and changing government policies resulted in reduced exploration spending in B.C., and a flight to offshore jurisdictions in the 1990s.

By that point, most of the major oil companies had long left the minerals business.

Mustard said the oil companies were initially interested in the coal and uranium (energy) sectors and expanded into minerals later.

"They never succeeded very well. One reason is that the oil cycle from conception to production is about five years, compared to ten years or more in the mining cycle. But one thing they did bring to us is the concept of land, the importance of having land."

Another benefit was the property and technical databases built up by the mining units of oil companies over the years, some of which ended up in the hands of junior companies.

One noteworthy example was the North American diamond exploration database of Superior Oil and partner Falconbridge gathered in the late 1970s and early 1980s. The program was managed by Superior's Hugo Dummett, with the help of two B.C. geologists, Charles (Chuck) Fipke and Stewart Blusson. When Superior left the mineral business, Dummett convinced the company to turn over the data to B.C.-based Dia Met Minerals, Fipke's and Blusson's company.

Fipke and Blusson continued the diamond hunt in northern Canada. When Dia Met made the first diamond discovery in the Lac de Gras region of the Northwest Territories in the early 1990s, Dummett convinced his new employer, BHP Minerals, to back the project.

The discovery was later developed into Canada's first diamond mine, Ekati. A second mine, Diavik, followed, developed by Kennecott in partnership with Aber Resources. Another nearby diamond mine, Snap Lake, was discovered by a Vancouver junior headed by geologist Randy Turner. Turner started his career with AGIP and Esso Minerals Canada.

Mustard had spent part of his early career at Mwadui, a diamond mine found decades earlier in East Africa by Canadian geologist John Williamson, a graduate of McGill University who mentored many of Canada's diamond exploration pioneers.

As these few examples show, endeavors of the past often bear fruit in the future.

The collective efforts of these and thousands of other talented individuals helped B.C. become a globally recognized centre of excellence in mining and mineral exploration.

David Barr passed away in 2009, but his legacy continues with a namesake safety award presented annually by AME BC to companies achieving the highest safety standards. Bob Cathro won many awards for his industry contributions, including AME BC's "Spud" Huestis Award in 1999, with co-winner Alan Archer. And AME BC annually presents the Hugo Dummett Diamond Award for excellence in this new, niche industry segment.

Rider Petch and Genevieve Morinville

B.C. expertise helped develop Ekati – and has been used since. Rescan fisheries work at Pigeon Stream at Ekati mine, c. 2006.

Junior miners welcome here. The historic home of the Vancouver Stock Exchange at the corner of Howe and Pender Streets, Vancouver

Junior Mining Companies in British Columbia and Yukon

AME BC has long recognized the important role played by junior mining companies in the discovery of mineral wealth, and have been staunch supporters of this vibrant sector for the past century.

Juniors are publicly listed companies without positive cash flow that operate by raising risk capital for mineral exploration or other early-stage ventures. During the past 100 years, thousands of juniors have been listed for public trading on the Vancouver Stock Exchange (VSE) and its successor, the TSX Venture Exchange. Many thousands of investors have purchased shares of junior mining companies over this period, hoping for high returns should a discovery be made. Using investor funds, juniors have contributed to the discovery and development of most mines in British Columbia and Yukon, as well as many elsewhere in Canada and around the world.

The discovery record of Canadian-based juniors is unmatched. Shareholders of successful juniors have been well rewarded for their risks.

Junior miners face immense risks in mineral exploration; few prospects ever become mines, and companies must rely on advanced technologies and methods to increase their odds of success. They have to be nimble, innovative and versatile in order to manage risk and adapt to change, whether from metal prices, capital markets or government policies. They have to decide whether to focus on specific metals and commodities, while also being mindful of long-term supply and demand fundamentals. And they must pay strict attention to social, environmental and Aboriginal issues, or risk stalled projects.

Juniors that are successful in discovery face challenges too, as they are often unable to finance expensive mine development on their own and are forced to seek a joint venture with a senior partner or a merger with a similar or stronger entity to survive. Accordingly, juniors must understand the objectives and commodity preferences of senior mining companies, many of which no longer conduct grassroots exploration, preferring, instead, to acquire a junior's proven discovery.

The changing commitment to exploration by major mining companies led to the expansion of the junior mining industry in the early 1980s. As senior companies shed their exploration staff, many explorers joined the ranks of the junior mining sector.

Junior company management has always needed to be versatile in order to adapt to changing availability of risk capital, metals prices, and investor focus. The investment community has always placed a priority on a junior's area of specialization (such as uranium, diamonds, base metals, and gold). As the number of juniors increased, more of them were capable of financing their discoveries into operating mines and, building on that success, acquiring other properties with near-term production potential.

As this chapter will show, many juniors overcame these risks and challenges in the past century. Some successfully developed mines on their own and grew into larger entities. A few evolved to become mid-tier or major companies.

Tommy Elliott, with his 47-year association with the mining industry and long-time secretary-manager of the Chamber, observed in 1977 that "By far the majority of mineral discoveries are made by prospectors and small public stock companies… I completed a study of who was responsible for the original discovery of seventy mineral deposits… revealing that at least eighty-five per cent of those deposits were originally discovered by the prospector and/or the small mining company."

Elliott's comments still hold true.

How did juniors achieve their remarkable track record of mineral discovery?

The Chamber's records show that it was not by luck alone.

Over the past one hundred years and continuing into this century, junior companies have relied on a tradition of teamwork, with the teams typically comprised of prospectors, geologists, engineers, financiers and promoters. And each member of this team plays an important part in mine-finding and development.

The Prospector

Although a few old-timers without a formal degree in geology still tramp the hills in search of the mother lode, the role of the prospector has changed with time. Some junior companies, in the early years, were formed by grass-roots prospectors as a vehicle to raise funds for their prospects. Many of the prospector-formed companies that grew into small mine producers were seen in the Kootenays, the Cariboo, Vancouver Island and Yukon.

Since the 1950s, prospectors were more likely to sell or farm out their mineral properties to juniors or major mining companies. Prospectors without their own funding would also seek financing or grubstaking from corporate or private backers.

In the 1960s, the role of the successful prospector changed substantially, spurred by improved metals prices and good economic times. Two B.C. prospectors, H.H. "Spud" Huestis and Egil Lorntzsen, took the initiative to form their own companies, in which they became significant shareholders, and then brought in management capable of turning their porphyry copper discoveries into major producing mines in British Columbia's Highland Valley. This was no overnight success story. It took faith and determination to overcome industry skepticism that these large but low-grade deposits could be economically mined.

Prospectors working for companies, or alone, have declined in numbers since the 1970s, yet they continue to make discoveries. One example is the Voisey's Bay nickel-copper-cobalt deposit in Labrador, found in the mid-1990s by Albert Chislett and Chris Verbiski, Newfoundland-based prospectors hired by a Vancouver junior.

More recently, prospector Shawn Ryan made several exciting new lode-gold discoveries in the South Klondike. Those discoveries, after 10 years of prospecting and geochemical sampling, were optioned to juniors Kaminak Gold and Underworld Resources. Ryan received generous cash and share payments for his Yukon discoveries, as well as industry recognition, notably AME BC's "Spud" Huestis Award for prospecting excellence.

Today's prospector is often a geologist or geoscientist, who begins the search for minerals with the assistance of geophysical and geochemical technology. As an example, B.C. geologists Stewart Blusson and Chuck Fipke started prospecting for diamonds near Golden in British Columbia and ended up with the first major diamond discovery in the Northwest Territories. Jimmy McDougall, although a long-time geologist with then major company Falconbridge, was also a prospector who spent many hours in the 1960s in a Super Cub and later a helicopter with his magnetometer, aerial photographs and keen eyeballs. He is credited with numerous B.C. discoveries, notably the Catface porphyry copper deposit and the Windy Craggy massive sulphide deposit.

The Geologist

More than 2,000 geologists graduated from the University of British Columbia from 1960 through 2010. In the 1960s, most sought employment with major companies, expecting career stability. Yet as many found, geologists, sometimes even entire exploration departments, were often the first people let go during industry downturns.

In 2010 most of the 1,380 geologists listed with the Vancouver Mining Exploration Group were directly employed by juniors. Many others act as consultants to juniors. Some geologists have formed junior companies that have subsequently found mines

The number of newly-graduated geologists joining juniors fluctuates with economic cycles. In the early 1990s, and again in the early 2000s, geologists often struggled to find steady employment. Starting in the mid-2000s there were not enough graduates to fill positions with the juniors. In 2011 juniors reportedly raided geological staffs of U.S.-based majors with lucrative offers of employment and stock options.

Over the past century, field and research geologists from the Canada Department of Mines, the Geological Survey of Canada, and the British Columbia Department of Mines have provided valuable exploration-related assistance to juniors in Yukon and B.C. The data include results from geological mapping, silt-sampling programs, airborne magnetometer surveys and metallogenic modeling, all helpful to the hunt for new discoveries. AME BC's Gold Pan Award

has been presented to several government geologists, including Atholl Sutherland Brown, Dirk Tempelman-Kluit and Jim Fyles.

The Promoter

The Oxford dictionary notes that the word "promoter" has been frequently used in an opprobrious sense since at least 1876, which isn't surprising as some promoters were rogues who flaunted whatever few rules existed in the early days of junior mining.

Rules and regulations are much tighter today, though even one bad apple can devastate markets, as was the case with junior Bre-X Minerals and its notorious salting scandal of the 1990s. (See Bre-X, page 58).

The role of the promoter has changed with time. The image of a cigar-chomping, fast-talking, hard-drinking Howe Street character has largely been replaced with investor relations professionals, whether in-house personnel or outside contractors.

For the junior, a stock exchange listing is a necessity for raising risk capital as well as providing shareholder liquidity. Yet their chances of finding a mine are slim. The rule of thumb is that for every thousand mineral prospects found, only 100 warrant advanced drill-testing and only one of those becomes a mine. The reality is that juniors need an element of promotion to raise risk capital.

Promoters have been part of the junior mining scene since the early days of the Vancouver Stock Exchange, starting with Alvo von Alvensleben who

made an estimated $25 million between 1907 and 1913 only to lose it all. A lesser role was played by Warburton Pike – a name familiar to some of the Yukon exploration fraternity. When not raising money, Pike prospected Yukon and Alaska by canoe during the 1890s.

In the 1960s, Martin "Mart" Gibbeson helped Chester Millar finance his new company Afton Mines, which became a great success story. In the late 1970s, he helped Orval Gillespie finance and bring the Carolin gold mine into production near Hope, B.C.

Gibbeson raised money for the Erickson gold mine in northern B.C., as well as for La Teko Resources, which financed Esperanza Explorations' Tillicum Mountain gold project near Burton, B.C. He also helped Alan Savage fund New Canamin Resources, which brought the now-producing Huckleberry copper mine to feasibility near Houston, B.C. He was a promoter of few words, when selling any project he only said it "looked good."

Morris Black, promoter of Endako Mines and numerous other endeavours, would introduce himself to geologists by saying, "Show me a rock and I'll make you a mine." He also helped promote Craigmont Mines, a junior with a copper project later developed (by senior companies) into B. C's first integrated large-scale open-pit mine.

Some promoters were less successful; particularly those who didn't like to hear much technical detail from geologists. One such promoter listening to a geological presentation mentioning "abundant favositides" didn't realize that fossils were being identified. He asked, "What does that stuff trade for on the London Metals Exchange?"

Harold Quinn was a unique promoter. With a PhD in geology, he ended the later part of his career forming "shell" companies – listed companies without material assets. Over a 10-year period he incorporated dozens of them with names like, "Black Sheep Mines" (named after him), "Popocatepetl" (a volcanic experience) and bearing a more obvious connotation "Last Chance." His selected list of "seed" investors would buy shares for 10 cents with a promise to Quinn that he could buy them back for 15 cents. Those 15-cent shares would then be purchased by the ultimate acquirer of the shell. Asked if anyone ever refused to sell back their 10-cent shares, Quinn said "Yes, a lawyer."

The most famous Howe Street promoter was Murray Pezim, subject of at least five books. The "Pez" arrived in Vancouver in 1964 to re-establish himself after experiencing regulatory issues with the Toronto Stock Exchange and Ontario Securities Commission.

Pezim promoted many VSE-listed companies, most of which weren't successes. Pezim often lost money on his deals too. He often said, "I always went down with the ship." Another occasional saying was: "Believe me, I'm telling you the truth this time."

John Brock considered Pezim a friend and served on a few of his boards, but also thought he was "… an agreeable rascal." Once while they were settling

the terms of a property option, a film crew for the television program *Lifestyles of the Rich and Famous* burst through the door and started recording the negotiation. Brock was gratified; the terms of the deal were settled in his favour. After the program was televised, Brock got a call from a friend who said, "That was a great performance, but you sure left a lot on the table for the Pez." It turned out Pezim had edited the tape to leave exactly that impression.

Through his company, Prime Capital, the Pez had an estimated 87 juniors under his management in the 1980s and 1990s, and raised more than a billion dollars for the stable of juniors. International Corona, Adrian Resources, Calpine Resources and Prime Resources were trading leaders on the VSE during this period. Corona financed the exploration and discovery of what became the 20-million ounce Hemlo gold deposit in Ontario, with its stock price hitting an all-time high of $85. Calpine financed the discovery and drilling of Eskay Creek in B.C., which became one of the highest grade gold mines in Canada. The Chamber presented him with its first award recognizing perseverance and success in financing mineral exploration, named in his honour, in 1999.

For tenacity and perseverance, promoter Frank Callaghan deserves an award. In 1991 he made a long-term commitment to the Barkerville and Wells gold camps. Twenty years later, his junior, Barkerville Gold, financed itself into production in 2011.

Another successful promoter was Robert Hunter, the 2001 winner of the Murray Pezim Award. He

started his career with Breakwater Resources, which developed the Cannon gold mine in Washington State. In 1985, he teamed up with geologist Robert Dickinson to form Hunter Dickinson Inc. (HDI), which became a highly successful exploration and mine development group. As George Cross, publisher of the *George Cross Newsletter,* said, "Bob had to get into mining, by that time he had seven kids."

HDI explored, financed and developed many B.C. projects that became mines, including Golden Bear, Mount Milligan and Kemess, as well as restoring the Gibraltar copper mine to production. The group also has many international successes. Between 1985 and 2011, HDI and its affiliated companies had raised roughly $1.4 billion of equity financing.

Neil Dragovan

Murray Pezim

Another well-known promoter, Bruce McDonald, formed Noramco Capital in 1983, along with Ray Cottrell. They managed 20 VSE-listed juniors, the most successful of which made a significant gold discovery later developed into a mine in the Casa Berardi region of Quebec. In 1994 McDonald sold his Noramco interest to Brian Bayley and Murray Sinclair, who changed the name to Quest Capital, that became a major financing house.

Don McLeod has made a substantial contribution to the mining industry, both in his own right and as the father of two extraordinary children: Catherine who is further described in the "Remarkable People" section of this book, and Bruce who steered the very successful Capstone mining group.

Don formed Northair Mines Ltd. in Vancouver in 1968. He and the Northair Group were responsible for the development of the Brandywine gold-silver-lead mine (1975), the Summit gold mine (1981) and the Silver Butte mine (1990s) in B.C. As a result, he received the E. A. Scholz award for excellence in mine development in 1988.

Ian Telfer would probably not mind being called a promoter, having raised a reported $1 billion for mining companies. In the early 2000s, he acquired Wheaton River, a VSE junior with the Skookum Jim gold mine in northern B.C. In 2003, Wheaton carried out an equity financing of $450 million (a TSX record at the time), and through mergers and acquisitions became Goldcorp, one of the fastest-growing, lowest cost senior gold producers in the

Americas. In 2011, Vancouver-based Goldcorp employed more than 11,500 people worldwide.

The Media

George Cross, publisher of the George Cross News Letter *"Reliable Reporting," was an icon within the junior community.*

Founded by his father, *The George Cross News Letter* published five days a week for 52 years, from April 1947 to December 2000 – a total of 13,388 issues. Most of the news reported the junior's activity and included personal interviews with management, junior news releases, and detailed reporting on the numerous exploration projects that George had visited in the field. His readers included investors, brokers, the junior sector and major companies looking for hints of the next discovery. No other mining-related publication ever matched the content in the News Letter. George said his only competition at the time was the *Northern Miner*.

The Stock Exchange

Fifteen stock exchanges were formed in B.C. between 1877 and 1910. The only survivor was the VSE, incorporated in 1907 with 14 listings.

By 1910 there were 32 listed companies, one of the first juniors being Green Lake Mining and Milling. The hot stock of 1911 was Lucky Jim Zinc Mines; its exact location today is probably unknown.

The VSE operated for 90 years until 1999, when it then merged with the Alberta Stock Exchange to

become the Canadian Venture Exchange (CDNX). CDNX and the Montreal Stock Exchange were acquired by the Toronto Stock Exchange in 2001. The Toronto Stock Exchange then created a subsidiary exchange called the TSX Venture Exchange (TSX-V) for the purpose of listing small-cap public companies. In 2011, its listing numbered approximately 1,100 junior mining companies. Toronto-based TSX-V maintains an office in Vancouver, where its services are mainly provided to juniors.

Stock exchanges today attract capital from across Canada, U.S., the U. K., Europe and Asia. Availability of risk capital varies from year-to-year, depending on world economies, metals prices and market cycles. The size of the junior financings has grown significantly over the recent decades; more money means finding more mines.

The Brokers

The combination of Vancouver-based juniors and brokerage firms has resulted in Vancouver becoming "…the undisputed capital of the global mineral exploration companies around the world."

This 2011 observation was made by *Engineering and Mining Journal* (E&MJ) as part of a special report on mining in B.C. and Yukon.

Brokerage firms have played an essential role in financing juniors for more than a century. Many of them started with humble beginnings in Victoria and Vancouver.

In the early 1900s a number of brokerage firms were doing business, including C. M. Oliver, whose name continued into the next century, and Wolverton Securities, which entered a new century under the management of fourth-generation Wolvertons.

In 1928, John McGraw started his career with Continental Securities and bought out that firm in 1931. Continental was later taken over by Gus McPhail, along with Bob Fay. McGraw, who also grubstaked prospectors, was responsible for 25 per cent of the VSE's volume well into the 1950s. Frank Giustra with Yorkton Securities bought out Continental in 1989. McGraw was also allied with George Tapp, senior partner of Doherty Roadhouse and McCuaig, known on the street as "Dorothy's Roadhouse".

Frank Giustra's successes via mining and the VSE were indirectly responsible for B.C.'s importance as film and television production centre, "Hollywood North". Giustra's Lionsgate Productions is an active and prolific player in B.C.'s film community.

Geological engineer Channing Buckland started his brokerage career with Dorothy's Roadhouse in 1962. One of his first successes was participating in financings of Dynasty Explorations in the mid-1960s, which led to the discovery of the Faro lead-zinc deposit in Yukon. He was known by juniors for participating in at least a portion of the financings that crossed his desk. In 1973 he moved to Draper Dobie, whose Vancouver officer was managed by Charlie Bawlf. (As an aside, Bawlf was a notorious short-seller. In 1974, his short position on the

Canadian dollar was so significant that he got a call from Governor of the Bank of Canada, Gerald Bouey, who wondered what the heck was going on).

Buckland joined Canaccord in the late 1970s, and then spent 19 years working with Peter Brown until starting his own firm, Bolder Investment partners. In 2010 Bolder merged with John Tognetti's Haywood Securities. Buckland met with hundreds of juniors seeking financing over the years, and would typically close these presentations with, "Oh geez, do I really have to have some of that?" before writing a cheque.

Haywood Securities, with John Tognetti as chairman and investment advisor, was also known for following and financing juniors. Tognetti could always be found strolling around the hundreds of junior company booths at mining investment conferences, looking for the next big story. Haywood raised more than $4 billion for the mining sector from 2000 to 2010, including $654 million for junior companies.

Since 1969, Peter Brown has maintained a commanding financing presence within the Vancouver junior mining community and beyond. At this time of writing (mid-2011), he was in his 70th year and still going strong, starting at 5. 30 in the morning taking phone calls in his bathtub. His legacy is based on hard work and a shrewd instinct for early recognition of, and capitalizing on, a deal. One exception was when he was with Greenshields in 1963. He tells of going home to Joanne, his wife, and announcing that "we have lost three hundred." Joanne was horrified. Peter

never told her that it was three hundred thousand. Many years ago there was a contest amongst his associates in order to determine who could make one million dollars the quickest. He won in 45 minutes, second place went to the guy who made it in a month, or so the story goes.

In May of 1976, Brown, recognizing the value of maintaining the junior marketplace, garnered enough votes to oust the VSE board of directors. He then became a dominant figure on the Exchange and remained on the board for nine years, including as chairman in 1982 and 1983. But his lasting legacy is building Canaccord (now Canaccord Genuity) into a leading independent investment dealer in Canada with capital markets operations in the United States and the United Kingdom and 46 worldwide offices, including 32 branches in Canada. As lead agent, Canaccord has raised $11 billion for juniors. As a participating agent, it has raised more $33 billion for companies in the mining sector.

Junior Mine-Finding in B.C. and Yukon: The Early 1900s

Many juniors of the late 1880s and early 1900s grew from prospectors discovering and developing small mining operations in the Slocan, Rossland, and Boundary camps in southeastern B.C.

Many of those involved came from Washington and Idaho, financing their efforts through the Spokane Stock Exchange, then the largest western stock exchange outside San Francisco. Some of those juniors were amalgamated into the Consolidated Mining and Smelting Co. (Cominco), now part of Teck Resources.

The growing importance of the Spokane financial community prompted B.C. mining companies and their financiers to establish the Vancouver Stock Exchange in 1908. Spokane declined in importance as the VSE grew during the next few decades.

A similar story developed in Yukon's Klondike. Joe Boyle's Canadian Klondyke and the Guggenheim's Yukon Gold — initially financed on the New York Stock Exchange curb market — were combined into promoter A. N. Treadwell's Yukon Consolidated Gold Company. Yukon Consolidated later traded on the VSE. The company and many other juniors maintained offices in the Rogers Building on Granville Street for decades.

1920s through the 1940s

During the lean Depression years, when capital was in scarce, many VSE-listed juniors survived through private financings with local businessmen.

Some of the larger gold juniors were financed privately in London and New York. Gold was a bright spot, which allowed many companies to survive the otherwise depressed markets, notably Yukon Consolidated Gold, the Pioneer and Bralone mines in the Bridge River gold camp, Cariboo Gold Quartz at Wells, and Hedley Amalgamated in the Similkameen.

Wartime demand for metals improved the fortunes of base metal companies. Cominco acquired Coast Copper on Vancouver Island. Reconstruction after the war helped spur metal demand and raise the fortunes of large companies, which in turn led to greater stability for juniors with discoveries. Silver Standard, listed on the VSE in 1947, remained (in 2011) the longest listed junior. In the 21st century it grew into an international major with producing silver mines.

Silver Standard's Bill Dunn served as Chamber president in 1977 and 1978.

The 1950s and 1960s

The post-war economic boom helped senior companies grow in size and stature.

As a result, most geologists worked for senior companies such as Canex Placer, Cominco and Eldorado. Some were recruited by the oil patch, then in a period of expansion.

Junior companies diversified their exploration efforts in this period to include base metals and uranium, resulting in new discoveries coveted by senior companies. Notable was the Granduc copper discovery made by prospectors near Stewart, B.C. The VSE emerged as a major source of risk capital in the 1960s. The Chamber also expanded, with membership totaling 251 companies: 171 juniors and 80 majors.

A transformative mineral discovery for B.C. in the 1950s was the Snowstorm copper prospect in the

Highland Valley by prospector "Spud" Huestis; it provided the first recognition of a porphyry copper deposit in Canada. But major companies were initially unimpressed by its low grades, and would remain so for some time.

In Yukon, Prospector Airways — following up on the Vangorda Creek discovery by Alan Kulan and native prospectors from Ross River — drilled a lead-zinc-silver resource that served as the geologic model for the subsequent discovery of the Faro deposit. This major discovery in 1965 was made by junior Dynasty Exploration.

With the assistance of Karl Springer, Granduc began preparing for production in 1961.

Bethlehem Copper Corporation, with Huestis as its first president, started production in the Highland Valley in 1962 (the company was absorbed by Cominco in 1983).

Egil Lorntzsen discovered the nearby Lornex copper deposit in 1963. Lornex Mining was incorporated a year later, with the prospector as president. He raised $400,000 by selling shares privately, bought a second-hand bulldozer, and proved up the merit of his claims. Rio Algom invested in the junior in 1965. The first production began in 1972.

The Craigmont discovery, in the region surrounding Highland Valley, was launched by a junior incorporated in 1946, and run by prospector Neal McDairmid and promoters Earl Oates and

Ray Collishaw. As the story goes, the geologists overseeing the drill program were "delayed" in a Merritt bar, so the drillers kept drilling and hit mineralization. Hole 15 graded 4.4 per cent copper over 640 feet, which got the majors excited.

Canex Placer brought Craigmont into production in 1961. About the same time, through juniors Torwest and Highmont, promoter Bob Falkins, along with John Leishman and Hec Waller, discovered the Highmont copper-molybdenum deposit. The deposit was later mined by Teck Corp. During the 1970s, after Teck moved its head office to Vancouver, Falkins and his partners maintained offices with the company.

Other juniors involved in discoveries that became mines in B.C. during the 1960s included Endako, a molybdenum property that Placer Development put into production in 1965. It was debt-free by the end of 1967. Gibraltar, brought to production by Canex Placer, was originally a penny stock deal involving promoter Paddy Bowes, mining engineer Jerry Wood, lawyer Ike Shulman, and broker Rudy Nosalek.

The Brenda copper-molybdenum mine was developed by a junior formed by partners Bern Brynelson and Archie Bell, both previously with Noranda. The low-grade deposit in the South Okanagan was later acquired by Noranda, and became a profitable mine.

In Yukon, resumption of production in the Whitehorse Copper Belt was financed by junior New Imperial Mines. Cantung's tungsten deposit,

accessed through Yukon but in the Northwest Territories, also came into production. Dynasty Explorations, led by Aaro Aho, a board member of the Chamber at the time, discovered the Faro lead-zinc deposit in the Anvil District in 1965. This led to the largest (10,000 claims plus) Yukon staking rush of the time. By way of joint venture, Cyprus Mining Corp. placed Faro into production in 1968. The Anvil rush also led to the formation of Archer Cathro and Associates, which provided consulting and exploration services to the numerous juniors participating in that rush. It was the same story with Bert Reeve and John Stollery's Cordilleran Engineering's entry into Yukon with the Norquest Syndicate.

Bob Cathro and Al Archer discovered the Casino copper-molybdenum deposit in 1969. In 2011 the deposit still awaited a production decision by Western Copper, originally incorporated as a junior company.

During the 1960s, regulatory compliance was minimal. A junior company's prospectus for its initial public funding might consist of about 15 pages and the cost of preparation would be in the order of a few thousand dollars. In 2011, a junior's prospectus could contain over 100 pages and be prepared at a cost of $300,000 to $400,000.

The 1960s closed with approximately 600 juniors listed on the VSE.

The 1970s and 1980s

The mining industry was hard hit by the election of a provincial NDP government whose onerous policies chased many companies from B.C.

The new premier Dave Barrett was described as "…the best premier the Yukon ever had" as many companies fled north. A staking rush took place in Yukon, triggered by the Howard's Pass zinc discovery.

Not everyone left B.C. Promoters Paddy Bowes and Ike Shulman optioned their Gibraltar claims to Canex Placer, which brought the property into production in 1972. In 1976, prospector Don McLeod's and "Moose" Manifold's Northair Mines, north of Squamish, began production. It was described as "B.C.'s first new gold mine in 40 years."

Chester Millar came to prominence for the discovery of the Afton copper-gold deposit during this period. He later incorporated Rennick Resources, subsequently re-named Glamis Gold. The pioneering junior went south to develop one of the first heap-leach gold mines in California, as well as other gold mines in the Americas.

A total of $362.5 million was raised in VSE financings during the 1970s, of which an estimated $250 million was on behalf of juniors.

The 1970s closed with approximately 1,000 junior companies listed on the VSE.

The 1980s began with gold prices reaching an all-time high of $850, with silver reaching a record of $49. Old-timers said, "With housewives lining up at the Bank of Nova Scotia to buy gold, this won't last," and they were right. But this was a transformative event notwithstanding, triggering a resurgence of exploration for precious metals not seen since the early 1900s, when world-class discoveries were made in B.C. and Ontario.

The junior market of the 1980s was tumultuous, with compressed market cycles during the decade. The first was a short-term downward correction on the VSE.

This "Black Friday" occurred on October 19, 1984, when heavily promoted Beauford Resources went "no bid" and dropped from about $11 per share to $2. This activity dragged five other juniors down it, resulting in paper losses in the order of $40 million. Two of the promoters involved were sentenced to seven years in prison.

The next market crash in October of 1987 slowed exploration financing for the next three years. Many great gold discoveries were made, notwithstanding, notably in the "Golden Triangle" of northwestern B.C., the site of one of the province's largest staking rushes. The Johnny Mountain gold-silver-base metals discovery made by Reg Davis' Skyline Exploration generated much of the early excitement and the rush was on.

Ron Netolitzky, with junior Delaware Resources, found the nearby Snip deposit, soon to be a gold mine taken over by Cominco. Netolitzky was also

behind Calpine, which optioned the Eskay Creek property from Margaret MacKay, who owned Stikine Resources. Her prospector husband, Tom MacKay, made the original Eskay gold-silver discovery in the 1930s. Stikine and Calpine became part of Murray Pezim's stable of juniors.

Among other key gold discoveries in the 1980s was the Brucejack Lake deposit in the Sulphurets camp by Newhawk (part of the Northair group).

Elsewhere in B.C., Bert Reeve, a long-time B.C. and Yukon explorer, put the Blackdome gold property into production through his junior Blackdome Mining Corporation.

The first success of the Hunter Dickinson Group in the early 1980s was with the Golden Bear mine in northwestern B.C. That was followed by Continental Gold Corp.'s Mount Milligan copper-gold discovery, where production was scheduled to start in 2012.

The 1980s closed with about 2,100 listings on the VSE.

The 1990s

The role of the juniors changed again during the 1990s as major companies (mining and oil and gas) began disbanding or downsizing their exploration departments.

During this period, many companies moved out of Vancouver, or merged with majors. Gone were the Vancouver-based exploration departments of Getty, Imperial Oil, Chevron, Kennecott, Noranda, Falconbridge, Placer Dome and Inco. But the silver lining for juniors

was that majors were no longer focused on exploration, and instead looked for projects of promise held by junior companies with an eye to possible buy-outs.

Ron Netolitzky continued his mine-finding career through Loki Gold's exploration of the Brewery Creek gold property, near Dawson City, which became Yukon's first heap-leach gold mine, later to be taken over by Viceroy Resource Corp.

Although many juniors retained offices in Vancouer, most of their activities were outside B.C. Of the 1,605 listed juniors in the decade, 868 had exploration programs. Almost half of the active juniors were exploring in 18 countries outside Canada and the U.S. Of those, 192 were in Mexico, 179 in Venezuela, 107 in Chile and 92 in Peru. During 1994, through the VSE, $500 million was raised for these Latin American exploration endeavours.

By 1993, it was estimated that only five per cent of funds raised through the VSE was being spent in B.C. This increased to 15 per cent of funds raised by 1994.

A stay-at-home exception was John Brock's American Bullion Minerals, which had optioned the Red Chris Copper property from Falconbridge and then drill-defined an overall resource of 355 million tonnes grading 0.45 per cent copper and 0.41 grams gold. Red Chris, now with Imperial Metals, was awaiting a production decision, expected in 2012.

The 1990s closed with about 1,450 listings, of which 870 were juniors

The 2000s

The latter part of the 1990s, and the 2000s, saw the consolidation of the major mining companies by way of merger and amalgamation, leaving fewer majors around to participate in traditional mineral property transactions with juniors.

In consequence, a growing number of juniors quickly became mid-tier mining companies; examples included Glamis, Bema, and Wheaton River. During the period 1999-2010, a total of 441 TSX-V listed companies graduated to the Toronto Stock Exchange senior market.

During the 2000s, junior exploration slowed in B.C. and Yukon, with continued growth of exploration opportunities elsewhere. Arequipa found Pierina in Peru (acquired by Barrick); Marwest found San Martin in Honduras (acquired by Glamis); Diamond Fields found Voisey's Bay (acquired by Inco), International Musto found Alumbrera (acquired by Rio Tinto); and on the diamond scene in the Northwest Territories, Dia Met Minerals found Ekati (BHP), and Aber found Diavik (Rio Tinto).

The 2000s closed with 1,178 mining issues listed.

The 2010s and Beyond

In the second decade of the new millennium, juniors made most new discoveries which were often bought out by acquisition-minded majors.

However, the abundance of risk capital available to the juniors during the 2000s allowed them to bring their own discoveries to a resource-definition stage, thus adding shareholder value when major company buyers appeared.

The Archer-Cathro stable of public companies was particularly active in Yukon in 2010 and 2011. The companies were managed under the umbrella of Strategic Metals, which held in its portfolio a number of juniors poised for discovery.

As junior companies moved into the mid-2000s and onward, a noticeable maturing of their role began. Some were once again becoming mine makers and operators. This was made possible by the increased availability of risk capital for both exploration and equity financing of capital costs. The transition included juniors such as Imperial Metals led by Brian Kynoch and Pierre Lebel. In the summer of 2011, Imperial was producing copper and gold from Mount Polley, and copper and molybdenum from Huckleberry, and was awaiting a production decision for Red Chris.

Jim O'Rourke, starting with Princeton Mining Corp., now Copper Mountain Mining Corp., saw the Copper Mountain deposit reach production in 2011. The Hunter Dickinson Group, led by Bob Dickinson and

Ron Thiessen, spawned Taseko Mines that brought the Gibraltar copper deposit in B.C. back into production in 2004. Hunter Dickinson was busy developing new mines, including Prosperity in B.C.,and the mega-giant Pebble copper-gold-molybdenum project in Alaska.

Not to overlook Yukon, the Minto copper-gold deposit was brought it into production in 2009 by Capstone Resources, which also had projects in Mexico and South America. Stephen Quin and Bruce McLeod were instrumental in bringing Minto on-stream.

Farallon Resources began producing zinc at the G-9 mine in Mexico in 2010. Great Basin Gold began trial mining at Hollister in Nevada in 2008 and began commercial production at Burnstone in South Africa in 2011. A production decision was considered likely for the Mount Milligan copper-gold project.

Continuing with exploration and mine-finding activity was Bob Quartermain who, over 25 years, grew former junior Silver Standard into an international silver producer. After leaving Silver Standard in 2010, he formed Pretium Resources, which then acquired Silver Standard's Sulphurets, Snowfield and Brucejack precious metals deposits in northwestern B.C. (Don McLeod, through junior Newhawk Gold Mines, conducted the first serious exploration at Brucejack and sold it to Silver Standard in 1999.)

No Stone Unturned

Exploration at Lucky Jem-Eldorado, 2011

Eldorado Mining & Refining airplane, c. 1940s

MINING & REFINING LIMITED

Rossland miners, early 1900s

AME BC

Grand Forks mining camp Yukon, 1900s

De Re Metallica – Georgius Agricola (1556) ~ An Early Text on Mining and Metallurgy

"De Re Metallica" was one of the first (if not the first) textbooks on mining and metallurgy, and was in use for over two centuries.

Even though written more than 450 years ago, it highlights many beliefs and social commentaries of that time, which are still with us today.

Written in Latin, it lay dormant for some 350 years until translated by Herbert Hoover; the same Herbert Hoover who went on to become president of the United States and his wife, Lou Henry Hoover. The translation was published in English in 1912.

Indeed, the Hoovers assert it had no equal until Schluter's great work on metallurgy published in 1738. Interestingly, the Hoovers intended the work only for private distribution amongst a small number of friends and acquaintances and, even when persuaded by Edward Rickard to allow a greater printing for wider distribution, they insisted the retail price of the book be set at no more than one fifth the cost of printing so it would be in reach of all interested readers. The original printing is now a rare collector's item.

There are a number of interesting statements by Agricola (who was trained and practiced as a physician) written in 1556 (or earlier) which still have relevance and resonate even today:

- *"None of the arts is older than agriculture, but that of the metals is not less ancient; in fact they are at least equal and coeval, for no mortal man ever tilled a field without implements.*

- *"When an art is so poor it lacks metals it is not of much importance, for nothing is made without tools.*

- *"Man without metals cannot provide those things which he needs for food and clothing. For, though the produce of the land furnishes the greatest abundance of food for the nourishment of our bodies, no labour can be carried on and completed without tools.*

- *"If we remove metals from the service of man, all methods of protecting and sustaining health and more carefully preserving the course of life are done away with. If there were no metals, men would pass a horrible and wretched existence in the midst of wild beasts; they would return to the acorns and fruits and berries of the forest. They would return to the herbs and roots which they plucked up by their nails. They would dig up caves in which to lay down at night, and by*

day they would rove in the woods and plains at random like beasts, and inasmuch as this condition is utterly unworthy of humanity, with its splendid and glorious natural endowment, will anyone be so foolish and obstinate as not to allow that metals are necessary for food and clothing and that they tend to preserve life?*

- *"In a word man cannot do without the mining industry, nor did Divine Providence will that he should.*

- *"How few artists could make anything that is beautiful and perfect without metals?*

- *"No just ruler or magistrate deprives owners of their possessions; that however may be done by a tyrant, who may cruelly rob his subjects not only of their goods honestly obtained, but even of life itself.*

- *"...inasmuch as the calling of the miner excels in honour and dignity that of the merchant trading for lucre, while it is not less noble though far more profitable than agriculture, who can fail to realize that mining is a calling of peculiar dignity?"*

Spirit of Haida Gwaii ~ Bill Reid

Myron Harris

The modern prospector – Craig Lynes exploring near Revelstoke, B.C.

Teresa Lynes

Sobering Advice

In 1959, the British Columbia Department of Mines offered much sobering advice to adventurous folks who thought they would like to try their hand at prospecting.

In that year the provincial government published a paper called *Placer Mining in British Columbia*. Actually, it was a re-print and up-date of several earlier publications on the subject, from as early as 1933. The voice of hard-won experience permeates its pages. In understated prose, they contain implicit warnings: Do not attempt placer mining unless you have physical stamina, good survival instincts, great patience and are willing to work hard to acquire local knowledge.

And, don't expect to strike it rich. Few do.

Here's what department officials had to say about getting around in the bush:

- *"Horses broken in to one type of country are amazingly sure-footed, but one accustomed, say, to the open ground of the Dry Belt is apt to get into trouble in the Coast woods or the northern muskegs. When the going is open and not steep a good horse can carry 250 pounds and even more for short spells, but for rough going where there are no trails 150 pounds is a good load.*

- *"Dogs are used for packing in some parts of Northern British Columbia. A good dog can carry*

35 to 50 pounds in canvas panniers when the brush is not thick. The use of dogs is not to be recommended, however, as the necessity of providing food is a serious problem and much valuable time is taken up by it.

- "Back-packing must be resorted to on many trips, whether for a day or so or for an entire season. The amount a man can carry depends upon stamina and necessity, and obviously varies greatly with the individual, but … 65 pounds is the heaviest load that should be attempted for day-long cross-country travel. For short hauls and relays on trails, a pack-sack with a tump-line may be used, but the universal choice is the pack-board. The pack-board is superior to the pack-sack; it keeps the back moderately cool and on it can be lashed almost any sort of load, and, what is most important the correct balance for the load is easily attained. A head-strap or modified tump-line may be attached to the board so as to ease the shoulders, if desired.

- "In back-packing … consider the element of time as against load. … a man, in addition to his equipment, can rarely carry more than two weeks' food, even of the simplest and lightest variety. If, then, several days are needed to get to his objective, say four days going in and three days coming out with a light load, he can only stay in a week. He can, of course, relay in almost any amount, but the time taken up and the food eaten during that time should be carefully figured. A man will eat between 3 and 3 ½ pounds of bush ration a day, and that is the fundamental basis of figuring.

- "If a man is working on a showing, it may be possible to augment store food with wild fruit, fish – either fresh, smoked, or pickled – or with game shot and canned the previous autumn. These, together with fresh vegetables from a garden-patch, do much to lessen the amount of groceries bought.

- "Careful planning must be done to prepare for a trip where food must be taken along. The average light-weight rations must provide 3 to 3 1/2 pounds per person per day, and cost, depending on where they are bought, from $1.75 to $2.25 per man per day. [1959 estimates]."

Until the 1970s or so, a very familiar part of field gear was the "Trapper Nelson" pack, Numbers 2 and 3. These simple, durable packs were standard kit for all bushmen and carried tons of material, one packload at a time, into exploration fields and gold camps. Produced by the Vancouver company, Jones Tent and Awning, they are one of the mining industry's little-known legacies to future generations that love hiking and camping. Vancouver is now home to a number of firms that cater to outdoor enthusiasts: Mountain Equipment Co-op, Taiga Sports and Deakin Equipment, to name a few.

The following provision list was suggested as a guide:

Provisions

	Pounds per Man per Month
Flour (white and whole wheat)	22
Baking-powder	1
Rolled oats (quick-cooking variety)	6
Beans	5
Rice	4
Dehydrated potatoes	4
Dehydrated vegetables (carrots, beets, turnips etc)	4
Canned bacon, ham, and corned beef	20
Cheese	3
Egg powder	1
Sugar (white and brown)	10
Tea	1
Coffee	2
Chocolate, semi-sweet	2
Milk (powdered whole milk)	2
Salt	1
Dehydrated fruit (prunes, apples, peaches, apricots, rasins, figs)	6
Canned butter	5
Jam, honey	5
Dessert powders (puddings or jelly)	2
Yeast if desired	
Total	107

Additional supplies should include matches, soup, mosquito repellent, simple first-aid supplies, needles and thread and no mention is made in the above about clothing, camp gear or tools.

A man going in to an unknown region should not count on living off the country at all but should be fully supplied with food and other necessities for the duration of his trip.

Britannia miners, 1937

Mining in Focus

A little book published in 1968 and titled Mining in Focus *by the late Bruce Ramsey is subtitled* An Illustrated History of Mining in British Columbia.

It's inexpensively produced, has no page numbers and no index, but what it does have in its approximately 150 pages is hundreds of photographs of mining camps, townsites, prospectors, geologists, investors and the like, spanning the years from 1835 to 1967.

You could read the entire text of the book in less than half an hour, but its value is in its mention of people and places that you can then research in more detail. For example, Ramsey makes a very brief reference to a Slocan prospector named Eli Carpenter who had once been a circus tightrope walker. A subsequent search on the Net for more information on that colorful fact found this: "In later years, Eli Carpenter ran a pack train between the mines and area towns, and also built a hotel in the neighboring community of Three Forks. On May 24, 1897, he astonished the entire Slocan district when, in order to win a bar bet, he walked blindfolded across a tightrope strung across Slocan City's main street, then doubled his winnings by stopping to cook bacon and eggs on a stove halfway across! By September of that year, Carpenter had departed for the goldfields of the Klondike, where he reportedly died a year later."

The discovery of gold in Wildhorse Creek Canyon led to the construction of the Dewdney Trail.

Lawlessness in the territory and Britain's desire to assert its claim to what is now Southeastern British Columbia led to the construction of the Dewdney Trail, one of B.C.'s most famous roads; another indication that mining was contributing mightily to the growth and development of the province.

"Under government contract, construction of the Dewdney Trail was undertaken in 1865 in order to provide coastal British Columbia merchants with access to the lucrative Kootenay market. The trail cut through the wilderness from Hope to Fisherville providing a route to Wild Horse Creek solely on Canadian soil. With the work of four section crews, Dewdney pushed the trail-building through rough and often inhospitable terrain. For the section from Fort Shepherd to Christina Lake, Dewdney hired a crew comprised completely of Chinese labourers. He made sure, however, that this crew was kept separate from his three white crews in order to avoid any racial disturbance."

Similarly, Ramsey's brief note on the White Pass & Yukon Railway related that, when the railway was being built in 1900, "…the workers encountered a large unnamed lake about 50 miles from Skagway near Lake Bennett. A construction engineer, A. B. Lewis, discovered that the surface of the lake was above the railway grade. To go around it would add as much as ten miles to the length of the line.

"Lewis decided if the water level could be lowered by about 10 feet the company would save a lot of money. A ditch was dug from the south end of the lake to drain away the excess water. The plug was pulled during the evening. But, to the dismay of Lewis and the workers, the force of the water flowing down the ditch washed the loose mud and gravel away causing a torrent of water which quickly drained the lake, not 10 feet, but nearly 80 feet. The flood washed out a considerable length of the recently constructed railroad bed below the lake. This held up construction, much to the embarrassment of engineer Lewis."

It's fun to read in Ramsey's book the names of mines of the past, and to wonder about how the men who staked them decided on those names: the Never Sweat, Ne'er Do Well, Sheepshead, Aurora, Mucho Oro, Tyee, Privateer, Spud Valley, Queen of the Hills, War Eagle and scores more.

It can't be counted as a major contribution to the history of mining in B.C., but for its photos and its brief evocative references to dozens of the province's mines and the people who found and exploited them Ramsey's little book has value. There is a copy in the Science Division of the main branch of the Vancouver Public Library, and perhaps your local library has one.

Rossland miners, early 1900s

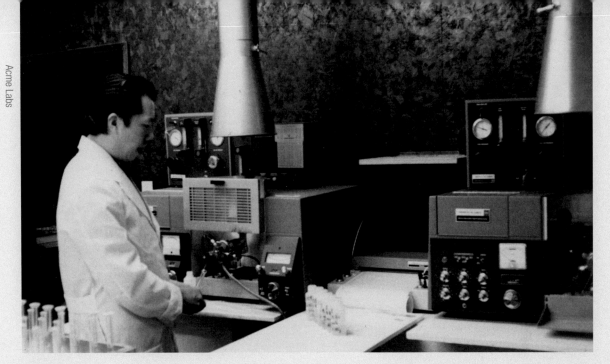

Dean Toye at Acme Labs

B.C. ~ Assay Capital of the World

British Columbia's status as the "assay capital of the world" was earned over the past century through a series of technical innovations and an enduring commitment to the highest ethical standards.

In the late 1800s, North America's fledgling mining industry was marred by rogue assayers who often worked with unscrupulous promoters to deceive investors about the true mineral content of certain properties. In response to public complaints about such practices the B.C. government introduced legislation in 1895 to ensure that assayers were fully trained and qualified. This move was supported by industry leaders who viewed the credibility of assay results as critical to investor confidence.

Before 1960, assayer training and examinations were carried out by the provincial government in its Victoria laboratory under the supervision of the Chief Assayer. Cominco also operated a training program for assayers at its Trail smelter laboratory for many years. Candidates now are tested by an independent Board of Examiners.

During the porphyry exploration rush of the late 1950s and early 1960s, only a few well-established commercial laboratories provided analytical and assay results. The largest was Coast Eldridge Laboratories, later acquired by Warnock Hersey. Others included Bondar Clegg Ltd., J.R. Williams & Sons Ltd., TSL Laboratories Limited and Rossbacher Laboratories. The large mining companies — Noranda Exploration, Kennco Exploration, Anaconda Copper, Placer Development, AMAX, Rio Tinto, Cominco and others — typically used private laboratories or built on-site labs at advanced projects and operating mines in order to achieve a quick turnaround of priority samples.

Early atomic absorption units were used for geochemical analyses for copper and other base metals. Molybdenum analyses were determined by colourimetric methods. Gold at $35 per ounce was of minor interest at the time, until it was recognized that significant amounts of gold were associated with some porphyry deposits (such as the Babine and the alkali suite of porphyry deposits). The traditional fire assay method is still considered the most accurate means of determining the gold and silver content of mineral samples.

Assaying and analytical methods changed dramatically with the introduction of Atomic Absorption Spectrographs (AAS) in the early-1960s, and Inductively Coupled Plasma Atomic Emission Spectroscopy (ICP-ES) technology in the mid-1970s. These technological breakthroughs, combined with computerized data output, provided laboratories with very fast, multi-element analyses for samples. In addition to significantly improving the volume of sample processing, the new instrumentation and procedures replaced the traditional wet-assay techniques, lowered analytical costs, and achieved lower analytical detection limits. Based on these advances and growing industry demand, several new commercial laboratories with state-of-the-art instrumentation were established during the mid-1960s and early-1970s in Vancouver and other strategic centres in British Columbia.

Before the downturn of the early 2000s, B.C. had almost a dozen commercial laboratories providing analytical services to clients around the world. Some have since closed, while others were acquired by or merged with large national or multinational firms. But they all made important contributions to the prestige and growth of B.C.'s minerals industry.

Chemex Labs

Chemex Labs Ltd. was founded by brothers Bruce and Bob Brown in 1966 as a family business, starting with a staff of fewer than 10 people. Bruce had previously worked at the Britannia Mine and also had installed a lab at a Yukon mine operated by United Keno Hill. He recognized the potential advantages of incorporating AAS and ICP technology into the business plan and hired experts in this technology to ensure a smooth start for the firm. Utah Mines Limited fortuitously opened an office next door to Chemex in North Vancouver, so Bruce arranged a contract to assay drill core from the company's Island Copper deposit on Vancouver Island. This developing mine supplied Chemex with large batches of samples throughout the year, including the traditionally slow winter period.

Chemex expanded rapidly and offered diversified services to clients around the world. The company's employees included as many as 36 different nationalities. Some were BCIT and UBC students and graduates with training and experience in lab procedures. Seven research scientists joined the company from a post-doctorate fellowship program set up by the National Research Council to initiate studies and tests on new laboratory equipment and techniques. In particular, studies and research related to pilot testing, monitoring and analyzing samples for environmental control projects were initiated to provide specialized services to industry.

Chemex was progressive in the introduction of innovative business and lab procedures to meet changing needs. Staff collaborated with the National Research Council and B.C. Ministry of Energy, Mines and Petroleum Resources on specialized technology for analyzing and determining finite concentrations of certain elements in samples. Financial assistance from these groups enabled Chemex to establish the world's first commercial cyclotron-based neutron activation analysis facility at UBC in 1978. The cyclotron was operated by TRIUMF, a consortium of UBC, SFU, and the University of Alberta. This sophisticated instrumentation provided Chemex with the ability to detect much lower concentrations for a range of elements, such as gold, uranium, arsenic, antimony, tungsten and thorium. The company also set up B.C.'s only radionuclide analytical facility to analyze isotopes of uranium and thorium in soils and water for exploration and environmental studies.

The 1970s were challenging years as NDP tax policies led to an industry exodus to more mining-friendly jurisdictions. Chemex responded by opening new labs in Reno and Elko to service the booming Nevada gold market. The firm then launched labs in other centres, such as Newfoundland, Quebec, Ontario, Alaska, Idaho, Montana and Arizona. By the mid-1990s, Chemex was also operating in Cuba, Mexico, Ecuador, Peru and Thailand.

In 1999, Chemex was purchased by Australian Laboratory Services (ALS), and the name was changed to ALS Chemex. This company, in turn, purchased Ottawa-based Bondar Clegg Laboratories, which also operated a number of labs worldwide. ALS Chemex subsequently changed its name to ALS Global.

In 2011, the ALS Vancouver laboratory staff comprised about 600 employees.

Acme Labs

Dean Toye's family escaped from China during the 1949 Communist revolution and found refuge in Canada. Nine-year-old Dean was placed in grade one as he couldn't speak English, but he learned fast and skipped grades three and five. He excelled in sciences and went on to UBC, receiving his bachelor's degree in 1962 with joint honours in chemistry and physics. His first job in analytical chemistry was with Warnock-Hersey Labs in 1965, followed by stints in the geochemical labs of Kennecott and AMAX.

Toye and his wife Mary opened Acme Analytical Laboratories Ltd. in 1970, during an exploration boom for porphyry copper deposits in B.C. The firm operated on a shoestring budget from a Burnaby garage in the early days. A bank loan allowed Acme to acquire an Atomic Absorption Spectrometer for performing its analyses.

The firm moved to a larger building on East Hastings Street in Vancouver in 1979. Toye understood the capabilities and potential of ICP-ES analysis and in 1980, Acme installed its first two ICP emission spectrometers. This new multi-element data soon found a home in Vancouver's exploration geochemistry community. Stan Hoffman of BP Minerals was among the first to apply the data not only to detect mineralized hot spots, but also to help define geology, alteration, surficial materials and glacial dispersion. Toye followed up his earlier success with the purchase of two ICP-mass spectrometers (ICP-MS) in 1997. The ultra-trace analytical capabilities of these instruments ushered in a new range of analytical procedures for geochemical and more finite lithogeochemical analyses. These became the standards used by governments and universities globally for baseline geochemical atlases and whole rock characterization research.

In 1996, Acme became the first mineral-testing lab in the Americas to achieve ISO 9000 certification, an achievement that helped open the doors to foreign markets.

Toye launched a government-sanctioned, employee share ownership program in 1995, and by 2005, employees were the majority owners. With wife Mary in ailing health, Toye passed the torch that year to new president John Gravel, who focused on expanding the business into South American and other markets, along with George Cartwright, recruited in 2006. A computerized system was put into place to track the flow of every sample through all stages of processing from the 24 globally-located sample prep facilities to the final stages at the two main assay labs in Vancouver and Santiago, Chile.

In 2009, Gravel was appointed executive chairman and Cartwright was named president. Acme grew nearly fivefold from 2005 to 2011, employing 650 personnel (230 in Canada) at 26 facilities in a dozen countries. The Vancouver lab, expanded in 2007, grew into one of the world's largest centres of excellence in ICP-ES and ICP-MS analysis, with 32 instruments operating three shifts per day, seven days a week. Sample prep facilities in Smithers, Whitehorse, Dawson City and Yellowknife rounded out Acme's Canadian presence.

Eco Tech Laboratories

Frank Pezotti established Eco Tech Laboratories in 1978, initially as an environmental testing lab operated by a few employees. The primary services offered by the Kamloops-based firm were water and stack testing for nearby municipalities and sawmill operations.

When gold exploration accelerated in the early 1980s, Pezotti added facilities for fire-assaying and classical wet chemistry procedures along with ICP equipment to provide much needed multi-element geochemical analyses for exploration companies. Eco Tech Laboratories expanded by opening a sample preparation lab in Flin Flon, Manitoba, followed by another sample preparation lab to serve exploration activity generated by the Eskay Creek and Sulphurets camps, near Stewart, B.C., in the 1990s.

Senior employee Jutta Jealouse purchased the laboratory in 2000, during an industry downturn. As the economy improved, Eco Tech grew by servicing exploration companies working in South Africa, Ghana, Mali, Portugal and South America. The firm also established a sample preparation lab in Whitehorse, Yukon.

The Stewart Group purchased Eco Tech in 2008 and established a sample preparation lab at Zacatecas, Mexico, with plans for a full analytical laboratory in Hermosillo. In 2011, the firm acquired G&T Metallurgical Services, a Kamloops lab and research centre specializing in metallurgical pilot-plant testing, mineralogical studies and analytical services. Eco Tech then employed about 55 people in Kamloops and was an integral part of the Stewart Group, which had a global network of more than 30 labs and 70 offices.

Bondar Clegg Laboratory

Bondar Clegg was founded in 1962 by geologists William Bondar and Malcolm Clegg, who initially set up their lab facility in a trailer in Fredericton, New Brunswick. Several years later, they set up a permanent lab and head office in Ottawa, followed by a branch lab in North Vancouver in 1967. Their first major West Coast client was Cordilleran Engineering managed by John Stollery and Bert Reeve, classmates of Bondar at Haileybury School of Mines. The branch lab also serviced companies involved in the B.C. porphyry copper exploration boom.

From 15 employees at the start, Bondar Clegg became the world's largest assaying and analytical company in its heyday, with more than 1,100 employees. Along with offices across Canada, the firm operated facilities in the U.S., Mexico, Peru, Ecuador, Argentina, Brazil, Chile and Bolivia. In late 2001, Bondar Clegg was acquired by ALS Chemex.

Min-En Labs

John Barakso, founder of Min-En Labs, came to Vancouver from the Faculty of Forestry at Sopron University in Hungary in 1956, along with others escaping the Soviet advance. UBC accepted the students and allowed them to continue their studies in Hungarian while learning English. Barakso graduated with a forestry degree in 1959, but became interested in geochemistry while working as a summer student for Kennco Exploration under renowned mine-finder Joe Brummer. He joined Kennco as an assistant geochemist and in 1961; then became a chemist at the Kennco laboratory in North Vancouver. Two years later, he was promoted to Chief Chemist and Geochemist for Kennco in Vancouver.

While working for Kennco, Barakso enrolled part-time at UBC to study geochemistry under Harry Warren and Robert Delavault and earned his M.Sc. degree in 1967. During his career, Barakso recognized fluorine as a key pathfinder element in geochemical samples at an exploration project, which led to the discovery of the Equity Silver deposit at Sam Goosly Lake. Next, he joined Anaconda Copper as Chief Geochemist at Britannia Beach until the program ended in 1972. Barakso then established Min-En on Pemberton Avenue in North Vancouver, home to at least five labs during the 1970s.

Min-En's facility provided assaying and analytical services for exploration and mining companies, with a staff of 75 people at full capacity. The firm expanded by opening a sample preparation and full laboratory facility at Smithers in 1991. Sample preparation facilities were set up in Sparks, Nevada; Thunder Bay and Timmins, Ontario; and Renforth, New Brunswick. Barakso also assembled portable sample preparation equipment in trailers that could be easily mobilized or air-lifted to various field projects.In 1992, Min-En Labs was acquired by

Assayers Canada, which in turn was subsequently acquired by SGS Mineral Services.

Vangeochem Lab

Vangeochem was a small analytical laboratory formed by Dick Woodcock and Conway Chun in 1965. The North Vancouver lab primarily tested samples submitted by close associates, prospectors and friends. A more permanent commercial laboratory was established a year later, which primarily provided only analytical services.

Bondar Clegg Laboratories was located next door to Vangeochem and the two labs often shared sample preparation workloads to help shorten their respective turn-around times. Vangeochem moved its lab to Vancouver and added fire assaying and multi-element analytical capabilities in the early 1980s. Approximately 40 employees worked at the lab in the busy mid-to-late 1980s period. Vangeochem Lab closed in the early 1990s.

Other Labs

Several small laboratories set up shop in the Vancouver area during the 1960s to 1990s. Fraser Labs operated for about three years in the early 1970s. Richmond-based Pioneer Laboratories operated continuously for more than two decades, while International Plasma Lab, also headquartered in Richmond, was acquired by the Inspectorate Group. AGAT Laboratories, which operated a network of labs across Canada and Mexico,

established laboratory and sample preparation facilities in Burnaby, Terrace and Prince George.

The British Columbia laboratory industry also has two facilities, CDN Resource Laboratories and WCM Minerals, which specialized in the preparation and distribution of a range of certified reference standards for groups of specific elements. The use of certified standards is vitally important for monitoring laboratory performance from sample preparation procedures, assaying and analytical precision and accuracy to data compilation stages. In accordance with best practices guidelines, the certified reference standards are the key component in the design and implementation of effective quality assurance/quality control protocols for early to advanced-stage exploration projects.

Another specialty laboratory was CF Mineral Research founded by Chuck Fipke. This independent lab in Kelowna specialized in techniques for separating and examining heavy and resistant mineral fractions from overburden and bulk stream-sediment samples. The procedure led to exploration success for base and precious metals and diamonds, most notably the discovery of Ekati, Canada's first diamond mine in the Northwest Territories.

Scott Heffernan

Mineralized rock – assaying a sample is part of early reconnaissance in mineral exploration

Analytical and Assaying Methods for Exploration Samples

The types of samples collected and submitted to laboratories for analyses and assays are contingent on the stage of exploration.

For grassroots and reconnaissance programs, stream and mineralized rock samples are typically collected. In the next stage, soil-sampling programs along grid lines are usually initiated together with samples collected from surface exposures, trenches and, depending on the terrain, possibly lithogeochemical samples of surface "rubble" or talus material. The follow-up stages of exploration involve drilling programs for the collection of samples of sub-surface rock.

Established labs have state-of-the-art instrumentation and equipment. Lab procedures and methods are tailored to analyze or assay for a single element, a multi-element suite of elements, or a select group of elements. Specialized analytical methods are also available at some labs for analyzing samples related to unique projects such as mobile metal ion (MMI) geochemical surveys.

Sample Preparation

As the laboratory receives samples from clients, a chain-of-custody protocol, including a sample status tracking system, is organized in order to ensure sample security. The initial process of sample preparation involves drying each sample, and then producing a small representative sub-sample of the original sample for analysis or assay. Soil and stream sediment samples are the most common geochemical samples submitted to the labs. The preparation involves sieving the samples to 80-mesh size fraction for geochemical analysis. Rock, drill core, reverse circulation and lithogeochemical samples are crushed and a 250-gram riffle-split portion is pulverized into a pulp sample for geochemical analysis or assaying.

Geochemical Analysis

The most efficient and economical method for analyzing geochemical samples is by ICP (Inductively Coupled Plasma) multi-element method, by which each sample can be analyzed for any number of elements up to a total of 51. A 32-element package is commonly selected for exploration geochemistry; this includes all the base metals, gold, silver, mercury, tungsten and a number of associated and indicator elements that are important for identifying and defining potential exploration targets. Labs also provide complementary analytical methods for geochemical samples, which provide more representative determinations with lower detection limits by analyzing larger size sample splits. Some gold occurrences present a nugget effect problem, and for such cases, the lab will usually recommend that larger 15-gram to 30-gram samples be analyzed.

In addition to exploration geochemical samples, early-stage diamond drill core and reverse circulation drill samples are often analyzed by geochemical analysis. The higher-grade samples are then selectively followed up by assaying techniques.

Exploration for rare earth elements (REE) has accelerated as these unique metals are in high demand by the electronics, hybrid battery and wind turbine industries. The 17 elements comprising the REE package are determined by multi-element ICP analysis.

MMI soil geochemical surveys are often conducted on early-stage exploration programs where extensive overburden masks the underlying bedrock and potential mineralized targets. These samples are collected in plastic bags from depths of 10 to 25 centimetres below the humus layer. The goal is to measure the concentration of metal ions released from mineral deposits that migrate vertically upwards to the near-surface soil horizons. A multi-element analytical method is available at SGS Laboratories for MMI samples.

Assaying

Assaying techniques provide a higher level of accuracy and precision for the metal content of samples than geochemical analytical methods, which are optimized for low detection limits. Assaying procedures are therefore recommended for evaluating well-mineralized samples. Drill core and reverse circulation samples from drilling programs to define mineral deposits are assayed to provide representative and reliable results for resource estimates.

Labs offer several different assay methods, depending on the type of mineralization. Multi-element ICP assaying methods are typically used to determine metal content for samples collected from sulphide deposits containing base metals and precious metals. In cases where mineralization may be extremely rich, a gravimetric assaying procedure is usually required to achieve acceptable determinations of metal content.

Fire assaying is preferred for determining the gold content in samples. This method is normally performed on a 30-gram pulverized sample split, with a 60-gram sample split used in some cases. Gold frequently occurs as comparatively coarse grains in veins or as tiny grains intimately associated with sulphides. Repeated assaying of the same sample with this type of gold will demonstrate a high nugget effect or erratic distribution of assays. In such cases, the pulverized sample can be screened for metallics and the small metallic fraction can be assayed for gold. Samples collected from platinum and palladium mineralization are also assayed by fire assay methods along with gold and silver.

Other Laboratory Services

Specific gravity measurements are important for evaluating mineral deposits. These measurements can be tested on-site by a field technician. The alternative is to collect a series of representative core samples, properly protected from dehydration, which are then delivered to the laboratory for specific gravity and bulk density measurements.

B.C.'s assay industry, of necessity, must meet the highest technical and ethical standards, which requires assay personnel to undergo exacting training and rigorous testing to attain accreditation. Assay personnel are all mandated to become B.C. Certified Assayers by successfully completing and passing a four-day theoretical and practical examination on fire assaying and analytical techniques as coordinated, invigilated and graded within the requirements of the British Columbia Assayers Certification Program. Additionally, laboratory facilities are accredited in accordance with standards governed by the International Standards Organization.

As leaders in providing quality service to the industry through breakthrough innovations, ideas and applications, the British Columbia assay and analytical laboratories were recognized worldwide.

From the ground up – traces of metals in dirt and vegetation can aid mineral exploration

B.C. ~ A Pioneer in Biogeochemistry

The association of metals in plants was recognized centuries ago as certain species of plants and trees were observed to occur near mineral occurrences.

Agricola in the 16th century recognized a form of biogeochemistry: "We search for veins by observing the hore-frosts which whiten all herbage except that growing over the veins, because the veins emit a warm and dry exhalation which hinders the freezing of the moisture, for which reason such plants appear rather wet than whitened by the frost." And: " in places where the grass has a dampness that is not congealed in frost, there is a vein beneath; also if the exhalation be excessively hot the soil will produce only small and pale-coloured plant. Lastly, there are trees whose foliage in spring-time has a blackish or leaden tint, the upper branches more especially tinged with black or with any other unnatural colour, the trunks cleft in two, and the branches black and discoloured."

In B.C., Harry Warren and his co-workers at UBC initiated research programs in 1945 to study the metal content in vegetation. The first biogeochemical prospecting began a few years later.

Biogeochemistry involves the collection and chemical analysis of whole plants, selected parts of plants or humus to determine if particular metals or indicator elements of a potential mineral deposit can be detected. These metals and other elements can be present in vegetation, as the root systems of growing trees and shrubs absorb groundwater that may contain dissolved metal-rich nutrients derived from a nearby mineralized source. These nutrients will commonly enrich or accumulate in the tips of the plant or trees. Sometimes the visual appearance of plants — such as discolouration, dwarfing and other physiographic changes — can be recognized as a result of metal intake by the plant.

Traditionally, various samples were collected, including whole shrubs such as fireweed, clover and Indian paint brush, scaly bark from spruce and lodge pole pine, coniferous cones, and new growth twigs, needles and leaves from a variety of trees. The technique has extended to harvesting humus samples and charcoal debris in the humus have also been collected from the forest floor as an experimental study to determine if copper-gold-molybdenum signatures could be defined in a deep overburden environment. With the aid of helicopters, studies have been undertaken to sample the tree tops of the taller old growth Douglas fir in the Quesnel terrane to determine if the deep tap root system of these trees might penetrate the water table to potentially absorb the copper, gold and associated metals and distribute them to its tree top.

Preparing biogeochemical samples for analysis normally involves procedures for drying, pulverizing and ashing the samples in a furnace. The resultant ash is then geochemically analyzed for metal content.

Britannia Mine shortly before its closure, c. early 1970s

Britannia Mine Museum

Driving up the Sea to Sky Highway, one can't help but notice a massive man-made structure tucked into a mountain slope south of Squamish, B.C.

Built in 1922, it was designed to process ore from the Britannia mine, once the largest copper producer in the British Empire. Almost a century later, the refurbished mill is the star attraction of the Britannia Mine Museum.

Copper mineralization was first discovered in the mountains behind present-day Britannia Beach in

1888, when Scottish doctor, Alexander Forbes, shot a deer and noticed that its flailing hooves had exposed mineralized rock below the moss. A decade later, mining engineer George Robinson convinced a group of financial backers to develop a mine.

The Britannia mine, controlled by the Britannia Mining and Smelting Company, shipped its first concentrates to the Crofton smelter, on Vancouver Island, in 1905. In 1916, *Mining Engineering Record* declared Britannia the largest copper mine in the British Empire.

The mine's early history was punctuated by tragedies. Bruce Ramsey's book, *Britannia: Story of a Mine*, describes how just after midnight on March 22, 1915, the mountainside collapsed, raining millions of tons of rock, mud and snow on the Jane Camp, killing 57 people. In 1921, heavy rainfall caused a dam to break above Britannia Beach. Within minutes 37 people were dead, 15 injured and rows of houses had floated away.

"On Friday, Britannia was a show place as industrial communities go, with pretty houses set in neat gardens," *The Province* newspaper reported. "Today, a tangled mass of trees, boulders and the wreckage of homes cut the village in two."

That same year, a mysterious fire started in the crusher and burned down the concentrator. Its replacement – the concentrator visible from the highway today – was designed and built in just 18 months. It used gravity to move ore from the top to the bottom level as it was crushed, ground and chemically treated to separate valuable minerals from the waste.

Another new town was built, offering tennis courts, swimming pools, a bowling alley and other amenities, as well as a busy calendar of community, cultural and social events.

While some open-pit mining took place at Britannia, most of the ore was extracted from underground, using 210 kilometres of tunnels (including one 500 metres below sea level). Copper was also obtained from the "precipitation" plant, a series of shallow troughs through which copper-bearing mine drainage water was directed over scrap iron and tin cans. Copper was precipitated from solution by replacing the iron and tin, which was then dried and bagged.

For much of its life, the only way to reach Britannia was by steamship from Vancouver. In the early days the original mine site — known as the Jane Camp and located high in the mountains 4.5 kilometers behind Britannia Beach — was supplied by packhorses on a 6.5-kilometre long trail from a wharf at Britannia Beach. After the Jane Camp was abandoned, following the 1915 slide, the lower "Tunnel Camp" (later named Mount Sheer) was serviced by a flat-deck open rail-car pulled by a cable up a steep 1,675-metre long slope from Britannia Beach. This was known as the "incline." A 5.6-kilometre long narrow-gauge electric railway (the "skip") ran from the top of the incline to the Tunnel Camp. The incline's thrilling ride became a tourist attraction.

The Pacific Great Eastern railroad from Horseshoe Bay to Squamish (now a CN line) reached Britannia Beach in 1956, and the highway from Horseshoe Bay arrived in 1957. The inauguration of the highway in 1958 was highlighted by a 600-car convoy led by Premier W.A.C. Bennett.

In the late 1950s, the price of copper plummeted and the Howe Sound Company sold the property to Anaconda American Brass Ltd. in 1963. Anaconda operated the mine until 1974, when it finally closed due to rising operating costs and taxes.

Some 60,000 people of many races, languages and religions lived and worked at Britannia between 1904 and 1974. During the mine life, more than 50 million tons of ore were extracted, containing

1.14 billion pounds of copper, 274 million pounds of zinc, 34 million pounds of lead, 500,000 ounces of gold, 6 million ounces of silver and 1 million pounds of cadmium. A major factor in the mine's success was the adoption, in 1912, of the newly developed procedure of froth flotation to separate valuable sulphide minerals from waste rock. Britannia was the first mine in B.C. to successfully adopt froth flotation.

To commemorate Canada's Centennial in 1967, a group of Britannia residents assumed the task of creating a history of the mine. They promoted the formation of the Britannia Beach Historical Society (BBHS), created in 1971 as a non-profit organization for the purposes of preserving the Britannia Beach mine site, the cultural legacy of the Britannia community and establishing a mining museum.

The museum opened its doors to the public in 1975, a year after the mine closed. When Anaconda sold the Britannia Beach land package in 1979, preservation of the museum site was made possible by a clause in the agreement stipulating that an area of approximately 16 hectares of land occupied by buildings of historical interest should be held in trust for the BBHS. In 1988, the mill building was designated a National Historic Site and for many years the museum was popular as the main tourist attraction on the Sea to Sky Highway. But it relied heavily on the industry it represented.

The beginning of the new millennium brought a change of fortune to the museum, starting with the province's pledge to deal with the acid mine drainage issue at Britannia. life. Acidic waters running from the mine, as well as natural runoff, inhibited aquatic life in Britannia Creek and left tidal areas of Howe Sound devoid of marine life. When Anaconda shut the mine it dammed the effluent and directed it into a pipe that discharged directly into Howe Sound, 50 metres below sea level, away from the sensitive tidal areas. The dam failed in the 1990s and with 200 kilometres of tunnels, an open-pit mine and contaminated soil, the environmental issue became even more serious. In 2002, Golder Associates started cleaning the contaminated soils, and in 2005, Epcor opened a water treatment plant to treat all water coming from the mine.

The museum says the water treatment plant removes 600 to 700 kilograms of metal sludge daily. The museum integrated information on acid mine drainage into some of its displays. This educational aspect resonated with the mining industry and proved to be a turning point for the museum.

At the same time, Michael McPhie, then with Natural Resources Canada, was seeking projects that educated the public about the mining industry in a positive light. He saw such an opportunity at Britannia and was instrumental in leveraging his department's original funding. He joined the board — along with mining veterans Bob Dickinson, Ross Beaty and Lukas Lundin — and played a key role in fundraising.

"At the time, the issues were big," McPhie says. "The historic buildings were falling down. The cladding was falling off the mill building and all the windows were broken. The province has a rich history of natural resource development. Britannia is a tremendous opportunity to tell that story."

As a National Historic Site and one of the last remaining gravity-fed concentrators in North America, the mill is a priceless artifact. To renovate the concentrator, the museum and its supporters raised $5 million through the federal and provincial governments and by donations from corporate and private sources. Completed in 2007, the metal cladding and each of the 14,416 panes of glass were replaced.

"Once the mill building was renovated people could see the vision more clearly," says Kirstin Clausen, the museum's executive director.

In 2008, a multi-million dollar museum redevelopment program, known as the Britannia Project and designed to enhance visitor experience, began.

"Those sitting on the edge jumped in," Clausen said.

Timely circumstances gave the project momentum. The 2010 Olympics were coming to Vancouver, the Sea to Sky Highway was about to be upgraded, mine site remediation was progressing and the mining industry was booming. In one year, $7 million was raised to support the Britannia Project. With matching funds from federal and provincial governments, the first phase of the $14.7-million makeover was completed in 2011.

"I'm not sure we would have gone any further without all those factors aligning," says Clausen.

"We were in the right place, with the right vision and the right economics."

The first phase renovated the whole museum site. With $1 million in personal donations from B.C. mining entrepreneurs Ross Beaty and Lukas Lundin, the museum built the Beaty-Lundin Visitor Centre, an attractive entrance to the museum grounds. It contains a small movie theater, interactive displays and exhibits showing how mining products are integrated into everyday life. It also houses a gift shop and is one of four Canadian sites that contain exhibits of the Canadian Mining Hall of Fame. An original mine building nearby is now the Britannia A-Z Exhibit Hall, where the history of Britannia is told with the aid of historic photos. Phase two, which involves behind-the-scenes seismic upgrades and other infrastructure projects was also tackled.

There's no doubt that the mill building is a unique and interesting feature.

"I love taking people inside it for the first time," said Clausen. "I don't say anything. They're always awe-struck. It's not impressive because of its size. It has a gritty element that makes it interesting and leaves an impression. We've got the underground railway and the outside attractions."

"The helicopter appears to be here to stay!" Modern-day exploration at the Lucky Jem-Eldorado project, 2011

Helicopters

"Exploration and prospecting by helicopter will soon be underway in British Columbia."

~Vancouver Sun, April 25, 1950

It's startling to realize that the use of helicopters for mineral exploration in B.C. began over 60 years ago. The *Sun* story quoted above goes on to say that Karl Springer, mining executive, was the head of a new syndicate called Helicopter Explorations Company, formed to prospect central and northern B.C. They had one helicopter (a Hiller purchased in 1949) and five prospectors. Springer – celebrated

for his ability to find valuable properties – is likely most widely known because of his connection with Granduc Mines, near Stewart, not far from the Alaska panhandle. Granduc, source of some 420 million pounds of copper over its lifetime, had originally been staked as far back as 1931 but the claims lapsed and were not looked at again until 1951 during helicopter exploration by Springer's syndicate. That marked the beginning of helicopter-based mineral exploration in B.C.

The first mention of helicopters in Chamber minutes comes a year later. The specific date was December 1, 1952, and the entry referred to: "…the success

story of another young man, George Smith, who attended our mining school at least 20 years ago, and who recently discovered a promising lode gold deposit on a tributary of the Kemano River, south of Prince Rupert. George spotted the rusty showing of gold-bearing quartz while flying in a helicopter in the employ of the Aluminum Co. of Canada." There's no reference in those minutes to the high-tech accoutrements used today: Smith just poked his head out of the aircraft and looked down.

Okanagan Helicopters' first use of the machines in mining operations also came in 1952, when they used a Bell 47 to haul freight for the Rico

Copper Mine near Chilliwack. Prior to that, they had used them for topographic surveys, spraying and dusting, freight hauling to new dam sites, and the like. Bob Petite of the Alberta Forestry Department, a helicopter buff, says Okanagan was using helicopters for geological surveys by 1954, and a Bell 47D-1 was used to search for radioactive ores around Bowen Island. (Okanagan Helicopters became CHC Helicopter Corporation.)

By 1953 the *Province* (May 20) was able to write: "Mineral prospecting has been revolutionized during the past few years. Helicopters … take prospectors to their claim areas in a few hours, where days were once required. Locations are more easily made and supplies follow men by the same air route."

In his book, *One Lucky Canuck,* the late Dave Barr cites a 1954 expedition in which he used a helicopter. He was working for Vancouver-based Northwestern Explorations at the time:

"I proposed an exploration program designed to search for massive sulphide copper-zinc deposits … in an area extending northwesterly from Toba Inlet to the head of Knight Inlet and northeasterly to … near Tatlayoko Lake. The area covered about 3,500 square miles (9,100 square kilometres) of relatively inaccessible terrain, which included the Mount Waddington massif, with its large system of glaciers and ice fields and many nearby unclimbed peaks. We felt that our target, a Britannia copper-zinc type deposit [like that] mined at Britannia

Beach, about 85 miles southeast of Toba Inlet, might be recognized with reconnaissance-type exploration and the aid of a helicopter, which was a new tool for prospecting at that time."

Some idea of that terrain – and an indication of how helicopters would prove useful – is given in Barr's mention of Mount Waddington. This is the highest mountain completely within B.C.; its rugged main peak, at 4,000 metres, had still not been climbed when Barr and his companions flew by. This was wild country.

"Helicopter-based exploration programs," Barr writes, "were in the pioneer stage in Western Canada and we were fortunate in having direct access in Vancouver to Okanagan Helicopters, which was to establish a worldwide reputation in the rotary-wing aircraft field. Our helicopter was a Bell 47-D1, piloted by Bill Legge …" The Bell 47, by the way, was the first helicopter certified for civilian use after the Second World War.

In a March 1960 article in *Canadian Geographical Journal,* writer Les Edwards calls the helicopter the "ugly duckling of the aviation world." But in that same article Edwards puts his finger on what would make this ugly duckling so valuable in mineral exploration.

"What a difference the helicopter would have made in the Klondike gold rush!" he exclaims. "The Chilkoot Pass would have been child's play." Edwards dates the earliest use of helicopters in B.C.

back to 1949, when Carl Agar – later of Okanagan Helicopter fame – ferried engineers around "…to chart the best power-line routes from Kemano to Kitimat through mountains subject to the severest weather conditions."

The use of helicopters began to intensify. In 1961 Atholl Sutherland Brown chartered a Hiller 12E from the Falconbridge Mine, at Tasu, as part of a mapping survey of the Queen Charlotte Islands. "This was part of the B.C. Geological Survey [Mineralogical Branch] program to map the Charlottes," Sutherland Brown said, "…specifically to stimulate prospecting for iron-copper skarns. The pilot was Roy Hepworth. The result was Bulletin 54 and a B.C. Geological Survey aeromag survey of the Kunga Formation as a target area. The Jib deposit among others was discovered."

Fixed-wing aircraft continue to be important, but they required landing sites of sufficient size – on water or snow or cleared land or beaches – that aren't always available in mountainous terrain. Helicopters had become a godsend for prospectors and geologists. This industry, says AME BC member, John Murray, has always been quick to adopt cutting-edge technical advances and, contrary to the pick-and-mule stereotype, has often been leading-edge.

One example among many: helicopters can tow aerial magnetometers that give the prospector or geologist a magnetic map of a large area. Some of those magnetometers look spookily like missiles, others like huge versions of the "dream catchers" some of us hang up on our walls at home. These dream catchers are towed aloft at about 50 metres above the ground. The helicopter – because of its variable speed and ability to hover, reverse, slip sideways and so-on – is uniquely qualified to do this kind of work. Even though most aerial geophysical surveys are still handled by fixed-wing aircraft the helicopter is the only practical way to maintain constant elevation above the ground on straight-grid survey lines in mountainous terrain.

Even into the 1960s horses were still being used to access remote areas of the province that fixed-wing aircraft couldn't get to. The introduction of the helicopter meant that a prospector could accomplish in one day what would have previously required a month or more. A section of rugged mountainous terrain that once consumed a field season of three or four months could be explored in a week.

Living conditions improved too. The days of packing in one's supplies by back or living off the land under often harsh conditions were much changed.

"There will never be another new mode of travel that will have such a significant impact on the exploration of the rugged Cordilleran terrain: B.C., Yukon, the Northwest Territories and Alaska," says consultant and AME BC past president Bob Cathro.

Another observation comes from AME BC member Brian Grant: "From my personal experience with helicopters there is an interesting feature of these machines of which most new geologists are unaware. The older Bell 47 series machines were far more useful for prospecting [from the air] than the newer, faster and more powerful models. Because the Bell 47 was so low powered and slow, a geologist or prospector had ample time to observe and think about the geology as they flew over. The more modern and 'efficient' machines have difficulty moving as slowly, so that a geologist or prospector has to think a lot faster nowadays."

A final note: Using helicopters has always been expensive. In that 1960 article Edwards says the hourly rental rates for the machines were high: $75 to $100 for smaller aircraft to several hundred dollars for larger transport types.

Fifty years later, Duncan Wassick, president of Dam Helicopters (based in Nelson and Castlegar), tells us that to charter a machine to take prospectors or geologists to and from a site costs $1,000 an hour plus about $200 an hour for fuel. A bigger aircraft, for transporting machinery and supplies, will run you $1,800 an hour, plus fuel. Sound costly? Not when time, distance and effort are factored in.

The helicopter appears to be here to stay!

Geological survey in the Mount Meager complex, 2003

John Hunter

AME BC president and CEO Gavin C. Dirom and Mel Stewart

Eldorado Mountain
~ The Lucky Jem Story

British Columbia's exploration industry is founded on a core of hard-working individualists dedicated to better understanding our geology and how to access the vast mineral wealth in our ground. They are at home in the wilderness, and work, often alone, under difficult and sometimes dangerous conditions. They walk softly and leave a small footprint, respecting our natural heritage and are puzzled by city folk who claim to but do not.

Mel Stewart's saga reads like something out of a youthful adventure novel: First, hints of buried treasure, gleaned from a stranger in a bar. Next, an expedition into rugged mountains, and promising discovery. Then, confrontation with a gang of adversaries determined to frustrate his endeavours. And finally, success — measured in gold.

Mel's case history illustrates the endurance and tenacity required to overcome the forces working against successful mine development in B.C. in recent decades. Let us hope that people of his character do not become discouraged, transferring their fortitude to more welcoming ground.

Ralph Sultan, P. Eng., MLA

ᘒ

In the spirit of sharing resources and respecting multiple land uses, the Mel Stewart story is one of great hope and incredible perseverance.

Mel Stewart's Lucky Jem-Eldorado story starts simply enough in 1956. He was a surveyor for B.C. Electric (now BC Hydro), surveying the power line for the Bralorne-Pioneer gold mine in the Bridge River mining camp, an important gold producer. The area sprang into prominence in the late 1890s, when the first claims were staked at Bralorne and Pioneer. Just 30 kilometres north of Bralorne, Eldorado Mountain had at one time become the focus of intense exploration. There are numerous old workings known on the flanks of the mountain.

Stewart's work took him to the old mining town of Minto City. One night in the town's hotel bar, Stewart met Paddy Lenahan, an old prospector. Lenahan saw that the younger man might benefit from his advice. On the back of a beer coaster, Lenahan drew a map to The Lucky Jem mine, on Eldorado Mountain, and sent Stewart on his way.

Years later, in 1962, Stewart decided to do some prospecting. He found himself slogging through 7,000-foot mountain passes, still in snow, searching for Lenahnan's old mine. He ultimately found what was left of the old mine; the old adit, a collapsed cabin, a log doghouse, a huge anvil and a number of pieces of equipment.

Several years passed. In the late 1970s, with gold prices rising, Stewart decided he had better stake the ground. He went back to Eldorado with the intention of staking four Crown Grants at the mine but he had missed his timing; he ended up staking adjacent ground.

Over the years, he did his assessment work to find out if he really had anything or, to keep his claims in good standing with the Gold Commissioner. Otherwise, he paid fees in lieu of assessment work on his claims.

One morning, in October 1996, Stewart found his access trail blocked by huge rocks. A sign had been posted by the provincial Wildlife Branch. In 1995, without notification, the Lillooet Land & Resource Management Plan process had been implemented, effectively blocking Stewart's access.

In 2001, the Spruce Lake Protected Area located in south Chilcotin BC, was created under Order-In-Council 524. This new protected area totally encompassed the Stewart claim group, staked by Mel Stewart in 1979, rendering the claims completely unexplorable.

Following this action, a seemingly endless succession of meetings to help resolve the conflicting values and interests of protectionists and mineral explorers ensued. At the end of seven years, the Lillooet land use management plan had not reached a consensus and an incomplete plan with a number of recommendations was sent back to the Ministry for Sustainable Resource Management to settle, which did not happen.

Faced with an unresolved problem, the B.C. government requested the assistance of the BC & Yukon Chamber of Mines (now AME BC). In 2004, the Chamber brokered a collaborative plan for Government approval, which was instrumental in gaining agreement among the parties, believing that it would allow for a reasonable amount of mining activity in what had historically been a very active mineral exploration territory known as the Bridge River Mining Camp. During this effort, the Council of Tourism Associations (COTA) and the Chamber established a working relationship while developing a Memorandum of Understanding. The MOU, which the Mining Association of British Columbia also signed, provided the ground rules for a discussion between members of their respective associations. Following this and through the extensive joint efforts of Mary Mahon Jones of COTA, Dan Jepsen of the Chamber and David Parker of Teck, the Wilderness Tourism Association and environmental activists, it was agreed that the boundaries of the protected area would exclude Stewart's claims and subsequent mineral exploration and possible development on the claims would not be opposed.

Based on this joint approach, the government was then asked for a final land use plan decision; but the response was that the plan would need to be discussed further with First Nations. So yet again, Stewart was effectively stymied and much hope was lost.

In June 2004 though, a determined Stewart, never a quitter, solicited assistance from Dr. Ralph Sultan, a former banker and mining executive and current MLA for West Vancouver-Capilano. Sultan proved to be a staunch ally, writing numerous letters in support of Stewart's situation, which dragged on for another four years, an incredible drain on a prospector's resources where little hope of a resolution presented itself. Nevertheless, the steadfast Stewart attended innumerable meetings with government officials and wrote letters to the Ministry, to deputy ministers, even to cabinet members explaining his plight. He even enlisted the support of the Lillooet town council and the Mayor of Lytton.

Then in late 2008, AME BC re-doubled its efforts and entered its second round of high level discussions to put an end to Stewart's saga by seeking a final decision on the unresolved land use plan. AME BC arranged a special meeting at Roundup 2009 with Ralph Sultan and the Minister of State for Mining, Gordon Hogg, and his staff. This critical meeting re-sparked the issue and gave Stewart and his partner Rudi Durfeld a fair chance to shed light on the challenging situation. They seized the opportunity to emphasize the potential of the Lucky Jem-

Eldorado properties and described to Minister Hogg how they had been rendered unmarketable, and how the Spruce Lake protected area had effectively and needlessly sterilized a huge block of highly prospective mineral territory. Hogg was convinced that the matter must be resolved fairly and he took up the principled cause to do the right thing and set government's course of action to find solutions in 2009 to rectify the problem.

In January 2010, a key meeting was held with Randy Hawes, Hogg's successor as Minister of State for Mining, where Stewart and Durfeld again laid out the case and asked for assistance. Eventually, with the dogged support of Hawes and help from Ralph Sultan; Gordon Hogg; Gavin C. Dirom, president & CEO of AME BC; and many others, legislation was drafted and finalized in order to change the protected area boundary, at last excluding the Stewart claims and opening up 15,000 hectares of land for mineral exploration and development.

July 5, 2010 was a landmark day. Thirty-one years since Stewart staked the claims, and after eleven years of petitioning and negotiating, the government finally made decisive adjustments in the protected area boundary which allowed Stewart to explore and develop his claims. On ground that had been caught up in the protected area discussion, Stewart staked additional land, including five former mine workings on the flanks of Eldorado Mountain. Stewart's additional claim acquisitions and the development work that he and

Durfeld had done now put the Lucky Jem-Eldorado properties on a solid footing and the pair were able to show the properties to a number of interested companies.

Then in February 2011, Gold Fields Canada Exploration, signed an agreement to option Lucky Jem-Eldorado. Under that agreement, Gold Fields can undertake an exploration program to prove up mineral resources which, hopefully, will meet their decision-making threshold to develop a mine project. This process could take a number of years, but will contribute to the economy of local communities and to the province's understanding of its mineral resources, overall.

Stewart, the eternal optimist and gentleman, never asked for a handout; he just did honest work in the belief he would be vindicated. His principled efforts and drive, with the support of Ralph Sultan, AME BC and many others, ultimately paid off. It took an excessively long time, but finally, Mel Stewart, got his just reward and was able to demonstrate to everyone that respectfully sharing the land is the best outcome for all.

The Old Ironsides copper-silver-gold mine at Phoenix – one of Canada's first open pit mines

Copper Craze

Copper has been good to British Columbia. It has been commercially mined in B.C. for over 100 years and will be for many years to come.

As recently as May 2010, the second-largest copper miner in Europe, Poland's KGHM Polska Miedź S. A., announced it would be spending millions of Polish zlotys in a joint venture to mine the Afton-Ajax copper-gold project near Kamloops. Later that month came word of $322 million in financing arranged by Japan's Mitsubishi Corporation, to construct a new mine at Copper Mountain, just northwest of Princeton. Production commenced in the summer of 2011.

It was at Copper Mountain that the first porphyry copper was mined in B.C., in the 1920s. It had been explored as early as 1884 and first staked in 1892. Granby Consolidated Mining, Smelting and Power Company took over the property in 1923 and high-grade portions of the deposit (averaging 1. 08 per cent copper) were mined in 1925-1930 and 1937-1957, mainly underground. Newmont Mining Corporation of Canada then acquired Granby's interest and operated the mine until 1985. Cassiar Mining Corporation (which later became Princeton Mining Corp.) purchased the project in 1988, and resumed operations at Copper Mountain until mining was suspended in 1996.

Porphyry copper, due to its relatively low grade, did not lend itself to production in 19th century British Columbia. Instead, copper first appeared as a byproduct of silver mining at the Hall brothers' mines near Nelson around 1893. By 1904, the massive sulphide deposit at Britannia was being mined.

In 1916, copper shipments in the province were worth $17.8 million, accounting for 56 per cent of B.C.'s mineral production values. At the time, copper still got little respect, at least from Ministry of Mines officials. At that time, the annual report of the minister of mines was an account of "Mining Operations for Gold, Coal, etc."

Copper makes its first appearance in the minutes of the B.C. Chamber of Mines in 1919 with a passing reference to its 26 cents a pound price. It pops up again in 1929 when the Chamber's executive publicly urged the construction of a copper smelter in B.C., so that the province's copper producers need not rely on a smelter in Tacoma, Wash. Three years later they again called for a B.C.-based smelter after the U.S. imposed a four-cents-a-pound tariff on imported copper, a move that prompted B.C.'s mines to stop sending their ore to the Tacoma smelter, opting instead to stockpile it.

In the 1960s porphyry copper came into its own with an upsurge in discovery, extraction and export. Copper's rising fortunes attracted increasing numbers of workers – engineers and geologists – to B.C.

The Japanese were particularly interested in copper. Chamber manager Tommy Elliott told of a visit in 1960 by two representatives of Sumitomo, who had called at the Chamber to express their thanks for cooperation and assistance given in making contacts with Canadian mining companies, and said the Chamber of Mines "…has done more than any other organization to encourage Japanese capital investment in the mining industry and in developing markets for a variety of minerals and metals in that country."

One of B.C.'s great mining stories began February 1, 1963, with the official opening of the mill at the Bethlehem Copper Company's property in the Highland Valley area, near Ashcroft. Sumitomo had financed the mine. About 400 mining people attended the opening ceremony, where great credit was given to H. H. "Spud" Huestis, a well-known prospector, for the important part he had played in developing this mine and bringing it into production.

In 1962, the full impact of copper's rise became apparent. In the previous year, the total amount of copper mined in B.C. was 39.61 million pounds, with a value of just under $9 million. In 1962 total output rocketed to 109 million pounds, with a value of $33 million. Similar numbers followed: $36 million in 1963, nearly $39 million the following year, $32.6 million in 1965. Then, another leap: $56 million in 1966, $88 million the following year, $87 million in 1968 and a whopping $111.5 million in 1969. The new decade began with a total of $121.3 million in 1970. Even a decline in the price of copper wasn't enough to lessen the impact of these impressive figures. Virtually all of this production was exported to Japan.

Bethlehem Copper Corporation

Copper craze officially underway: the Bethlehem mill in the Highland Valley opened on February 1, 1963

Industrial Minerals Mined in British Columbia

Courtesy of Mineral Resources Education Program of British Columbia

Commodity	What it is	Main Uses
Aggregate / light weight aggregate	Either river/beach sand or gravel, or crushed hard rock (e. g. granite, limestone) or loose volcanic rock fragments	Commonly used to build roads and make highways, to make asphalt and concrete, as railroad ballast and to improve icy and snowy road surfaces.
Basalt	A dark-coloured, fine-grained igneous volcanic rock; may have vesicles (trapped gas bubbles) like pumice, but is very dense and heavy.	May be crushed into granules that are used to make asphalt roofing shingles. Larger basalt pieces are also used in landscaping.
Dimension Stone	Refers to any number of sedimentary, metamorphic, and igneous rocks, especially sandstone, granite, and marble that can be cut in different sizes and used in construction in various ways	Used as decorative rock, ashlar (rectangular block of chiseled stone used in buildings), and facing rock. Cut pieces of solid rock are used to face buildings, make monuments, and to make floor tiles and countertops.
Dolomite	A mineral $(Ca,Mg(CO_3)_2)$ that makes up the sedimentary rock dolostone.	A source of lime (calcium oxide) and magnesium, used to neutralize acidic soils, as a flux in steelmaking, as an ingredient in glassmaking, in cement production, fertilizer, and paint.
Flagstone	Refers to rock that can easily be split into flat pieces, commonly, but not always referring to a metamorphosed sedimentary rock – slate, phyllite or schist.	Used to make floors, and to build retaining walls (layers placed horizontally one on top of another), to build fireplaces or make sidewalks and pavements.
Granite	A light-coloured, coarse-grained, igneous plutonic rock that is made up mostly of potassium feldspar and quartz, plus mica and hornblende.	May be quarried in large pieces that can be cut and polished for interior floor tiles and counter tops or cut for facing stones on buildings or tombstones and monuments. Crushed at some B.C. quarries to make aggregate for road base and to make concrete.
Granodiorite	A coarse-grained igneous plutonic rock similar to but generally darker in colour and poorer in quartz than granite, and which also contains mostly feldspar minerals plus mica, and hornblende.	May be quarried in large pieces and used in ways similar to granite. In south central B.C. and elsewhere it may be melted and spun to form mineral wool insulation.
Gypsum	A soft, white evaporite mineral $(CaSO_4\text{-}2(H_2O))$, which makes up a layered sedimentary rock also called gypsum.	A main ingredient in wallboard and building materials, plaster of Paris, and Portland Cement. Also ground and used as a soil conditioner to allow water and air to penetrate the soil, and to prevent it from compacting and losing its leaching ability. Gypsum is also used as a filler in paint.

Commodity	What it is	Main Uses
Jade	The common name for the minerals jadeite (Na (Al, Fe)Si_2O_6) (a type of amphibole) and nephrite (Ca_2(Mg, Fe)$5Si_8O_{22}(OH)_2$) (a type of actinolite) which form by metamorphic alteration of other sodium- and calcium-rich minerals.	This hard, green mineral is commonly used to make jewelry, gemstones, carved objects, and ornamental objects.
Limestone	A common sedimentary rock composed mostly of the mineral calcite ($CaCO_3$).	Used as an ingredient in cement; roasted in a kiln to produce lime; used in construction aggregate, flux in steel manufacturing, in fertilizer, in poultry feed, a filler and whitener in paint and plastics, glass, soil conditioner; also used for sewage and water treatment.
Magnesite	A magnesium-rich carbonate mineral ($MgCO_3$) commonly occurring in the sedimentary rock dolostone.	Source of magnesia (magnesium oxide); used as a refractory in steel furnaces and cement kilns because it is very resistant to heat; used in animal feeds, stucco, Epsom salt, special cements and magnesium chemicals. Small chunks are used for landscaping. In its powdered form, it is used by gymnasts and weightlifters for grip.
Magnetite	An iron-bearing mineral (Fe_3O_4) occurring in small amounts in all types of rocks. (In B.C., it is recovered from a tailings deposit at a closed copper mine near Merritt.)	Mixed with water to form a dense liquid that is used in the coal mining industry to separate coal from rock. Mined elsewhere as a main source of iron used in the manufacture of steel.
Marble	A metamorphic rock that originated as the sedimentary rock limestone.	Used as ornamental stone for buildings, memorials, and statues; used as filler in paint and plastics.
Monzonite	A light-coloured, coarse-grained, igneous plutonic rock that is rich in sodium-rich feldspar minerals, lesser amounts of potassium-rich feldspar, and poor in quartz.	Quarried in south central B.C. for processing into mineral wool.
Opal	A type of very finely crystalline quartz, a (SiO_2-H_2O), which occurs in veins associated with some volcanic rocks.	Cut and polished into cabochons and used to make jewelry such as rings, earrings, necklaces, pendants, and mounted on gold or silver settings.
Pumice	A light-coloured, light-weight igneous volcanic rock that is full of vesicles (trapped gas bubbles).	Pumice naturally occurs in pebble to boulder size pieces that are used in landscaping, lightweight aggregate, abrasives (stonewashing), baseball diamonds, and sport tracks. It is also used as a cosmetic abrasive (removing calluses), and to make stonewashed jeans.

Industrial Minerals Mined in British Columbia (cont.)

Commodity	What it is	Main Uses
Shale	A fine-grained sedimentary rock made mostly of clay minerals and silt.	Crushed and processed for brick-making and ceramic tiles; ground and used in cement-production.
Silica	Generally refers to the silicon-rich mineral quartz (SiO_2). It is common in many kinds of rocks, but is a dominant mineral in many ancient sand stones.	Source of elemental silicon; used to make glass, as a flux in steel making, to cast metal, a main ingredient in cement, and used to make memory chips in computers.
Slag	A glassy-looking by-product of the smelting process.	Produced by water-cooling molten slag into a granular form or crushed to sand-size grains that may be used in road bases, asphaltic aggregates, abrasives, fills, mineral wool, cement, and concrete applications.
Slate	A fine-grained metamorphic rock that originated as shale, and has strong cleavage planes along which the rock readily breaks apart.	Used as decorative building stone, ornamental stone, roofing tiles, and in flooring; the original blackboard.
Sulphur	A bright-yellow element (S) derived as a by-product of crude oil, natural gas, and tar sands refining.	Used to make sulphuric acid, used in many industrial processes, one important use of which is the production of fertilizer; ingredient in match sticks.
Tufa	A type of limestone formed by the precipitation of the mineral calcite from hot springs in volcanic areas.	This unusual deposit displays internal layers and smooth, irregular surfaces so it is decorative and commonly used in gardening, landscaping, water fountains, ponds, and sculptures.
Zeolite	One of several sieve-like minerals that form by weathering of feldspars in volcanic rocks or weathering of volcanic glass.	Uniquely capable of absorbing gases and liquids, and capturing metals. Used to produce absorbent pellets for animal litter, for example in kitty boxes and livestock pens (e. g. used in stables along with horse bedding to prevent ammonia fumes from damaging the horse's lungs and coat); used as molecular sieves in oil refining and other industrial processes; component of some fertilizers.

Granduc Slide

The threat of avalanches has been an ominous presence for miners in B.C. since the very beginning, with numerous deaths – and many miraculous escapes – over the years.

Snow will slide even on surprisingly gentle slopes when fresh snow falls on an unstable layer of frost crystals. Often there is no warning, just a faint rustle of frost crystals as the slide passes – "whispering death." (And many of the slopes where miners work are decidedly *not* gentle!)

For the most part, deaths in B.C.'s mining community have come in small numbers, but in 1965, a large slide at Granduc killed 26 men. The Britannia Mine, on Howe Sound, was hit by a rock and snowslide at Jane Camp in March 1915, which killed 54 people and demolished many buildings – Canada's second worst rock slide.

At Granduc, an 11-mile-long tunnel was being driven to a camp at the foot of the Leduc Glacier end with four bunkhouses, a dining hall, recreation hall, auditorium, offices and powerhouse. This area gets some of the heaviest snowfalls on earth, averaging 800 inches each year, with the record at over 1,100 inches. In the second week of February 1965, 16

feet of snow fell and at 10:16 a.m. on February 18, millions of tons of snow broke loose without warning. Of the 140 men in the vicinity of Portal Camp, 68 were directly exposed to the avalanche. Forty-two were saved, although 20 were injured, but 26 men died.

The radio operator managed to get out a brief "Mayday," before communication was lost, but fierce storms impeded the arrival of rescuers from Canada and the U.S. Still, within hours a massive international rescue effort was underway, battling fog, snow, 50 to 60 mile per hour winds and white-out conditions to reach the mine.

Most survivors were soon found although one had been carried 50 feet and buried under 3 ½ feet of snow, lying face down with arms outstretched and knees immobilized by debris. He survived 79 hours in that position, mostly conscious. This area was flat and was being used as a helicopter landing zone; he was found when someone realized it hadn't yet been searched and dispatched a bulldozer which partially uncovered him. His first words after being placed on a stretcher reportedly were, "Give me a shot of whiskey!"

Virtually the entire camp was wiped out by the avalanche. Demolished buildings were scavenged for fuel for fires, food was recovered from the collapsed cookhouse and steaks were cooked on shovels over

the fires, and eaten with fingers. As one chronic complainer was finishing his steak, the cook chided him, "This must be fine food – it's the first time you never complained!" To which came the reply, "Shut up and put another steak on the shovel!"

The Madam of Sandon

As is sometimes the case, moments of high drama can produce moments of humour – even in the case of avalanches.

Gene Petersen wrote of one slide near Sandon that took out a "house of comfort" early one morning, burying the Madam.

Many would-be rescuers leapt into action; a local minister one of the most energetic. The assumption was that she had most likely been abed when the disaster struck and soon there were heated arguments as to the exact location of her bedroom.

An impressive number of the good minister's flock seemed to have initimate knowledge of the house and of her bedroom's exact whereabouts in it. It was the minister who found her. It was later said she was never quite the same again "…and the same was said of the men whose wives had overheard the argument that night on the snow."

John Murray

The historic Windsor Hotel in Trout Lake, a hub of Lardeau district exploration

The Lardeau District

The Lardeau district of southeastern British Columbia has over 200 precious and base metal deposits and showings in a belt stretching northwest from the north end of Kootenay Lake to the northeast arm of Arrow Lake.

It is a region of precipitous mountains reaching over 9,000 feet, with huge snowfalls up to 27 feet, copious rainfalls and spring run-offs, rushing glacial streams; old-growth forests of fir, cedar and hemlock and luxuriant, impenetrable vegetation of slide alder and devil's club.

For many years the only access to the Lardeau area was by foot, horse, boat or limited rail service. Moreover, many mines were above the timberline so even firewood had to be packed in. Sometimes mine buildings had to be bolted to cliff faces on the edges of precipices. Snow-slides, often fatal, were common.

David Thompson first explored the area from 1807 to 1811. Map-maker James Turnbull explored the Incomappleux and Trout Lake region in 1866 reporting, "I am of the opinion that gold will be found on the bars of the river separating the Upper and Lower Kootenay Lakes, and also in the banks of the river." Lardeau Creek had been worked unsuccessfully by placer miners before the 1880s, and there are records of prospectors being in the Lardeau Valley by 1883.

In 1890 the *Sherman Silver Purchase Act* authorized the U.S. Treasury to buy 4.5 million ounces of silver each month, igniting a silver exploration boom in the Lardeau area. In 1891 Charlie Holten and Thomas Downs discovered the Great Northern deposit on the mountain of the same name north of Ferguson townsite, and rediscovered the Silver Cup deposit, which was found but not staked three years earlier.

By spring of 1893, hundreds of prospectors were in the field, and on one occasion as many as 300 men were camped at one spot on the banks of Duncan River waiting for the snow to melt. However, initial field results were discouraging. The *Sherman Silver Purchase Act* was repealed in 1893, which caused the price of silver to plummet and precipitated a major crash in the Canadian mining industry. Interest shifted to gold and the placers along Lardeau Creek.

While gold was the main target in the southern Lardeau area, it was still silver that attracted attention in the more northern Trout Lake/Camborne region, where nearly 200 claims were staked in 1893. All this mining activity attracted both the Canadian Pacific Railway and the Great Northern Railway. Rail access to Trout Lake, Ferguson and Camborne was critical; without it, transportation costs were very high.

The Lardeau's "coming out" year was 1895: Silver Cup Mine had sacks of ore ready to ship, Badshot Mine announced the discovery of a large orebody, and in July a wagon road to Trout Lake was completed from Thompson's Landing on the Northeast Arm of Arrow Lake. The first wagonload of ore from Silver Cup arrived at Thompson's Landing on February 26, 1896 – a milestone. This delivery of ore to smelters "proved" the district, but there was still much more talk than activity. At the time over 900 claims had been recorded but only a half dozen were even partially developed.

Timber for underground mining was expensive. Every hundred feet of underground tunnelling required an average of 4,000 to 6,000 board feet of timber. Shafts used up to 20,000 board feet, and stoping consumed 500 to 4,000 board feet for every 100 tons of ore mined; for those mines located well above timberline, such as Triune, supplying timber was a tall order.

By1900 the CPR was satisfied there was enough ore in the district to begin building a line from Lardo on Kootenay Lake to Arrowhead on Arrow Lake, but construction stopped when it reached Gerrard at the south end of Trout Lake in 1901.

Hope rose in 1902 with construction of a smelter at Ferguson, offering the prospect of making lower grade ores economic. The existing mill recoveries during this period were poor, which meant mines were transporting a lot of waste as well as metal, so a local smelter was important. Unfortunately a main component cracked in its trial runs and the smelter was never used again. Plans were made to address the lower grades at the Nettie L and the Silver Cup by building a mill at Five Mile with new aerial trams from each mine to the new site.

The new rail access to Gerrard stimulated exploration resulting in a rich gold strike at Poplar Creek. In July 1903 a group prospecting within 100 feet of the CPR tracks rediscovered the Lucky Jack, and between 1903 and 1905, Poplar Creek boomed to over 5,000 people, but the strike was not repeated. Yet this discovery assumes an important place in the annals of B.C.'s mining law.

An issue arose when Edward Tanghe staked a placer claim that overlapped the Lucky Jack lode claim, and proceeded to stake the perimeter ore despite being ordered to remove his posts by the gold commissioner. Upon appeal, three judges in Vancouver ruled that Tanghe's property was a legitimate placer claim. Recognizing the potential negative consequences, Chief Justice Hunter recommended that the *Placer Act* be changed to prohibit over-staking of lode claims by placer claims.

The year 1905 was pivotal. Since the first staking in 1890, much had been spent but doubt was rising. As the working season was short, access was difficult at high elevations and there was still no completed railway, adequate mineral processing technology and poor equipment availability. There were also disastrous fires. Five Mile Mill, once seen as key to the future of the area, had closed because of poor design, and by 1905 the initial boom was over. Another problem may have been a lack of competent, experienced mine managers. It was said the area was affected by "…smelter and refining trusts, excessive transportation charges and a host of mine managers who knew as much

about mining as the miners did of wine suppers." By this time, investor sentiment in the district was sour, and between 1906 and 1909 the number of mines shipping ore had dropped from 154 to 89.

The onset of the First World War exacerbated the investment drought. Geologist Newton W. Emmens painted a picture of a region rich with deposits but noted problems such as discontinuous veins, uneconomic grades, dangerous terrain, too much zinc that incurred a smelter penalty and poor engineering, which meant tons of metal ended up in waste dumps. Still, between 1905 and 1916, lead prices had soared and zinc now had value due to advances in process technology and its new importance in the production of brass and bronze for manufacturing armaments and shell casings for the war.

Gold brought over 200 prospectors back to the Lardeau during the Depression. A positive development was a U.S. proposal to accept $100 million in silver from foreign nations to cover war debts. Another boost came with the revaluation of gold from $20.67 to $35 per ounce in 1934.

Silver Cup Mine, which operated from 1893 to 1914 and re-opened in1937, closed in 1941, as did the Winslow.

The Triune Mine, which operated intermittently from 1900 to 1918, was the most inaccessible mine in the district. It comprised literally a portal on the side of a 1,000-foot cliff, with the mine building anchored on steel rods drilled into the rock face at an elevation of 8,500 feet. The last two miles of the trail from Ferguson to the base of the cliff climbed 3,000 vertical feet. Access to the mine and portal were via an aerial tramline. Fortunately, the ore was high-grade, averaging 0.9 ounces per ton gold, 250 to 400 ounces per ton silver and 33 to 50 per cent lead.

Another high-elevation mine was the Teddy Glacier, which operated in 1929. There, it was said it was nothing to get four feet of snow in one night. The trail to the Teddy Glacier, 13 miles from the valley bottom, was known as the "Golden Staircase."

Yet another hard-to-reach property was the Mammoth, at Camborne; it too was above the tree line and the access trail crossed a precipitous bluff on a four-foot-wide trestle supported by timbers resting in niches cut into the mountainside. "This was a hair-raising task for it is a drop of a mile-and-a-half to Fish River which flows directly below," notes the Arrow Lakes Historical Society in its book *Circle of Silver*. "The face of the mountain rises perpendicularly from the river bank." A bottle of Seagram's Nervine was cached near the trestle to assist those wishing to cross.

The CPR abandoned the Gerrard-Kootenay Lake line, possibly because of the wartime need for steel. Access to the region became even more difficult until 1954, when the road from Kaslo was completed.

Much like Sandon during the Second World War, a number of Japanese-Canadian internees were interned at Trout Lake City, where abandoned buildings were available.

The war had ushered in a period of rising metal prices, generating renewed interest and capital in the Lardeau, which continued well into the 1950s. A new company, Sunshine Lardeau, was incorporated in 1947, with production from the Spider Claim to be processed at a new mill installed at the old Camborne townsite.

The Sunshine Lardeau operation was quite modern, with new equipment, but the cost of transporting ore to the mill from the many mine portals developed on a rugged mountain slope was high. Sunshine Lardeau mined ore from 10 levels, and toward the end of the mine life, accessed the Eclipse vein through a winze until it was too costly to operate economically. In 1957 the bunkhouse burned, killing one man, and the mine closed in 1959. Prospector Stu Barkley subsequently leased the mine, salvaged some high-grade pillars and made $60,000. Some believe as much ore came from this deposit – ironically nearly missed – as the rest of the Lardeau combined.

Official records suggest the Sunshine Lardeau operation was the biggest producer in the district, accounting for over 141,000 tons of the camp's estimated total of 295,000 tons, yielding 38,831 ounces of gold, 3,964,672 ounces of silver, 34,583,392 pounds of lead and 26,482,760 pounds of zinc, with minor copper, cadmium, silica and antimony, molybdenum and tungsten values. Using September 2009 metal prices, the total value of the Lardeau Camp production today would be in the order of $165 million.

All the promotion over the years set against the lack of success gave the district a bad reputation.

Still, some work was undertaken in the 1980s at the Silver Cup and Wagner/Abbott, and on the Independence, Goldfinch and other properties.

And there have been recent successes. Alan Marlowe purchased Lucky Boy in the 1960s and found molybdenite. Subsequently, Barkley persuaded Newmont Mining Corporation to explore the property; a mile-long drift was driven and extensive diamond drilling was completed to define a large deposit, but molybdenum prices dropped and work stopped in 1980. In 1997, key claims covering the deposit expired and the property was re-staked by Nelson prospectors Lloyd Addie and Bob Bourdon, who subsequently optioned them to Roca Mines Inc. Renamed the MAX mine, from 2007 to 2011, it produced molybdenite concentrate from a high-grade zone of about 280,000 tons of 1.95 per cent molybdenum disulphide (MoS2), developed in an intrusive complex that is host to a much larger resource at depth totalling 43 million tons, grading 0.20 per cent molybdenite at a 0.10 per cent cut-off grade.

Also, Taranis Resources has explored its Thor property, which included the past-producing True Fissure, Great Northern, St. Elmo, Blue Bell and Broadview properties. The company's 2007-2008 exploration program comprising over 36,000 feet of drilling was focused on exploring the massive sulphide potential of the large property. Also, Jazz Resources reported bulk sampling results and the discovery of a new extension to the Teddy Glacier deposit. Jazz also held the Spider property, which was formerly mined by Sunshine Lardeau Mine.

Sandon, B.C.

Sandon ~ The "Sunless City" ~ Misfortune's Playground

Newspaper publisher, Col. Lowery, claimed, "Silver, lead and hell are raised in the Slocan and unless you can take a hand in producing these articles your services are not required."

In 1891, Eli Carpenter and Jack Seaton set out from Hot Springs camp (Ainsworth) prospecting the rough country to the west where, despite falling out, they discovered high-grade galena and staked the Payne claim. Back in camp, Carpenter had samples assayed and falsely told Seaton (and the rest of the camp) that the results were poor. Taking on a new partner, he set off to return to the discovery. However, he had been overheard discussing his plans. Seaton set out with four others and reached the Payne first. Following the ridge they found more rich showings, which they staked as the "Noble Five." On their return they reported assays of 400 ounces per ton silver and 75 per cent lead. The rush was on!

Sandon became the centre of the Slocan Mining District. Nakusp, Rosebery, New Denver, Silverton and Slocan City all sprang up to serve Sandon and area mines.

Total production statistics for the camp are difficult to compile but as of June 1988 cumulative recovered production at the Silvana mine complex alone was 376,750 tons grading 514.7 grams per tonne silver, 5.8 per cent lead, and 5.1 per cent zinc. The all-time peak production (for Slocan camp as a whole) was in 1918. In its heyday over 300 mines operated in Sandon's vicinity and, since 1892, several billion dollars in today's value worth of metal was produced.

Mining and sacking of ore occurred in summer and the ore was shipped in winter with horses pulling raw-hides packed with ore sacks, or "go-devil" sleds over the snow. Some horses learned to sit on their loads and ride the rawhides down the mountains while steering with their front legs. Some even wore snowshoes.

Later, aerial trams were extensively used carrying timber, supplies and sometimes people up to the mine site, and ore down. Between 1896 and 1920, some 60 tramways operated in the camp. Many were made by Riblet Tram Company of Spokane.

Two railways served Sandon and rivalry was intense. The Kaslo and Slocan railway arrived in Sandon first; the CPR's branch line, Nakusp and Slocan Railroad, was just a few days behind. When the CPR arrived, K&S workers, angered at what they felt was a CPR trespass on their right-of-way, hooked a line from a locomotive to the CPR station and pulled it into the creek.

Initially ore and concentrates were shipped to U.S. smelters, but CPR's purchase of the Trail smelter removed the Americans' advantage.

The camp's history was one of rapid initial growth followed by booms and busts dictated by metal prices, accompanied by disasters, including fire, avalanches, flood and labour unrest.

There was also lots of innovation and initiative.

In 1897, Sandon became B.C.'s first city to be completely electrified. The last plant built in Sandon was the Silversmith powerplant in 1916, which, as of October 2011, was still operating with some machinery over 100 years old. It was thought to be the oldest (almost) continuously operating hydroelectric plant in western Canada, with over 750,000 hours. Some believed it to be Canada's oldest operating machine.

The Slocan Miner's Union, affiliated with the militant Western Federation of Miners, was one of the first in B.C. The province's unilateral introduction of an eight-hour workday in 1899 ended the boom. Mine owners cut the daily pay rate to reflect the shortened work hours — and the strike/lock-out was on. Eventually, a compromise of $3.25 per day was reached, but the dispute caused severe hardship for Sandon residents. By the time the dispute was settled, silver prices had collapsed (again) and many workers departed for the recently discovered Klondike. By the time of the devastating 1900 fire,

which destroyed downtown Sandon, the population had declined from around 5,000 to about 2,000.

In the wake of the 1919 Winnipeg General Strike, the Sandon local joined the One Big Union (OBU), which struck CM&S in Trail. Failing there, the OBU tried again in Sandon in 1920. The Mine, Mill and Smelter workers (who had helped CM&S beat the OBU) supplied workers to the mines. The fight was on. Once more, metal prices chose this time to slump, and desperate workers again moved on. By 1920 the city was broke, and disincorporated. Neither the unions nor Sandon ever really recovered; both Sandon mining peaks had ended in strikes.

The union played an important part in community life. In 1899 it built, funded and operated a hospital open to rich and poor alike at a time when there was no social safety net, or medicare. It, too, was destroyed in the 1900 fire but was rebuilt and was still in use as late as the 1930s, when it finally closed during the Depression.

After Pearl Harbour, Sandon was used as an Internment camp for over 950 Japanese from the coast. Because of its severe winters, the internees called it "Camp Hell-Hole." No fishing, no farming, and idle mines made for scarce employment opportunities. The internees were so isolated, no guards were considered necessary.

Carpenter and Sandon creeks had been channeled into a narrow flume to conserve space in the

narrow valley bottom (which the sun didn't reach in winter); the flume was planked over to become Main Street. It also, seemingly, solved the sanitation problem as all sewage was now discharged directly into the creek and flushed through the flume. All the hotels, stores, restaurants, the school, even the hospital ran raw sewage lines directly into the flume. At least one hotel, the Denver House, had a trap door through which sweepings were deposited directly into the current. There was even a trap door opening on Main Street for dumping garbage directly into the flume. (There always seemed to be a lot of sickness downstream, in New Denver.)

In 1955, the spring runoff burst out of the flume and destroyed much of the town, washing out the railway down valley, and spelling the end of the community.

Treminco Resources suspended production at the Silvana in 1993 because of low metal prices and placed the mine on care and maintenance. In the last eight months, the company milled 18,000 tons averaging 15.79 ounces per ton silver, 6.54 per cent lead and 6.28 per cent zinc. Some further work was done in 1997 and 1998.

In 2011, Klondike Silver conducted exploration in the area and had periodic production.

Rossland miners, early 1900s

Rossland

Rossland, "The Golden City", was B.C.'s second most prolific gold-producing camp (to the end of 1989) with production of over 85,387 kg gold and 107,020 kg silver from 5,623,200 tonnes.

The Dewdney Trail passed by Rossland in 1865 but it wasn't until 1887 that the first claim was staked. It soon lapsed and was re-staked in 1889. In the spring of 1890, Joe Moris and partner Joe Bourgeois staked five claims (at the time mining law allowed only two claims per man) on Red Mountain, trading the fifth, the Le Roi, to the Mining Recorder, Col. Topping, in exchange for the $12.50 recording fees for all five claims.

Initial assays from the Le Roi returned over $217 per ton and Topping sold out to a Spokane syndicate for $35,000 – a good return on $12.50! The Le Roi eventually sold for $3 million and went on to produce almost $30 million during its lifetime.

By 1892, a wagon road was built to link with a rail line that D.C. Corbin was building from Spokane to Northport in Washington State and in 1893, a wagon road reached from Trail to Rossland. The Le Roi hit a large high grade orebody and paid its first dividend. The rush was on.

Fritz Augustus Heinze, a 24 year old millionaire metallurgist from Butte, Montana, arrived in Trail to build a smelter and a narrow gauge railroad to Rossland; D.C. Corbin began extending his Red Mountain Railway from Northport to Rossland. Heinze stole the march on Corbin by negotiating a deal guaranteeing him 75,000 tons of ore from the Le Roi.

In 1895, the War Eagle and Centre Star both hit rich ore and others were finding good values, too. All this was occurring at a time when mining elsewhere was generally depressed. In the early 1890s, the silver price had dropped 40% (especially after the repeal of the *Sherman Silver Purchase Act* in 1893), crippling many mines – especially those in nearby Idaho. Rossland's population exploded from 300 to over 3,000 and the three main railroads (D.C. Corbin's Northern Pacific, J.J. Hill's Great Northern and the CPR) began jockeying for position to challenge Heinze.

In 1896, Heinze's smelter at Trail began production. West Kootenay Power and Light was established to provide hydroelectric power to the Rossland mines from the distant Lower Bonnington power plant on the Kootenay River, thus pioneering long distance power transmission, yet another B.C. innovation. And two railways were now racing to Rossland: Heinze's Columbia and Western and Corbin's Columbia and Red Mountain Railway.

However, Heinze fell out with the Le Roi interests in 1897; the Le Roi, by now, was paying dividends of $25,000 a month and they built their own smelter at Northport to the good fortune of D.C. Corbin and his Columbia and Red Mountain Railway, which began operation in January 1898. Canadian Pacific Railway was also keen to expand and acquired Heinze's Trail smelter in February 1898. Corbin sold his Spokane-Rossland line to J.J. Hill's Great Northern Railway thus exacerbating the long-standing rivalry between CPR and GNR. (Ironically, Canadian-born Hill controlled the American GNR, while the CPR was controlled by American born W.C. Van Horne.)

Between the CPR's main transcontinental line through Revelstoke, and the GNR's transcontinental line through Spokane lay not just the Rossland camp but also the mining camps of the Boundary, Slocan and East Kootenays. So the stakes were high: Which railway would dominate the Canadian west?

The north-south trending valleys provided better access to the Canadian mines for the American railway; most supplies came in from the U.S. The main shipping mines were American controlled, at least until 1898, and much of the ore was treated by American smelters so the GNR had the initial advantage. However, in the late 1890s several mines passed into British control and expansion of Trail's smelter capacity ensured most of the Canadian ores could now be handled domestically. A federal government decision to subsidize the CPR's Crowsnest Pass line signalled a determination to support the CPR.

Until Northport opened, Trail had a virtual monopoly on Rossland production. The Northport smelter posed a serious threat to the Trail operation. Now, not only was a substantial portion of that production lost to Trail, the ores were being transported to Northport by CPR's archrival, Great Northern Railway.

The CPR had wanted only Heinze's railway charter to counter the threat posed by Hill's GNR to their southern B.C. interests but Heinze, facing lawsuits and possible loss of his properties in Montana, insisted the smelter be included in the deal. He drove a hard – and somewhat sharp bargain but CPR brought in Walter Aldridge to negotiate. Aldridge threatened to build a new smelter at Blueberry and Heinze capitulated. Aldridge faced the Northport challenge by diversifying and upgrading the Trail facility's ability to treat not only Rossland's copper-gold ores but also the lead-silver ores of Slocan and St. Eugene, and later, the Sullivan.

Another unexpected threat to Canadian mines emerged in 1901. American Smelting and Refining Co. (ASARCO) was establishing a monopoly on the American ore treatment industry – the smelter trust – and now controlled the lead market in the U.S.

B.C.'s lead-zinc mines had nowhere to ship their production for refining. The federal government quickly established a temporary (and limited) $5 per ton lead bounty for lead produced from Canadian ores at a Canadian refinery. This encouraged CM&S to add a refinery at Trail in 1902 utilizing the first application of the new Betts process of electrolytic refining. In 1906, a recent advance in lead smelting, the Huntington-Heberlein process, was installed allowing more efficient and less costly operation.

Meantime, the Le Roi had become involved in serious and protracted litigation and was sold to British interests. The sale was disputed by minority American shareholders who insisted that because the company was registered in Washington, it was subject to state law and not British law. Also, because Washington law stated that no aliens could own property in the state, the British American Corp. (BAC), part of the Whitaker Wright group of companies, was ineligible to run the Northport smelter.

The impasse produced a host of shenanigans, including struggles over possession of company documents, substitution of the company seal and an injunction forbidding members of the majority group from leaving the U.S., enforced by deputies stopping all trains leaving Spokane for Canada.

The BAC chartered a special train whose departure a sheriff tried to prevent but the railroad President, Austin Corbin, ordered the train to depart. The sheriff held a gun on the crew but left the train at Northport when informed he would be arrested in Canada for carrying a weapon.

A series of injunctions and legal maneuverings ensued. The manager was ousted and later reinstated until eventually a compromise was reached and BAC took full control. However, the Whitaker Wright financial empire collapsed in late 1900, and in 1901 the BAC was liquidated. In 1904, Wright was tried in London for fraud, convicted and sentenced to seven years imprisonment. He retired to an anteroom to discuss matters with his lawyer, had a last cigar and drink, then excused himself. Upon his return he collapsed, having swallowed cyanide.

The scandal had a lasting effect on the investment climate; Canadian, especially British Columbian, mines were branded in the public mind as scams. Twenty-five years later in 1936 an industry journal noted "…even today in London, the Le Roi fiasco is still remembered."

Still, production boomed until 1901, when the Rossland mines were hit by a bitter and lengthy strike from which they never really recovered. The miners were represented by an American union, the Western Federation of Miners (WFM), a local being formed in 1895. The WFM had a reputation for confrontation and violence and began pushing for an eight-hour workday for underground workers, which became law in 1899.

Mine owners responded by cutting pay rates proportionately. In June 1899, Slocan miners, who had formed a second WFM local in 1898, had struck. Two months earlier miners had blown up the buildings of the Bunker Hill mine in Idaho, causing much consternation amongst Canadian government officials who took a hard line and appointed a Royal Commission. Eventually the strike failed but the Slocan mines never really recovered.

The miners in Rossland adopted a somewhat different tack: they quietly resolved to produce more in eight hours than they previously had in 10, and when the mine owners complained to the Royal Commission of their 'serious losses' the owners were caught out by evidence the miners had actually produced more – and at less cost. That effectively ended that particular debate.

However, unlike the Slocan mines which had been quite profitable and had built up cash reserves, which enabled them to ride out their strike, the Rossland mines were struggling: For example, in 1899, the Le Roi lost $2.64 on each ton shipped and the eight-hour law added another 72-cent cost.

Rumours of mine closures ran rampant over the winter of 1899 to 1900 and, in mid-January, the mine owners petitioned government to repeal the new law saying "…the expense of carrying on the work in the mines that are at present being operated is so great that it has become burdensome and un-remunerative. The necessary alteration will be a reduction of wages, and upon such reduction … your petitioners are afraid consequences will ensue." They were right.

Government refused, and in February the Centre Star and War Eagle closed, followed soon after by the Le Roi, ostensibly "for repairs." But before reopening the owners insisted miners accept a switch to a contract system of payment whereby pay would be based not by the day but on the amount of drilling completed or lineal feet of excavation – a radical departure the miners had rejected in a vote six months previously.

The advantage to the companies was they would only pay for work actually done, not just time spent, and they could hire their best workers; it diminished and threatened the role of the union. Royal Commissioner Clute couldn't see the union's objections and the miners returned to work under the new system. But a legacy of bitterness and suspicion was entrenched and mine owners asked for special police protection which the local police chief provided.

Mining costs were still too high, ore grades were falling and the owners continued a campaign to limit union influence, culminating in a strike vote in April 1901, after the mine owners banned union representatives from their properties in February and began to import workers from Europe, especially Italy, and the eastern U.S.. The union narrowly lost the strike vote.

However, the WFM managed to provoke a showdown by organizing a local at the Northport smelter. Le Roi management closed the smelter and reopened with only non-union men. The union struck the smelter which put the Rossland local in a dilemma – the fruits of their labour would now be going to a strikebound smelter. A second strike vote in Rossland was held in July 1901, and, though the result was disputed, Rossland mines were then struck too.

Interestingly, the WFM national leadership in Denver tried to mediate and settle the dispute but ran up against their Rossland local's leadership.

The union was unable to prevent growing numbers of strike-breakers from moving in. William Lyon Mackenzie King (later to become Canada's longest serving Prime Minister) was then a young labour expert sympathetic to the cause and serving as federal Deputy Minister of Labour. King was invited to Rossland but after analysis concluded the strike had not been declared "…at the wish or by the vote of the workers…themselves, but was … forced upon them by subterfuge and a great deal of crooked work on the part of the executive committee." Basically, he accused the union executive of declaring the strike and then refusing to allow the miners to call it off. He lost all sympathy for the union leadership and recommended the strike be called off, declaring the situation "… the grossest tyranny of a labour organization."

The costly strike was stressing the WFM's financial capabilities and Denver leaders, after visiting Rossland, concluded prospects for settlement were not good. In January 1902, WFM, running out of money, cut support to the strikers. The local soon settled with the Le Roi.

The strike had been a complete failure and WFM leadership felt the Rossland local had not negotiated seriously because they could rely on the WFM national strike fund (until it ran out). Moreover, in October 1901, the mine owners won

an injunction to stop union members "besetting" the train station, which prevented union members from engaging with strike-breakers.

After the strike was settled, both the Centre Star and War Eagle won damages from the union for unlawful activities and the local was forced into receivership; the union never regained its prominence at the centre of the B.C. mining labour movement. However, loss of the strike did encourage new and more radical leadership from which emerged a group that went on to establish B.C. as "…a bastion of the Socialist Party of Canada."

Peak production occurred in 1902 but ore structures were pinching out and grades declined with depth. Labour, smelter and transportation costs remained high, as did government taxation – and provincial legislation was seen to be 'unfavourable.' Rossland began to see an exodus.

In 1905, the Centre Star powder house blew up with one fatality and fires destroyed much of the town centre. The need for consolidation was evident and the War Eagle and Centre Star, along with the smelter and the St. Eugene mine at Moyie, and Rossland Power Company were amalgamated to form Consolidated Mining & Smelting Company.

The Le Roi continued as an independent operation until 1911 when CM&S bought the assets after the Le Roi Company was wound up the year before. Eventually the majority of the producing operations saw the benefits of consolidation and CM&S

integrated their operations operating as a single mine from the 2200-foot deep Centre Star shaft, the deepest in Canada at the time. (Eventually, underground workings would total about 97 km of tunnels.)

During the period 1901 to 1916, over 50 per cent of B.C.'s total gold production came from Rossland mines but production waned until operations ceased in 1929. By then, however, the Trail smelter was no longer dependent upon Rossland ores and Rossland continued as a bedroom community for smelter workers.

In 1892, four American prospectors had located what was to become the Sullivan mine. A group from Spokane tried to develop it in 1896 but the low grade 'lead-silver' ore stymied them when lead prices fell. In 1904, it passed into the hands of an ASARCO subsidiary. The high zinc content of the ore complicated recoveries; too much zinc for a lead smelter and too much lead for the primitive zinc processes of the day. ASARCO gave up trying to resolve the metallurgical problems and, with the St. Eugene ores running out, CM&S bought the Sullivan in 1910.

The metallurgical problem was solved by the advent of World War I when zinc suddenly became a strategic metal and prices soared. Shell casings are made of brass, an alloy of copper and zinc, and in 1915 Canada had no refineries capable of producing either – Canada relied on U.S. imports of the refined metals. The Imperial Munitions Board decided Trail was the place best-suited for copper and zinc production and recommended CM&S be asked to expand their plant to produce metallic zinc. The federal government was reluctant to advance funds for this expansion – and the company reluctant to accept the funding because of the known metallurgical challenges.

However, the CM&S Board signed several contracts committing the company, so a zinc plant was built, a world first "…although it shared the honour with an Anaconda plant in Montana…."

The new plant was immediately plagued with problems and it quickly became clear that the feed needed to be higher grade. That meant finding better ways of concentrating the ore and CM&S turned to R.W. Diamond, a Canadian with considerable experience with a new flotation process developed in Australia. Diamond succeeded in pioneering a selective flotation process that could treat Sullivan ores and a concentrator was built at Kimberly in 1923, thus ensuring the viability of the Trail facility.

In 1934 – with the gold price now at $35 per ounce – CM&S, partly as a Depression relief aid, began leasing their Rossland holdings, and leasers recovered over $1 million from old workings and dumps that first year but by 1942, with the world preoccupied again with war, the leasing phase ended.

In the years since there have been sporadic attempts to further explore the camp with some limited production (for example, Iron Colt produced 1,434 tonnes yielding 21,586 grams of gold and 466 grams of silver in 1995).

Also, from the early days of the camp the presence of molybdenum was recognized and serious exploration for moly began in 1962 when Torwest Resources began drilling old showings. Red Mountain Mines, a consortium formed by Torwest, Metal Mines Ltd. and Canadian Nickel Company, (an INCO subsidiary), from a series of small open pits, produced some 6 million pounds of molybdenum sulphide concentrate from 1,040,000 tons of ore between 1966 and 1972.

Mining's contribution to the Rossland community went beyond producing mineral wealth. Between 1971 and 1981 a mining school operated there, ultimately teaching 1,400 students who went on to contribute to Rossland's, the provincial and the national economies.

Remarkable People

Gold brick poured at
Barkerville, 1930s

Chamber mineral exhibit

At Johnston's Roadhouse, Alaska; date unknown

Aaro Aho

Aaro Aho

Aaro E. Aho was a geological engineer and prospector who explored Yukon, including the Keno Hill district, for almost twenty seasons.

Born of Finnish-Canadian pioneer parents at Ladysmith, B.C. in 1925, he spent his youth on a farm on Vancouver Island. A love of applied science and outdoors led him to choose geological engineering as a profession, graduating from the University of British Columbia in 1949. After a stint with the Geological Survey of Canada in northern British Columbia and Yukon, Aho went on to study petrology, mineral deposits, structure and volcanology at the University of California at Berkeley, earning a PhD in 1954.

Fascinated by the beauty, frontier challenge and individualism of Yukon, he returned there as exploration manager for the White Pass & Yukon Corporation, which operated the railway between Whitehorse and Skagway and ships between Skagway and North Vancouver. His fieldwork led to a strong conviction that major mineral deposits were to be found which could open up Yukon despite its remoteness, lack of development, short seasons and severe climate.

Aho began an independent consulting practice and explored many areas in Yukon from 1959 to 1964, including the Keno Hill district, where he experienced many years of hard work, disappointment and frustration. Those years made him a more determined and tenacious explorer. Aaro was also an amateur historian; while working in the Keno Hill district, he interviewed more than a hundred pioneer prospectors and miners who had worked there. When studying in California, he also interviewed surviving managers living in San Francisco who had been involved in the mine before World War Two. He used this original research to prepare a 480-page draft of a book on the Keno Hill camp, but it was incomplete when he died. An excellent edited version was published in 2006.

He formed a junior mining company, Dynasty Explorations, and headed the exploration team that discovered the large Faro lead-zinc deposit near Ross River, in central Yukon in 1965. This was developed in a 60/40 joint venture with Cyprus Mines, of Los Angeles, as the Cyprus Anvil mine, in 1969. It was the largest Yukon mine ever developed and it was in production for 20 years. Its production was worth several times the combined value from the Klondike and Keno Hill and it became the biggest contributor to Yukon economy. The capital cost to bring it into production was over $100 million.

In 1973, Aho formed AEX Minerals Corporation and discovered the 30-million ton Grum lead-zinc-silver deposit, located near the Faro deposit, in a joint venture with Kerr Addison Mines Ltd. The ability to lead two separate projects that found commercial deposits in a very competitive district, the first while working independently with a junior mining company, and the second time while working with a different team in partnership with a major company, was an outstanding achievement. The Grum deposit was mined in 1997 to 1998 by a different company.

AEX Minerals Corporation later became part of Canadian Natural Resources.

For a time, when not working in Yukon, he explored in Chile, where he discovered the Sierra Gorda copper-molybdenum deposit in 1970. It was awaiting a production decision by Quadra FNX Mining in 2011.

Aho was an active participant in many of the endeavours of the Chamber. During the 1960s and 1970s he participated in lobbying efforts for tax reforms and land use regulation, and led a fund-raising drive that successfully raised most of the cost of a new UBC geology building.

He died prematurely in 1977 at the age of 51 in a tractor accident on his farm. At his funeral Tommy Elliott, recently retired manager of the Chamber said "Aaro Aho had a nose for ore, in my 45 years of association with the mining scene, I found him to be one of the most productive men I have known. He had a natural ability to go out and find ore deposits of importance … there have not been many like him in our history."

AME BC

Jerry Asp

Jerry Asp

Jerry Asp is a proud member of the Tahltan Nation, a defender of Aboriginal issues and a crusader for opportunities for Aboriginal Peoples in the mineral exploration and mining sector.

Still active as this book goes to press, he is a visionary, a savvy negotiator and a businessman recognized locally, nationally and internationally as an expert on Aboriginal relations.

Born in 1948 and mostly raised in Lower Post, B.C., Asp's character was influenced by many factors but it was his grandfather's teachings that shaped his drive and work ethic. "Our grandfather, George Edzerza, was the last true hereditary Chief of the Tahltan Nation. He taught us three things: Family is important, education is important and how to work hard," said Asp. He did not initially take to heart his grandfather's words regarding education. He dropped out of school when he was a teenager

to work on diamond drill rigs, his first encounter with the mineral exploration sector but returned to school when he was 33 and earned his high school equivalency certificate in Whitehorse. Prior to this, he had already taken business, bookkeeping and taxation courses.

Of all of his career accomplishments, Asp said he was most proud of three: Starting the Tahltan Nation Development Corporation, his role as co-founder and Vice President of the Canadian Aboriginal Minerals Association and his work in developing the Aboriginal Toolkit for Mining and delivering it to indigenous communities around the world.

The Tahltan Nation Development Corporation, which grew to become the largest Aboriginal-owned and -operated heavy construction company in Western Canada, was formed in order to move the Tahltan Nation forward. "Our people had to leave the Bush Economy because they could no longer sustain themselves and provide for their families; they needed to enter the Wage Economy," he said. It was not a fluid transition but the time was ripe to take advantage of construction opportunities in the development of the Golden Bear mine and other construction ventures.

He had the support of his Nation's leaders, in particular the late Chief Ivan Quock, Pat Edzerza and Vernon Marion; and a belief that this was the best move for his community at that time and for the future. "When I started TNDC, we had 98 per cent unemployment on our reserves in the winter

and 65 per cent unemployment in the summer; in my last year as chief (2002 to 2006), we had zero per cent unemployment in the summer and five per cent in the winter."

He said this turnaround occurred because the Tahltans embraced mining and the mining industry. During his tenure as general manager of the TNDC he graduated 18 journeyman carpenters, four journeyman heavy duty mechanics, two welders and numerous heavy equipment operators and truck drivers.

Negotiations did not always proceed smoothly. At one point, after some equipment was surreptitiously moved onto the mine site, Tahltan women blocked the road to the reserve thereby preventing the workers from accessing the mine site. Asp announced there would be an auction for about $1 million worth of equipment that was "… littering our reserve." A day later he triumphantly signed an agreement, the first Impact and Benefits Agreement (IBA) in British Columbia's history and only the fifth one in Canada. This IBA became the template for many First Nations to use when working with resource development companies.

IBAs have become the standard operating procedure in Canada, as is the duty of government to consult when a resource development company wants to work on First Nations traditional lands.

It was not always thus. As recently as 1988, such agreements were unknown. Asp sowed the seeds of change, in 1985, when he founded the Tahltan

Nation Development Corporation (TNDC). As general manager of the TNDC, he broke new ground in his demands for an IBA with North American Metals Corp. over what eventually became the Golden Bear Mine, an open pit and underground operation within the Tahltan traditional territory.

As proud as he is of the historical IBA that he signed with North American Metals Corp. on behalf of the TNDC, after a quarter century structuring other IBAs, he said that first IBA was only a partial success for the Tahltan people and wished that the agreement had addressed the social issues that arose from the influx of wealth into the community.

Later economic agreements signed by the TNDC addressed social aspects and impacts. Another issue that was not identified in the IBA was how mine access roads affected the sanctity of the Tahltans' traditional territory. Eventually, all roads were gated, which put an end to the unrestricted access previously enjoyed by non-Tahltan hunters, snowmobilers and four-wheel-drive enthusiasts.

Asp believes there were invaluable opportunities for careers for Aboriginal youth in all aspects of the industry, from early stage exploration right through to remediation. "It is my opinion that while a well-thought-out Participation Agreement may not be the panacea for all our problems, Mining and Mining Participation Agreements could be an important step on the way for First Nations to once again enjoy the self-sustaining, healthy and enterprising economies we once had," he said.

The Canadian Aboriginal Mining Association (CAMA), which Asp founded with his friend Hans Matthews in 1990, forged the missing link between Aboriginal peoples and the mining industry. "When Hans and I started CAMA, Aboriginal peoples and the mining industry didn't know how to talk to one another. One was talking Greek and the other was speaking Chinese. We had our 18th annual conference in 2010 and we had over 500 delegates, half were Aboriginal and half were non-Aboriginal, and they were all talking to one another in the same language," he said in 2011.

The Aboriginal Toolkit for Mining was a collaborative effort by Natural Resources Canada, Indian Affairs, the MAC, PDAC and CAMA; Asp was the project lead from CAMA. The Toolkit was released in 2006 and won the Developmental Merit Award from Natural Resources Canada for the best Aboriginal mine training document. The next year it was awarded the International Award for the best Aboriginal mine training document in the world. (This should not be confused with AME BC's Aboriginal Engagement Toolkit).

For many years Asp acted as an advisor to AME BC on Aboriginal culture, heritage and communication and was instrumental in assisting and guiding AME BC's strategy and approaches to Aboriginal relations. He served as a founder and an editor of the AME BC *Stepping Stone* newsletter designed to increase Aboriginal understanding of minerals and mining, and was a member of the B.C. Mineral Exploration and Mining Labour Shortage Task Force.

Throughout his career, Asp has always looked for ways to increase capacity within Aboriginal communities for economic sustainability. In 2007, he became a Certified Professional Aboriginal Economic Developer. He sits on the Regional Provincial Management Assessment Committee (Indian and Northern Affairs Canada) for which he assesses, designs and implements policies concerning Aboriginal economic development in B.C. In 2011, he was appointed to the Yukon Mining Advisory Board.

In 2010, PDAC awarded Asp the Skookum Jim Award for Aboriginal achievement in the mineral industry. "I feel that receiving the Skookum Jim Award was a crowning achievement for me for two reasons: First, Skookum Jim was a great Aboriginal person so it's a real honour to receive an award named after him, and secondly, I am very thankful for the recognition of my small contributions to the mining industry," he said.

In 2008, Asp co-founded C3 Alliance Corp., a consulting company working to build positive relations between Aboriginal Peoples, resource developers and government. In 2010, he co-founded the National Aboriginal Energy and Power Association to bring together Aboriginal communities and the power and energy sector to explore mutual opportunities.

David Barr

David Barr

Dave Barr graduated from the University of Toronto in 1950 with a B.Sc. degree in Mining Geology. Shortly thereafter he embarked on a career in mineral exploration with Kennecott Copper's subsidiary, Kennecott Canada, in Vancouver.

The Kennco organization was the place to be for a young geologist at that time; very forward-thinking, with a number of top-flight technologists in their leadership. Under Kennco's president, John Sullivan, the company formed a formidable exploration team, including such greats as Jack Gower, who managed the team and later went on to teach economic geology at UBC; and Charlie Ney, Kennco's Chief Geologist and a noted member of B.C.'s mineral exploration community.

Kennco's geochemical consultants included such noteworthy practitioners as Herbert E. Hawkes and Canadian Mining Hall of Famer, Harry V. Warren.

Barr was the consummate geologist. He was passionate about exploration geology and much-admired by his colleagues for his complete dedication. He joined the Kennecott team in 1951 and, along with his boss, James S. Scott, another young geologist, John Anderson, and the office secretary, Irene Wright, set up the company's first Vancouver office in May 1952.

Barr oversaw the first wide-scale exploration of northwestern B.C.'s Galore Creek copper-gold deposit, leading to the first expansion of the deposit in 1959, culminating in 1965 with what was then a pioneering 14-drill, helicopter-supported program.

In 1970, he led an exploration party to the coast of Labrador, acting on his hypothesis that it could host magmatic sulphide deposits. In 1994, his theory would eventually be confirmed with the discovery of the Voisey's Bay nickel deposit by Newfoundland prospectors, Albert Chislett and Chris Verbiski.

Barr rose from junior geologist to vice-president of exploration for Kennecott Canada in less than twenty years.

Later in his career, in 1980, when serving as vice-president and general manager for DuPont Canada Exploration, four of his exploration staff and their pilot lost their lives in a helicopter crash in northwestern B.C., Barr became a champion of mineral exploration and mining safety.
(See A Safe Day, page 86).

British Columbia began an intensive period of land-use planning in 1990. As a firm believer in engagement and public process, Barr immediately got involved. He chaired the Chamber's sub-committee on the Parks '90 Open Houses and Public Meetings. He joined the Vancouver Island land-use planning table as a representative for the exploration industry, the first of four regional land-use planning tables established under the Commission on Resources and the Environment (CORE). Participation required a commitment of at least one monthly meeting in various locations throughout the region over the next few years, as well as review of extensive material, meetings of the mining exploration sub-group and reporting to the Chamber on the progress of the planning exercise.

He and his peers faced many challenges at that table trying to work through the process and represent the "hidden resource" that tended to be overshadowed by conflicts between the forestry sector and the environmental movement.

He strongly opposed the government's largely opaque process under CORE, which led to the establishment of the Alsek-Tatshenshini Park in the early 1990s, encompassing the rich Windy Craggy deposit and nearby areas of favorable mineral potential. He worked for several years to compile data and submit letters to newspapers and the government to challenge the lack of process regarding this decision.

Barr joined the Lower Stikine Advisory Committee, a predecessor to the Iskut Stikine Land and Resources Management Plan, and was an active member of that group for five years. When the Province changed from regional to district planning under Land and Resource Management Plans (LRMP), he became the sector's representative on the Iskut LRMP table for the next four years.

Barr neither became cynical nor did he give up in frustration. His input was professional and respectful. He collected and analyzed data and carefully considered and presented the results. He listened to and considered the opinions of others but was not averse to stating his own alternate view. He challenged the Chamber's decision to leave the land use planning processes in 1999 as he believed that only through education would other people learn about the importance of exploration and mining and its contribution to society. He continued to provide an alternative view to the "development is bad" stance of some members of the public and independently developed brochures, for example, "Co-Existence of Wildlife and Mining-Related Infrastructure". His message was that industry was concerned about the environment. Exploration and development could occur without negative impacts.

Barr's contributions to the Chamber and industry as a whole were exceptional and have been widely recognized:

1994 – One of the first recipients of the AME BC's Frank Woodside Award recognizing long and distinguished service to the association and British Columbia's mineral exploration industry.

1998 – Mining Person of the Year Award from MABC.

2001 – Christopher J. Westerman Award from the Association of Professional Engineers and Geoscientists of British Columbia.

2005 – The Health & Safety Committee of the AME BC established the David Barr Award to recognize leadership and innovation in mineral exploration health and safety. Barr was the first recipient of the award.

2008 – Distinguished Service Award from PDAC for his contributions to health and safety in mineral exploration

Barr died on January 25, 2009.

Courtesy of the Barr family

A passionate explorer and mountaineer: Dave Barr with son Rob and Brent Hawkins on Mount Whitney, California

Ross Beaty

Ross Beaty

Ross J. Beaty was born in Vancouver in 1951, and was educated at the University of British Columbia, B.Sc. (Honours Geology) 1974, and LLB (Law) 1979, and at the Royal School of Mines, University of London, England, M. Sc., Distinction (Mineral Exploration) 1975.

He speaks English, French and Spanish as well as some Russian, German and Italian, and has worked in more than 45 countries.

Beaty has founded, built and sold a number of public mineral resource companies. In 1985, he founded Equinox Resources Ltd., which held two producing gold mines and a portfolio of gold properties. It was acquired by Hecla Mining through a $107-million merger, in 1994. Beaty then founded Da Capo Resources Ltd., a gold company active in Bolivia. Da Capo was acquired by Granges Mining Corp. (to form Vista Gold Corp.)

in a $57-million merger in 1996. In 1997, Beaty founded Altoro Gold, which held gold and platinum projects in Bolivia and Brazil; it was acquired by Solitoro Resources in a $30-million merger in 1999.

Beaty was once described as a "broken slot machine" for his remarkable consistency at creating shareholder wealth. In 1994, he founded Pan American Silver Corp., one of the world's leading primary silver producers. He was still the company's chairman in 2011.

Pan American Silver was his most significant company, with a market value of about $850 million, over 4,000 employees and operations in six countries. The company operated four large silver mines in Peru and Mexico and had major silver development projects in Mexico, Peru, Bolivia and Argentina. As these came on stream, Pan American's annual silver production increased from 13 million ounces in 2004 to over 24 million ounces, in 2011.

In 2002, Beaty founded Lumina Copper Corp., a copper development company, and also served as its chairman. He also founded Magma Energy Corp. to focus on international geothermal energy development. In 2011, Magma and Plutonic Power merged to create Alterra Power Corp., with three geothermal power plants in Nevada and Iceland, two hydro plants and a large wind farm in British Columbia, as well as an extensive portfolio of geothermal, hydro and wind projects worldwide at various stages of development.

Beaty was a past president and member of the executive committee of the Silver Institute in Washington, D.C., and a founder of the Pacific Mineral Museum in British Columbia. He was also a Fellow of the Geological Association of Canada and the Canadian Institute of Mining; and a recipient of the Institute's Past President's Memorial Medal.

In 2007, Beaty received AME BC's Colin Spence Award for excellence in global mineral exploration. In 2008, he won the Mining Person of the Year award from the MABC, as well as the Natural Resources & Energy Entrepreneur of the Year Award by Ernst & Young. And in 2010, he was awarded PDAC's prestigious Viola MacMillan Award.

Beaty supports many worthy causes. He was a director of The Nature Trust of B.C. and patron of the Beaty Biodiversity Centre at the University of B.C. He also served on the board of the Vancouver Youth Symphony Orchestra, where he chaired the funding committee.

Fred Connell

Fred Connell

Fred M. Connell was a gifted mine-finder, mine-maker and company-builder who left an indelible mark in many of Canada's most productive mineral districts. He was born and educated in Ontario, yet had some of his greatest successes in western Canada.

In Yukon, Connell is known best for his leadership role in establishing Keno Hill Mining Company (later United Keno Hill Mines) as Canada's largest single silver producer in the late-1940s and 1950s. In British Columbia, he is best known for developing claims into a successful mine operated by Cassiar Asbestos Corp.

Donald Coates, founder of drilling company D.W. Coates Enterprises Ltd., worked extensively with Connell over the years on various mineral projects from coast-to-coast.

"He was my mentor, a terrific man, and I can't say enough good things about him."

Coates said Connell relied on the best geological maps and exploration techniques available, but also believed in having lots of prospectors in the field.

"Conwest was one of the largest Canadian exploration companies of the time," Coates said. "This was before the U.S. companies started coming in a big way."

Conwest was willing to explore highly prospective areas that competitors often avoided for lack of infrastructure. If a significant mineral deposit was proved to exist, Connell would find innovative ways to overcome the logistical challenges.

"He was a truly amazing person with a big, big brain, who was as honest as the day is long," Coates said. "He was known as a fair man and lots of companies would go to him to settle a deal."

Fred Connell was born in Spencerville, Ontario, in 1883, and graduated from Queen's University in mining engineering in 1906. Northern Ontario was generating intense exploration excitement at the time, so it is no surprise that Connell started his career by exploring for silver in the famous Cobalt camp and taking part in the Timmins and Kirkland Lake gold rushes.

Early in the 1920s he gave Noah Timmins a right of first refusal on any properties submitted to Timmins, with Connell retaining an interest; when the Waite mine was merged with Amulet to form Waite-Amulet, in 1928, Connell became a director of Noranda in which office he served many years.

In the 1920s, Connell launched Central Patricia Gold Mines, which operated a gold mine of that name from 1934 to 1951 in the Pickle Lake region of Ontario. He also played a role in the development and financing of the Kerr-Addison mine, once Canada's largest gold producer, in northeastern Ontario.

In 1938, Connell formed Conwest Exploration as a vehicle for his very successful exploration in Western Canada and Alaska. (Conwest later absorbed Connell Mining, founded in 1930.)

During World War II, Connell served, without remuneration, first as Deputy and later as Wartime Metals Controller. In 1945, he formed a Toronto-based partnership with legendary mine-finder Thayer Lindsley of Ventures Ltd. (later Falconbridge) to investigate the potential of the dormant Keno Hill silver camp in the Mayo district, of Yukon.

Connell and Lindsley sent two respected consultants, John ("Turn-em-down") Reid and Frank Buckle, to examine the camp, which had closed during the war after an intermittent (depending on silver prices) production history starting in 1919.

Reid lived up to his reputation, but Buckle saw potential for operating improvements and to expand resources. In 1946, Connell and Lindsley formed Keno Hill Mining to acquire the assets, as a partnership between Conwest and a Ventures subsidiary.

The start-up phase proved to be a challenge, as the winter of 1946-1947 was one of the coldest on record. Milling began in April 1947 and, by 1948, newly discovered major ore-shoots had greatly enhanced project economics. The revived complex also benefited from rising prices for silver, lead and even zinc in these post-war years.

Connell helped bring about infrastructure developments that improved the long-term viability of the Keno Hill camp. A 467-kilometre gravel highway was built from the mine to Whitehorse in 1950 and a hydroelectric power plant was built in 1952.

The Keno Hill camp continued to operate through the 1980s and became famous for its rich silver-lead-zinc deposits. It closed in 1989, owing to a slump in silver prices.

Conwest Exploration moved into British Columbia, in 1950, after catching wind of an asbestos property near McDame Mountain. Established asbestos companies felt the area was too rugged and remote but Conwest saw an opportunity and seized it.

A feasibility study confirmed the quality of the chrysotile asbestos and the town of Cassiar and an access road were built to service the mine. Operations began in 1953 and continued until 1989 and, again, for a short period until final closure, in 1992.

Fred Connell died in 1980. He was inducted into the Canadian Mining Hall of Fame in 1989. He received other awards for his achievements, including the Order of the British Empire, the Inco Medal and an honourary degree from Queen's University.

The Metals Controller was appointed in 1940 with absolute power to "… buy, sell, mine, process, store, transport, or otherwise deal with all minerals, ores, metallic products, metal s and alloys thereof, except coal,and other solid fuels, oil, steel and iron". The Metals Controller had three divisons: Administration, Development and Allocation and Conservation (the latter responsible for finding substitutes for critical metals and allocating available supplies).

In 1942, Wartime Metals Corp (WMC) was established to increase metal production and the Wartime Metals Advisory Committtee was created.

Some of the BC projects undertaken by WMC included Emerald Tungsten, Kootenay-Florence, Granby, and Britannia Copper.

Raeff Miles

Bob Dickinson

Bob Dickinson

An unparalleled level of convincing and contagious enthusiasm for projects with promise… an ability to provide funding to permit such projects to maintain momentum… the vision to look past setbacks, to heed and support the technical-geological team when decisions are needed… and the capacity to remain totally informed without micro-management, reading every report, remembering every comment – and remaining instantly ready to refer to them. This is how B.C. geologist Mark Rebagliati, has summed up Bob Dickinson.

Dickinson grew up in West Vancouver, not far from his future family home in Lions Bay. He considered himself lucky in that, as a young student, he knew precisely what he wanted to do with his life and career.

"At a career night I met some geologists and was immediately hooked," he said. "The creation of wealth really attracted me coming out of grade twelve. Every summer while I was at university I worked for mining groups. I had some fantastic years out in the bush, living out of tents with supplies dropped in by helicopter. I keep telling everyone that when I retire I want to go prospecting again. It's a very peaceful pursuit."

Dickinson earned an undergraduate degree in economic geology at the University of British Columbia. During one of those summers of "peaceful pursuit" he earned enough for an exploratory venture into the stock market, netting a $200 profit. Beginner's luck or youthful insight, it was a harbinger of future financial success. With that introduction to the capital markets under his belt and back at UBC, Dickinson followed up with a master's degree in finance.

After a few years working for others, he embarked in 1976 on a career path that would leverage his technical background and natural ability as a mining entrepreneur. In 1983, he founded his first public companies, Dimac Corporation and Trader Resource Corporation.

In late-1985, Dickinson teamed up with Robert Hunter. Together, over the next decade, they acquired a series of notable mining projects in B.C., including Golden Bear, Mt. Milligan and Kemess. They advanced the projects to the permitting stage of development before dealing them to major mining companies. During this period, the "Two Bobs" (as they were often known) acquired several additional partners, and the foundation for Hunter Dickinson Inc. (HDI) was established.

By 2011, HDI had evolved into one of Canada's most respected mineral exploration and development groups, known for its relentless pursuit and efficient development of high-quality mineral properties, as well as its commitment to responsible mining practices. HDI provided a broad range of management, technical, financial, investor and administrative services. Its capabilities were similar in scope to a large integrated mining company but were provided to private and publicly traded companies associated with HDI at significantly less cost.

As one of HDI's founders and principals, Dickinson was instrumental in the identification, delineation, development, financing and operation of a number of globally significant mineral deposits. The Mt. Milligan, Kemess, Golden Bear and Prosperity deposits in British Columbia were just a few of the discoveries made or significantly advanced by HDI-associated companies. Those outside B.C. included the Pebble Project, in Alaska, one of the world's largest accumulations of copper, gold and molybdenum; the Campo Morado zinc-copper-silver-gold deposits, in Mexico; the Hollister gold deposit, in Nevada; the Burnstone gold and Drenthe platinum group metals deposits, in South Africa; and the Xietongmen and Newtongmen copper-gold deposits, in China.

As these and other projects advanced, the public companies created and fostered by HDI to manage them became increasingly self-sufficient and independent, or were purchased by larger mining companies. Along the way, HDI continued its search for promising new mineral projects around the globe and established new companies to acquire and advance them. In 2011, Dickinson and his HDI colleagues were involved in VMS projects in Alaska; zinc-lead exploration and development in Ireland and Poland; a feasibility-stage, bulk tonnage tungsten-molybdenum deposit, in New Brunswick; an in-situ copper recovery development, in Arizona; and a bulk tonnage gold delineation project, in British Columbia. Additional acquisitions were brewing.

An active member of the mining community for four decades, Dickinson was a director of the Britannia Mine Museum and a trustee of the Mineral Resources Education Program of B.C. His career accomplishments were recognized through numerous industry awards, including: PDAC's Mine Developer of the Year Award for Canada (1990 with Bob Hunter); B.C.'s Mining Industry Person of the Year (2000); the Ernst & Young Entrepreneur of the Year 2004 Pacific Award (with HDI management); PDAC's Thayer Lindsley International Discovery Award for the discovery of the Pebble East deposit (2007 with Northern Dynasty geology team); the Canadian Institute of Mining, Metallurgy and Petroleum's A. O. Dufresne Award (2007); and the American Institute of Mining, Metallurgy and Petroleum Engineers Charles Rand Award (2010). Bob Dickinson and Robert Hunter were inducted into the Canadian Mining Hall of Fame in 2012.

Gavin A. Dirom was awarded the Gold Pan Award by the Chamber in 1980.

Gavin A. Dirom

Gavin A. Dirom's life and mining career spanned most of the 20th century. His work in British Columbia began with the use of horses, canoes and primitive aircraft and advanced to the employment of satellite mapping, 3D geophysics and computer modelling.

Those who worked with or knew Dirom found him to be a straight shooter. He was a big man who approached people and projects in an easy, unexcited way. He described mining properties clearly and concisely, with well-illustrated and accurate maps prepared from his field work. He excelled at summing up data on the prospects of a given area – its regional geology on a district-wide scale – all valuable traits in an exploration manager.

Dirom attended UBC from 1927 to 1932, graduating with a Bachelor of Applied Science in Mining Engineering. Born in Duncan, he was keenly involved in sports on Vancouver Island, an interest he continued at university. His favorite sports were track and field and football, at which he excelled. He was a Big Block holder and was elected president of the Men's Athletics Society in 1931. His athletic ability went hand-in-hand with the strength and endurance he built up; qualities he would need for the rugged outdoor existence to come.

Dirom began fieldwork while still at university. In the summer of 1928 he worked for the Geological Survey of Canada in the Stikine area of B.C. He joined a party headed by Forrest F. Kerr, mapping a large area from the Stikine River north to the Tulsequah and Taku Rivers. He spoke of the time when he was navigating the wild waters of the Taku on his own. His outboard motor failed and his boat drifted downstream until it hit a bank of fallen trees and overturned. He saved his life by pulling himself up the river bank. He was forced to beat the water from a small evergreen to build up a small fire he had started. This was a demonstration of his toughness, strength and ability to survive in the unforgiving terrane of backcountry B.C. This perhaps is why a 1,800-metre mountain, 26 kilometres north of Tulsequah, was named Mt. Dirom in his honour in 1933.

He gained his first mining company experience working for Cominco Ltd. during the summers and immediately after graduation from university. From 1929 to 1934 he carried out property examinations in the Northwest Territories and British Columbia. Then, in 1934 he moved back to the Stewart and Stikine areas working for Premier Gold Mining Company at its mine north of Stewart. Premier was one of the many companies controlled by the Guggenheim brothers of New York. The brothers also controlled two other companies active in British Columbia: American Smelting and Refining Company (ASARCO) and Federal Mining and Smelting Company.

While working at the Premier mine, Dirom met fellow employee, Tom MacKay. Along with a group of other Premier employees, and on their own time and with their own money, MacKay acquired two groups of gold claims near the Unuk River about 100 km. north of Stewart.

MacKay called his group Unuk Gold and another group had adjoining claims called the Unuk Valley Gold Syndicate claims. In 1935 Dirom was assigned the job of examining these claims. Access was by float plane from Stewart. The aircraft was the Junkers W34, a plane with an open cockpit for the pilot and one passenger. On the flight north the plane encountered extreme turbulence and plunged suddenly. Dirom, who wasn't wearing a seat belt, suddenly found himself floating up and out into space. He was able to pull himself back into the cockpit. A similar aircraft CF-ATM was later flown for many years on the B.C. coast as a charter aircraft by PWA and is now on display at Uplands airport museum in Ottawa.

Much later, in the 1990s, the Unuk syndicate claims developed into the important Eskay Creek gold mine; they were the subject of a talk Dirom gave to the MEG Group in 1990.

In 1939, Dirom was transferred to Premier's Vancouver office and became its resident engineer. In 1945, he joined ASARCO in Vancouver and worked in the Bridge River gold country on copper prospects in Alaska and B.C., and even travelled to Saudi Arabia to examine a gold prospect for the New York office. He also worked on lead-zinc-silver properties in Yukon, particularly the McMillan property north of Watson Lake. In 1951, he was made Assistant Chief Geologist for the Northwest Mining Department of ASARCO, covering exploration work in Western Canada and the U.S.

In 1955 through 1958, while he was in charge of ASARCO's Vancouver office, Dirom was involved in the option of Bethlehem Copper in the Highland Valley district of B.C. and the exploration on the property, which resulted in delineation of the first orebodies at Bethlehem.

ASARCO's work on Bethlehem signalled the start of porphyry copper exploration in B.C., which grew to great importance in the area. Mapping, drilling and sampling by ASARCO proved up 30-40 million tons of +0. 5 per cent copper. This work also proved up new ways of mapping alteration in porphyry copper deposits and saw the first use of truck-mounted portable percussion drills for evaluating large low-grade Bethlehem type deposits. In 1958, ASARCO-Vancouver planned to begin evaluating newly-staked claims based on aeromagnetic anomalies in the southwest part of the property.

ASARCO's head office decided to drop its Bethlehem option as copper prices were low and the company faced large investments to put new Arizona desposits into production.

In the mid-1960s, Dirom and the Vancouver office were involved in joint ventures with Silver Standard Mines Ltd. in a large area of the Stikine country on Galore Creek where the Galore Creek copper deposit was being explored by Kennecott Copper Corporation. The joint-venture area was initially evaluated by stream-sediment geochemical surveys and prospecting by prospectors and geologists. Claims were then staked and mapped and sampled in detail and a few properties were then drilled. From this program the Schaft Creek copper-molybdenum-gold porphyry deposit was discovered and extensively drilled by ASARCO before being given up. This property was then held by Copper Fox Metals Inc. and Teck Corporation and, after extensive work, boasted a mineral resource of something like a billion tonnes of about 0.2 per cent copper, with low values in molybdenum and gold.

Gavin Dirom was elected president of the Chamber in recognition of his great contributions to mining and exploration in B.C. and elsewhere in western Canada. He retired from ASARCO in 1966 and continued consulting work for Guggenheim and Strauss Exploration until 1973. He never officially retired but kept in touch with mining developments until he died in 1996.

Gavin A. Dirom in the field in the Unuk region

Early days for airborne geophysics, Al Kulan (right) holding airborne geophysics "bird,"1963.

Al Kulan

After the Second World War, Al Kulan vowed never again to work for someone else and became a prospector in Yukon.

In 1953 he, with the help of several members of local First Nations, located a strong gossan near Vangorda Creek and in 1964 he helped form Dynasty Exploration to explore the area.

With Cyprus Anvil they formed Anvil Mining to develop the Faro Deposit, once Canada's leading lead producer.

He also formed and ran several other mineral exploration companies including Sparton Explorations and Welcome North Mines.

In addition Kulan discovered several new species of minerals including a group of new phosphate minerals found nowhere else in the world. Kulanite is named after him.

In 1972, the CBC deemed the community of Ross River to be too small to have a satellite-serviced TV. Due to bureaucratic delays, it didn't even have radio.

When residents had to drive to Faro to listen to the Canada-Russia hockey series, Kulan hired a helicopter and flew from mountaintop to mountaintop searching for the signal from Faro's 5-watt transmitter. Finding a spot on Grew Creek Hill, where it could be picked up, he paid for the necessary equipment and, with community labour, he pushed through a road where they set up their own transmitter to serve Ross River. The feds were not amused; the residents demanded a licence. In 1975 radio was finally installed.

Tragically, Kulan was murdered in Ross River in 1977. He was inducted into the Canadian Mining Hall of Fame in 2005; his citation specifically credits him with helping educate First Nations people about prospecting and mineral identification.

Mifflin Wistar Gibbs

Mifflin Gibbs

Once in a while, characters pop up and make one wonder how they could possibly have packed so much activity into one lifetime.

Consider Mifflin Wistar Gibbs. He was black in an age when a person's colour, especially if it was of dark pigmentation, largely determined one's education, social position, wealth and opportunities. Gibbs was born a free man, in Philadelphia. Supremely intelligent, shrewd, self-confident and enterprising, he became a businessman, investor and politician who, throughout his life, championed the welfare of coloured people. He spent eleven crucial years in British Columbia, prospered and was an important fixture in the political life of Victoria. Of particular interest to these pages is the record he left of pioneering coal mine operations in the Queen Charlottes in 1869.

The title page of his autobiography, *Shadow and Light*, published in 1902, already leaves one breathless.

His career is summarized thus: "A Fatherless Boy, Carpenter and Contractor, Anti-Slavery Lecturer, Merchant, Railroad Builder, Superintendent of Mines, Attorney-at-Law, County Attorney, Municipal Judge, Registrar of United States Lands, Receiver of Public Monies for U.S., United States Consul to Madagascar – Prominent Race Leaders etc."

Gibbs was born in 1823, the son of a Wesleyan Methodist minister who died leaving a wife and four small children and little money.

Eight-year-old Mifflin, the eldest child, was sent to work, driving a doctor's horse. In time, he became a carpenter's apprentice. In 1839 he joined the Philadelphia Library Company, an African American literary society, which included prominent abolitionists and he soon was involved with the Underground Railroad, helping slaves escape to Canada.

Gibbs arrived in San Francisco in September 1850 and, by working as a carpenter and bootblack, accumulated savings which enabled him to join a clothing business. Later he became partner in a firm importing fine boots and shoes. He helped found the first black newspaper west of the Mississippi, The Mirror of the Times (1855). But life for a black man in San Francisco became unendurable with growing racial prejudice, violence and discriminatory legislation.

Hearing of the Fraser River Gold Rush, he was part of an exodus of six hundred blacks who sailed north seeking a better life in British territory.

Governor James Douglas had encouraged the new arrivals and promised them protection under the law so long as they behaved peacefully. Gibbs arrived in Victoria in June 1858 with a large supply"…of miners' outfits, consisting of flour, bacon, blankets, picks, shovels etc." He sold this inventory immediately and straightaway sent for fresh supplies.

The day after his arrival he bought a one-storey house for $3,000 and it became the site for a mercantile business, reportedly the first outside the Hudson's Bay Company, which Gibbs operated with his old San Francisco partner. Gibbs became a leader of the coloured community. He joined the short-lived Victoria Pioneer Rifle Corps, an all-black defence militia established to safeguard British rule. He also became involved in local politics, eventually winning a seat on Victoria City Council in 1866, despite fierce racist opposition. He served two terms in office and was briefly chairman of the finance committee. In 1868 he was an elected delegate to the Yale Convention, where members of the Confederation League presented their views on union with Canada.

Involved in other business concerns besides his store, Gibbs became a director of the Queen Charlotte Coal Company. He writes in his autobiography:

"The most rapid instrumentalities in the development of a new country are the finding and prospecting for mineral deposits. The discovery of large deposits of gold in the quartz and alluvial area of British Columbia in 1858 was the incipiency of the growth and prosperity it now enjoys. But although the search for the precious is alluring, the mining of the grosser metals and minerals, such as iron, lead, coal, and others, are much more reliable for substantial results.

"The only mine of importance in British Columbia previous to 1867 was at Nanaimo, where there was a large output of bituminous coal. In that year anthracite was discovered by Indians building fire on a broken vein that ran from Mt. Seymour, on Queen Charlotte Island, in the North Pacific. It was a high grade of coal, and on account of its density and burning without flame, was the most valuable for smelting and domestic purposes. A company had been formed at Victoria which had spent $60,000 prospecting for an enduring and paying vein, and thereafter prepared for development by advertising for tenders to build railroad and wharfs for shipping. Being a large shareholder in the company, I resigned and bid. It was not the lowest, but I was awarded the contract."

(The B.C. Ministry of Energy and Mines notes that coal deposits on the Queen Charlotte Islands have not been fully mapped because of thick vegetation, lack of outcrop and complex geology. All the deposits are on the larger northern Graham Island and are either Tertiary or Jura-Cretaceous. Tertiary lignites are exposed in the northeast coastal areas and the older anthracites and bituminous deposits outcrop in the southwestern part of the island. The variation in rank of the older deposits is attributed to the presence of younger volcanic rocks in the area. According to the ministry, the Jura-Cretaceous deposits were discovered in 1865 and were mined in the period 1865 to 1872, when a few thousand tons were extracted. The ministry observes: "Preliminary exploration by a number of companies … has failed to identify sufficient resources to justify continued development.")

In January 1869, Gibbs took a leave of absence from Victoria City Council and embarked for the Queen Charlottes on the steamship *Otter* with a crew of fifty workers: surveyors, carpenters, blacksmiths, and labourers.

The *Otter's* destination was a rough camp, a few miles up the Skidegate River. The Haidas, despite their reputation for ferocity, gave the newcomers a friendly reception. A decade earlier, Governor Douglas had complained of the unreliability of Indian workers, but Gibbs' experience with them was better. The original samples of coal had been carried down the slopes of Mount Seymour by Haida workers who were paid in tobacco for each bag of coal delivered to the ship.

Gibbs' objective was to build a tramway over the more difficult terrane to get the coal from mine to shipside more efficiently. Construction work was hampered by almost constant rain, and by the effects of liquor. Gibbs found the engineering problems of the tramway formidable. It took him months longer than he expected to overcome them. From the mouth of the mine, the tramway ran a third of the distance down the mountain to a chute; the coal went down this chute to a second tramway, and thence to the wharf. Largely because of his endeavours "…the first cargo of anthracite coal ever unearthed on the Pacific seaboard…" was sent to San Francisco.

Gibbs stayed on briefly to manage the operations but left later the same year. Author Crawford Kilian speculates that Gibbs' energy and restless nature would not allow him to stay in one place long.

For reasons unclear, Gibbs' wife Maria Ann had left Victoria with their five children in 1865 and returned to the States. He rejoined his family and, in 1870, entered the law department of a business college at Oberlin, Ohio. In 1871, he moved to Little Rock, Arkansas and was hired by a law office but resigned the next year to form his own firm. An active Republican, he subsequently held various judicial and governmental positions until October 1897, when he was appointed American consul to Madagascar. In 1901 Gibbs returned to the United States and became president of the Capital City Savings Bank, a mainly African American institution located in Little Rock. This position afforded him time for travel, and he again visited Victoria in 1907. He died a wealthy man, at his home in Little Rock eight years later, aged 92.

Louis LeBourdais

The Last of the Camels from the Cariboo Road;
Photo taken at Grand Prarie, Westwold

Louis LeBourdais

It would have been a treat to be in the Cariboo in the early 1860s and see the faces of the prospectors and others when they turned a corner on the trail and came face to face with a camel.

You don't expect to see camels in the B.C. interior and how they got there—and the work they did in hauling supplies—is an interesting story.

That story was told back in 1936 during Mining Week in Vancouver, a big event sponsored by the Chamber of Mines to help Vancouver celebrate its 50th birthday. Louis LeBourdais, a well-known Quesnel man, who would become the MLA for Cariboo the following year had offered his services as a historian and lecturer on the Cariboo country out at UBC's Mining Department. He wrote out a brief account of the camel adventure for the Chamber's Mining Week brochure.

"Camels were introduced," he tells us, "in an effort to increase the loads and decrease the freight charges. The animals—a band of 21—were part of the American Camel Company importation of Bactrian camels from the Highlands of Manchuria, and were supposed to carry twice the load of an ordinary mule (the camels could carry some 500 to 600 pounds). They were fairly successful on the Harrison-Pemberton portages, and were later moved to Quesnel for packing over the sixty-mile stretch of boggy ground between that point and Barkerville, on Williams Creek, then the mecca of men from every part of the civilized world.

"It was hoped that their splay feet would prevent them from sinking into the series of holes made by the iron shod hooves of passing pack train mules and horses. But the camels' feet, already sore from travel over rocks and gravel in the lower country, sank into these water filled holes and there, spread flat by the weight of heavy loads, frequently stuck fast!

"The peculiar odor which escaped from the sweating beasts, together with their double humps and otherwise strange appearance, frightened all other animals off the road. But, other than cursing, no one did anything about it, so long as the damage was confined to pack loads of provisions. When one day a pack train load of whisky was crowded over a cliff, the outraged packer brought suit against the camel owners and the camels were court-ordered off the road."

The last surviving camel was known as "Lady." Like the other camels, she is wearing special boots intended to protect her feet. Lady ended up on a ranch near Westwold and, if reports are accurate, died sometime in the late 1890s—which means she was around for more than 30 years. The man aboard her is W. H. Smith.

The American Camel Company cited by LeBourdais was still going in Texas in the 21st century. It had been active since 1854.

≪⊃

Louis LeBourdais' story is interesting too. Born in Clinton (about 50 km north of Cache Creek) in 1888, he was elected MLA for Cariboo in 1937. He was re-elected in 1941 and again in 1945, with heavy majorities in all three elections. He was a very popular man and a friend to the industry. It was LeBourdais who arranged the spectacular Cariboo Gold Rush display at Mining Week in 1936. With the help of Cariboo friends, Chamber minutes show that he brought in a pack train of 10 horses, complete with all equipment, a bull-team with four yoke of oxen with driver and swamper, a 10-horse jerkline freight outfit (a jerkline is a single rein that runs to the lead animal in a team of mules or horses), a six-horse stage outfit with an old-time Cariboo coach and a deluxe Dufferin Coach with stage driver and many relics of the early days.

"It was a fascinating sight," the minutes tell us, "to see the team of oxen, stage coaches and pack trains, being driven down Georgia Street past the old Medical Dental Building!" That spectacular parade is also cited in an admiring article on LeBourdais by Winston Shilvock published in the Summer 1992 issue of *B.C. Historical News*. (Shilvock had met LeBourdais in 1934.)

Shilvock's article tells us that Louis started breaking wild stallions at age 13; then, at 15, became a telegrapher at Fort Alexandria; then, he was a cowboy. Next, with his brother, he ran a small sawmill at Barkerville, went back to telegraphy working for the CPR at Golden; then Grand Forks, Vancouver, Vernon – and finally back to Quesnel. On the night of January 17, 1916, half of Quesnel burned to the ground and 27-year-old Louis LeBourdais telegraphed a story of the event to *The Vancouver Daily Province*. The story was a great success and led Louis to a lifetime of writing about characters and events in the Cariboo.

Image A-03357 courtesy of Royal BC Museum, BC Archives

Cariboo Gold and Quartz mine at Wells

McDame Creek

Harry McDame

Among black pioneers who, like Mifflin Gibbs, responded in 1858 to Governor James Douglas' invitation to escape discrimination in California, were two rugged adventurers whose names now grace maps of British Columbia. They were Harry McDame and John Robert Giscome.

McDame, born in the Bahamas in 1826, prospected in both the California and British Columbia gold rushes. Giscome hailed from Jamaica and trekked to the goldfields of California via Panama. He was an adventurer, explorer and gold miner. The two men became neighbours at Quesnelmouth (now Quesnel). Together they explored and established a major route to the Peace River Gold Rush at what became known as Giscome Portage. They explored the Peace, Nation and Smoky Rivers. They prospected on Germansen Creek in the Omineca area in 1870, but in 1874, like thousands of others, went to the Cassiar Country where rich gold deposits had been reported around Dease Lake.

The pair focused their prospecting on the northern portion of Dease River, and McDame discovered rich gold-bearing bars along McDame Creek. This creek is a tributary of Dease River, about 165 kilometres north of Dease Lake. Gold was found in the stream bed gravels, in the gravel bars and along the banks of this fast-flowing creek. In order to access and mine the gravel, the miners had to construct wing dams at the head of the gravel bars and sluice boxes to wash the gravel. This required whip-sawing lumber and packing it several kilometres to the site. In 30 days, eight miners in the McDame group, now established as the Discovery Co., recovered gold from rich pay-dirt valued at $6,000 when the gold price was about $17 per ounce. Another group of miners started mining on an adjacent claim to the Discovery Co. and they were recovering an average of two ounces per day per man. At the height of the season in 1874, there were about 50 men working along McDame Creek. Interestingly, a number of large yellow quartz veins were exposed on some of the

rock outcrops along the creek and it was believed that these were gold bearing.

In 1877 a gold nugget weighing 72 ounces was recovered from McDame Creek.
(See Gold Nuggets, page 4).

The creek that bears McDame's name soon became a hive of prospecting and mining activity. In addition to McDame Creek, the legacy of the man included the naming of the settlement of McDame; this outpost was originally known as McDame's Creek Post and also Fort McDame. McDame and the Discovery Co. mined along the creek until the early 1880s when he returned to the Ominecas and later died in the region around 1901.

In 2011, small-scale placer mining was still ongoing on McDame Creek.

Catherine McLeod-Seltzer

Catherine McLeod-Seltzer

Catherine McLeod-Seltzer is an accomplished mining executive and entrepreneur best known for her role as the CEO of Arequipa Resources, a Vancouver-based junior that discovered and marketed one of the world's hottest gold prospects in the early-1990s.

But this is only a small part of the story. Over the next 20 years, she raised more than $400 million of venture capital for mineral exploration and development and was directly involved in more than $4 billion of mining-related corporate transactions.

McLeod-Seltzer has been described as having "an innate ability to translate geology and the potential that lies within it into words that satisfy and motivate investors." She grew up in a mining family — her father founded the Northair Group — with deep roots in B.C. and the city of Vancouver, where many junior companies have germinated new mining opportunities

around the world and where the environment was particularly receptive to her skill set and career goals.

After graduating from university with a degree in Business Administration, McLeod-Seltzer was employed by Yorkton Securities Inc. as an institutional trader and broker from 1985 to 1993, and as Operations Manager in Santiago, Chile from 1991 to 1992.

From 1994 to 1996, she was the President, Chief Executive Officer and a director of Arequipa Resources Ltd., which she co-founded with well-known porphyry geologist David Lowell in 1992. Arequipa went public in 1993, based on a number of properties in Peru identified by Lowell over 20 years. Most of the projects were soon overshadowed by a discovery of gold and silver discovery at the Pierina prospect.

The first drill hole confirmed results from surface exploration, returning an 88-metre intersection grading an average of 6.58 grams gold per tonne that started at surface. Drilling progressed and Arequipa's share price increased to $34 over the next few months. The discovery attracted the attention of mining giant Barrick Gold, which made a cash-only bid of $969-million for the shares of Arequipa in 1996. Arequipa held out for a better deal. With the growing interest of other majors threatening its acquisition, Barrick later increased its offer to a combination of shares and cash worth more than $1 billion, which was accepted by Arequipa. The deal was an extraordinary coup for the first-time executive but also proved to be

a shrewd move for Barrick. The major developed Pierina from an exploration property to a producing mine with mineral reserves of 7.2 million contained ounces at a capital cost of only $260 million in just over two years. For her part, McLeod-Seltzer received the Award for Performance from the Association of Women in Finance in 1997. In 1999, she and Lowell were jointly recognized with *The Northern Miner's* Mining Man of the Year Award.

Building on that success, McLeod-Seltzer was a founding director of Francisco Gold Corp., a company that was sold to Glamis Gold Ltd. in 2002. Its main asset, the El Sauzal deposit, led to a merger of Glamis with Goldcorp Inc., in 2006, creating one of the world's largest precious-metal producers that year. McLeod-Seltzer was also a co-founder of Peru Copper Inc., purchased by Aluminum Corp. of China for $792 million, and a director of Miramar Mining Corp., which was bought by U.S. giant Newmont Mining Corp. for $1.5 billion in 2007.

Currently McLeod-Seltzer is chairwoman and director of Pacific Rim and Bear Creek Mining Corp. Pacific Rim has an advanced-stage gold exploration project in Central America, while Bear Creek is focused on the development of two silver projects in southern Peru. Her work with these companies requires patience and tenacity — talents recognized by majors such as Kinross Gold Corp., of which she is a member of the Board, and emerging producers such as Stornoway Diamond Corp., where she was lead director until late-2011.

Viola MacMillan

Viola MacMillan

"Sometimes it seems that the worst that can happen to a mining district is to start with a boom for the inevitable bursting quite often presents an insuperable obstacle to future development. This observation applies with particular force to the Slocan. For a few brief years a region of extravagant promise it has for nearly 50 years been a land of abandoned hope …although both geology and common sense suggest this does not correctly reflect the possibilities of the region. Mine developers and others have continued to give the country the go-by. An exception is Viola MacMillan, President of PDA [PDAC], and of Violamac… the property was worked in the early Slocan days. [The] present company has conducted operations only since 1945 … average grade is 22 oz/ton silver, 8% zinc and 10% lead."
~ D. M. Lebourdais, 1957

All of five feet tall and weighing less than 100 pounds, Viola MacMillan was an extraordinary person, much more than her diminutive size suggested. She was driven by a sheer force of will and a refusal to take no for an answer.

Over four decades she was one of the country's most successful prospectors and developers, with substantial mineral deposits across Canada. She helped find major deposits in Kirkland Lake, northern Quebec, Saskatchewan and in B.C. And she was the driving force behind the transformation of a small regional prospector's association into an internationally recognized association of professionals that is PDAC today.

MacMillan served time in prison for stock manipulation in the sixties; in 1992 she was appointed a member of the Order of Canada. She is a member of the Canadian Mining Hall of Fame and her contributions to Canada are recognized in the Viola Macmillan National Mineral Exhibition Gallery in the Canadian Museum of Nature in Ottawa.

The 13th of 15 children in an impoverished family, Viola Huggard knew hard work from an early age. She never finished high school but managed to complete a business school course and become a stenographer.

Her first permanent job was with a law firm in Windsor, Ontario, where she acquired a working knowledge of law that she put to practical use in her future

mining career. In the evenings and on weekends she moonlighted in real estate (directing any resulting legal business to her day-time employers).

Viola married George MacMillan in 1923. He came from a prospecting family; his uncle was known as "Black Jack MacMillan." Her brother, Joe, had worked at the Coniagas mine in Cobalt and she talked her way into going underground disguised as a man; women were considered bad luck underground at the time.

"It was the most glorious experience of my lifetime and I was completely hooked on the glamour of mining."

In 1926 "Black Jack," aging and going blind, asked George and Viola to do the assessment work on his claims in northern Ontario for a half interest.

A bear had ruined their intended shack, so they bunked and shared beans with four other prospectors. Listening to those prospectors the first night in the bush, she began to realize what it is that makes men take to prospecting. "It is not just the chance of finding a pot of gold at the end of the rainbow. It is something more than that. The real attraction is the life itself…[to be] their own masters,"she recalled.

During the Depression, the MacMillans decided to spend their summers prospecting; and engage in real estate the rest of the year to earn money for grub-stakes and syndicate financing. The more she learned about the mining business the more she realized "…the people who owned the

Viola MacMillan 197

companies, because they were able to spread the risk, I suppose, were likely to make more money than the prospectors who made the discoveries."

Other prospectors often consulted Viola because of her legal knowledge. Knowing the problems and difficulties often faced by prospectors, the MacMillans were both strong supporters of the aims of PDAC from its inception, although they didn't join until 1935.

As secretary, MacMillan made many trips to Ottawa to lobby government of behalf of PDAC members. She lobbied to have the Geological Survey of Canada provide classes to prospectors on how to recognize and search for the strategic metals that were in such short supply.

The classes, held in Kirkland Lake and Toronto, were so successful that within days over 600 prospectors fanned out over Ontario.

With the outbreak of World War II, three PDAC members, including MacMillan, were appointed to the War Metals Advisory Committee. The committee worked with the Wartime Metals Controller who, in the interests of the war effort, had virtual control over everything to do with mining.

The committee decided that fifteen strategic metals were high-priority, "…of which practically …none had been produced previously in Canada." This list informed and guided mineral exploration throughout Canada during the war years and was highly influential in the allocation of manpower, supplies and equipment.

There had been a dramatic reduction in prospecting as younger men went overseas, also because government red tape had become an impediment. Revival of prospecting became the PDAC's priority.

During the early years of World War II Canada needed American dollars to purchase war materials; increasing gold exports was a good way to get them. Gold mines were given priority in allocations of manpower and supplies. But, when Congress passed the Lend-Lease Bill, the need for hard currency became less important and the gold industry lost its importance; priority switched to base metals production.

By early 1947, the industry's future looked bleak and the very existences of gold-mining towns like Timmins, Yellowknife, Val d'Or and Kirkland Lake were threatened. MacMillan lobbied the federal government for assistance. In response, the federal government introduced a $7-per-ounce subsidy for all Canadian gold producers. However the IMF objected and the plan was shelved. Ottawa replaced it with a "cost plus bonus plan" – *The Emergency Gold Mining Assistance Act*, a complicated system specifically designed to keep high-cost producers and their communities alive.

In 1947, Arthur Cockshutt (part-owner of the MacLeod-Cockshutt mine, in the Little Long Lac camp) acquired an option on the Slocan-Rambler mine and invited MacMillan to take an interest in it. She incorporated a Golden Arrow subsidiary, B.C. Slocan-Rambler Mining (1947) Ltd., and

reactivated the mine that had been idle for nearly 25 years. She and George purchased a house and acreage near New Denver, in the Slocan Valley.

Ernest Doney had been working the Victor mine by himself on another mountain across from the Rambler. It had begun producing in 1923 and, when the owner died, his daughter leased it to Doney. In early-1948, the aging Doney suggested Viola buy the property, which also included two other inactive mines, the Lone Bachelor, and the Cinderella. (The Lone Bachelor had operated from 1905 to 1922, the Cinderella between 1904 to 1924). The owner would sell for $50,000 and Doney would assign his lease for $15,000.

The MacMillans put the Victor property into Violamac Mines Ltd. and raised money selling shares at 10 cents each; the market high in 1954 was $4. Doney was offered a job as long as he wished. His response was grateful and gracious.

"I hope you make a million, Mrs. Mac," he said.

She would later say, "Violamac Mines Ltd. was the most successful company I ever formed."

Realizing reopening the Rambler wasn't likely, they switched their focus to the Victor property and had it geologically mapped. In the fall of 1948 they hit the main vein of the Victor. Doney refused to go see it until "Mrs. Mac" arrived. They viewed it together, a solid wall of blueish–grey galena. When Viola told Doney she was very sorry he hadn't found it, he replied: "Mrs. Mac, I told you I wanted you to make a million!"

The company did retire Doney in time – he had trouble adjusting to the new-fangled machinery, and they worried about his safety.

In 1948, the Victor mine produced 220 tons; next year production rose to over 1,700 tons, reaching its peak, of over 27,000 tons, in 1953. It yielded gross smelter returns of over $1.4 million from 8 million pounds of lead, 4 million pounds of zinc, 0.5 million ounces of silver, 25 pounds of cadmium, and 217 ounces of gold.

In mid-1955, exploration at the Victor had found new ore shoots and results from the neighbouring Lone Bachelor seemed encouraging, though they eventually disappointed. Also, in 1955, lithium was thought to be an important metal for the coming space age and Violamac acquired the Cat Lake property, in Manitoba, outlining 1.7 million tons grading 1.3 per cent lithium. Lake Cinch began shipping in May 1957 and, in 1958, earned $1.7 million after custom-milling charges, just as the Victor mine's production was declining.

In 1959, MacMillan had also taken over, reorganized and reactivated operations of another Slocan area company, Carnegie Mines.

She had a heart attack in 1960 and doctors advised her to give up her business activities. In July 1960, she sold Violamac to Art White's New Dickenson Mines.

However, MacMillan couldn't stay away. She still had a number of companies (including Consolidated Golden Arrow, with its interest in the Slocan Rambler) and the next company she acquired, which plunged her deep into scandal…and into prison.

"Things that were accepted practice in the mining business and had been done that way since time began were described by reporters who didn't understand the events they were writing about as though they were at least immoral if not downright criminal," she wrote in her autobiography.

The MacMillans bought Windfall Oils and Mines in December 1961. In the winter-spring of 1963 to 1964, Texas Gulf Sulphur (TGS) discovered the Kidd Creek deposit, one of the largest volcanogenic massive sulphide and largest base metal deposits in the world.

When Windfall began diamond drilling in July 1965, Windfall's stock took off, jumping from 56 cents to $2 on July 6, later peaking at $5.70.

The knock against the MacMillans was that they withheld assay results on the first hole; she maintained they were following accepted practice of waiting for the hole to be completed before sending the core for assay. (Later both the Toronto Stock Exchange and the Ontario Securities Commission agreed that not assaying and publishing the results until holes were complete was proper procedure.)

On July 10, the TSE demanded explanations. Together with the OSC, they ordered that the core be placed under guard until assayed – the air of mystery sent the shares still higher. Then telegrams containing false assay results – the core hadn't yet been sent for assay – were sent from New York to Toronto newspapers, supposedly over George's signature.

Assays were finally received on July 30. They showed some copper, but not much, and the stock collapsed to 23 cents. The conductive material producing the geophysical anomaly that had guided their drilling decisions turned out to be graphite. George was criticized for not reporting results of his visual examination; today he would be criticized if he did.

Viola speculated in her autobiography that all the money paid into the treasury so suddenly at the Exchange's "express order" fueled the speculation that drove the stock price up. As underwriters of the stock the MacMillans had a responsibility to maintain a stable market – the only way she could do that (and – perhaps not incidentally – fund the purchase/rescue of the options), was by selling into it.

A Royal Commission of Inquiry and a parallel investigation by the Ontario Securities Commission were announced. MacMillan resigned from PDAC, which was seriously damaged by the scandal, and several years of volunteer effort were needed to recover. There was no convention in 1965.

She was charged with share manipulation in 1967 and was convicted. She had used 52 different accounts at six different brokerages. She was sentenced to nine months in jail but was paroled after just seven weeks, though she still faced fraud charges.

MacMillan was the first woman convicted of wash trading and the oldest woman (at age 64) imprisoned in Ontario at the time. The broker who did the trade for her was found not guilty. Prison was "…a lot more comfortable than some of the places I lived in when I was on the trail prospecting," she said, but "…being cooped up like that was terribly frustrating when I had always been so active."

In February 1969 both she and George were acquitted of the wash trading charges. Judge Harry Deyman, in February 1969, found no evidence that the Macmillans had influenced the price or falsely promoted Windfall stock. He blamed the TGS discovery and the large volume of buy orders emanating from the Timmins area. He held they had acted correctly and in accordance with accepted practice.

"She was probably no different an operator from the rest of the crowd, upholding the code of the day, making a market in her shares" said Robert Ginn, government geologist in Timmins at the time. Wrote Cameron Darby in *Saturday Night* magazine: "She was convicted of a practice…that is almost as common but just as illegal in Canada as contraception."

An outspoken advocate for her own and for industry's interests, Viola had made enemies on Bay Street and in government. The royal commission found she made $1.46 million in profit on trading through controlled companies while others lost $2.7 million. There were implications that several politicians, including cabinet ministers, were involved in Windfall but the royal commission found no connection.

However, the OSC director was involved in trading and was charged with breach of trust.

The TSE was partly to blame for the debacle; they did little to tame the frenzy or to insist on full disclosure.

The Windfall scandal changed the dynamics of share trading in Canada. The royal commission and OSC investigations led to an improved securities act, a better defined TSE/OSC relationship, and the TSE cleaned house, discouraging new speculative listings and tougher rules for juniors. Between 1964 and 1967, many promoters such as Murray Pezim and most of the Toronto penny market decamped for the Vancouver Stock Exchange.

In 1989, Viola pledged $1.25 million to a fund-raising effort to raise $5 million to purchase the William Pinch Mineral Collection, which put them over the top. The collection now resides in the Viola Macmillan National Mineral Exhibition Gallery in the Canadian Museum of Nature in Ottawa. It is one of the finest in the world and consists of over 10,000 specimens from around the globe, including over 500 radioactive specimens housed in a specially designed vault – the finest radioactive collection in the world.

Viola MacMillan was appointed a member of the Order of Canada on October 21, 1992 and received the award on her 90th birthday. She was still active and planning to drill her properties, although she hadn't been in the bush for four years. She died in 1993.

Viola MacMillan equipped for winter prospecting

Jim Morin

Jim Morin with Dean John English of BCIT, federal natural resources minister Hon. Gary Lunn, MABC president and CEO Michael McPhie, AME BC president and CEO Dan Jepsen and AME BC chairman Robert Stevens at AME BC Breakfast Series, 2007

Jim Morin

Jim Morin loved fishing with his father in the waters near the small town of Pine Falls, Manitoba, though he would often spend more time looking at colourful outcropping rocks than casting his rod. The young man fell in love with rocks when he was 13; they became his lifelong passion.

"Every day I walked along the railway tracks, and then one day I actually looked at what I was walking on and realized that beneath my feet lay treasure," Morin said. "Each stone was unique, told a story, had a history and marked time in some way. I was hooked by the mystery of rocks!"

When his grade-eight science teacher skipped the chapter about geology, Jim began his own quest to find out everything he could about rocks. By the end of high school he had read every book about geology he could find in the local library and there was no question about what he would study in university.

By 1975, Morin had a PhD in geology and was on his way to Whitehorse to work with the Department of Indian Affairs and Northern Development. In the mid-1980s, he headed back to Vancouver, where he worked for Inco (now Vale Inco); in that job, he travelled all over North America working on mineral exploration projects.

During a trip to Alaska, Morin visited an exploration site discovered by Inuit prospectors and quickly realized they could have used some training to make their prospecting more successful. He got involved with the Yukon Chamber of Mines and the B.C. & Yukon Chamber of Mines to pursue this objective. Through organizing conferences and teaching prospecting courses, he discovered his second passion: Teaching.

In 1998, he started teaching at the post-secondary level, mainly to Aboriginal students. This provided a vehicle for him to explore his Métis ancestry.

Everything came together when the British Columbia Institute of Technology (BCIT) and the B.C. & Yukon Chamber of Mines hired him in 2005. Rob Stevens and Dan Jepsen were instrumental in the decision to develop a training program involving Aboriginal people and the mining industry. There were challenges at the start, including ensuring sustainable funding for the program. But working with industry, BCIT put together an Aboriginal Minerals Training Program consisting of three elements: The first phase involved mining community awareness sessions over one to two days. This was followed by basic prospecting, mineral exploration and mining (MINING 1001) over ten days. The final phase, a wide-ranging Associate Certificate, involved academic and field components (up to 15 weeks).

The courses were given in Aboriginal communities across B.C. and Yukon. Since 2006, more than 20 sessions have been held with over 300 people. As well, sixteen deliveries of MINE 1001 were made to over 300 people, along with seven deliveries of blocks of the Associate Certificate.

Much of the teaching was done in three venues: The Chief Louis Centre in Kamloops; Prince George Nechako Friendship Centre; and the Saikuz Community Centre near Vanderhoof. The courses were also taught in communities that included Dawson City, Watson Lake, Anahim Lake, Alert Bay and Vernon.

Participants aged from 18 to 60 years. Their enthusiasm was always present, most having an earnest interest and desire for employment in the minerals industry. Many of the former students went on to work in mining as drillers, first aid attendants, geophysical survey workers, miners, geological assistants, truck drivers, and office workers, among other positions.

At the outset, in 2006, the provincial government provided funding of $500,000 through the Ministry of Energy, Mines and Petroleum Resources, which allowed for additional workers including another instructor, Mary Lou Malott and several part-time assistants. New Gold Inc., AME BC and the Mining Association of B.C. also contributed to the program. The continuing search for funding led AME BC and other partners to the federal Aboriginal Skills and Employment Program and in 2009, success was achieved with formation of the B.C. Aboriginal Mine Training Association.

Morin observed that one of the most rewarding things about teaching is reconnecting with former students: "There's nothing better than running into people I've taught when I'm on a field trip to a working mine, or a mineral exploration project. When the students I'm teaching at the time listen to former graduates of the program share their experiences, it's so inspiring for all of us. These people are real life examples of Aboriginal people working in mineral exploration and mining and they become role models for what is possible."

What is his advice to Aboriginal students and people thinking about what to do next?

"Finish high school, if you can. It's free education, available to everyone, and there are many different ways you can get it done. After that, try to find something you are passionate about. I was lucky; I knew early on I wanted to work with rocks. But I didn't think about teaching for many years. I worked really hard, stuck at things even when the going was tough, and today, I have a rewarding career, sharing something I love with Aboriginal people across B.C."

Mihajilo Samoukovic

Schaft Creek, northwestern B.C.

John Brock

Pete Risby

Pete Risby

Clifford Leroy ("Pete") Risby started his prospecting career as a heavy equipment operator at the Cassiar Asbestos mine that led him to work in the company's assay lab. Cassiar geologists Bill Plumb and Lomer Daigle introduced Pete to rocks and minerals and he started prospecting out of Watson Lake and Lower Post.

Attracted by Yukon's Anvil staking rush, he moved to Ross River in 1966. For the next five years he prospected on his own with Aboriginal partners Esau Dick and Arthur John, as well as for Spartan and Atlas Explorations. During this period, he discovered tungsten in the Pelly Mountains. His prospect, Risby Tungsten, had an inferred resource of 8.5 million tonnes grading 0.78 per cent Tungsten trioxide.

During the early 1970s, Pete found numerous carbonate-hosted zinc-lead occurrences in Yukon-NWT Mackenzie Mountains, where properties were optioned to Al Kulan's newly formed company Welcome North

Mines. This activity resulted in a notable staking rush throughout the Mackenzie Arch and into Yukon.

Pete had an exceptional eye for mineralization. He said that if he couldn't see mineral, there was nothing there. He disdained geophysics and geochemistry, saying that the only thing soil sample bags were good for was to light the airtight heater. Pete was one of the first to hire women as field assistants, "they don't talk back". He also had a large crew of Ross River native Indians who were also good prospectors. Pete stayed with Welcome North as its Chief Prospector for 10 years, during which time he found over 80 prospects, all of which Welcome North farmed out to major companies.

Pete loved to prospect in the dark with an ultraviolet lamp to detect scheelite, a tungsten mineral. He found a spectacular showing in mountainous terrain in eastern Yukon where his helicopter pilot would drop him off at dusk and pick him up in the morning. A major company came to examine the property but

lost heart when faced with the prospect of flying in rough terrain after sunset. Pete's solution was to bring a truckload of scheelite to the Welcome North's Vancouver office. He piled up the tungsten mineralization against a wall and lit the "outcrop" with UV lamps. The fluorescence under ultraviolet light was spectacular. The major signed an option agreement on the spot.

Pete left Welcome North in 1982 to establish a placer mining operation on the Indian River in Yukon's South Klondike. In 1996 he and his wife were named *Mr. and Mrs. Miner* by the Klondike Placer Mining Association and Pete was also inducted into the Yukon Prospectors Hall of Fame. He spent many Yukon winters teaching prospecting courses in Aboriginal communities as well as prospecting for John Brock and Wayne Roberts' Northern Crown Mines in Mexico and Nevada. Pete continued to prospect in the Yukon until a year before his death, in 2011.

AME BC

Ed Scholz

Ed Kimura

Craigmont ore conveyor to transport ore from pit to plant site

Ed Scholz

Born in Sand Coulee, Montana, Edgar A. Scholz began his working life as a miner in Butte. He earned a B. Sc. in geological engineering from the Montana School of Mines in 1941. From 1942-1945, he worked with the United States Geological Survey in its Western Mineral Deposits Branch.

During this period, he conducted the fieldwork for two scientific publications: USGS Professional Paper *Geology and Ore Deposits of the Bagdad District, Arizona* (published 1955), co-authored with C. A. Anderson, which developed a model for understanding the geological environment for porphyry copper deposits; and USGS Bulletin *Molybdenum Deposits of the United States* (published 1964), which quickly became the handbook for those seeking molybdenum deposits.

Over the next 10 years he managed several successful small mines producing gold, copper,

zinc and tungsten in Montana and Arizona. In 1956, he joined Placer Development's subsidiary in San Francisco, American Exploration and Mining Co., as senior exploration geologist, later becoming vice president and a director. Scholz transferred to Placer's Vancouver head office, in 1961, as manager of exploration, becoming vice president exploration in 1965.

He was a pioneer in applying large-scale open pit mining methods to low-grade porphyry copper, molybdenum and gold deposits. His knowledge of mineral deposit geology, mining technology and mineral economics, combined with business acumen and entrepreneurial instincts, gave him a rare ability to recognize the potential of low-grade deposits, to negotiate their acquisition and to oversee their evaluation. His expertise and enthusiasm contributed greatly to the success of Placer Development Limited (later Placer Dome) in low-cost bulk mining worldwide.

Scholz was a man of strong and independent convictions, one of the strongest of which was his unwavering belief, even in the 1950s, that the price of gold would, in time, rise dramatically. His indoctrination of exploration staff and company management in this belief, combined with the company's low-cost mining skills, prepared Placer, when the gold price did rise, to be a pioneer in the open-pit mining of large, very low-grade gold deposits, and ultimately to become primarily a gold company.

A believer in a team approach and a great teacher and developer of the staff, Scholz often invited junior geologists as well as seniors to sit in on property negotiations and he took in all opinions. He was an optimist and a realist who believed that a good deal was one where both parties were happy. He was a great believer in being a generalist rather than a specialist. He felt that a geologist wasn't doing his job well if he didn't pay attention to other aspects of the mining business beyond exploration — such as mining, metallurgy, mineral economics and the national and local politics related to a project. He insisted that younger exploration staff be involved in all exploration activities, and that they have a remarkably free hand, but be responsible for their decisions and actions. This approach allowed rapid decision-making at critical stages in a project's development and was fundamental to Placer's success.

He was a visionary and a leader, as well as a teacher. At a very early stage, he recognized that good quality exploration properties represented low-cost, long-term product inventory for Placer and encouraged his staff to be very forward-thinking in their project assessments.

He explored the Marcopper porphyry copper prospect in the Philippines, in 1956, and proposed further exploration, which continued until the property was brought into production in 1969.

In 1961, he was involved in an examination of data on the Craigmont property, near Merritt, B.C., and recommended Placer's participation. His understanding of the economics of open pit mining was instrumental in the decision to develop the property as an open pit.

He made an initial field examination of the Endako molybdenum property, in 1962, and recommended that Placer option the property. An aggressive exploration program was undertaken and the property was brought into open-pit production, in 1965. The mine opening was two weeks short of three years from the first diamond drill hole.

Endako's economic success caused Placer to pursue exploration projects that were orientated towards low-grade, bulk, open-pit mining. An example in B.C. was the Gibraltar Mines property, near Williams Lake, originally a joint venture with Duval Corporation.

Scholz was the first Placer geologist to see Porgera in New Guinea and an enthusiastic backer of its exploration. His knowledge of Montana gold projects was instrumental in the exploration and development of the Golden Sunlight property.

In the 1970s, he was aware that a heavy reliance on copper was not desirable for the company in the long term and a move into other metals was needed. Gold was one of his favorite commodities and increased exploration was directed towards the yellow metal. This met with so much success that Placer essentially became a gold company.

Scholz believed that one should belong to, and be active in, professional and industry associations. He did so and, among other duties, he served as president of the Chamber in 1973-74 and, in 1978, was general chairman of the annual general meeting of the Canadian Institute of Mining and Metallurgy in Vancouver.

Scholz retired from Placer, in 1976, and established a consulting firm, Scholz International Mining. His knowledge of the Zortman and Landusky gold deposits in Montana had much to do with the early success of Pegasus Gold.

His untimely death, in 1980, cut short a distinguished career. Ed Scholz was an outstanding creative explorer and great communicator; truly a leader in the mining industry.

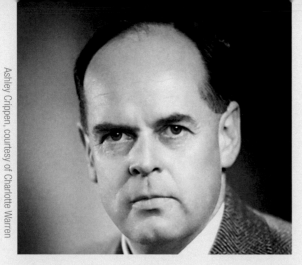

Ashley Crippen, courtesy of Charlotte Warren

Harry Warren

AME BC

Harry Warren teaching at Chamber prospecting school, 1970s

Harry Warren

Harry Warren changed forever the way prospectors look for buried mineral deposits.

He discovered that, if you analyze the chemical content of grasses, trees and other plant life for the trace elements they contain, you can learn about minerals in the earth beneath them.

Born in Anacortes, Washington in 1904, he lived an extraordinarily active life and a long and productive one. He got off to a rapid start, being awarded four degrees in four years: a BA and BASc. from UBC in 1926 and 1927; and, as a Rhodes Scholar, at Oxford, a B. Sc. in 1928 and a D. Phil. (Doctor of Philosophy), in 1929. After working on research projects for a few years he joined the UBC faculty in mid-Depression 1932 as a lecturer. His annual salary was $800, about half the average wage in Canada at the time. He rose to professor by 1945, a post he would hold until 1973, when he was named Honourary Professor

and Professor Emeritus. His links to UBC covered 75 years, from his entry as an undergraduate in 1923 to his death in 1998, aged 93.

Warren's early research interests were mineralogy and economic geology, but his major interest became biogeochemical prospecting. His early work in the field was not without critics. Ray Lett of the B.C. Geological Survey wrote, "Geochemical exploration techniques were once regarded with mild amusement by the mining community…" Today, thanks to Harry Warren, "…geochemistry is considered a key discipline contributing to the search for new mineral deposits."

His groundbreaking work in biogeochemistry, although very important, was just part of his varied career. Among other things, he published 198 articles and scientific papers, gave lectures on mining and prospecting to many thousands of young people, joined in effective lobbying for the rights and benefits of the prospecting and mining

communities and was associated with the Chamber for more than 50 years – being its vice-president for 12 years, from 1939 to 1951, and its president for three years: 1952, 1953 and 1954.

He was also a member of the 1928 Canadian Olympic team, and the founding president of the Canadian Field Hockey Association. Warren can, with no exaggeration, be described as a renaissance man.

One of the little-known facts of Harry Warren's career was that he pioneered the use of dogs to find minerals in Canada; more on that later.

As for the Chamber, Warren first appears in its minutes in 1932, the same year he began his UBC lectures. He was 28 years old and, as part of his duties at the university, he was conducting prospector training classes. In later years, one of his students was his son, Victor, who said, "I, and some of my buddies, spent hours and hours gathering tree samples and rock samples (from holes we had to dig down to bedpan), so my dad could have all these samples analyzed at his lab. I attended his prospecting class at Point Grey Secondary, and was privileged to have him lecture me in one of my classes at UBC. I got the odd lecture at home, too, but not in geology!"

Chamber minutes for 1951 note that "... one large company, the Kennecott Copper Corporation, will have several parties in the field using the biogeochemistry method of detecting orebodies...." The minutes credit Warren for the concept. More than one B.C. mine has been found based on analysis of trace elements in the surrounding trees and soil.

Chamber minutes are dotted with mention of Warren's efforts on behalf of the industry over five decades. In 1955, for example, he was particularly busy: He began the year with a visit to Ottawa as a Chamber representative to argue against new and unwelcome changes in Yukon mining laws. Later that year he began a series of night lectures at Point Grey Secondary School to future prospectors. He ended the year as head of a special Chamber team presenting a brief, *The Mining Industry in British Columbia and Yukon Territory*, to the Gordon Royal Commission on Canada's economic prospects.

At the 57th annual meeting of the Chamber on January 14, 1969 a presentation was made to Warren as a token of gratitude for the time and service he had freely given to the Chamber over a period of many years – some 37 at that point. Charles Ney, a longtime volunteer and lecturer for

the Chamber, paid Warren tribute, emphasizing his keen interest in the mining industry and the training of prospectors.

In March 1973 Warren was a speaker at a special general meeting (attended by 1,100 people) in the Hotel Vancouver Pacific Ballroom to protest unfavourable provincial legislation affecting the mining industry. The NDP government, under Premier Dave Barrett, had just introduced Bill 31, the Mineral Royalties Act.

Almost exactly one year later, in the same place, another special general meeting was held – this one with an audience of 1,600. Again, Warren was a key speaker. The meeting's purpose was to consider the effects of Bill 31 and other adverse legislation. The following resolution was passed unanimously by those attending: "That this Special General Meeting of the British Columbia and Yukon Chamber of Mines go on record as urging the Provincial Government to drastically amend its legislation and particularly Bill 31, the Mineral Royalties Act."

In 1974, under the auspices of the Mining Emergency Fund, Warren, now 70, toured the Okanagan, speaking on behalf of the industry in Peachland, Penticton and Vernon.

In 1986 the Chamber presented Warren with its "Spud" Huestis Award for excellence in prospecting and mineral exploration.

Now about those dogs. An article by J. Stirling in the November 1972 issue of the *Canadian Mining Journal* tells the story. Back in the 1960s someone in Finland discovered that dogs, properly trained, could sniff out sulphide-bearing rocks "not normally indicated by conventional prospecting methods." Apparently "...a prospecting dog located some pyrite and chalcopyrite boulders which diamond drilling investigation revealed to have a copper orebody of economic significance." Harry Warren was taken by the notion and introduced it to Canada. He was assisted by Bob Wright, recently retired from the B.C. Research Council, and an expert in scent detection.

They had financial backing from a group formed for the purpose, whimsically named Syndicate K-9 and consisting of Kennco, Falconbridge, El Paso and Dynasty. With the assistance of Warren, Falconbridge's Jimmy McDougall, Aaro Aho and other Chamber members, the program was initiated. Members of the Vancouver Police Department Dog Squad taught German shepherds to sniff out sulphide mineralization; "... the dogs responded very well and within a few weeks were infallibly selecting sulphide-bearing boulders from amongst ordinary rocks." Often they would find such rocks where the prospector had not and "...one of the major difficulties was maintaining the dogs' interest when natural finds were slow. The dogs were not fooled by planted rocks designed to bolster their enthusiasm. They seemed to know the real thing."

The dogs didn't seem to perform as well on wet days; because of the moist climate of Western Canada, the K-9 program did not contribute to any new discoveries. Dog prospecting never caught on, here. Not even Harry Warren could win 'em all.

And then there were fish. Warren's friend and colleague Alex Burton recalls: "In 1960 Harry had me collecting trout livers to analyze for molybdenum at Boss Mountain. It was fun fishing in the creek before I brought it to a production decision. Didn't catch many fish, though."

Burton has another keen memory of his long-lived friend: "A few years before his death we were discussing the number of people we knew who were dying and he said he had so many acquaintances who were dying that he had to ration his funerals so he had time left for his own activities."

With all he did, it's astonishing Harry Warren was also very active in sports. He was part of Canada's presence at the 1928 Amsterdam Olympic Games, coaching the ladies' track team – for the first year women competed in Olympic track and field. And he was a reserve athlete for the sprints and relay runners, sharing a room with an old friend from Vancouver, legendary sprinter Percy Williams. Warren was later responsible for Canadian involvement in Olympic field hockey for the first time in the 1964 Games.

One of the Olympic team members was Victor Warren, Harry's son. Warren held high office in rugby, cricket and field hockey organizations, both men's and women's. He was the founding president of the Canadian Field Hockey Association and did a great deal to promote the sport in B.C. He received awards for his support of sports organizations and in 1990 was named to the B.C. Sports Hall of Fame.

For his lifetime of accomplishments he became a holder of the Order of Canada in 1991 and the Order of British Columbia in 1991.

AME BC

Harry Warren receives Chamber honourary life membership from Chamber past president Robert Sheldon and mines minister James Chabot, 1977

Tom Waterland

Tom Waterland

Tom Waterland's name first appeared in the Chamber's minutes in 1969. (Waterland would go on to play an important role in the province's mining and forestry portfolios – and would subsequently become President and CEO of the Mining Association of B.C.)

Chamber manager Tommy Elliott had suggested that the organization's honourary advisory board should be broadened to include area members from "such important centres as Kamloops, Prince George, Smithers, etc." Nelson and Whitehorse were already represented. Appointment of members from different geographical areas would help blunt criticism that the Chamber was exclusively a Vancouver organization.

The minutes note that Waterland, a mining engineer associated with Versatile Mining Services Ltd. of Kamloops, was a former provincial government mines inspector and chairman of the local CIM branch. (He was back with the provincial government as a mines inspector in Kamloops immediately prior to seeking election in late 1975.)

Waterland, a self-admitted political neophyte, loved mining and only entered public life because he was aghast at the policies of the Dave Barrett's NDP government in the early 1970s. Waterland had not even seen inside the provincial legislature in Victoria prior to his election as MLA in the Social Credit victory of December 1975. Premier Bill Bennett (son of long-serving W.A.C.) asked him to take on the mining portfolio; he was delighted.

When, during the cabinet swearing-in ceremony at Government House in Victoria, he heard his name called: "Thomas Waterland, Minister of Mines and Forests." He turned to the premier: "What's this forestry bit, Bill?" Bennett's response was that he would not ask Waterland to carry the forestry role indefinitely. But the premier must have been impressed by his rookie minister. He asked him to soldier on for a while longer with both portfolios, half-joking that, in Alberta, one minister handled both jobs.

Waterland would go on to scrap the NDP's mining legislation and replace it with laws more amenable to the industry. Thereafter he turned his attention to forest policy; he found it fascinating though, at first, complex. He could not always suppress his engineering interests. On field trips an advisor had to remind him he was supposed to be investigating policy issues, not figuring out how mill machinery worked.

Fred Wells displaying gold bricks at Barkerville, 1933

Fred Wells

The hunt for gold in British Columbia boasts many fascinating characters. But few come as physically tough, determined, opinionated and eccentric as Fred Wells who, despite skeptics' scorn, found a mother lode in the Cariboo and got his name on a town.

Wells, born in 1861, hailed from Whitefield, New Hampshire. He was involved with various mining enterprises before venturing to the Cariboo: Prospecting on the Columbia River, at Spillamacheen; and developing the Nickel Plate Mine, near Rossland, among others.

Prospectors in nineteenth-century B.C. hoped to find an elusive mother lode, source of the nuggets and gold dust widely scattered throughout rivers and creeks. Richard Willoughby noticed pieces of quartz still attached to the gold he found on Lowhee Creek in the Cariboo 1861. He paid little attention.

In the 1920s, Fred Wells went to Barkerville obsessed with the idea that the quartz-bearing nuggets indicated a buried orebody. He must have irritated a few people. A department of mines official wrote that he was "…an opinionated prospector, devoid of geological knowledge."

Wells found backers who shared his hunch. These included a Vancouver doctor, W. B. Burnett. They formed the Cariboo Gold Quartz Mining Company and, in 1930, Fred Wells found his mother lode on the Rainbow group of claims covering a spur of Cow Mountain.

He took the first gold brick produced at the mine – actually two gold bars worth $22,116 at 1,410.62 troy ounces – to Vancouver. He drove by limousine from the docks to Birks, where the treasure was displayed in the store window. In May 1933, about a hundred shareholders, in Vancouver for the company's annual meeting, met him at the Union Steamship wharf. Wells stepped down the gangplank with gold bullion worth more than $36,000 wired to a packboard on his back.

Cariboo Gold Quartz was wildly successful. It paid dividends of more than $1.6 million between 1935 and 1943. Gold valued at over $40 million was mined from the faults on Cow Mountain.

The new town of Wells, laid out in 1933, became a centre of culture and activity in the Cariboo, with a population of over 1,500. Cariboo Gold Quartz chose employees not only for their mining skills but also

their interest in art, music or sport. The company built a large community hall with a dance floor and gym, a racetrack and a baseball park. Eventually the town boomed to 4,500 when Newmont Mining Company opened equally rich holdings on Island Mountain, in 1934. The town is still there with a small population, an attraction for summer tourists.

A vigorous man with great physical strength, he was Snowshoe Champion of British Columbia three years running. When he was well into his seventies, he still travelled by snowshoe around his claims. Although he built a fine house in Wells and ate his meals there, he preferred to sleep in a tent in the backyard. Even in his nineties, he worked on an iron and copper prospect in the Namu area, about 150 kilometres north of Vancouver Island. When he died in Vancouver, aged 95, though, the "Father of the Cariboo" was living in a small, humbly furnished room with tables covered with ore samples. He died penniless and was buried by the Salvation Army.

Fred Wells and other Cariboo mining men, date unknown
AME BC

Companies Key to B.C.'s Economic Growth

Endako Mine near Fraser Lake, B.C.

Thompson Creek Metals

Underground at Bralorne, 1934

Bralorne Gold Mines Ltd.

Gold was discovered at the historic Bridge River Camp, 180 kilometres north of Vancouver, in the summer of 1896. Over the next two years, key claims of the future high-grade Pioneer and Bralorne mines were staked.

With the news of the discovery, throngs of prospectors scrambled over the rugged terrain to uncover numerous gold-bearing veins, many seldom more than a few feet wide. By the start of the 20th century, Bend'Or Mines, under Arthur and Delina Noel, was developed as a producing mine, and *arrastras* – crude rock-crushing devices that utilize water power – were installed at the Lorne Gold Mines (as it was called then) and Pioneer properties.

In 1923, mining engineer David Sloane was called in to examine the Pioneer mine, which had been operating on a small scale since 1913. He recognized the mine's potential and, after a few fruitless attempts to raise financing, he negotiated a lease-purchase arrangement. Within four years he had transformed the Pioneer mine, producing $100,000 worth of bullion each year.

Drawn by Sloane's success, a major Toronto brokerage firm incorporated Lorne Gold Mines in 1928 to acquire and explore the ground between the Pioneer boundary and the Lorne property. Work commenced on an eight-level adit to test the Lorne The project ended when the brokerage firm declared bankruptcy in 1930.

Many major mining companies examined the Lorne holdings; all walked away. In 1931, Vancouver industrialist Austin Taylor took a $300,000 gamble on the property. In return, he and his backers received a 40 per cent interest in Bralorne Mines, the new operating company. Ira Joralem, a consulting geologist already familiar with the Pioneer ground, examined the Bralorne property that summer. It is assumed that it was he who suggested the workings on Lorne's eight-level be extended through a major fault, to facilitate a search for a continued king vein.

After 60 feet, the new workings struck a bonanza that extended six to 10 levels. Bralorne had arrived. Joralem's persistence in drifting other veins located between Lorne and Pioneer workings led to major new discoveries.

In the 1930s, the success of the Pioneer and Bralorne mines attracted a host of exploration companies and job seekers searching for the next bonanza. Pioneer paid its first dividend in 1931 and, Bralorne, after a shaky start, followed suit in 1934. The best years for the area were between 1933 and 1941, when Bridge River was a bright spot in sharp contrast to the economic gloom blanketing much of Canada.

In 1959 the two mines, then controlled by a group headed by former Pioneer geologist, Franc Joubin, merged as Bralorne Pioneer Mines. The mines continued to operate until they were trapped between the fixed price of gold and ever-increasing inflationary costs. The Pioneer operation shut down in 1960; Bralorne followed in 1971.

Smaller producers remained active at the Bridge River camp, which, by 1978, had produced 4,178,363 ounces of gold, (2,821,567 ounces from Bralorne and 1,333,074 from Pioneer).

In 1986, Louis Wolfin, chairman of Bralorne Gold Mines, visited the tiny gold mining town and was impressed with the area's potential for resuming operations. However, it took two and a half decades to assemble the properties of interest, discover significant new gold zones, redesign the mill, build a tailings pond, stockpile ore and receive permits.

Under the guidance of William Kocken, president and CEO, director David Wolfin and chief operating officer Matthew Ball, the team's exploration strategy was to drill the area between the historic Pioneer, King and Bralorne gold mines. The plan paid off with significant new gold discoveries. In 2011 mining was taking place in the gap (named the BK Zone), located between the King and Bralorne mines. This new high-grade resource had expected head grades of 0.38 ounces per ton gold or greater and new zones in the gap remained open for expansion.

Exploration on the North Vein in the King Mine targeted a historic resource block that extended over a strike length of 85 metres from the 800 to the 700 level. The Bralorne Camp mines were deep; in an interview, Ball commented that the old-timers had discovered 30 veins and mined down some 6,000 feet.

"It's a classic gold mine just like you would find in the Timmins or Red Lake Camp but it's out in B.C. and hasn't drawn a lot of attention."

Guests at the re-opening ceremony filed into the mill building where they eagerly anticipated the pouring of a gold bar. About 60 per cent of Bralorne gold characteristically occurs as fine to coarse grains that are recovered on a jig. The remaining 40 per cent is concentrated in the 100 tonne-per-day mill and shipped to a Barrick Gold facility in Nevada for processing. Always exciting to watch, the gold pour yielded a doré bar worth about $450,000. The doré bars go to a refinery in Richmond, B.C.

Kocken explained that the property was originally developed as three separate mines that were subsequently combined. "The gap areas were owned by residents that would not accept mining activity below them," he said. "Now we have shown the gap areas have exploration potential and recent exploration has found a new vein in the Bralorne-King gap – the BK Vein, which has been the focus of exploration and development for the past three or four years. It's right in amongst the old workings, so it only required about a thousand feet of drifting (tunnelling) to reach the zone." Drill-indicated, measured and indicated resources stood at 75,000 tons grading about 0.35 oz/ton with another 220,000 tons of similar grade in the inferred category.

Ball speculated that gold mineralization in the BK Zone could continue to depth, as with the other nearby veins, but deeper drilling on the vein had not yet been done. "The similarities are that the ore is more vertically continuous than laterally continuous," said Ball. "I think the real future of this mine is following those gap areas down deeper and parallel to the old workings. It will take a lot of work, drilling and reopening some of those old workings. Eventually, we have to look at dewatering the old mines."

The company used an underground diamond drill to test for more mineralized zones on the BK structure. Later, it planned to move over to the other gap area between the Bralorne and the Pioneer to try and drill the upper segment of the 77 Vein. "The 77 Vein went all the way to the bottom of the mine and there's still some potential for the 77 in the gap between the old Bralorne and Pioneer mines," said Ball.

Mill expansion plans were in the works. While the mill was operating at 100 tons per day, it was permitted for a 500 ton-per-day operation. "We have equipment on site to increase mill production to 280 tons per day," said Ball. "So it will be a minimal capital cost; however, we're waiting to develop the ore zones that we have at hand before we go into that." The company planned to conduct about 4,000 metres of surface drilling and 3,300 metres of underground drilling to define these ore zones.

"Shrinkage stoping is the most common mining method used, which means blasting and working your way up in the vein on top of the broken ore and, when the zone is mined out, pulling all the broken material out of the stope," continued Ball.

Kocken added, "We haven't been able to find enough underground workers. We're trying to get them in from anywhere. Maybe we should put a bonus program together, not only for underground miners, but for everybody working at Bralorne."

Director Gary Robertson told *Resource World* that building a mine is a hugely capital intensive process; however, the company had enough money to get the mine up and running. "I guess it depends on how fast we want to move, at some point we're going to expand the mine and have to raise more capital," he added. "I don't think that should be too much of problem with the price of gold at $1,500 an ounce."

Bralorne Gold Mines was expected to produce about 6,000 ounces of gold in 2011. While the cash cost per ounce had not yet been calculated, historically and with what the company processed in 2003-04, management estimated it to be about $450. For 2012, production was estimated at about 500 ounces of gold per month.

It's taken a long time but efforts have finally paid off and Bralorne Gold Mines has now joined that select group of gold producers in British Columbia.

Drilling at Bralorne, 1934

Present-day McDame Creek near Cassiar

Cassiar Asbestos

Early prospectors and First Nations told of mountain sheep bedding down in matted fibre accumulated from the weathering of an asbestos outcrop and birds' nests that withstood brush fires.

According to an information booklet given to all employees by Cassiar Asbestos Corporation Ltd., existence of the deposit had been known for many years. It was located in northern B.C., just south of the Yukon border on McDame Mountain in the Cassiar range at an average altitude of 6,100 feet.

Development of the orebody began in 1951 thanks to improvements in transportation and technology as well as a promising economic climate. Prospectors, Vic Sittler, Hiram Nelson and brothers Bob and Ron Kirk, staked the property. Conwest Exploration Company of Toronto acquired their holdings in the fall of 1950. A rough road was available from the Alaska Highway to the Moccasin Mines dredging site, a distance of about 60 miles. Conwest managed construction of a ten-mile extension before freeze-up.

Cassiar Asbestos, formed in May 1951, took over the claims from Conwest, which remained a major shareholder. The road was then extended the remaining distance to the Cassiar camp.

In January 1952, active work was started on the planning and construction of a pilot mill and ancillary shops to handle the asbestos talus material. Mill construction was completed that November. The property then consisted of 40 claims in the McDame Lake area of the Liard Mining Division. The mine was about 86 miles by road southwest of Mile 648 on the Alaska Highway.

When work started there was sufficient asbestos in evidence to provide a mill feed for three years at an average of 250 tons a day. Encouraged by test results indicating that the fibre was an iron-free chrysotile asbestos with very good spinning qualities, company directors decided that the main orebody should be immediately investigated by driving an adit to intersect the ore zone at an average depth of 250 feet "…with a view to making early plans for a larger scale of operations." In the company's 1952 annual report, consultant William V. Smitheringale said the results of this work were "…most satisfactory". He estimated there were 5,892,000 tons of reasonably assured fibre-bearing serpentine grading $30 per ton in spinning grade fibre. In addition, undetermined amounts of crude fibres would be recovered. The company immediately raised funds to support a much larger operation.

A 500-ton milling unit was in operation by July 1954. The company spent over $1.5 million on plant and equipment that year. This work included the completion of the milling unit and additions to the power plant, general camp facilities and housing, and the start on construction of an aerial tramway. The tramline went into service with a capacity of 100 tons of ore an hour; its installation was expected to materially extend the mining season.

A research report dated December 1959 by brokers James Richardson & Sons of Winnipeg called the Cassiar discovery "…one of the most significant developments in the asbestos industry in recent years." For some time the fibre was declared a strategic commodity by the U.S. government.

Production rose gradually from 500 tons of ore daily in 1954 to 1,000 tons by 1957. Throughout 1958 and 1959, the mill averaged around 1,065 tons per day and, in 1960, capacity was expanded to 1,500 tons per day.

"The mill produces four grades of spinning fibre, and four grades of the shorter fibre used in cement and shingles. One-third of Cassiar's production is sold to the U.S. 20 per cent in Australia, 10 per cent in the U.K. and the rest in other markets," the Richardson report noted.

"The importance of the Cassiar deposit is well illustrated by the fact that prior to its discovery… Southern Rhodesia was the Free World's only source of low-iron spinning fibres. Even during the [Second World] War supplies to the U.S. had declined drastically because of mounting British requirements and, by 1954-55, exports of the Rhodesian fibre to the U.S. had practically ceased. It was at this critical point that the Cassiar deposit was discovered and developed."

In 1958, Cassiar purchased three additional properties from Conwest Exploration: The Clinton Creek, Caley and Letain properties. At the time, Clinton Creek, 40 miles northwest of Dawson City in Yukon, had received the most extensive development. Reserves were estimated at five million tons of high-grade fibre that compared very favourably in characteristics and grade with the main Cassiar deposit and it was available for open-pit mining.

The company's 1964 annual report noted that the asbestos-cement industry was continuing to expand throughout the world. This was evidenced by the encouraging number of machines that were being installed and new plants that were to be constructed in the next three or four years. It appeared that the imbalance between consumption and productive capacity, which had plagued the industry for a number of years, was coming to an end.

By 1964 the mill was treating 1,611 tons of ore and concentrate each day. A 4-1/2-yard electric shovel was put into service on the stripping operations in April 1964. The cost per ton of rock removed was reduced from an average of 86 cents per ton in 1963 to 65 cents per ton in 1964. Further economies were anticipated in 1965 with the introduction of 40-ton trucks to replace part of the existing 20-ton fleet and with the use of a new rotary drill.

Bagged fibre produced by the mill was hauled by truck to the White Pass & Yukon railhead in Whitehorse and then by rail and ship to Vancouver. By 1964, it was clear that facilities in Vancouver Harbour would not be able to handle the growing tonnages that Cassiar expected to ship. In October 1965 a new dock, warehouse and foreshore improvements were completed and put into service in North Vancouver at a cost of $991,594. At the same time White Pass &

Yukon commissioned its new 6,000-ton container-tanker vessel, the *MV Frank H. Brown*. The new facilities, which included an asbestos wharf, provided an efficient warehousing and shipping operation with sufficient capacity to handle additional fibre forthcoming from the Clinton Creek mine.

Cassiar's 1976 annual report noted that Clinton Creek, in Yukon, Canada's most northerly open-pit mine, had produced over 861,000 tons of asbestos valued at over $219 million since it opened in the fall of 1967. In addition, through local purchases, taxes and payroll, the mine and its community have made a major contribution to the economic and social development of Yukon. Clinton Creek had reached full production in April 1968, although its first load of fibre was delivered by truck to railhead at Whitehorse late the previous year.

Exporting asbestos had become a major international enterprise as the company's report noted: "Transporting fibre is an ongoing and continuous process. By ship, train and truck, container and palletized loads of fibre arrive in Vancouver for onward shipment to such ports at Sydney, Valparaiso, Buenos Aires, Penang, Amsterdam, Barcelona, Melbourne, Liverpool, Tokyo and Bangkok – to name a few."

But the industry had to face criticism that asbestos posed a serious – indeed lethal – health hazard. In 1973 Cassiar's president, J. D. Christian, felt obliged to respond. He told the company's annual meeting:

"Once again, I must refer to the repeated attacks … in the press and on television concerning implied hazards to the environment and to the health of the workers and to the public at large. These reports are emanating from a small group of over-enthusiastic people who apparently have excellent access to the media, labour unions and aspiring politicians. Unfortunately, reports from reliable doctors and scientists are not receiving the same publicity. Asbestos, like many other materials, including some sitting in our own kitchen cupboards, has to be handled in the proper manner.

"The three known diseases, Asbestosis, Bronchogenic Cancer and Mesotheliomia, which to varying degrees, have been associated with exposure to asbestos fibres, are time-related. It is important to realize that the cases being reported today involve people who experienced severe exposure many years ago when little was known of the problem, and dust controls were minimal or non-existent. All the evidence that I have before me indicates that if the present standards and approved practices for handling asbestos and its products are adhered to, the risk if any, of contacting any of the diseases in question will be extremely low and socially acceptable. Throughout our operations we are endeavouring to meet and surpass these standards. At the present time, the major problem in this area is hiring sufficient men to get the required jobs done."

Christian said there were already signs that "emotional publicity" was having an effect on some segments of the industry. It would be regrettable, if not disastrous, he said, if thousands of uses, many in the safety, insulation and fire protection field, were ruled out by panic legislation.

WP&YR

The MV Frank H. Brown in action.

Extracting what had become a controversial product from a remote mine in northern B.C. was hugely expensive. Attracting and retaining skilled staff was not easy; in its quarter century anniversary year of 1976, the Cassiar's annual labour turnover was 119 per cent, an improvement over 157 per cent in 1975. Maintaining an attractive company town with a school, hospital, cafeteria and social amenities added significantly to the cost of doing business.

A two-month strike in July and August 1976, plus the residual effects of an earlier three-week labour stoppage in late 1975, cost the company a 12 per cent loss of sales volume. This was offset by price increases of eight and 15 per cent. In 1976, the company spent $2.2 million on townsite, cafeteria and hospital improvements; $1.3 million on an employee change house and almost $3.8 million on a new mill air system. The company's bank debt at the end of 1976 was $20 million. Dividends had not been paid since early 1974. The 1976 annual report noted:

"During the past three years, cash flow…has been adversely influenced by the need to accelerate the waste removal program at Cassiar, the construction of a new tramline and concentrating plant, and improvements and modernization of other plant facilities and the townsite. In addition, major capital expenditure commitments have been undertaken to meet the new and more stringent environmental standards with respect to asbestos.

"The directors expected the company's finances would improve when its development and capital

The Cassiar mine, 1976

spending programs were completed. The report noted that demand for asbestos cement fibre grades remained strong, but demand for [higher priced] textile grade fibres had softened.

"Regarding the company's working environment, the report noted that improved procedures, coupled with better equipment design and maintenance, had reduced the average in-plant count to a level below the current required standard. Personnel working in areas that do not yet meet the required air cleanliness standards are provided with respirators which offer the wearer complete protection from airborne fibres and dust. It is the company's intention to reduce airborne

asbestos fibres to the lowest concentration practicable using the best available technology."

In late 1980, Cassiar was taken over by Canadian-controlled Brinco Limited which, through subsidiaries, had interests in the exploration, development and production of energy resources (oil and gas, uranium and coal), industrial minerals and base and precious metals. The year 1981 started well for Brinco. Deteriorating economic conditions in Canada and elsewhere, however, then resulted in reduced demand for mineral products, including asbestos. This severely hurt sales from the Cassiar mine and Brinco's net earnings. The mine was shut for 30 days in 1981; sales were 88,409 tons versus 105,431 tons in 1980. Brinco, expecting demand for asbestos to remain depressed in 1982, planned a one-month Cassiar mine shutdown at mid-year to conserve cash. It also decided to reduce its waste removal program and meet customer demand from inventory, which was at an all-time high. Cassiar continued to serve over 100 customers in 40 countries and had expanded its sales in India and the Middle East.

The B.C. Ministry of Energy and Mines website reports that asbestos reserves at the Cassiar mine were finally exhausted in June 1989, after 38 years of production. Stockpiled ore (1.4 million tonnes) from the pit supplied sufficient millfeed while the underground McDame deposit was being prepared for production, which began in November 1990 using block caving methods. At the end of 1990 mineable reserves were 18,900,000 tonnes averaging 6.1 per cent fibre. In February 1992 the B.C. government placed Cassiar Mining Corp in receivership.

Large quantities of jade were also produced in the later years. Bill Plumb (Cassiar chief geologist, 1958-1974, and later a Chamber employee), subsequently said, "I am reluctantly proud to admit that it was Clancy Hubbell, a garage mechanic at the pit and an ardent rockhound, who first recognized the jade and brought it to my attention. From then on we arranged to stockpile the jade separately and it was used to provide financing for some of the amenities at Cassiar. It was often difficult to identify as jade and separate from the waste rock along the hangingwall of the pit."

Len Werner, Cassiar geologist, 1970-73, wrote, "In 1970, the first jade boulders were hauled down from the pit…and Bill Plumb asked me to go see if I could diamond-drill some core samples from them with a little 'packsack' diamond drill we had…it was those samples – about a total of 6 feet of 1" core pieces – that went overseas to be determined if the jade quality was good enough to market. The rest is history; Clancy Hubbell's history mostly, I guess."

Brian Pewsey, mine superintendent and general manager, 1974-83, remembered, "When I joined Cassiar as the mine superintendent in 1974 the mine …never stockpiled Nephrite…every time we drilled in the area of the Nephrite our drill bit replacement cost went out of sight. I have no doubt in my mind that hundreds of tons of Nephrite were sent to the waste dumps.

"In 1975-76 a young geologist came to me with a polished block of jade stating that the product was valuable. It was his initiation that started a long journey through marketing in Vancouver to find a market and sell the Nephrite. The shovel operators were the experts in separating the Nephrite from the waste material …the board of directors agreed in 1975 to allow the proceeds from the sale of the jade to be spent on additional recreational facilities in Cassiar…Unfortunately for Cassiar Town the sale of the jade increased to such an extent that the income from the sale had to be included in general income for the benefit of the shareholders."

In the mid-1980s, reserves at the Cassiar mine in a low-grade stockpile (waste from the former dry-milling operation) were approximately 17 million tonnes grading 4.2 per cent asbestos and 23.5 per cent magnesium.

Jedway Enterprises recovered 50 tonnes of jade from the old asbestos dumps in 1998. Cassiar Mining Inc., a wholly-owned subsidiary of Minroc Mines Inc., expected to produce at a rate of 1,000 tonnes of asbestos fibre per month from August to October 1998. A total of 20,000 tonnes was shipped. Minroc was conducting a feasibility study to assess magnesium recovery in the tailings. Minroc changed its name to Cassiar Mines & Metals Inc. in June 1999.

In July 1999, Aluminum of Korea Ltd. entered into an agreement with Cassiar to acquire 35 per cent of the Magnesium Metal Project. The serpentine stockpile of 20 million tonnes contained 3,630 million kilograms of magnesium metal and 700 million kilograms of chrysotile fibre, according to a Cassiar Mines & Metals press release in December 1999. In April 2000, Cassiar changed its name to Cassiar Magnesium Inc. In 2000, Cassiar Magnesium Inc. dry milled surface stockpiles of chrysolite, with approximately 6 million tonnes of 7 per cent fibre outlined, to produce 60 to 70 tonnes per day of long and intermediate fibre. The dry mill facility was damaged by fire in December 2000 and production was suspended.

Endako haul truck and driver, c. 2008

Endako Mines

Molybdenum is a rising star on the commodity chart and B.C. is home to the world's fifth-largest pure or primary producer of its primary mineral source, molybdenite, at the historic Endako Mine.

Molybdenum is a relatively rare, silvery white metal that did not garner much attention until the latter part of the 18th century. What was once a laboratory curiosity is now heavily in demand with ever-widening uses. The main use of molybdenum is as an alloying agent in specialty steels used primarily in furnaces, high-temperature applications in the lighting and glass industries, electronics, nuclear energy, aerospace and natural gas and oil transmission.

In ancient times, for want of a better definition, a number of lead-like minerals were collectively referred to by the Greek word *molybdos*. Molybdenite, the predominant source of molybdenum, was one of those nameless substances. It was not until 1778 that Swedish scientist Carl Wilhelm Scheele positively identified molybdenum. Scheele decomposed molybdenite by heating it with nitric acid and then heating it in air to yield a white molybdenum trioxide powder. In 1782, Peter Jacob Hjelm reduced the oxide with carbon to obtain a dark metallic powder that he named molybdenum.

Molybdenum remained little more than a scientific curiosity until 1891, when it was used as an alloying element in the production of armour plate. Molybdenum was quickly recognized as an effective substitute for tungsten in numerous steel-alloying applications. During the First World War the demand for tungsten soared and supplies were severely strained. Molybdenum was successfully substituted in many hard and impact resistant steels, which spurred exploration for new sources. In the 1930s, after much research and testing, scientists finally determined the critical temperature ranges for the forging and heat treatment of molybdenum-bearing steels. They also determined how molybdenum imparts its many cost-effective benefits as an alloying element to steels. Molybdenum became a hot commodity.

It was at about this time that two hunters from Fraser Lake, Charles Foote and Alfred Langley, found fragments of mineralized boulders scattered along a ridge 8.5 kilometres southwest of a village called Endako. Being enterprising individuals, they staked the claims, discovered a quartz molybdenum vein, sank a shaft and drove a small adit below the shaft. However, that was the extent of it and not much else occurred on the claims until the Second World War and its aftermath pushed molybdenum

into the spotlight. Post-war reconstruction of Europe brought with it new demands for structural steels, many of which contained molybdenum. At that point, those molybdenum claims in central B.C. became much more interesting.

Endako Mines Ltd. was incorporated in May 1962 and began a full exploration program, the results of which drew the interest of Placer Development Limited (later Placer Dome). By August of that same year, Placer and Endako Mines entered into an option agreement. Clearing and construction began in March 1964; 14 months and $22 million later, the Endako Mine went into production with mill throughput of 9,100 tonnes per day. In 1971, Endako Mines amalgamated with Placer Development and became a division of that company. The mine was processing molybdenite ore at full capacity, a rate of 28,000 tonnes per day by 1980, making it the largest molybdenum mine in Canada and the second largest in the world.

Unfortunately, the global molybdenum market collapsed shortly afterwards; in 1982, operations at the mine were suspended. Mining and concentrating resumed on a limited scale in 1986 and, by 1989, when the market recovered, the mine and milling facility returned to full capacity.

In 1997, Thompson Creek Metals Company Inc. and a Japanese joint venture partner acquired the operations from Placer Dome. Endako Mine was operated as a joint venture (Thompson Creek 75 per cent interest and Japan-based Sojitz Corporation, 25 per cent).

A relatively young company, Thompson Creek Metals believed in the star quality of molybdenum. It had in its portfolio the world's fourth (Thompson Creek Mine, Idaho) and fifth (Endako) largest open-pit primary molybdenum mines. It was one of the world's largest publicly traded pure molybdenum producers. It also owned a metallurgical facility in Pennsylvania and the established Davidson molybdenum deposit (formerly known as Yorke-Hardy) near Smithers, B.C. It also had another copper-molybdenum-silver deposit, the Berg, near Houston, B.C.

Although the tale of Endako spanned more than 40 years of near-continuous production, the story seemed far from over. A consultant's study in mid-2007 estimated that proven and probable reserves would support a mine life of 27 years, based on an assumed price of $10 per pound for molybdenum. In late 2007, Thompson Creek commissioned a feasibility study on a proposed mill expansion from 28,000 to 50,000 tonnes of ore per day. In March 2008, the company announced a decision to proceed with the expansion plan that included the modernization of the aging 1965 mill and the amalgamation of the three existing pits into one super pit.

Kevin Loughrey, president and CEO, Thompson Creek Metals, said, "The combination of the super pit and the expansion of the mill capacity will allow us to increase our annual production. Also, as time moves on, we will be able to maintain higher production than we otherwise would because as the grade gets lower towards the back end of the mine life, we will be moving more tonnage through, therefore we can continue to keep up production. And, we can do it all at a lower cost because we have a more modern mill, an improved grinding system and in-process flow control, which allows us to get a better recovery from the ore."

Endako has long been a major contributor to the economic wellbeing of Fraser Lake and many of the smaller communities in the vicinity.

Prior to the feasibility study, the mine was forecast to be mined out around 2010. The news that the mine would last another 16 years was warmly greeted by the town. Exploration work on the Endako property outside the pits was ongoing and involved aerial geophysical and geochemical soil sampling surveys. There was a good likelihood that the resource would be further expanded.

In March 2012, Endako completed its expansion, including the completion of a new mill. The $500-million expansion increased milling capacity from 28,000 to 55,000 tonnes per day. The expansion created 160 new jobs, leading to sustained employment of 400 people in northern B.C.

The Endako mine from the air, 2007.

Artist's view of the Endako mill and mine complex upon opening, 1965.

Hauling waste rock at Phoenix, 1917

Granby Mining

Destined to overshadow all other mining operations in B.C. at the time, the Granby Mining Corp. was virtually synonymous with copper for the first half of the 20th century.

Although the name changed throughout the years, the value of its sustainable and innovative ideas made Granby one of the first mining powerhouses in the province's history. Granby developed a rare talent for discovering and developing mines, enabling it to play a large role in shaping the province's future. It had operating mines in B.C. for about eighty years and was among the province's greats.

Granby's most influential mine was Phoenix Mountain. Its story began in the late 1850s as prospectors searched the banks of Boundary Creek for placer gold. In the surrounding area, they stumbled upon a large copper deposit in the remote and undeveloped hills. While big, the deposit was low grade and was untouched until the 1890s.

Henry White (Knob Hill Mine) and Matthew Hatter (Old Ironsides Mine) staked the first claims in 1891. Interest heightened when the ores were found to be self-fluxing (requiring only the addition of coke for direct smelting, an affordable treatment). In 1896, J. F. C. Miner, president of Granby Rubber Company, of Granby, Que., along with mining promoter Jay P. Graves and A. L. Little, from Spokane, Wash., formed the Miner-Graves Syndicate and began buying claims. In 1901, they consolidated all of the syndicate's companies and properties under a new company, Granby Consolidated Mining, Smelting and Power Company Limited (shortened to Granby Mining Company Limited in 1963).

Seeking a favourable site for their smelter and a reliable water supply with beneficial tax incentives, the promoters approached the city council of Grand Forks. On May 16, 1899, a deal was announced that gave Granby Consolidated as much flow from the north fork of the Kettle River as they required, as well as a nearby site to construct a smelter. By late 1899, Granby's first smelter was completed at the confluence of the Granby and Kettle Rivers. A long, earth-filled dam, constructed across the Granby River, created Smelter Lake.

On April 11, 1900, the first batch of processed ore was delivered by wagon from Phoenix. That year, Canadian Pacific Railway built a spur line to the smelter, hauling its first ore in June. On October 11, the small settlement of Phoenix celebrated the railway's arrival by incorporating itself as a city.

The Phoenix mine now employed over 500 men and became generally known as the "Granby Mine" as it dwarfed all other operations on Phoenix Mountain. It was the largest copper smelter in the British Empire during its period of operation, from 1900 to 1919 and, by 1904 the Phoenix mine was the largest underground copper operation in North America. In 1906, Granby accounted for nearly three-fourths of the mineral wealth pouring out of the Boundary District. The smelter shipped its blister copper as far as New York and Liverpool.

As the operations advanced, Granby began an aggressive modernization program. The company ordered two giant steam shovels but, more significantly, it also invented a new style of ore car, described below.

The town of Phoenix at 4,500 feet had a peak population of 2,500, and was serviced by two railroads. *The Western Miner* reported: "It also had 17 saloons, all operating 24 hours a day, and supporting 30 professional gamblers." Old timers remembered that Phoenix had 12 houses of ill repute; business boomed.

In 1919, a strike by coal miners at Fernie stopped the flow of coking coal to Granby's smelter. The entire operation shut down. (This incident encouraged Granby to engage in coal mining itself with the Cassidy Coal Company on Vancouver Island, thus allowing it to supply coal directly to the Anyox copper smelter.) Phoenix re-opened in the early 1930s and then again in the late 1950s as an open pit.

While the Phoenix mine prospered for years, clearly it could not last forever and alternatives were sought early on. In 1901, the Hidden Creek copper deposits had been discovered at the head of the Observatory Inlet, 145 kilometres north of Prince Rupert. The first inhabitants of the area, the Nisga'a of the Nass Valley, called the area Anyoose.

Many prospectors searched for the place after hearing native legends of a "golden mountain" in the area. These supposed riches were, in fact, large amounts of pyrite or fool's gold. But the early prospectors also found copper showings, enough evidence to encourage Granby to take over the existing claims and begin construction of a mine, plant and town it would name Anyox.

Construction began in 1912 and production started just two years later. The Anyox plant consisted of a smelter, a 5,000-ton mill, concentrator, coke plant, powerhouses, dam and an electric railway. Almost everything was owned by Granby, including a hospital, schools, library, and even a movie theatre.

The Hidden Creek mine became the company's most important property. Anyox produced 685 million pounds of copper, 140,000 oz of gold and 7 million oz silver by the time the plants were closed in 1935, owing to low copper prices and the exhaustion of richer ores. The town (population 2,500) was more or less abandoned. It was estimated that there were nearly two and a half million tons of low-grade ore still in the mines. Granby sold the property to Cominco for $300,000.

As the years went by, Granby grew in stature and portfolio. In 1923, the company acquired the Copper Mountain mine, located about 15 kilometres southwest of Princeton. A milling facility was built in the nearby town of Allenby. Production began in 1923 and continued until the Depression forced its closure in 1930.

In 1936 Granby put itself into voluntary receivership. When it proposed receivership, the price of copper had dropped to two cents per pound, and Granby had volumes of unsold copper stockpiled at Anyox. In 1937, it received a "stay of proceedings" and resumed production at Copper Mountain. Business had picked up again.

In the 1970s, a junior company discovered the Ingerbelle deposit on the north (highway) side of the Similkameen.

John Jewitt, one of the last presidents of Granby, recalled that instead of negotiating the acquisition of the Ingerbelle, Granby's president (Larry Postle) and controlling shareholders decided to sell the Copper Mountain property to Newmont Mining for $10 million cash. Newmont subsequently developed Similkameen Mining into a major producer, and created a spectacular bridge and conveyor system across the Similkameen valley to convey ore from Copper Mountain to Newmont's mill on the Ingerbelle side.

(Ownership changed several times over the next two decades. Its owner in 2011 was Copper Mountain Mining Corporation. With support from Mitsubishi Materials Corporation, the company put Copper Mountain back into production with a conventional open pit mine and a 35,000-ton per day mill in the summer of 2011.)

The Jedway iron-copper mine was also added to Granby's portfolio. The mine, located on the Queen Charlotte Islands, operated from 1906 to 1920 with the original town site located at Ikeda Cove. The mine re-opened from 1961 to 1969 and is now within Gwaii Haanas National Park.

In 1965, Granby opened its open-pit copper mine on McDonald Island on Babine Lake; as a result, the town of Granisle was forged with an economy based on copper mining. The name Granisle was created as a combination of "gran" for Granby and "isle," for the island where the mine was located.

The Granisle mine was another example of Granby innovation. During the winter, a bubbler system maintained an ice-free channel on Babine Lake so barges could easily pass through. Compressed air was injected into a pipe suspended between sinks and floats, forming a parabolic curve under the lake's surface all the way from the townsite at Granisle to the island where the mine was located. Tiny holes were drilled at intervals along the length of the pipe and by the time the tiny bubbles reached the surface they had expanded to form large bubbles, thereby maintaining an ice-free channel. Crews were transported to the mine daily and concentrates were barged in transport trucks back to Granisle and thence to Prince Rupert.

Jewitt had an interesting perspective on the company's eventual change of ownership. He recalled: "Around 1970, when Granby was shipping iron and copper concentrates to Japan from Jedway Iron, and copper-gold-silver concentrates from Phoenix Copper and Granisle Copper, a guy named Rene Wolcott (president of Pacific Clay & Pipe in Los Angeles) stood on the New York Stock Exchange and paid any asking price to acquire control of Granby. On average, he paid about $36 per share, at a time when it had been trading at around $22 (I think)."

At this time, Larry Postle resigned as president of Granby, and Bob Matthews became president, and John Jewitt became vice president and general manager (promoted from Phoenix). But the clay sewer-pipe manufacturer was unable to hang on and sold Wolcott's 50 per cent controlling interest to Zapata Corporation of Houston, Texas.

George Bush (Sr.), who would later become president of the United States, had formed Zapata in the 1960s as an offshore drilling company. Bush took it to about $300 million in revenue, then sold out in order to enter politics. Subsequently, according to Jewitt, Zapata became a classic 1960s conglomerate with annual revenues over $1 billion.

"Zapata re-organized Granby with Bob Matthews continuing as president, Roger Taylor became vice president operations and I became vice president exploration," said Jewitt. After about two years, Matthews resigned to become managing director of MABC. Jewitt became president of Granby, and subsequently moved to Houston in 1975 as vice president mining for Zapata Corp. Taylor was then appointed president of Granby.

Jewitt wrote: "Zapata went on to acquire over 90 per cent of Granby, but was unable to achieve its target of 100 per cent because they were blocked by Ottawa under FIRA (Foreign Investment Review Act). It had been Zapata's intention to use Granby as its worldwide mining vehicle. After several attempts to acquire Noranda's Bell Copper operation near Granisle Copper and to acquire the Equity Silver deposit southeast of Houston, B.C. (subsequently developed by Placer Development),

Zapata sold Granby to Noranda — end of story!"

Throughout Granby's history, the company was also involved in the early exploration of many projects still in operation today.

In 1931, mineralization was discovered on Granduc Mountain in northwest B.C., with claims staked in 1946. Exploration and development began in 1953 as a joint venture between Granby and Newmont Mining Corp. Ltd. After completing development on three mining levels at the Leduc Deposit, Granby sold its interest to Newmont in 1956. Newmont, in turn, sold a 50 per cent interest in the project to ASARCO and formed Granduc Operation Company, which operated the mine from 1971 to 1978. Esso Minerals re-opened the mine and operated it from 1979 until closure in 1984. Bell Copper acquired the property in 2004 and drilled successfully within a four-kilometre range of the original mine. In 2010, Castle Resources Inc. acquired a six-year option to acquire up to 80 per cent of Bell's interest in the Granduc mine by spending $25 million on exploration and drilling; providing project financing, it could acquire a further ten per cent.

Granby was also involved in the early exploration of the Sulphurets Creek Camp, located in the Iskut-Stikine River region, about 65 kilometres northwest of Stewart, B.C. Seabridge Gold Inc. of Toronto subsequently acquired the Kerr-Sulphurets-Mitchell (KSM) project. In May 2011, Seabridge released a preliminary KSM feasibility study that put proven and probable reserves at 38.5 million ounces gold, 10 billion pounds copper, 214 million ounces silver and 257 million pounds

molybdenum. Seabridge said KSM was one of the largest undeveloped gold projects in the world.

Granby Cars

Granby Consolidated Mining and Smelting Company's lasting innovation was the self-dumping Granby mine car, designed at the Phoenix mine. Originally based on a wooden car, the Granby car, in its ultimate form, was first introduced in 1905 when twenty 10-ton steel cars were built for use on the main haulage levels. With one edge of the box hinged to the side of the car's frame and a wheel assembly on the opposite edge which engages an elevated rail parallel to the track at the dump site, the box is raised to an angle of 45 degrees, spilling the contents sideways into the ore or waste pass. This self-dumping feature was a significant time-saver, and an order of magnitude step forward in safety.

Granby cars are still widely used today. They are rugged and can handle large volumes (up to 180 cubic feet capacity) of material.

Other innovations at the Phoenix included a drill sharpening machine, which saved time and money by eliminating the need for many blacksmiths and forges; and an automatic furnace charger at the smelter, again enhancing and greatly reducing time and labour requirements.

Drilling at Copper Mountain Mine, 1947

Playing on the Granby Car, 1961

Core sheds at Mount Polley mine

Imperial Metals Corporation

Imperial Metals has a comparatively long history for a junior company. In the late 1950s – when it was Imperial Metals and Power – its prospectus described it as seeking to develop a wide range of products: coal, coke limestone, electricity, iron, copper, gypsum, amongst others.

The company's early years culminated in 1981 with the formation of Imperial Metals Corporation, with the amalgamation of Invex Resources, Western Rolling Hills and Risby Tungsten, under the leadership of Alan Savage.

In the early 1980s, E&B Explorations, a German drilling fund operator, was seeking to monetize its Canadian investments, prompting management to look for suitable reverse-takeover candidates. Dr. Hugh Morris, E&B's president, led the initiative.

Morris soon focused on the newly-created Imperial Metals. Dr. Peter Geib, then chairman of Imperial recalled: "We saw, in Imperial, a junior company with an excellent track record led by Alan Savage, a highly-regarded dealmaker and John McGorran, a geologist with a keen eye for good properties." Morris and Savage skillfully rolled E&B's assets into Imperial for shares, achieving their liquidity objectives and launching E&B as an independent public mining company via Imperial.

The company then entered a long period of rationalization, selling off non-core assets and gradually focusing Imperial's growth on copper and precious metals; its oil and gas assets provided a solid cash flow.

When Savage left Imperial in 1986 to pursue other initiatives, Pierre Lebel became president. What started out as a temporary assignment continued for a decade and a half, until the early part of the 21st century, when Lebel took over as chairman.

Highlights of the period 1986 to 1993 included the creation, financing and listing of Cathedral Gold Corporation on the Toronto Stock Exchange and Anglesey Mining Plc. on the London Stock Exchange; the permitting and development of the Crow Butte *in situ* leach uranium project in Nebraska (which was subsequently sold to Cameco Corporation) and numerous exploration programs in British Columbia, including Bronson Creek, Takla, Rainbow, Porcher Island and Ato. Imperial also owned a majority stake in the Sterling gold mine in Nevada.

It was also during this period that Imperial began focusing on Mount Polley.

Mount Polley
Copper-Gold-Silver Mine

The Mount Polley deposit was discovered in 1963 during follow-up prospecting of an anomaly highlighted on a government aeromagnetic map sheet. Mastodon Highland Bell Mines Limited and Leitch Gold Mines had staked claims in 1964 on the property 100 km northeast of Williams Lake. In 1966 the two companies merged to form Cariboo-Bell Copper Mines Limited. Teck Corporation assumed control of Cariboo-Bell in 1969. Highland Crow Resources, an affiliate of Teck, acquired control in 1978.

During 1966 through 1979, extensive geophysical work (magnetic, seismic and induced polarization surveys) plus diamond drill core and percussion drilling were undertaken at Mount Polley.

In 1981, E&B Explorations Inc. optioned the property from Highland Crow and by 1982, had acquired a 100 per cent interest. E&B conducted exploration on the property with joint venture partners Geomex Partnerships and Imperial.

E&B subsequently merged with Mascot Gold Mines, which merged with Corona Corporation and then became Homestake Canada. In 1987 Imperial purchased Homestake's remaining interest in the property.

During 1988 to 1990, Imperial conducted a comprehensive exploration program before commissioning a feasibility study by Wright Engineers, based on a 5-million tonne-per-year plant. The study incorporated new ore reserve calculations, metallurgical testing, geotechnical evaluations and environmental impact assessments.

Imperial tried to move the project forward but got caught when metal prices declined. Its partner, Corona (Homestake Canada), sold its 38 per cent interest in the project to Imperial for $6 million in cash and shares. Imperial continued to advance the project in other ways. In 1992 it obtained a mine development certificate, also completing acquisition of Geomex Limited Partnerships, which gave Imperial a 100 per cent interest in Mount Polley.

After six profitable years, the company incurred operating losses in 1992 and 1993 forcing a decision to re-organize and downsize.

Imperial's fortunes were soon to rise again with the acquisition of control in 1994 by Calgary entrepreneur Murray Edwards.

That year the stock almost doubled to $1.15. Edwards wanted Imperial to move forward as quickly as possible with Mount Polley but the company's downsizings had left it too lean. Edwards encouraged Lebel to hire the needed talent.

Lebel immediately called Brian Kynoch who, at that time, was president of Bethlehem Copper, chaired by Henry Ewanchuck. Kynoch and Ewanchuck had impeccable credentials, a great track record in mine development and operations and an established relationship with Sumitomo Corporation.

Although Kynoch was intrigued by the challenge, he could not bring himself to abandon his Bethlehem shareholders. The talks then turned to the possibility of a merger. Imperial's board recognized the value of the people and Bethlehem's relationship with Sumitomo. Seeing real value for these intangibles, it approved the merger.

Ewanchuck and Kynoch immediately got to work on Mount Polley, putting together a strong management team. Project development financing was provided by Sumitomo Corporation, which acquired a 45 per cent interest.

Imperial completed an update of the Wright Engineers study and loan financing was arranged with Sumitomo Corporation through a joint venture with SC Minerals Canada Ltd. , which culminated in the formation of Mount Polley Mining Corporation in April 1996.

Construction of the 18,000-tonne-per-day Mount Polley mine and milling facility began in May 1996 and was completed in June 1997. The estimated cost was $123.5 million with a 17-month construction time. The project was completed under budget, for $115 million, and five months ahead of schedule. The mill startup and commissioning occurred in late June, with the mill rising towards design capacity by year end.

With Mount Polley in production, Imperial sought to consolidate its position in the mine and pursue other opportunities for growth and, in 1998, merged with Princeton Mining Corporation, which held a 60 per cent interest in the Huckleberry copper molybdenum mine near Houston, B.C.

However, Imperial found itself in difficulties as it struggled to break even under adverse conditions during the late 1990s. Project debt was restructured, costs were rolled back. With two mines in production in British Columbia and one in the U.S., Imperial seemed poised for significant growth but low metals prices kept the mines from achieving their expected financial returns.

The B.C. government provided a financial support package, which included cheaper power for both Mount Polley and Huckleberry. These measures enabled the Huckleberry Mine to remain in production, but the outlook for Mount Polley, facing pre-stripping costs of $15 million for the Springer pit, was less hopeful. Sumitomo decided to exit the project, selling its entire debt and equity in Mount Polley to Imperial for $11 million.

Mount Polley operated for four years from 1997 to 2001. Then, in September 2001, due to sustained low metal prices, mining operations were suspended and the property placed on care and maintenance. During the shut down, exploration activities continued. Kynoch's thinking was that, with flow-through funds readily available for exploration in Canada, the company should

be exploring at Mount Polley to add to resources already in place, making the project more robust when mine operations eventually restarted.

In a surprisingly short period, prospecting at the northeast end of the property identified some promising outcrop. Subsequent trenching exposed a large zone of high-grade copper, gold and silver mineralization. The first hole drilled into the zone intersected 57 metres grading 2.54 per cent copper, 1.15 grams per tonne gold and some 17 grams per tonne silver. It was a significant discovery located two kilometres north of the mill. In less than six months, the company's stock rose from a low of 31 cents to $7. "After all the company had been through, it was great to see support coming back for Imperial," Lebel recalled.

In 2002, Imperial completely re-organized its operations into two businesses, one concentrating on mining, and the other focusing on oil and gas. The latter assets were eventually sold, refocusing the company's business solely in base metals.

In 2003, the discovery of a new high-grade zone on the Mount Polley property, together with the rise in metal prices, led to the decision to re-open the mine. In August 2004, Imperial completed additional feasibility study work on Mount Polley that included an updated ore reserve statement, a new mining plan, and confirmed the viability of restarting mine operations.

Exploration work continued on the new discovery, the Northeast zone, and also located new high-grade ore

beneath the existing Springer pit. Imperial was able to hang on to most of these gains with the stock trading strongly between the $5 and $6 range.

In October 2004, a mining permit amendment and a mining lease were granted to include mining of the Northeast zone. Milling operations commenced in March 2005. The first copper concentrate shipment of approximately 11,500 tonnes from the re-opened mine was dispatched in July 2005.

Huckleberry Copper-Molybdenum Mine

Copper mineralization at Huckleberry was first discovered by Kennco Explorations (Western) Limited in 1962. Several companies had options to the property until 1994, when New Canamin became the sole owner of the Mount Polley property for a short period. It was Princeton Mining Corporation's acquisition of New Canamin and subsequent merger with Imperial that led to Imperial's involvement in both Mount Polley and Huckleberry

In July 1995, Princeton Mining Corporation acquired all the shares of New Canamin. A strategic alliance with the Japan Group (a consortium of Japanese copper smelters, Mitsubishi Materials Corporation, Dowa Mining Co. Ltd. and Furukawa Co. Ltd.) was established to assist in financing the project. A feasibility study was commissioned by Princeton in early 1995 and completed by H. A. Simons in August 1995.

In June 1996, the Japan Group purchased a 40 per cent equity position in Huckleberry and entered into an agreement to provide $60 million of project loan financing based on the positive feasibility. The Japanese consortium also entered into a long-term contract for the purchase of all copper concentrates from the Huckleberry mine.

The British Columbia government provided financial assistance in the form of a $15 million loan to Huckleberry for infrastructure including roads and power lines.

An additional $4.5 million of equity was injected into the project by Princeton and the Japan Group in November 1997. Marubeni Corporation provided a $10 million loan to Huckleberry for working capital. With financing in place, the construction of the mine commenced in June 1996. The total cost to construct, install and commission the facilities was approximately $142 million.

Imperial's 1998 merger with Princeton Mining Corporation netted Imperial a 50 per cent interest in Huckleberry Mines Ltd., owner of the Huckleberry mine.

In 2011, a new mine plan was completed for extension of the mine to 2021. Huckleberry had the funds to complete the extension, and on January 3, 2012, announced that it had received permits to confirm the extension of the mine life.

Sterling Gold Property

Imperial's Sterling gold property and mine northwest of Las Vegas, Nevada, operated as an underground and open-pit mine from 1980 to 2000. During its 20-year life, the mine produced 194,996 troy ounces from 941,341 short tons of ore with an average grade of 0.217 ounces per ton (7.44 grams per ton) gold.

In 2001, Imperial's exploration team discovered a deep high-grade gold zone, the "144," located south of the historic Sterling mine workings in an entirely new setting similar to the gold deposits in the Carlin Trend.

Between 2002 and 2005, the company conducted aggressive exploration programs, and in 2006 obtained permitting for construction of an underground ramp to access the 144 zone. The 1,021-metre ramp and two exploration drifts off the main decline below the 144 zone were completed in 2007, followed by exploration focusing on delineation and expansion of the 144 zone and underground development for additional underground drill stations.

During 2011 plans were underway to complete construction of a new leach pad and recovery plant that would allow the restart of gold production at Sterling. These facilities would be put in place to generate cash flow to fund further development and exploration of the 144 zone. The total capital cost of implementing this plan was estimated to be $8 million.

Red Chris Copper-Gold Property

The Red Chris property was acquired by Imperial in 2007 following a takeover battle for bcMetals Corporation. The property, located 80 km south of Dease Lake, in northwest British Columbia, had become a game-changer for both Imperial and the Province of British Columbia as a prospective address for world class deposits.

The deposit, to be developed as a 30,000-tonne-per-day open-pit mine in tandem with construction of British Columbia's Northwest Transmission Line, is situated only 20 km from Highway 37. Plans are to tie in to the Northwest Transmission Line, which would occur at the Bob Quinn power station approximately 120 km from the proposed mill site.

Red Chris has provincial and federal environmental approvals for mine development as well as Mines Act permit. Viewed by industry analysts as one of the most important discoveries ever made in British Columbia, the start of production is contingent on the completion of the Northwest Transmission Line in 2014.

Examining a core sample at a Noranda property.

Noranda

Only a handful of mineral deposits in the world are known as "company-makers," one being the great Horne copper deposit discovered by prospector Edmund Horne (1865-1952) in Quebec's Rouyn Township during the early 1900s.

Rarer still are companies that grow from a single mine into a diversified resource conglomerate with a global presence, as Noranda Mines ultimately did after it was established to develop the Horne deposit in 1922.

James Murdoch (1890-1962), the first president of the fledgling company, had the vision to develop the Horne mine and nearby copper smelter as a foundation for growth into other mines and commodities. His successors, notably John Bradfield (1899-1983) and Alfred Powis (1930-2007), further elevated the status of the company through global expansion, resource diversification, technical innovation and the value-added production of refined and finished products from raw materials.

The name is no more, as Noranda became part of Falconbridge, which was acquired by Swiss-based Xstrata in 2006 but the company's legacy endures as a uniquely Canadian success story. As Murdoch once commented, Noranda's growth could not have happened if Canada had not been what it is, "…a great and rich young nation whose frontiers beckon the man in whom the spirit of high adventure is strong."

Noranda looked towards western Canada for much of its growth in the post-war years, says John Kalmet, who spent 25 years with Noranda Minerals, including as General Manager, Western Canada, from 1983 to 1989. "Commodities go up and down, so they believed they could achieve a degree of revenue stability by being exposed to a lot of different [resource] products," Kalmet said.

Copper was Noranda's cornerstone in the early years, hence initial exploration efforts were focused on finding replacement deposits for the Horne mine, expected to be depleted by the mid-1970s, and securing feed for the Horne smelter. Noranda created an exploration arm to pursue these objectives, which achieved great success in 1947, when geologist Archibald Bell (1906-1991) discovered the high-grade Needle Mountain deposit on a copper prospect he had optioned a decade earlier in the Gaspé region of Quebec. Needle Mountain and the nearby Copper Mountain deposit were placed into production by Gaspé Copper in 1955, and operated for decades.

Bell, who took the helm of Noranda Exploration in 1947, embraced new frontiers of technology to aid the company's post-war exploration efforts across Canada. Noranda's exploration arm helped pioneer geochemical exploration, portable geophysical instrumentation and rock alteration studies as guides to ore deposits.

The discovery of porphyry copper deposits in the Highland Valley region in the mid-1950s prompted Noranda and other senior producers to step up their exploration efforts in British Columbia. Bell launched an exploration program near Babine Lake, which led to the discovery of a copper deposit in 1963. A mine hosting reserves of 46 million tons averaging 0.5 per cent copper was developed, named in Bell's honour.

Bernard Brynelsen (1911-2004), a B.C.-born mining engineer known as "Noranda's man in the West," led the development of the Brenda copper-molybdenum mine in the Okanagan district – no easy task with a grade of 0.183 per cent copper and 0.049 per cent molybdenum.

"It became a very successful mine and operated for twenty years," says Betty O'Keefe, who worked with the Noranda group of companies from 1974 to 1988.

The introduction of new technology contributed to the mine's success, such as computerized control and monitoring of the milling process. "The mine also had some outstanding managers over the years," she adds.

Noranda had other operations in B.C., including the Boss Mountain molybdenum mine in the Cariboo region, the Granisle copper mine situated near the Bell mine, the Goldstream copper-zinc mine near Revelstoke, and the Kennedy Lake (iron) and Yreka (copper-silver-gold) mines, both on Vancouver Island.

Based on past experience, Kalmet says, "Four elements are essential to making a successful mine: the markets, and understanding where they're going; the deposits (grade, tonnage and detrimental elements if any); infrastructure; and dedicated people.

"People are most important. There has to be a champion who carries the project forward.

"And that applies to people who lead exploration, as well as running mines," Kalmet says.

Kalmet cites John Harvey, Gavin E. Dirom and Lawrie Reinertsen as having played important roles in Noranda's exploration efforts in the West.

Kalmet says, "Juniors are often better at making discoveries than senior producers such as Noranda, which typically acquire most of the projects later developed into mines But large companies have to be involved with the exploration scene, in the field, because that's the best way to learn about and acquire positions in new discoveries."

One such example for Noranda was the acquisition of a gold project in the Hemlo region of Ontario from Vancouver-based Golden Sceptre and Goliath Resources in the early 1980s. Noranda developed the project into the Golden Giant mine, which produced more than six million ounces of gold from 1985 until its closure in 2006.

Noranda's exploration team contributed to several B.C. discoveries, including several being advanced by other companies today. Noranda also acquired interests in various mining companies over the years, including 27 per cent of Placer Development (later Placer Dome), which operated the Craigmont (copper), Endako (molybdenum) and Gibraltar (copper) mines; and Western Mines (later Westmin), operator of the Myra Falls zinc-copper-gold-silver mine, on Vancouver Island. Noranda also held various interests in Falconbridge before it merged with the nickel giant in 2005.

Foreign frontiers beckoned to Noranda as well. Long-time Noranda veteran Michael Knuckey is credited with the discovery and development of at least ten deposits in Canada and abroad, eight of which later became mines, including the world-class Collahuasi copper mine, in Chile; and the Antamina copper-zinc mine, in Peru.

Kalmet says, "Noranda was a leader in safety and research, but adds that an often over-looked element of its success was its management style, which evolved over time to one where employee empowerment became a guiding principle. They gave their people a fair amount of latitude, let them grow and innovate and I think that brought out the best in the team."

As an example, Kalmet points to the 1980s, when many copper mines were facing closure because of low metal prices. The company eliminated layers of management and negotiated lower power rates with the B.C. government's Critical Industries Commission as part of a joint effort to keep B.C. mines operating and save jobs. "We placed Bell Copper back in operation, with a much smaller crew, who also shared in the mine's profitability. It was wonderful to see this operation prosper even in an adverse economic environment."

O'Keefe agrees that people were one of Noranda's most important assets.

"In the mining end, I must say they were all clever and conscientious people."

Global exploration and development – a Placer Dome trademark

Placer Development Ltd. / Placer Dome Inc.

Placer Development, later Placer Dome Inc., began when two men got together in Vancouver in January 1926. One was William Addison Freeman, a successful Australian entrepreneur and president of the Austral-Malay Tin Company.

The other was Charles Arthur Banks, a New Zealand-born mining engineer who managed the B.C. Silver Company for the Victoria Mining Syndicate, of London.

Freeman, seeking investment opportunities, had been advised that Banks might suggest promising placer gold properties. The pair got along famously. Freeman offered to underwrite a new mining venture if Banks would manage it. They shook hands on it. The men quickly recruited dredge designer Frank W. Griffin and dredging engineer Harold Peake as directors. Within weeks, the four met in San Francisco, decided to hire a geologist to test promising properties and budgeted $40,000 for the first year's operations. Vancouver, where Banks lived, was chosen for the company's headquarters as, at that time, Canadian tax laws were favourable.

Placer Development Ltd. was incorporated in B.C. on May 26, 1926 with $200,000 in share capital. In its first two years, it investigated gold properties in Alaska, Colombia, California, Oregon and B.C. without success.

The company scored a major success, however, in 1929, dredging for gold on the remote Bulolo River in Australian-administered New Guinea. Australian prospectors had earlier discovered rich deposits of alluvial gold on the Bulolo and its tributaries. An enterprising government official, Cecil Levein, convinced that much of the gold had been widely scattered by the river, staked out 1,500 acres of the

Bulolo Valley. William Freeman acquired Levein's leases in 1928 on the understanding that the Australian government would build a road to the inaccessible gold field. When test drilling indicated the Bulolo riverbed contained still richer gold deposits, Placer purchased adjoining leases and equipped the property with dredges. The company increased its capitalization to $500,000 and organized Bulolo Gold Dredging Ltd. to develop the New Guinea leases. But, when the Depression hit, the Australian government decided it could no longer afford to build the access road.

Undaunted, the company bought three German Junkers G31 tri-motor aircraft, built an airstrip on the banks of the Bulolo and flew disassembled machinery in over the mountains. The first reassembled steel bucket-dredge began operations in 1932. By the end of the decade, seven more dredges, hydroelectric power, a machine shop, and living and recreational facilities for more than 1,000 employees had been constructed at the site.

Bulolo was spectacularly successful. The gold-bearing gravel deposits ran much deeper than estimates had indicated and, in 1934, the United States raised the official price of gold from $20 to $35 an ounce. Placer declared its first dividend in 1933 and, in the next year, its authorized capitalization was increased to $1 million. In 1935, when the world economy was stagnant and unemployment soared to record levels, Placer's net profit increased from $108,000 to $1.5 million.

The company invested surplus capital in new ventures: Canadian Exploration Ltd. (Canex) was formed to explore for minerals in Canada; oil leases in Texas were purchased; and two other companies (Rutherglen Gold Dumps Ltd. and Gold Dumps Proprietary Ltd.) were set up in Australia to reclaim gold from tailings. Subsidiaries Pato Consolidated Gold Dredging Ltd. and Asnazu Gold Dredging Ltd. were also organized in Colombia. These subsidiaries would play a prominent role in Placer's growth. Although conditions in Colombia were incredibly difficult, by 1940, Pato and Asnazu were producing more than 125,000 ounces of gold a year.

World War II forced Placer to abandon mining and exploration work in Australia, Canada and the United States. In January 1942, Japanese planes destroyed the company's three Junkers aircraft. When the Japanese captured the nearby coast, the Australians hastily razed Bulolo. The army built a road to the coast, obviating expensive air transportation. Following the end of hostilities, the Australian government awarded Placer a subsidy of $4 million to rebuild Bulolo.

Placer's most important venture shortly after World War II occurred in Canada, with its acquisition in 1947 of the Emerald underground tungsten mine, on a mountain near Salmo, in southeastern B.C. Big deposits of lead and zinc were discovered the next year. With a drop in the price of tungsten, the mill was converted to lead-zinc production from the nearby Jersey mine. Another large tungsten orebody was discovered in 1950 beneath the lead-zinc deposits. The Korean War bumped up the price of tungsten and a lucrative seven-year contract with the U.S. government enabled Placer to re-open the Emerald mine. A new tungsten mill was built on the mountainside and Placer began extracting two entirely different types of ore from interconnected underground mines.

More than a thousand people worked at the height of construction on the Emerald and Jersey mines, and much innovation and ingenuity was applied to mining activities, including the first adoption of trackless mechanized mining in Canada. Many came to refer to "Salmo Mining University." People trained at Canex spread across Canada and left a large imprint on the development of the international mining industry.

The B.C. venture had a profound impact on Placer's future. Earnings from the new mine gave the parent company a record profit of $11 million in 1955. The highly profitable Salmo operation came at a time when Placer's gold dredging operations in New Guinea and Colombia were past their prime.

In 1957, Placer leased an entire floor in Vancouver's first modern high rise office, the Burrard Building, to house the rapidly growing staff and its new subsidiary, Canex Aerial Exploration Ltd. formed in January of that year to undertake mineral exploration in Western Canada, Yukon and NWT. The company embarked on still more aggressive exploration and development. Then president, John D. Simpson, recalled: "A Texas corporation made us an offer [in 1959] that was difficult to resist. We had equity of only $950,000 in [the Texas oil company] Coronet, but we got more than $12 million for it."

This windfall did not lie idle. The company bought S & M Fox, an Australian mining and manufacturing company in 1960, and Placer joined Noranda and several other mining companies in financing the Mattagami zinc-copper mine in northwestern Quebec. When drilling near Merritt revealed the existence of a massive copper orebody, Placer, Noranda and Peerless Oil negotiated a substantial development loan from Canadian and American banks to develop the Craigmont mine.

Craigmont sparked the investment interest of Canadian banks and was the first of a series of bank-financed copper mines that stimulated B.C.'s mining industry in the 1960s and made the province one of the world's important suppliers of copper concentrate. Placer was now able to attract the large sums of loan capital required to develop major mining ventures like the open-pit molybdenum mine at Endako, B.C. Low-grade deposits of molybdenite had been discovered near the village of Endako in 1927, but several companies had concluded that they were not economic. Finally, after an intensive program of test-drilling, Placer negotiated an agreement in 1963 to construct a mine and thereby earned a substantial interest in the property.

The mill was brought into production in 1965 at a daily capacity of 10,000 tons of ore. Demand for molybdenum proved so strong that mill capacity was increased to 27,000 tons per day in 1967, and development loans were retired within three years. Tax advantages brought the amalgamation of Endako and Placer in 1970. With improved production methods, mill throughput was increased to 31,400 tons per day in 1980.

Dividends from Endako and Mattagami mines, the latter having been brought into production by Noranda in 1964, further enhanced Placer's capital position and assisted the company's continuing search for viable properties.

The company's operations were shut down in Colombia (1957) and in New Guinea (1965) as ore reserves were exhausted. Placer accelerated its search for new mines. Between 1965 and 1968 the annual sum earmarked for exploration increased from $1 million to more than $5 million.

In the late 1960s and early 1970s the company's activities increased dramatically in both size and international scope. Massive open-pit copper mines in British Columbia and the Philippines contributed most to Placer's growth in that period.

The development of the Marcopper mine, on Marinduque Island in the Philippines, was unusually venturesome. Before it could develop the mine, Placer had to create port facilities and build roads. To finance this work the company pledged all its assets to secure a $40-million loan in 1968 from a consortium of U.S. banks.

The venture proved enormously successful. Marcopper retired its development loans within two years and declared its first dividend in 1972.

Development of the giant Gibraltar mine in central B.C. demonstrated that careful engineering can make risks worthwhile. The presence of low-grade copper deposits in the area had been known since 1917 but Placer's geologists discovered in 1970 that there were additional reserves sufficient to support mining operations. Long-term sales contracts were arranged in Japan and Placer secured a development loan of $74 million, purchased a fleet of 100-ton trucks and proceeded to construct one of Canada's most important open-pit copper mines. Gibraltar began producing in 1972, ahead of schedule and under budget, with the concentrator operating well above the design capacity of 30,000 tons per day.

Both Marcopper and Gibraltar came into production during years of world economic expansion. The price of copper rose from 46 cents to 86 cents a pound in 1973 and continued rising in 1974. In 1973, with world metal prices climbing, Placer's net earnings rose to $71.8 million (versus $16.6 million in 1972).

In the years that followed, Placer experienced good and bad times.

In its 1976 annual report, the company complained about the Canadian investment climate that, it said, had deteriorated since the initiation of tax reforms nearly a decade earlier. "Government policies and practices at both federal and provincial levels, coupled with a worldwide recession, have reduced the attractiveness of investment in industry."

As a diversification into the energy field, Placer acquired 86.7 per cent control of Canadian Export Oil & Gas Company (CEGO) that had working interests in oil and gas leases in Canada, the North Sea and the United States.

Placer described 1977 as "An Unimpressive Year for Mining." Molybdenum was the only metal that contributed significantly to company earnings: (74.13 per cent versus copper 6.28 per cent and oil & gas 16.24 per cent). Ore reserves were nearing exhaustion at Craigmont, an important producer since 1961, and Gibraltar was losing money in the face of low metal prices.

Placer acquired a 70 per cent interest in Equity Silver Mines Ltd. , owner of the Sam Goosly silver property near Houston, B.C., which it decided to put into production. Construction began on a 4,500 metric ton-per-day plant early in 1979. In its day, Equity was the largest primary producer of silver concentrate in the world.

In its 1979 annual report, Placer announced that its earnings for the year were the highest in its history. Consolidated net earnings of $74.5 million were boosted by an extraordinary item of $38.5 million relating to a share swap of its 27.1 per cent interest in Mattagami Lake Mines Ltd. for a 5.5 per cent interest

in Noranda Mines Ltd. Placer subsequently increased its Noranda ownership stake (indirectly) to 7.7 per cent.

A deepening recession in 1981 was marked by severely depressed metal prices and reduced demand for molybdenum. The news got grimmer. In 1982 Placer reported a consolidated loss of $16.3 million. Economies had weakened through most of the year and the metals sector was especially depressed by poor industrial demand. The prices for Placer's most important products, molybdenum and copper, plummeted. Molybdenum was especially hard hit.

The Endako molybdenum mine was closed as markets worsened. Mining at Gibraltar was suspended in July 1982 although production continued with milling of low-grade material from stockpiles. Total employment by the Placer group in British Columbia was reduced by almost 1,000. Mineral exploration was significantly reduced and some further budget cutbacks were planned for 1983.

C. Allen Born, company chairman and CEO, who looked pensive in the 1981 annual report (and whose photo was absent in the austere corporate

Placer Dome

Environmental monitoring – a key element of mineral exploration and development by the 2000s

communiqué of 1982), had a smile on his face in 1983. As well he might. He reported to shareholders that, while most mining companies continued to report losses for 1983, Placer was an exception with consolidated net earnings of $29.2 million. He noted this was a significant improvement over 1982, when the company's restated loss was $20.2 million.

The company's decision in the late 1960s to emphasize precious metals, especially gold, led to the development of the comparatively small Cortez Gold mine in Nevada. Eventually, with the discovery of the Pipeline deposit in the 1990s, Cortez became a world-class gold mine. Following Cortez, a line-up of gold mines were developed in the 1980s starting with Golden Sunlight in Montana; Kidston, Granny Smith and Big Bell in Australia; Misima and Porgera in Papua New Guinea; and, finally, Musselwhite in northwestern Ontario.

Significant developments for Placer in 1985 were the successful start-up of Kidston, Australia's largest gold mine, and completion of the integration of an important new U.S. oil and gas unit into the Placer group. To comply with Australian laws, Placer sold off 20 per cent of the Kidston gold property, for a gain of $22.4 million. Reluctantly, it would reduce its Kidston ownership still further in coming years.

In 1987 Placer Development amalgamated with Dome Mines Ltd. (founded in 1910) and Campbell Red Lake Mines Ltd. (founded in 1944), both of Toronto, to become Placer Dome Inc. Placer Dome, with headquarters in Vancouver, made several acquisitions: Kiena Gold Mines Ltd. and Sigma Gold Mines Ltd. in 1988; Placer Pacific Ltd., in 1997; Getchell Gold Corporation, in 1999; Aurion Gold Ltd., in 2003; and East African Gold Mines Ltd., in 2003.

Despite a strong operating performance, Placer Dome recorded a loss of $236.2 million in 1991 due to a write-down on the carrying value of investments in mining properties. Still, it poured $480 million into exploration in the years 1991 to 1995. In doing so, it discovered an estimated 30 million ounces of gold (reserves, and other mineralized material) at an average finding cost of about $16 per ounce.

Placer Dome's growth continued. By 2005 it had interests in 17 mining operations in seven countries. Collectively, these operations produced 3.65 million ounces of gold. Two copper mines, including world-class Zaldivar direct-to-metal mine in Chile, complemented the company's gold business.

Placer Dome's 2004 exploration programs defined new reserves of 3.6 million ounces at existing mine sites. At the end of 2004, proven and probable gold reserves totalled 59.9 million ounces. In 2005, Placer Dome planned to spend $50 million on exploration. Its annual report declared: "2005 will be a defining year for Placer Dome."

Defining it was. But, presumably, not in the way the report's authors had in mind.

A predator pounced.

Obviously impressed by Placer Dome's rich potential, Barrick Gold Corporation, of Toronto, came calling that October. It offered $9.2 billion for the company. The offer was rejected. Not discouraged, Barrick dug deeper into its pockets and came back in December with an increased bid of $10.4 billion. Placer Dome's directors recommended acceptance.

Formalities completed, Placer Dome's common shares stopped trading on the Toronto and New York Stock Exchanges the following March. It must have been a sad day for many. Placer's name disappeared after 80 years and Barrick became the world's largest gold producer. At December 31, 2008, Barrick's proven and probable gold mineral reserves stood at 138.5 million ounces.

Image D-00251 courtesy of Royal BC Museum, BC Archives

THIS · GLACIER · LIES · NEAR · THE · GREAT · PREMIER · MINE · AT · STEWART · B.C.

The setting of the Premier Mine

Silbak Premier Mines Ltd.

The Silbak Premier Mines property, near Stewart, B.C., consists of about 5.3 square miles on the west slope of Bear River Ridge on the Alaska-British Columbia border. The Cascade Falls Claims 4 and 8, which cover the principal orebodies, were discovered and staked by William Dillworth and the Bunting brothers in June, 1910.

They probably were attracted by an oxidized capping that still forms a bare ridge west of the main glory-hole. Claims Cascade 4 and 8, along with an adjoining group, were taken over by O. B. Bush, who organized the Salmon-Bear River Mining Co. in 1910-1911 to develop them.

During the next two seasons, short tunnels (Nos. 1 and 2) and surface cuts were put in on low-grade showings, but nothing was done on adjacent quartz-pyrite-native silver mineralization.

In 1914, surface work directed by W. J. Rolfe traced the silver showing 800 feet downhill to the west and discovered good grades in gold and silver along this length. Possibly as a result of the First World War, work was discontinued until H. R. Plate, representing a New York syndicate, began work on the Nos. 1, 2, and 4 tunnels.

In 1918, R. K. Neill, of Spokane, bonded the property from Pat Daly and commenced work on the No. 1 tunnel, where Plate had stopped in apparently barren quartz. With a small amount of blasting Neill exposed ore, which showed native and ruby silver, and high-grade ore that was shipped to ASARCO's Tacoma smelter.

In the fall of 1919, ASARCO acquired a 52-percent interest in the property from Neill and his associates, R. W. Wood, A. B. Trites, and W. R. Wilson, of Fernie, for $1 million cash.

Premier was officially opened in April 1921, and construction of the aerial tram-line began that same year. It was to take one million feet of lumber, 150 timber towers, 12 tension towers, three angle stations and two terminals. In all, 160 supports were built. One-inch steel stationary cable and five-eighths-inch steel traveling cable was used. This was to be the second largest tramline on the continent and the longest cable aerial tramway in the world.

The original cable for the tramway was installed in 1922. The upper terminal was at Premier, B.C. and the lower at the Stewart harbour, while the cable passed over the extreme southeastern tip of Alaska.

Crude ore shipped during 1919 and 1920 from Premier averaged 4.24 ounces gold and 141 ounces silver per ton; milling began in 1921 at 200 tons per day. This rate increased in 1926 to 400 tons tons per day.

B.C. Silver Mines Ltd., which held two claim groups adjoining the Premier, began exploration in 1922 and, in 1925, after considerable exploration, intersected ore 1,500 feet east of the Premier ore zone in the 3-level area. Sebakwe and District Mines Ltd., which gained control of the adjacent Bush property in 1926, started a tunnel from the east fork of Cascade Creek (now Cooper Creek) and intersected the mineralized zone at about 1,050 feet.

Independent operation of the various mining companies and syndicates continued on the zone until 1936, when the Premier Gold Mining Co. Ltd., B.C. Silver Mines Ltd., and Sebakwe and District Mines Ltd. were consolidated to form Silbak Premier Mines Limited. The latter two groups were controlled by Selukwe Mining Company of London, which, upon merger, received a substantial interest in Silbak Premier Mines.

In November 1934, a fire broke out and the tramway was not able to operate without power so all supplies for the mine had to be hauled by motor trucks until the tramway was fixed.

In March 1935, pedestrians traveling between the government pier and the Premier ore bunkers and Hyder were greeted with real music. It was the sound of ore bucket sheaves rolling and clicking along the tramway cable to and from the Premier mine. One could see that the big gold mine on the hill was, at last, back on a production basis.

For the four months since fire destroyed its diesel power equipment, the Premier mine had to rely on the output of the 500 horsepower hydroelectric unit to supply power. This capacity was sufficient only to take care of the lighting load and a few small motors necessary to the continuous operation of essential devices and the occasional operation of the tramway transportation system.

During the extreme cold weather, which lasted longer than usual that winter and resulted in a shortage of water for power purposes, there was a considerable period when even the tramway could not be operated and supplies for the mine were taken up with sleighs hauled by tractors.

Citizens of the two Hyders and Stewart were delighted that the Premier mine would soon be running full blast again, turning out gold in quantities that made this great mine world famous.

In May 1937, a work crew installed 120,000 feet of three-quarter inch steel cable in 20 hours with only eight, 40-minute interruptions to traffic on the Silbak Premier aerial tramway.

During World War II, many of the miners were unable to enlist as their work was regarded as essential war service. The mine stopped gold production and concentrated on producing base metals.

After many years of continuously profitable operation, low base metal prices forced Silbak Premier to close in 1953.

During the period from 1918 to 1953, when continuous operations ceased, Silbak Premier Mines Limited, and operators before and since, produced about 4,700,000 tons of ore from the deposit with gross earnings about $30 million. Of this, approximately $22 million was paid in dividends.

Development work resumed in 1955 under the direction of Henry L. Hill and Associates. In 1956 the property was rehabilitated but fire destroyed the mill and surface buildings at the No. 4 level portal after only a few months' operation. At this time, underground work was concentrated on the 790, 940, and 1060 levels.

Low metal prices in 1957 again forced closure of the property, except for geological studies.

In 1959, Silbak Premier granted a one-year lease on the upper levels of the mine to Blermah Mines Ltd. The lessees mined the upper part of a small high-grade ore lens found on the south side of the abandoned glory- hole. This oreshoot was discovered after waste rock had sloughed from the pit wall and exposed silver-gold mineralization.

Image D-52575 courtesy of Royal BC Museum, BC Archives

Interior of No. 1 power house, Premier Gold Mine at Stewart, B.C.

At the termination of the one-year lease, Silbak Premier mined the lower part of the high-grade sulphide lens from 1960 to 1962. Production from this one lens amounted to roughly 2,736 tons of ore containing 18,595 ounces of gold, 394,933 ounces of silver, 16,258 pounds of copper, 215,999 pounds of lead, and 322,118 pounds of zinc.

Stimulated by this bonanza ore, the company reviewed the potential of the property but work at the mine was severely hampered when the Salmon River section of the Stewart-Premier road was washed out by overflow of water from Summit Lake in November 1961. The washed-out section of the road, entirely within Alaska, was largely rebuilt by Silbak Premier. However, the mine was unable to sustain operations because of a lack of continuous funds.

Since 1953, the Silbak Premier Mines Limited glory-hole has produced another 26,000 tons of good ore.

Crew going on shift at the Sullivan mine, 1948. Operating for more than 90 years the Sullivan mine is a key part of Teck's history and the history of British Columbia.

Teck Resources Limited

Teck Resources Limited is the result of the 2001 combination of Teck Corporation and Cominco Ltd., two of the oldest mining companies in Canada.

Cominco had its origins in southeastern British Columbia 106 years ago, and Teck began as a new gold company in northern Ontario a few years later, in 1913. Both moved their head offices to B.C. from eastern Canada in the early 1970s.

Cominco's life began as The Consolidated Mining and Smelting Company of Canada (CM&S), the result of the amalgamation of several units controlled by the Canadian Pacific Railroad. It was not until 1966 that it took on the name Cominco. Teck began as The Teck-Hughes Gold Mines Limited, after Jim Hughes, who discovered its gold deposit and Teck Township, where it was located. Teck-Hughes became Teck Corporation in 1962 as the result of a series of mergers and acquisitions.

Teck acquired an initial significant shareholding in Cominco from CPR Limited in 1986, gradually increasing this over the years until acquiring the balance of the company in 2001. The combined company was known as Teck Cominco for seven years before the name was changed to the present Teck Resources Limited.

ರಾ

CM&S and Cominco

Around the dawn of the 20th century, CPR purchased a package of B.C. assets created by American entrepreneur Frederick Augustus Heinze. These included a smelter Heinze had built at Trail, along with mining interests, railway lines, railway charters, and associated land grants. CPR was really only interested in Heinze's rail lines, but to get them, they had to buy the entire package.

The railway hired Walter Hull Aldridge, a smelter manager from Montana, to conclude a deal with Heinze. Under Aldridge's leadership, CPR bought Heinze's company, including the mining interests that he had assembled. CPR also put in a branch line to Kimberley in 1899, mainly to serve the North Star Mine.

In 1892 lead-zinc mineralization of the Sullivan Mine was discovered and staked by Pat Sullivan, Walter Burchett, John Cleaver and Ed Smith while prospecting north of the North Star Mine,

In 1892 lead-zinc mineralization of the Sullivan Mine was discovered and staked by Pat Sullivan, Walter Burchett, John Cleaver and Ed Smith while prospecting north of the North Star Mine, which had been discovered by others earlier that year. Sullivan was killed by a cave-in at an underground mine near Coeur d'Alene, Idaho the following winter so they named their property in his memory and it stuck. Systematic development began in 1900, to feed lead-rich ore to a small smelter built in nearby Marysville. The property was acquired by the Federal Mining and Smelting Company, later ASARCO, in 1908 but the venture failed due to metallurgical difficulties in 1910.

Aldridge apparently arranged for examinations of properties in the vicinity of CPR's lines. This unsigned carbon copy of a letter was found in about 1974 in Cominco's files:

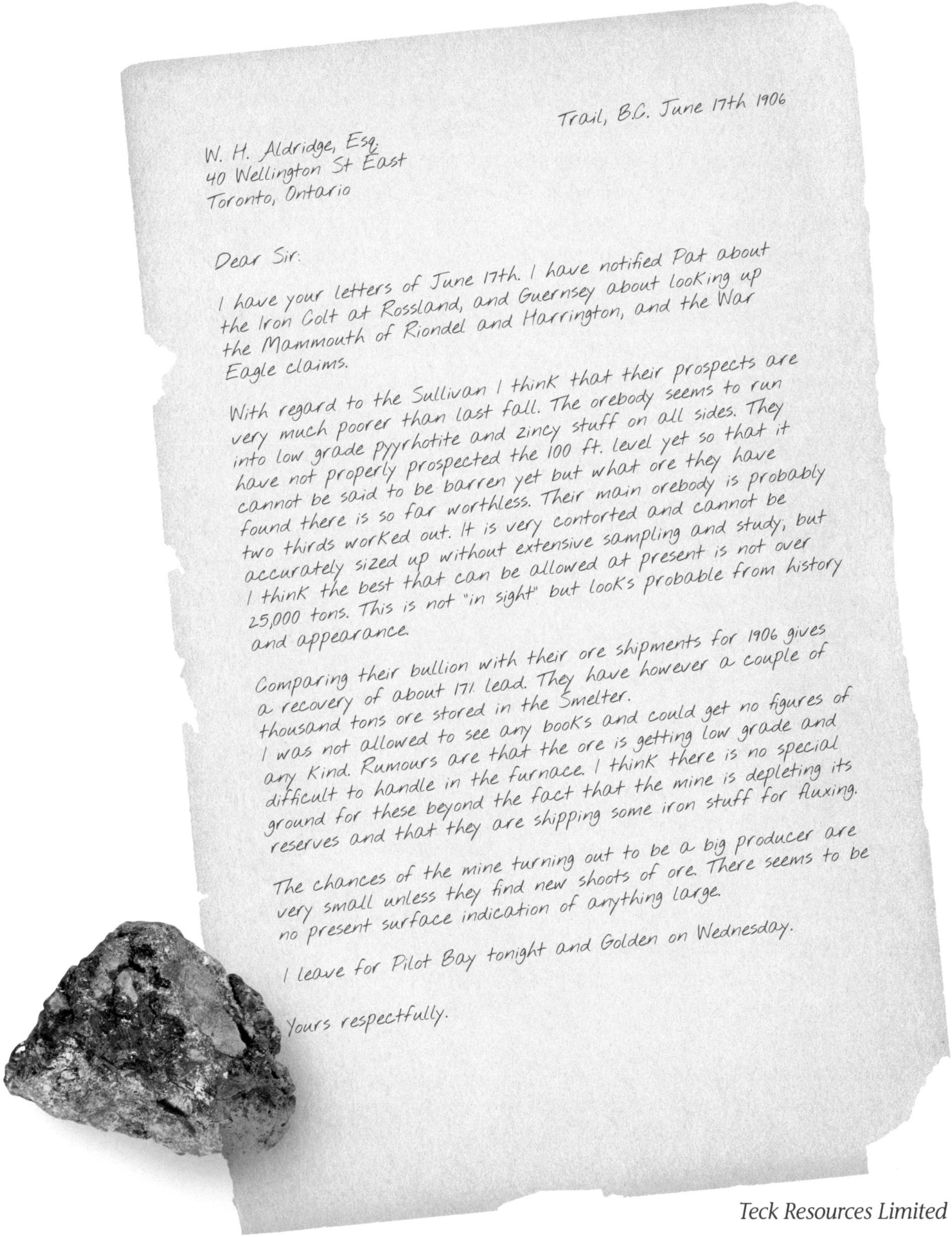

Trail, B.C. June 17th 1906

W. H. Aldridge, Esq.
40 Wellington St East
Toronto, Ontario

Dear Sir:

I have your letters of June 17th. I have notified Pat about the Iron Colt at Rossland, and Guernsey about looking up the Mammouth of Riondel and Harrington, and the War Eagle claims.

With regard to the Sullivan I think that their prospects are very much poorer than last fall. The orebody seems to run into low grade pyyrhotite and zincy stuff on all sides. They have not properly prospected the 100 ft. level yet so that it cannot be said to be barren yet but what ore they have found there is so far worthless. Their main orebody is probably two thirds worked out. It is very contorted and cannot be accurately sized up without extensive sampling and study, but I think the best that can be allowed at present is not over 25,000 tons. This is not "in sight" but looks probable from history and appearance.

Comparing their bullion with their ore shipments for 1906 gives a recovery of about 17% lead. They have however a couple of thousand tons ore stored in the Smelter.
I was not allowed to see any books and could get no figures of any kind. Rumours are that the ore is getting low grade and difficult to handle in the furnace. I think there is no special ground for these beyond the fact that the mine is depleting its reserves and that they are shipping some iron stuff for fluxing.

The chances of the mine turning out to be a big producer are very small unless they find new shoots of ore. There seems to be no present surface indication of anything large.

I leave for Pilot Bay tonight and Golden on Wednesday.

Yours respectfully.

Mercifully, the identity of the author of this very early geological examination report remains unknown. Thankfully, Aldridge didn't agree with this estimated potential of Sullivan, but we will never know how close he might have come to accepting it. CM&S took a lease and option on the property in 1909 and had completed its purchase by 1913.

During the next five years, selective mining and sorting produced high-grade lead and silver ore that was shipped on the CPR to Trail where it caused little metallurgical difficulty. In fact, during World War I, this was the largest single source of lead in the British Commonwealth. In the meantime, deep drilling revealed an immense lens of complex sulphide ore. A main adit (tunnel) was started in 1915 to provide access to the orebody and a major effort was started to solve the milling and metallurgical difficulties.

By 1920, a differential froth flotation process that produced separate lead and zinc concentrates suitable for smelting had been developed by Randolph W. Diamond and five others in Trail. The first concentrator of its type, based directly on Diamond's research, was commissioned at Kimberley late in 1923. Shipments of raw hand-sorted ore quickly tailed off but shipments of very significant amounts of lead and zinc concentrates continued until the end of 2001.

Total production from the Sullivan orebody was 150 million tonnes of 6 per cent lead, 5.5 per cent zinc and about 65 grams per tonne silver, with subsidiary values in tin, cadmium and indium. About 30 million tonnes of that was dilution that occurred during mining of pillars after stopes had been extracted. Accordingly, mining recovery of the orebody was virtually 100 per cent.

Bruce McKnight, then executive director of the B.C. & Yukon Chamber of Mines, wrote an eloquent tribute to Sullivan Mines for the Fall 2001 issue of *Mining Review*. Here, in part, is what he had to say:

Forget about corporate strategy, scientific investing, or whatever. Think about luck coupled with perseverance. Many of the largest mining companies in the world grew up by having the good fortune to stumble over one huge mineral deposit, plus having the skill to recognize it and the financial resources to exploit it. This was largely the case with the Sullivan Mine.

These company-making deposits are" so rare and important that they are known as "world class" mines; the Sullivan is clearly one of them. They even spawn their own nomenclature such as "Sullivan-type" environment or geology, or looking for "another Sullivan." Conferences are held to discuss them; their technical attributes, including geological features, and, in particular, how to find more. And for very good reason, because deposits like Sullivan are fantastic economic prizes for all the participants in their development – the company, employees, suppliers, customers, communities and governments. In many ways this one mine is tied to

not only the history of Cominco, but also the history of mining in B.C. and the history of B.C. itself.

No other mine, and no other corporation, arguably had a larger influence on British Columbia's development than Sullivan and Cominco. The entire pattern of southeastern B.C.'s development – towns, railways, highways and ports as well as numerous offices, warehouses, processing and research facilities – was strongly influenced by this one mine and the developments that it spawned.

And the rest, as they say, is history. And a colourful and varied history it has been, all largely fuelled by millions of dollars of Sullivan profits and staffed by thousands of Sullivan graduates. Along the way at Sullivan, the milling rate was increased to 8,500 tons per day in 1934, a tin circuit added in 1945, and numerous technological, safety and environmental improvements were made. These advances should come as no surprise, for Sullivan operations began deep in the horse and buggy era and continued well into the space age – touching three centuries and using the technology of all three. It also continued well into the age of "Sustainable Development" and over the past 30 years the mine has made major investments into the environmental and socio-economic sustainability of Kimberley, the mine's host town, and the community where four generations of Sullivan employees have lived.

So we at the Chamber of Mines say "so long Sullivan," we salute you for your enterprise, your technological innovation and your contributions to our community. We only wish there were more "Sullivans" now ready in B.C. to replace you, because we know there is potential for more. We just have to overcome those same technological and transportation barriers which you overcame a century ago.

CM&S got into the chemical fertilizer business as it sought a means of utilizing by-product sulphuric acid and preventing environmental damage that had been a major problem. By 1930, the company had three sulphuric acid plants in operation and it had begun the construction of a fertilizer complex. Its Elephant Brand fertilizers were used on the Canadian Prairies and sold abroad. Demand for fertilizers fell off during the Great Depression but, by 1935, it was clear that grain growers desperately needed them and the company returned to the Prairie fertilizer market.

Prospectors heading for the Klondike gold rush in Yukon in 1898 were the first to find gold near Yellowknife, and lead-zinc near what was to become Pine Point. To back its interest in northern exploration, CM&S began assembling its own fleet of bush aircraft to transport employees and supplies to its properties in 1925. Uniquely, these were piloted by geologists and mining engineers. The last two company aircraft, both Cessna 180s, were sold off more than 40 years later.

The first visible gold in the Yellowknife area was discovered in 1934. This set off a claim-staking rush that transformed the quiet bay into an overnight boomtown of shacks, tents and dugouts.

Cominco staked the Con Mine property in 1935 but winter stopped further work that year. Numerous gold veins were discovered the next summer. The Con Mine went into production in 1938 and continued operations until 2003. It produced over five million ounces (160,000 kilograms) of gold from 12. 2 million tons of ore processed. Cominco retained ownership until 1986.

CM&S ventured profitably into the mining of other minerals, thanks to its sophisticated technology and the changing needs of the market. During World War II, it opened new mines in British Columbia to provide tungsten for armour-piercing shells and to supply coal to the Trail smelter. The Pinchi Lake mine, located on a prominent limestone hill on the north shore of Pinchi Lake, about 25 km from Fort St. James, supported the Allied war effort by producing mercury needed for bomb detonators. Consolidated also secured wartime contracts to supply zinc and lead to the British government.

During World War II the company engaged in highly-secret work that ultimately helped the American government to develop the atomic bombs that destroyed Hiroshima and Nagasaki. The company certainly knew that by supplying the Americans with heavy water, it was engaged in immensely important war production. It is uncertain if anyone in the company knew of the ultimate use of the heavy water in weapons development. Heavy water, consisting of two deuterium atoms instead of two hydrogen atoms, was used in the control of neutron particles resulting from atomic fission. This was necessary for an atomic

chain reaction to be possible. CM&S was chosen because it already had an electrolytic hydrogen plant, a natural concentrator of heavy water.

The first inquiry about CM&S's capacity to make heavy water was made in February 1941 by the National Research Council of Canada on behalf of the British government. It took almost 22 months of intensely complex negotiations before the company (with the Canadian government's blessing) concluded negotiations with the United States government for the supply of heavy water. Under the contract, the Americans would build the production plant at their expense and the company would sell them the heavy water at cost. The company shipped 100 pounds of heavy water a month to the United States. In 1945, the plant began supplying heavy water to a uranium facility owned by the Canadian government.

The company ventured into lead fabricating with the Canada Metal Company and die casting with National Hardware Specialties Ltd. In the 1960s it formed Cominco Binani Zinc Ltd. in India (an electrolytic zinc smelter, refinery and sulphuric acid plant); in Japan it joined with Mitsubishi Metal Mining Company to build a lead smelter that would process concentrates from Cominco operations. Its foreign expansion plans led it into the United States (Cominco American Incorporated), Australia (Aberfoyle Limited) and Spain (Exploración Minera International). Exploration discovered profitable mines in each of these countries, and the company became respected worldwide for its exploration prowess.

The company's discoveries that resulted in mines, with the year they went into production, are as follows: Sullivan, 1910; Montana phosphate, 1930; Con gold, Yellowknife, 1938; Pinchi mercury, B.C., 1940; Tulsequah copper zinc silver, B.C., 1951; Bluebell zinc lead silver, B.C., 1952; H. B. zinc lead, B.C., 1955; Wedge zinc lead silver, New Brunswick, 1963; Pine Point zinc lead, NWT, 1964; Magmont lead zinc, Missouri, 1968; Vade (Vanscoy) potash, Saskatchewan, 1969; Black Angel zinc lead silver, Greenland, 1973; Rubiales zinc lead silver, Spain, 1977; Hondeklip alluvial diamonds, South Africa (with Trans Hex), 1978; Que River zinc lead silver, Australia, 1981; Polaris zinc lead, NWT, 1982; Valley Copper, B.C. (with Lornex and Teck), 1983; Buckhorn gold, Nevada (with Equinox), 1984; Troya zinc lead, Spain, 1986; Hellyer zinc lead, Australia, 1987; Red Dog zinc lead silver, Alaska (with NANA Regional Corporation), 1989; Ajax Monte Carlo copper, B.C. (with Teck), 1989; Stratmat zinc lead silver, New Brunswick (with Noranda), 1989; Maria copper, Mexico (with Empresas Frisco), 1990, Snip Gold, B.C., 1991; Quebrada Blanca in Chile (with Teck), 1994, and Pend Oreille zinc, lead in Washington, 1994.

Few other companies have a list of developments that has the geographic scope, commodity diversity and time span equal to Cominco.

In 1966, CM&S officially changed its name to Cominco Ltd. Two years later, it joined with Canadian Pacific Investments to create Fording Coal Ltd. to develop coal deposits in southeastern B.C. Cominco sold these interests to CP in 1985.

Cominco sailed into turbulent waters in the 1980s. A severe economic downturn in the U.S. economy, resulting from high interest rates and a slump in consumer demand, saw the company's earnings drop dramatically in 1980 and 1981, and by 1982, Cominco had suffered its first loss since 1932. By 1985 it was more than $1 billion in debt. Even so, the company was building for the future. In 1984 it completed the first phase of its Trail modernization program, which had begun seven years earlier.

Cominco's next big step forward looked to be a development decision on its Red Dog Project, under an agreement with the North Alaskan Native Association (NANA), who had selected Cominco to be their mining and development partner. However, that commitment was something that CP, Cominco's controlling shareholder, was ambivalent about pursuing. CP then set about trying to sell its Cominco interest.

That control almost ended up with a major South African company in 1986, but in the end a Canadian-led consortium, headed by Teck Corporation, was formed to buy CP and keep control in Canada.

Cominco returned to profitability by 1987 and had trimmed its debt to $344 million through the sale of some surplus assets.

The highlight of the decade for Cominco was the 1989 startup of the Red Dog zinc-lead mine, which it had discovered and then developed into one of the world's largest producers of zinc concentrate. The mine resulted from an innovative operating agreement with the Inupiat people of northwest Alaska.

In 1993, Cominco decided to begin exiting its main fertilizer business, including the Vade potash mine in Saskatchewan. Cominco Fertilizers was taken public in an initial public offering, and eventually the balance was sold and it became Agrium Inc., now a major independent fertilizer company.

The company celebrated its 90th birthday in 1996. By that point it had experienced further success with the start of production at the Quebrada Blanca copper mine in Chile. In 2001, Teck acquired the balance of Cominco and the combined company was re-named Teck Cominco and later changed to Teck Resources Limited.

Teck

Teck traces its lineage back to The Teck-Hughes Gold Mines Ltd., formed in 1913 to develop a gold discovery on claims in Teck Township on the shore of Kirkland Lake, Ontario. The discovery was the result of prospecting by the team of James Hughes and Sandy McIntyre. Hughes would lend his name to the new company; while McIntyre would go on to discover gold in what is now Timmins, with his discovery becoming the McIntyre Porcupine mine.

Interestingly, the name Teck was selected at random from British history when an unknown cartographer was placing names on square blocks called townships in the wilderness of northern Ontario. It originally came from a titled German family whose castle still stands near Stuttgart. Princess Mary of Teck was a member of both the German and British royal families and the grandmother of the present Queen Elizabeth.

The Teck-Hughes mine produced gold for half a century until 1965, when it finally exhausted its ore reserves. In the 1930s, Teck-Hughes developed a second major gold mine at Val d'Or in Quebec, the Lamaque mine, which also produced for 50 years until closing in 1984.

In the mid-1950s, Teck and five other companies formed the Mattagami Syndicate, inspired by the entrepreneurial Karl Springer, to search for base metals using the new airborne electromagnetic geophysical technology. In 1957, the group discovered the Mattagami orebody, but did not proceed to develop it themselves. Instead, it was financed to production by Noranda, after a bitter competition with McIntyre. Five of those discovering companies, Leitch, Highland-Bell, ISO Mines and Area Mines, would become part of Teck Corporation through amalgamations in later years.

Meanwhile, at the same time as Mattagami, another geophysical discovery was being made which would eventually impact Teck-Hughes in a major way.

Exploration at a Teck property in British Columbia

Norman Keevil Sr. was a chemist who had left teaching at MIT and the University of Toronto to pioneer the new art of applied geophysics. He introduced areomagnetic surveys into Canada, using technology that had been developed in World War II to hunt for submarines. Working mainly as a consultant for established mining companies, he used his spare time to explore for his own account, especially in the Lake Temagami area of Ontario where he had long had a cottage.

Using a new and now largely forgotten geophysical technique called Self Potential (SP), he began surveying on Temagami Island near an old copper showing. In due course he outlined a large, almost circular SP anomaly which he wanted to drill, but without much funding, his company Temagami Mining, farmed the property out to Anaconda, a major U.S. copper miner. Anaconda put a hole down smack in the middle of the anomaly, but it just encountered a barren diabase dyke. The company gave the property back to Temagami.

Keevil was undeterred, reasoning that a diabase dyke couldn't have caused the SP anomaly, so he continued surveying on closer and closer spacing until it transpired that the big anomaly was actually made up of two smaller lobes with a gap in the middle, where the dyke was. Temagami scrounged up enough money to drill another hole a few feet away from the Anaconda hole and this bored into 28 per cent copper over 58 feet, an unheard of grade over that length. Further drilling confirmed two separate, high-grade pods under only 30 feet of gravel. Both could be mined by simple truck and shovel methods, without sinking costly shafts and both were high enough grade to be shipped directly to smelters at either Noranda or Inco, without building a costly mill, and so Temagami was able to become an operating mining company without having to hand the property over to a larger company for development.

Haul trucks at Highland Valley Copper

Temagami would eventually build a mill and go underground, but it was largely self-financed off those first two pods, and would mine two dozen separate orebodies over its 15-year life. Anaconda's loss could be said to be Canada's gain, because the new company, small as it was, had the vision and ambition to take an historic company like Teck-Hughes and infuse it with that new vitality.

Control of Teck-Hughes and its affiliate, Lamaque Mining Company became available from a group of older holders a few years after the Temagami discovery and, in a series of quick moves, the group including Consolidated Howey, an old gold producer from the Red Lake District, acquired control of Canadian Devonian Petroleums, an oil producer, and the four merged to form Teck Corporation in 1962.

Meanwhile, Keevil's eldest son, also Norman, was working on his own PhD at Placer Development's Craigmont mine near Merritt, where his friend Bob Hallbauer was pit superintendent and later mine manager. Both were influenced heavily by the legendary John Simpson, who had built Placer into arguably the best mine operator in the world with a strong engineering bias and this influence would later prove important to Teck's own growth.

Throughout the next ten years, Teck participated in the mining exploration activities of the "Keevil Mining Group" of related companies, which resulted in a number of mines including Silverfields, in the historic silver mining town of Cobalt, Tribag in Ontario and Madeleine in The Gaspé. The Teck-Hughes mine finally closed in 1965, but Lamaque would carry on for another 20 years. However, Teck Corporation, with the important Steelman Field oil production in Saskatchewan brought in by Devonian, emphasized oil exploration more than mining for a period.

This would change as the 1970s began, when the decision was made to begin consolidating the diverse group of companies into one, so that for both management and the market, there would be a more obvious focus on building a single, major mining company.

An essential part of that plan was to establish a dual class share structure, with all 4.8 million pre-existing Teck shares being reclassified as Class A shares, now with 100 votes per share, and a new Class B share with one vote created to be used for future mergers and acquisitions. The new Class B shares were used to merge with Leitch Mines and Highland-Bell Mines, both acquired from Karl Springer, Area Mines, acquired from Dick Corbet and Silverfields. Later Temagami; ISO Mines, acquired from J. P. Dolan, and other companies would be folded in in the same way and the new Teck Corporation became the single focus of the team.

Without this share structure it is almost certain that the new, growing Teck would have been swallowed up by one of its larger competitors before it could prove its mettle. With it, the company was able to maintain its independence and over time would become one of the new Canadian champions.

The second part of the plan, motivated by the two Keevils and Hallbauer, all of whom were now key players at Teck, was based on the Placer model. This meant focusing not just on grass roots exploration, with its long odds against early success, but more on new mine acquisition and development. The emphasis would now be on continuously increasing the quality and mine life of its projects and operations, whether by discovery, development contract or acquisition. This was easier said than done given the relatively small capitalization of the company, but it would be achieved in spades. It was in fact a precursor to Deng's famous dictum for China a few years later: "It doesn't matter if a cat is black or white, so long as it catches mice."

The first new mines to be put into production by the new, consolidated Teck were Newfoundland Zinc, a high-grade zinc deposit that, coincidentally, had been optioned to Cominco by Leitch earlier, and was returned to the Teck fold when the option period ended without exercise, and the Niobec niobium mine, a joint venture with Soquem, the Quebec government mining exploration company. Both reached production in 1975, on budget at capital costs of only $18 million each. "On time, on budget" would become Teck's mantra for years to come.

Meanwhile, Brameda Resources had been formed to combine the exploration, development and promotional talents of an illustrious group including ex-Noranda professionals Morris Menzies and Bernie Brynelsen, Merv Davis and lawyer Jack Austin. Financed with a major initial public offering, for its day, in 1970, the new company would acquire extensive copper and coal properties in B.C. and Yukon. Unfortunately it became over-extended in the market euphoria of the time, and fell on hard times. Teck would be invited in by its bankers to take over management, and Hallbauer would be sent back to live in B.C. with a team to work it out.

Teck Corporation moved its head office from Toronto to Vancouver in 1972, a year after Cominco did. The attraction of British Columbia was both personal and professional, given both the quality of life and the fact that major orebodies were being discovered and there were more to be found. As well, the junior exploration sector, which had historically discovered the bulk of Canada's mines, was increasingly working out of Vancouver, whose stock exchange had eclipsed Toronto's as a source of venture financing. Teck wanted to be near the centre of the action so it could keep close to those companies.

Also in 1972, Chester Millar discovered a native copper deposit near Kamloops through a junior exploration company called Afton Mines Limited. Teck saw the potential and was able to acquire 51 per cent of Afton shares on the open market. This was eventually increased to 74 per cent through a senior financing arrangement. Teck brought the Afton mine into production at 7,000 tonnes per day in early 1978, at a capital cost of $90 million. The project included a new copper smelter, the first of its kind in the province. The smelting operation closed in 1983 when it became commercially more efficient to send the concentrate offshore, but the mining operation continued until 1997.

In 1977, Teck acquired a controlling interest in Yukon Consolidated Gold Mines Limited (YCGC). The company held a number of placer leases in the famous Klondike Gold district in Yukon. Teck operated a seasonal placer operation on these claims from 1981 until 1997. YCGC also held a 21 per cent interest in Lornex Mining Corporation, which had a large copper molybdenum mine in the Highland Valley, next to the Highmont property in which Teck held an interest.

In 1981, Teck placed the Highmont mine into production at the rate of 25,000 tons per day and a capital cost of $150 million. In 1989, the Highland Valley Copper Joint Venture combined the Lornex mine and mill, Cominco's Valley Copper orebody and Teck's Highmont mill to create one of the largest open-pit copper mines in the world, processing over 130,000 tonnes per day. This was an amazing engineering feat. It involved moving the Highmont concentrator by wheeled trailers a distance of five kilometers and combining it with the Lornex mill. All of this was accomplished in a mere 18 months.

In 1981, Teck sold off its remaining oil interests as part of a debt control program, but also took a chance by optioning a property that would return it to the gold business in a big way. David Bell, a consulting geologist for Corona Resources, had discovered the Hemlo gold deposit in Ontario. Teck entered into a 50/50 development contract with Corona shortly afterwards and the David Bell mine was placed in production in 1985. In 1989 the Williams mine, an extension of the orebody discovered by David Bell, was awarded by the courts to Teck and Corona, and the combination was for years Canada's largest gold producer.

Meanwhile, Bill Bergey, a Teck geologist, had discovered a promising open-pittable metallurgical coal resource on a property near Brameda's original Sukunka prospect, and Teck had proven up what would become one part of B.C.'s Northeast Coal Project, along with Denison's nearby Quintette mine. This was a $2.5 billion northern development program that included a new 136-km railroad, transmission line, town site, and port facility at Prince Rupert. The Bullmoose mine, with Lornex and Japan's Nissho-Iwai as partners, was built at a capital cost of $275 million, $35 million under budget, and would be one of Teck's most successful new mines. It operated until 2003 before its coal reserves were exhausted.

The Quintette mine did not fare so well, for a variety of reasons, and in 1991 Teck was appointed the operator of its mine in Northeastern B.C. In 2000 the operation was closed. But in June 2010, with world met coal markets again stronger, Teck initiated a feasibility study to potentially reopen the mine to produce approximately three million tonnes of coal per year.

In 1986, Teck acquired a controlling interest in Cominco Ltd., a company that had once been much larger but had been overtaken as Teck expanded. Canadian Pacific, the seller, had controlled Cominco for years and wanted to sell its 54 per cent interest but, given conditions at the time, there were no buyers for the entire bloc. Teck, joined by two minority foreign mining partners, agreed to buy a 31 per cent slice of the company for $280 million, with CP selling the rest to the public. It was a bold move, and not entirely obvious. George Albino, CEO of Rio Algom, which was affiliated with Lornex, Teck's partner in Bullmoose, asked what discount factor Teck had used, and then quipped: "I didn't think Teck used discount factors."

Cominco's very first item of business under the new regime in 1986 was to approve building of the Red Dog mine in Alaska, which would become the company's next flagship mine.

Throughout the 1990s, Teck Corporation incrementally increased its stake in Cominco, attaining 100 per cent ownership in 2001; whereupon a new company, Teck Cominco Limited, was formed.

In 1991 Teck would enter into an agreement to develop AUR Resources' copper-zinc discovery at Louvicourt in Quebec, with an affiliate of Noranda being a partner. It would also join with Cominco in agreeing to develop a copper mine in Chile known as Quebrada Blanca (QB). In proof of how small the mining world is, Teck and Cominco would later sell their interests in QB to AUR, and still later Teck would acquire AUR and prove up a major deep orebody now in feasibility study under the original QB supergene deposit.

In 1992, Teck was awarded the Sparwood area's Balmer coal mine, then in bankruptcy proceedings. Teck re-opened it as the newly-named Elkview Coal mine in 1993. By 2002, production had increased from 2.5 million tonnes per year to 5.5 million tonnes and Elkview became Teck Cominco's biggest source of mine operating profits.

In early 2003, Teck instigated the formation of the Elk Valley Coal Partnership, combining all of the coal operations of Teck Cominco, Fording Coal (previously also part of CP) and Luscar Coal into a single business. This included five coal mines in B.C. and one in Alberta. Teck Cominco was the managing partner and owner of a 40 per cent partnership interest. This development made Teck Cominco a major global player in the production of steelmaking coal, as well as a significant producer of copper, zinc and gold.

In 1996, Teck acquired an 11 per cent share interest in Diamondfields Resources, which had discovered a high-grade nickel deposit at Voisey's Bay in Labrador. Teck's objective was to eventually become the mine development partner, but this was thwarted when Inco and Falconbridge became involved in a bidding war to see which could take over Diamondfields. Which company won or lost is arguable, but Inco bought Diamondfields and Teck was left with almost a half a billion dollar gain, which it would redeploy into South America.

Rio Algom and Inmet had been exploring a copper-zinc deposit in Peru called Antamina, and in one of those periodic cyclical downturns, Inmet found it necessary to sell. Teck, with its Louvicourt partner, Noranda, bought out Inmet and part of the Rio interest and the three of them proceeded to build a new mine on the property.

Antamina was not a slam dunk. Nobody had ever built a large project, mining or otherwise, on budget at an altitude of over 14,000 feet, and the cost of

this one would be a massive $2 billion. The "Street" knew this risk and the partners' market values were penalized accordingly for a time, but they accomplished it. Norm Keevil points out that one reason for their success was that the three partners had worked together on engineering construction projects before; Teck and Noranda, at Louvicourt; and Teck and Rio at Bullmoose; and their people knew each other's strengths and how to work together. With Teck's Mike Lipkewich playing a leading role, Antamina was one of the mining industry's major success stories at the turn of the 21st century.

While the mining industry suffered through what has been termed "20 years of declining prices, in real terms" as the last century neared its end, Teck's willingness to take a chance, developing new mines it knew would eventually be needed by an expanding world economy, has been rewarded. Since 2006 commodity prices have turned the corner, and the future belongs to those that prepared for it.

In July 2008, Teck announced an agreement with the Fording Canadian Coal Trust to acquire all of its assets, essentially the remainder of the Elk Valley Coal Partnership that Teck did not already own, for $14 billion. When the worldwide financial crisis occurred shortly thereafter, Teck was left with substantial short term debts as a result of this acquisition but, just as in the earlier 1981-82 financial crisis, it was able to recover through careful divestments of non-core assets and new partnerships.

With 100 per cent of these coal assets, Teck became the largest producer of steelmaking coal in North America, and the second largest exporter of seaborne metallurgical coal in the world.

By 2011, after almost 100 years of production, Teck operated six mines in British Columbia and one of the world's largest integrated zinc and lead smelting and refining operations at Trail. In addition, it had mining operations in the United States, Peru and Chile as well as a 20 per cent interest in the Fort Hills oil sands project and a 50 per cent interest in other oil sands leases in Alberta. It had become the largest diversified mining company in Canada, a tribute to all those in Teck-Hughes, Teck Corporation and Cominco who had dared to dream.

Myra Falls mine, 2006

Westmin Resources

From humble beginnings, Westmin Resources became a significant player in Canadian mining.

The company started life in 1951 as penny stock Western Mines Ltd. and had to battle environmental opposition to build a copper-zinc-lead mine in Strathcona Park on Vancouver Island. The mine didn't get into production until 1967.

The mineral showings were already known in 1917 when the park was opened for prospecting. One of the early claim holders, Paramount Mining Co. of

Toronto, conducted exploratory work between 1919 and 1925. With metal prices depressed and the remoteness of the site, early activity petered out.

In 1930, the Geological Survey of Canada reported "extensive copper, zinc and lead mineralization" in zones extending about three miles and over widths "up to at least 25 feet" containing mineralization "of probable milling grade…"

The Reynolds Syndicate (whose members included H. H. "Spud" Huestis, P. M. Reynolds, and J.A. and W.J. McLallen) acquired and consolidated the claims in 1959. Two years later, Western Mines

negotiated an option-purchase agreement with the Reynolds Syndicate for 250,000 Western shares and $166,500 cash.

Since incorporation in 1951, Western had tried, unsuccessfully, to find and develop a viable property. Now it set to work in earnest. Its emphasis was on claims known as the Lynx group that had excellent surface showings. By mid-1964, ore zones had been defined and opened up on five levels. Underground work and extensive diamond drilling indicated 810,300 tons of "assured" ore and 689,999 tons of possible ore at the Lynx property, plus 113,300 tons assured and possible at the Paramount claim (later named Myra). First production began in 1967.

Initially, a small fleet of company boats and log rafts brought everything to the mine site on Buttle Lake. Among the first shipments was a portable sawmill that produced lumber for mill construction from timber on the property.

Although Westmin was operating legally in Strathcona and fastidious in following the requirements in permits governing its activities, the company came under public attack. Then president, Harold M. Wright, revealed his frustration to shareholders in December 1966. First he described the unusually complex problem of creating a mine at a site lacking road access, building a deep-sea dock and ship-loading terminal at Campbell River, generating the mine's own hydro power, arranging finance and so on. He then said: "It has been most unfortunate that in the face of many natural problems involved in the project, the unnatural problems based on emotionalism and lack of facts have required heavy costs which were not budgeted for and many hours of time and patience from our senior staff. It is therefore with considerable relief that we are now able to say that our plant is in the tune-up and initial production stage."

During the first year of production, 82 per cent of the ore milled came from an open pit; this grew to almost 97 per cent in 1968. From 1969 onwards, the pit was phased out in favour of underground ore. By the end of 1974, the pit had yielded over 1.6 million tons of ore – far in excess of the reserves of 300,000 to 400,000 tons originally estimated.

Early in 1970, drilling revealed a rich ore deposit on the Myra property. A 9-foot-by-9-foot decline for trackless mining and haulage equipment was driven 2,200 feet to the vicinity of the high-grade drill intersections.

With steady production, a road linking Campbell River to the mine site was completed in 1970.

During the first decade of operations, production settled at the rated capacity of 1,000 tons a day. Concerned about future mill feed, the company renewed exploration efforts, which resulted in the discovery in 1979 of the H-W orebody. As a result, the company began to build a new mill and auxiliary facilities to triple capacity by the end of 1984.

H-W in-place reserves at January 1, 1983 stood at 15.2 million tons grading 0.07 oz/ton gold, 1.1 oz/ton silver, 2.2 per cent copper, 0.3 per cent lead and 5.3 per cent zinc.

In 1980, Western experienced a major transformation. From a single operation on Vancouver Island, it became a major diversified company, a force to be reckoned with in the Canadian natural resources sector. Effectively, it became an operations, exploration, development and acquisition arm of Brascan Ltd., which had acquired an 84 per cent interest in the company.

In 1980 (while still known as Western Mines), the company had spent $23.6 million to become the largest shareholder in Lacana Mining Corp., which

owned large majority interests in two precious metal mine/mill complexes in Mexico and a producing gold mine in Nevada.

In 1981, Western changed its name to Westmin Resources Ltd. Westmin engaged in an active exploration program for base and precious metals and uranium throughout Canada. It also became involved in exploration for thermal and metallurgical coal in western North America. It also entered the oil and gas industry. In 1980, its oil and gas interests generated $48.6 million in revenues (pre-tax income of $27.5 million) – about half the corporate total.

Western Miner reported in May 1983: "In the midst of a $225 million expansion that will see new production from the H-W mine and a tripling of the mill rate to 3,000 tons, the future of Westmin Resources' Vancouver Island mine has never looked brighter."

Added to the H-W discovery was the recent discovery of an extension to the original Lynx zone. The mine was already bustling with activity in preparation for a busy construction period in summer 1983. As well as the H-W development, the project involved building a new 2,700 ton/day mill to replace the existing 875 ton mill; a new warehouse and office complex; a conveyor system from the H-W mine to the mill; a new tailings disposal and water management system and a small hydro-electric power plant. The ship and barge loading facilities at Tyee Spit in Campbell River would also be upgraded to handle increased shipments.

Westmin began a process of corporate transformation that took to years to complete. Westmin's 1996 annual report explained that the changes were largely fuelled by market response to the high-grade zinc and silver Wolverine deposit in Yukon and the promising high-grade zinc developments at Myra Falls. As a result, Westmin was successfully re-launched as an independent public company in December 1995. This was achieved when its controlling shareholder Brascade Resources Inc. sold its 76 per cent interest into the market place and Westmin raised $67 million (net) by issuing new equity capital. With a favourable market, the company went on to raise a further $96 million of equity in April 1996.

With a much-improved balance sheet from two equity issues and the sale of its coal assets to Brascan Ltd., Westmin was in a mood to go shopping. It acquired Gibraltar Mines Ltd. for $272 million. In addition to its very efficient, low-grade copper mining operation in the Cariboo, Gibraltar also had a large, low cost oxide development project at Lomas Bayas in northern Chile. In line with its focus on base metals, Westmin announced it would be selling its Premier Gold Operations, which it considered non-core.

Business seemed to be bubbling along nicely for Westmin. Its 1996 annual report contained an enthusiastic *Outlook* section dated March 14, 1997. Chairman Paul M. Marshall and President and CEO Walter T. Segsworth wrote: "Management is pleased with the significant progress made in the Company over the past year and is excited about prospects for the future."

Others had taken note; Westmin's prospects excited them too.

On a Friday afternoon that November, representatives of the Swedish mining giant Boliden Ltd. called on Segsworth and the new Westmin chairman, Terry Lyons. They had an unsolicited surprise takeover offer. Boliden proposed to buy all Westmin common shares at $5.40 per share.

(Boliden engaged in mining, processing and selling metals and mineral products, principally copper and zinc, with operations in Europe, Chile and Canada.)

From the tone and detail of the directors' response, they were outraged. They unanimously urged shareholders to reject Boliden's offer. Nor did they mince words. They described the offer as "inadequate, opportunistic and coercive." In urging rejection – a battle they would ultimately lose – the incumbent directors offered shareholders a snapshot of Westmin's major assets. These included:

The combined Lomas Bayas Mine and Fortuna de Cobre Project, Northern Chile.

Westmin's management believed the combined geological resource could justify a combined production rate for the two properties of 150,000 tons (331 million pounds) per year of cathode copper. The combined resource would rank fourth on the list of contained copper resources for world-wide leachable copper deposits.

The underground zinc-copper mine at Myra Falls had a 3,850-ton-per-day milling facility, which was then operating at about 3,600 tons per day. Myra Falls had become a highly competitive producer of zinc and copper concentrates as a result of changes in technology and work practices along with the discovery and development of the high-grade Gap and Battle ore deposits. The 1997 year-to-date break even cost for producing zinc (after netting out by-product credits for copper, gold and silver) was $0.30/lb. For the nine months ended September 30, 1997, operating cash flow from Myra Falls was $26.3 million.

Westmin had an option to earn a 51 per cent interest in the Vizcachitas Exploration Property in Central Chile. The property had a near surface, high-grade resource of 24 million tons of enriched sulphide mineralization grading 1. 02 per cent copper, which was part of a larger resource of 310 million tons grading 0. 52 per cent copper. There was excellent potential to expand the high-grade near surfaced resource thereby enhancing project economics.

Westmin and its partner made a high-grade zinc-silver-gold-copper-lead discovery at Wolverine in southeastern Yukon in 1995. In the first two years of drilling, Westmin intersected the main zone with 45 drill holes and defined a resource (as at January 1, 1997) of 5.3 million tons grading 1.81 g/t gold, 359.1 g/t silver, 1.41 per cent copper, 1.53 per cent lead and 12.96 per cent zinc. Exploration work was continuing.

Despite the directors' appeal, shareholders voted 95 per cent to accept Boliden's offer. The takeover was completed in March 1998 at a cost of $360.7 million.

Less than 18 months later – in July 1999, Boliden sold its newly-acquired Gibraltar interests to Taseko Mines. Taseko clearly had ambitious long-term plans for Gibraltar. In March 2010, it sold a 25 per cent interest in Gibraltar to a Japanese consortium for $187 million. Taseko extended the orebodies at Gibraltar. It already held the Prosperity property and later acquired Harmony and Aley.

In July 2004, Breakwater Resources Ltd. acquired the Myra Falls operation when it purchased all the outstanding shares of Boliden (Canada) Ltd. from Boliden Ltd. It was still the only mine in B.C. located within a provincial park. Although mining began with an open pit, later operations were all carried out underground. The mine produced zinc, copper, gold and silver. In recent years all mining occurred in two distinct mines – the H-W and Battle/Gap, which were connected underground by a 1. 8 km drift. In 2009, 375 people worked at the Myra Falls operation.

Yukon Zinc Corporation

Wolverine – a former Westmin exploration project – now in operation, 2011.

Companies and Mines Key to Yukon's Economic Growth

Caribou swimming in
Stewart River, 1938

Gold dredge below Bonanza Creek,
mid-20th century

Mines have been a key driver of Yukon's growth. They have spawned new towns, new and improved highways and expanded hydroelectric facilities as well as increased employment and population and significant tax revenues.

Trevor MacInnis/Creative Commons

Cantung mine and townsite, 2008

Cantung Mine

The Cantung tungsten-copper deposit lies in the Flat River Valley in the Mackenzie District in the Northwest Territories

It is only accessible from the Yukon side of the border via a 300-kilometre highway from Watson Lake. The deposit was discovered in 1954 by Northwestern Explorations, a Kennecott subsidiary. Kennecott failed to recognize the presence of scheelite in the mineralization and abandoned it in 1958 because of its low copper grade. The Mackenzie Syndicate restaked it immediately;

members of its field crew had worked at the Emerald tungsten mine owned by Canex Placer at Salmo, B.C., which had similar mineralization.

Scheelite is an oxide and one of the principal tungsten minerals. In the northern Cordillera, it is usually colourless and can easily be mistaken for common silicate minerals. Its only diagnostic feature is a bright-bluish-white fluorescence under ultraviolet light. Tungsten has the same specific gravity as gold (19.3) and has the highest melting point and tensile strength of all the metallic elements.

Canada Tungsten Mining Corp. (owned by American Mining Climax Inc., Falconbridge Nickel Mines Ltd., and Dome Mines Ltd.) placed it into production in late 1962, based on open-pit reserves of about one million tonnes grading 2.47 per cent tungsten trioxide and 0.45 per cent copper. It was one of the richest tungsten deposits in the world.

The early years of production were marred by the first of many interruptions that marked the mine's history. In mid-1963, tungsten's price dropped to its lowest level in 40 years and the operation had to be suspended for a year. At the end of 1966, it was suspended for another year when fire destroyed the mill and crusher.

A new deposit was discovered in 1971 beneath the pit and was accessed through an adit collared at the valley bottom, close to the town site. The mill began to process the underground ore in 1974. After several expansions, mill capacity reached 900 tonnes per day in 1979. In 1985, Amax consolidated ownership of Canada Tungsten Mining and sold it to Aur Resources Inc. in 1995. Canada Tungsten and Aur merged in 1996. In 1997, North American Tungsten Corporation Ltd. purchased the Cantung mine and other assets of the former Canada Tungsten from Aur. Periodic closures due to low tungsten price occurred many times since. Some were due to manipulations by China, which controlled the world market with production from small, labour-intensive mines. Other closures were caused by corporate re-organizations and unpaid creditors. The most recent ended in 2010, leaving

the mine with indicated resources of 2.25 million tonnes grading 1.11 per cent tungsten trioxide, and inferred resources of 0.35 million tonnes grading 0.84 per cent tungsten trioxide.

The Cantung mineralization occurs in a dark green, skarn alteration zone composed of diopside, garnet, quartz, orthoclase feldspar, and pyrrhotite, with minor amounts of epidote and actinolite. The skarn has developed near the contact between lower Cambrian, massive crystalline limestone and a small intrusion of biotite granite. Narrow dikes of porphyritic rhyolite cut the orebody.

Capstone Mining Corp.

Drills at the Minto Mine

Minto Mine

Minto Mine

When the Minto mine, held in 2011 by Capstone Mining Corporation, began production of copper concentrates in 2007, it became the first mine to open in Yukon since the Brewery Creek gold mine began production in 1996.

The mine experienced many changes in control since its discovery as a geochemical anomaly in 1970 by the Dawson Syndicate, a Silver Standard Mines-ASARCO joint venture.

When Dawson staked the anomaly in July 1971, it triggered a staking rush with a competitor, a joint venture consisting of United Keno Hill Mines, Falconbridge Nickel and Canadian Superior Exploration (a unit of Superior Oil, which became the controlling shareholder of Falconbridge in the early 1970s). Both groups ended up with portions of the deposit.

The groups explored their properties independently from 1971 to 1974 with mapping, geochemistry and geophysics, and a combined total of 232 drill-core holes. They also participated in a joint feasibility study in 1975 to 1976, which indicated that approximately 60 per cent of the mineral resource occurred on the Dawson Syndicate claims, and that the deposit was not then economic.

Between 1984 and 1989, Silver Standard transferred its interest to Teck Corp. In the mid-1990s, Lutz Klingmann negotiated a deal with the various parties to bring 100 per cent of the Minto property into a new junior company, Minto Explorations Ltd. Asarco and Teck sold their interests for shares in the new company, while Falconbridge, the parent of United Keno Hill, sold its interests for $1 million, due (and paid) in 1996.

Minto Explorations became a publicly-traded company in 1994, with ASARCO as its 55.8 per cent majority shareholder. Drilling campaigns in 1993 and 1994 resulted in a new resource calculation, followed by a positive feasibility study in 1995. A year later, ASARCO announced that it was prepared to invest $25 million to place the mine in production for a 70-per cent interest in the project. Minto Explorations was to retain a 30-per cent interest and remain as operator.

Access road construction to the mine site, including a barge landing on the Yukon River, was completed by 1997. By 1998, a new camp was built and concrete for mill foundations was poured in advance of installing milling equipment already on site.

Weak metal prices and market conditions in the late-1990s brought the project to a halt, and by 2004, ASARCO-controlled Minto Explorations was put up for sale.

Sherwood Mining Corporation, then led by Stephen Quin and Bruce McLeod, negotiated with the various parties to acquire Minto Explorations, which was achieved in June 2005. Soon after, Sherwood announced the first National Instrument 43-101 measured and indicated mineral resource of 8,340,000 tonnes grading 1.83 per cent copper, 0.55 gram gold per tonne and 7.95 grams silver per tonne, using a 0.5 per cent copper cut-off.

Exploration drilling from 2005 to 2007, while development work and mill construction was underway, was remarkably successful in finding new surface zones. The first concentrate was produced in May 2007. In 2008, Sherwood was taken over by Capstone.

Additional exploration drilling from 2008 to 2010 continued to find new zones and increase the reserves. As a result, mill capacity was steadily increased, achieving an average of 3,729 tonnes per day in the quarter ended September 30, 2011.

The mine was located about 120 kilometres north of Whitehorse, and was accessed via the Klondike Highway to Minto Landing on the east side of the Yukon River. A ferry was used to reach the property on the other side. The mine was connected to the Yukon electrical grid in 2008. The ore was mined in open pits using conventional shovel and truck methods.

Copper-gold-silver concentrates were trucked to Skagway, Alaska, and then shipped to smelters in Asia.

The Minto property is underlain by granodiorite of the Early-Jurassic Minto Pluton. Copper sulphide mineralization is confined to rocks that have a structurally imposed fabric, ranging from weak foliation to strongly developed gneissic banding. It is generally believed by geologists that this foliated granodiorite is just variably strained equivalents of the granodiorite and not a separate lithology. The contact relationship between the foliated deformation zones and the massive phases of the granodiorite is very sharp. These contacts do not exhibit chilled margins and are considered to be structural in nature.

Hypogene mineralization consists of chalcopyrite, bornite and rare chalcocite, which may occur in combination or as individual blebs of massive to semi-massive mineralization. Gold and silver occur as microscopic inclusions within bornite. Free native gold is rare. Environmental studies indicated that the deposit was not acid-generating and that the tailing solids were low in heavy metals and were strongly acid-consuming.

Geologists have long argued about what type of deposit Minto is. In October 2011, two possible deposit types were favoured, magnetite skarn or iron oxide copper-gold (IOCG). The lack of typical calc-silicate skarn mineral assemblage seemed to preclude the skarn deposit type, thus leaving the IOCG type or, alternatively, a previously unrecognized deposit type.

Faro, Yukon

Cyprus Anvil and the Faro Mine Complex

The area around what is now Faro, Yukon, was prospected in the 1950s and 1960s by Al Kulan, credited with discovering several significant lead-zinc deposits and playing a major role in the discovery of the Anvil Mine, which became Canada's largest lead-zinc mine.

Kulan discovered and staked the nearby Vangorda lead-zinc deposit in 1953. The property was optioned to Prospector Airways and diamond drilling was carried out between 1953 and 1955. Kerr Addison Mines Limited eventually acquired Prospector Airways but its interest in the property waned for a number of years because of depressed metal prices, declining metal markets and the remoteness of the area.

In 1962, Kerr Addison resumed exploration in the Vangorda plateau area, and the Swim lead-zinc deposit, eight kilometers southeast of Vangorda, was discovered in 1963. At the same time, Dynasty

Explorations, under the direction of Aaro Aho, commenced a detailed exploration program on several claim groups in the Faro area in 1964 and discovered the Faro lead-zinc deposit in 1965. Anvil Mining Corporation (AMC), a joint venture between Cyprus Mines (60 per cent) and Dynasty (40 per cent), was formed in December, 1965 to develop the Faro deposit.

AMC (later Cyprus Anvil Mining Corporation) began open-pit mining on the Faro lead-zinc deposit in late 1969, at rates of up to 10,000 tonnes/day and established the town of Faro. A new highway was built between Carmacks and Ross River to serve the Faro area – initially numbered Highway 9; it became part of the Robert Campbell Highway, Yukon Highway 4.

A forest fire in 1969 destroyed the newly-built homes, and work had to start all over again. The mine was officially opened on January 28, 1970.

In 1973, the Grum lead-zinc deposit was discovered by a joint venture between AEX Minerals and Kerr Addison while testing a gravity anomaly. Cyprus Anvil Mining Corporation purchased the Grum property in 1979.

Until 1982, the mine remained in more-or-less constant production. Trucks carried the ore concentrate from the mill by highway to Whitehorse, where the buckets were lifted from the trucks and lowered onto cars of the White Pass and Yukon Route railway. The trains took the buckets another 106 miles to Skagway where the contents were poured out into ships' holds.

By then, Cyprus Anvil had been taken over by Hudson Bay Oil and Gas, which in turn was taken over by Dome Petroleum. Dome Petroleum announced an indefinite shutdown due to declining metal prices, low productivity, high operating costs and high debt. Between June 1983 and October 1984, some open-pit waste-stripping was carried out but production ceased altogether by the end of 1984.

The Anvil Range mineral assets of Cyprus Anvil, including the Grum and Grizzly deposits, were acquired in November 1985 by a predecessor partnership of Curragh Inc. With government assistance, a waste-rock stripping operation began in 1985.

The new owners, Curragh Resources, resumed production in 1986. This time, bypassing the railway, ore was trucked from Faro directly to Skagway. This operation ended in 1993, not long after Curragh had suffered a disaster at the Westray coal mine in Nova Scotia.

In 1989, development of the Vangorda Plateau was begun with stripping of the Grum and Vangorda deposits. Curragh carried out extensive surface drilling on the Grum deposit to delineate reserves and obtain samples for metallurgical testing in preparation for production. Preparation of Grum for mining began in 1989.

In early 1990, an underground operation was initiated just southwest of the Faro pit from a portal in the pit. This operation closed in October, 1992, after mining 1.8 million tonnes of ore.

In 1991, Curragh began stripping the Grum deposit. As of October 1991, the total waste requiring stripping from Grum was 193.2 million tonnes for a stripping ratio of 6.7:1.

A third operation, Vangorda, was opened by the Anvil Range Mining Corporation in 1995. By the end of 1996, the Vangorda pit was mined out and mining operations were suspended because of low metal prices and other factors, including lower head grades, mechanical problems in the mill and lower metal recoveries, which contributed to less than planned production. The mill continued to process low-grade stockpiles at 50 per cent capacity until March 31, 1997.

In February 1997, Anvil Range Mining Corp. announced a private placement of 4.1 million common shares for a total of $9.4 million with Cominco. ARM also secured a $15 million loan from its principal shareholder, Cominco, in July 1997.

Stripping of the Grum pit started in August 1997. The mine re-opened at full production in November 1997. Production ceased in January 1998, and Anvil Range filed for bankruptcy. With liquidation of the company's assets, much of the heavy mining and milling equipment was sold and removed from Yukon.

The federal government began covering the costs for the interim care and maintenance of the Faro site.

In July 2008, a new contract for care and maintenance at the Faro Mine Complex was awarded to Denison Environmental Services. Reclamation and environmental work at the mine site was continuing in the summer of 2011.

Any prospect for further mining of the lead-zinc resource would now require significant new investments.

The Elsa mine and camp in the Keno Hill district, 1989.

The Keno Hill Silver Camp

*The Keno Hill silver camp –
460 kilometres by road north
of Whitehorse and 55 kilometres
northeast of Mayo, the nearest
town – was the second largest
primary silver producer in Canada.*

It ranked among the richest silver-producing districts on earth. The camp consisted of 16 "important" deposits (defined as those that have produced over 15.55 tonnes or 500,000 ounces), another 19 that shipped lesser amounts to a smelter, and 35 smaller occurrences.

One of the most daunting challenges faced by operators of the Keno Hill mines was the high cost of transportation. In the early years, between 1920 and 1923, hand-sorted ore had to be hauled 70 kilometres in 50-kg (110-pound) sacks on horse-drawn sleighs over rough winter trails to Mayo, where it awaited stern-wheel steamboats that operated only four to five months a year. The next step was an 860-kilometre river trip to Whitehorse, where ore was transferred to the White Pass &

Yukon railway for a 106-kilometre trip to tidewater at Skagway, Alaska. This was followed by a voyage to Vancouver or Seattle, and another train trip to a smelter. Transportation was greatly improved in the early 1950s with construction of a highway from Whitehorse to Mayo, which became truly all-weather when large bridges were completed over the Yukon, Pelly and Stewart Rivers.

The Keno Hill silver camp was one of the mainstays of Yukon's economy from the decline of the Klondike Gold Rush to the Second World War. For example, it provided the bulk of the freight that allowed the steamboat service to continue operating on the Yukon and Stewart Rivers until the highway system was built in the 1950s. Without Keno Hill, there would have been no reason to build the highway from Whitehorse to Mayo or the Mayo Lake hydro project. At its peak in the 1950s and 1960s, the Keno Hill camp supported about 15 per cent of the Yukon population.

From 1920 to 2005, production in the camp totalled 6,657.24 tonnes (214 million ounces) of silver, 322,700 tonnes of lead and 198,150 tonnes of zinc from 4,847,164 tonnes of ore mined. The ore consisted mainly of the lead mineral, galena, and the zinc mineral, sphalerite, in a siderite gangue. Because the two sulphide minerals were often mixed together, they had to be mined together and separated by a flotation process. Geologists estimated the average zinc grade at between 8 and 9 per cent, which would have made zinc an important by-product if the camp had been near

a railroad. But with low zinc prices (until later years), much of this material was not mined or was discarded after mining.

Mining was continuous at Keno Hill from 1913 to 1989, except for two brief wartime shutdowns. The two largest deposits produced most of the ore from the camp.

The Hector-Calumet mine produced 50.9 per cent of the total tonnage, 45 per cent of the silver, 57.3 per cent of the lead and 76.6 per cent of the zinc.

The Elsa and Husky mines, thought to be parts of the same deposit offset by a fault, together accounted for 18.2 per cent of the total tonnage, 23.2 per cent of the silver, 11.8 per cent of the lead and 4.1 per cent of the zinc.

Silver historically accounted for about 80 per cent of the value of the ore, with most of the balance in the lead. Even though Keno Hill galena had a relatively high silver content, the value of the lead sometimes barely paid for the cost of shipping. The principal importance of the galena was in its role as the host or carrier of the silver.

The production history of the camp can be divided into five important phases:

1. Discovery and the Silver King mine ~ 1913 to 1917.

Silver-lead mineralization was first discovered in 1901 by a placer gold prospector, who found an outcropping vein of galena in a creek bank at the west end of the camp. He didn't stake a claim because lead was of no value in this location. It was first staked in 1913 and became the Silver King mine, from which Thomas P. Aitken shipped 3,230 tonnes of hand-picked ore by 1917, earning a profit of $500,000.

2. Keno Hill, Limited and the Keno mine ~ 1918 to 1923.

Louis Bouvette discovered rich galena float on top of Keno Hill in 1918, which was at the east end of the camp. He returned the next year after breakup and found the veins that became the Keno mine. They were sold to Keno Hill Ltd. , a subsidiary of the Guggenheim-owned Klondike gold dredging company, Yukon Gold Company. The Guggenheim name was almost synonymous with copper at the time. By 1920, the new town of Keno City had been established and like other frontier towns, it had all the necessities: hotels, saloons, brothels and electricity generated by a wood-fired powerhouse. By 1923, mining was terminated after 8,425 tonnes of high-grade, hand-sorted ore had been mined underground and hauled to Mayo with horse-drawn sleighs. It had an average grade of about 6.9 kilograms per tonne (200 oz/ton) silver and 54 per cent lead, and contained 57.8 tonnes (1.8 million oz) of silver. Because of the complete lack of access or services at the start of mining and the difficult location above timberline, this was an amazing accomplishment.

3. Treadwell Yukon Company, Limited ~ 1921 to 1941.

Prospectors discovered several new deposits northwest of the Keno mine in the early 1920s while it was operating, including the Ladue, Sadie, Lucky Queen and Shamrock. Although Keno Hill Ltd. was interested in optioning them, they were outbid by an aggressive competitor from Juneau, Alaska. The newcomer was Fredrick Bradley, who purchased the Gambler claim, adjacent to the Keno mine, for $10,000, sight unseen. He had been attracted to the new silver camp by the success of the Keno Mine and sent his senior mining engineer-geologist, Livingston Wernecke, to acquire prospective properties. Bradley, from San Francisco, was the successful operator of huge Alaska Juneau mine and the Treadwell Complex, which consisted of four adjacent mines across the channel on Douglas Island.

Wernecke was both a skilled explorer and efficient developer who would go on to become the most important figure in the history of the camp. He examined all the prospects as soon as he arrived in June 1921 and soon purchased the adjoining Sadie and Ladue claims for $260,000, a precedent-setting price for this camp. It also demonstrated his astute exploration approach, which was based on his recognition that the prospectors in the camp were a diligent and independent group of former placer prospectors and miners, many of them war veterans. He could see that they had already devised many clever exploration methods to overcome the problems caused by permafrost and the vegetation and overburden cover that made outcrop scarce. He implemented an incentive system that paid large bonuses for new discoveries, supplemented by grubstakes and free supplies such as explosives and services such as assays. The results proved him right.

One of the best prospecting techniques that was developed was to sink small shafts to bedrock to explore for buried veins. It was a method that had been used in northern placer creeks to explore for buried gold paystreaks, and was similar in a general way to modern deep soil sampling to collect samples for geochemical analysis. It turned the permafrost from a problem into a safety advantage because timbering wasn't needed. It was only practical where overburden was less than 20 to 25 mettres thick. Panning the overburden and bedrock and assaying any galena present was an easy way to determine its silver content.

If no evidence of a mineralized vein was present, it showed that the area uphill was unmineralized, whereas evidence of mineralization showed that the shaft was located in the dispersion train below the vein. Dispersion trains of galena could extend 50 metres or more downslope along bedrock from the subcrop of a vein, and were sometimes rich and thick enough to mine.

By the spring of 1922, the Sadie-Ladue mine had been developed with two shafts and 3,600 tonnes of shipping ore grading 230 ounces per ton silver was ready for the trip to Mayo. The transportation costs and difficulties of travel to Mayo were improved by replacing the horses with trucks and bulldozers. A comfortable townsite named Wernecke was established, a road was constructed to Keno City and by early 1925, sufficient lower grade milling ore had been blocked out to construct a 90 tonne-per-day bulk flotation mill, the first in the camp. The concentrate was shipped to a smelter at Kellogg, Idaho.

In 1928, as milling ore reserves were declining, Wernecke acquired the Lucky Queen mine, the richest ever found in the camp, from a prospector for $60,000. Samples assayed up to 1700 ounces-per-tonne silver. The Lucky Queen orebody was comparatively small but ideally located just above the Wernecke mill. The ore was transported there cheaply using an aerial tramline (similar in operation to a ski gondola).

When silver prices dropped sharply during the Great Depression and reserves were exhausted, mining operations were suspended on Keno Hill in late-1932. Before and during the closure, Wernecke began to turn his focus to Galena Hill, where prospectors had made several impressive discoveries since 1920. He had established a reputation with the prospecting community as a tough but fair negotiator who was always willing to give free advice and encouragement. During the closure, he acquired, by option or purchase, the new Elsa mine in 1928 for $150,000, the former Silver King mine for $425,000 in 1929 and the Hector claim in 1935 for $200,000. He also acquired the adjoining Calumet claim soon after for an unknown price. The Hector-Calumet mine eventually became the largest producer in the camp.

The cumulative ore reserves from the Elsa, Silver King and Hector-Calumet properties, along with rising silver prices, encouraged Treadwell Yukon to move the mill from the Wernecke camp to the new Elsa townsite, expand its capacity to 225 tonnes per day, and build a 4325-metre aerial tramline to transport ore from the Hector-Calumet mine to the Elsa mill, which was topographically 400 metres lower. Milling was resumed at the end of 1935 and the mines produced more ore than the riverboats could haul to Whitehorse. Mining had to be stopped at Silver King in 1939 because the ore changed from galena-rich to more zinc-rich as it went deeper.

Economic and political problems forced mining to be suspended at Keno Hill near the end of October 1941. Lower silver prices were compounded by labour shortages following the start of the war in the fall of 1939. The final straw was a decision by the U.S. government to restrict the purchase of foreign silver. The company was almost broke because management had been diverting the Keno Hill profits to other projects in an unsuccessful attempt to diversify.

Wernecke had devoted the best twenty years of his life to overcoming all the geological, technical and economic problems at Keno Hill and must have been disappointed as he headed back home to San Francisco after closing the mine. It was a terrible irony that he and his pilot were killed when their floatplane crashed in bad weather on Salal Island, in Millbank Sound, 200 kilometres north of Alert Bay, B.C. Their plane didn't burn and, in a strange twist of fate, their emergency gear and food saved the lives of two other men who were able to swim to Salal from their plane that had crashed and overturned a few minutes earlier.

4. United Keno Hill Mines Ltd. ~ 1946 to 1989.

In early 1945, two well-connected legends in the Canadian mining industry, Thayer Lindsley of Ventures Ltd. (a predecessor of Falconbridge) and Fred Connell of Conwest Exploration Company, were intrigued by the camp's geological potential. They hired two Toronto consultants, John Reid (nicknamed Turn 'em Down) and Frank Buckle, to examine the potential for further exploration and development and prepare separate reports. Not surprisingly, Reid concluded that the camp was essentially mined out and turned it down. Buckle, on the other hand, believed that the main deposits would extend to greater depth, particularly the Hector-Calumet and Elsa mines, and he recommended more exploration. Lindsley and Connell accepted Buckle's conclusions and asked him to supervise a program in 1946 to access the old underground workings and rehabilitate the mill and equipment. They then formed a new company, Keno Hill Mining Company Ltd., with Conwest as the operator, and optioned all the Treadwell Yukon assets. This included all the most important mines in the camp except the Husky, which was not discovered until much later because it was covered by thick overburden.

Buckle's program was successful and milling resumed in April 1947. To reduce power costs, the company bought a coal mine at Carmacks and installed a new coal-fired generator. That was satisfactory until the government built a hydroelectric power plant on the Mayo River in 1952. Lindsley and Connell were also able to persuade the federal and territorial governments to construct a 467-kilometre gravel highway from Whitehorse to Mayo, which was completed in 1950.

A huge exploration breakthrough was achieved in 1948 with the discovery of a major deep ore shoot at the Hector-Calumet mine. Subsequently, two additional associated ore shoots with widths exceeding 10 metres were defined, which were so wide that square-set timbering had to be introduced to support the wallrock. The huge new reserves guaranteed the camp a much longer life.

Even more important was the support the new ore gave to the theory that commercial ore could persist at depth and not turn into a zinc deposit. The debate had arisen because the Silver King, Keno, Sadie-Ladue, Hector-Calumet and Elsa mines all appeared to become more zinc-rich as they were mined deeper. It was demonstrated later that most individual ore shoots have a characteristic internal zoning, with a silver-lead-rich top and zinc-rich bottom. The larger mines were composed of separate ore shoots that were stacked above one another within favourable structural and stratigraphic settings. The ore could also extend to considerable depths as long as the veins remained within the favourable quartzite member. The deepest was Hector-Calumet at 365 metres but Keno was mined to a depth of 290 metres and Elsa to 250 metres.

With the depth potential appearing more optimistic, plans were made to enlarge the operation. The company name was changed to United Keno Hill Mines Ltd. in connection with a new underwriting to finance an enlargement of the Hector-Calumet mine and construction of a new townsite named Calumet. A fire in 1949 destroyed the Elsa mill but it was rebuilt and became operational within four months at an increased rate of 225 tonnes/day. Increased zinc prices in 1950 made it economically feasible to install the first zinc flotation circuit, with the concentrates being shipped to the Cominco smelter at Trail. In 1951, another stage of mill expansion to 450 tonnes/day was completed and by 1953 the company was producing almost 625,000 ounces of silver per month.

Silver recovery exceeded 217 tonnes (7 million oz) in eight of the ten years between 1953 and 1962, with peak production achieved in 1960. However, the Hector-Calumet ore was again becoming richer in zinc and the economics of deepening the shaft weren't favourable. At this point, Conwest sold its interest to Falconbridge, which became the operator.

In early 1963, United Keno Hill Mines enlarged the underground exploration effort and launched an intensive surface exploration program to determine if new ore zones could be identified. The Husky deposit was discovered along the lower slopes of Galena Hill just west of Elsa and developed in 1972, as production at Hector-Calumet was winding down. With production declining in all the mines, silver prices declining, and costs increasing, the end came slowly until mining ceased in January 1989.

5. Alexco Resource Corp. ~ 2006 to the present.

In 2006, after a period of 17 quiet years since the closure, and following a long period of ownership changes and debt settlements, Alexco Resource Corp. purchased the mine site and carried out exploration. In 2011, production began at the former Bellekeno mine on Sourdough Hill. Alexco and the Na-Cho Nyak Dun First Nation were working together under the provisions of a cooperation and benefits agreement.

Calumet Mine

Panorama of the community of Whitehorse looking southwest from across the Yukon River. Eleven sternwheelers including the 'Yukoner' either docked or on shore. Mountains are visible in the background.

Whitehorse Copper Belt

A 32-kilometre long belt of small copper deposits was discovered between 1897 and 1900 parallel to the Yukon River and a few kilometres from the new gold rush town of Whitehorse.

The copper belt was ideally located because the town was situated at the head of navigation on the river and would soon become the transhipment point between the White Pass & Yukon Railway and

the steamboats carrying supplies downstream to the Klondike Gold Rush and Dawson City.

The belt contained 28 old mines and showings. Between 1900 and 1920, several short-lived companies participated in the exploration and mining program. Seven different deposits became producers and about 147,300 tonnes of hand-sorted ore averaging about four per cent copper was shipped to smelters. The largest producer was the Pueblo mine, between 1912 and 1917, prior to a disastrous cave-in. Between 1924 and 1929, Richmond Yukon drilled 20 holes at Pueblo, worked underground at the Carlisle mine, and shipped

about 900 tonnes. The copper belt was then idle until 1948, when Noranda conducted geophysical surveys and drilled 17 holes in three deposits. In 1953, Hudson Bay Mining drilled 10 holes on the Cowley Creek deposit.

The modern era began in 1954, when Imperial Mines & Minerals Ltd (renamed New Imperial Mines Ltd in 1957) began to consolidate the ownership by staking, option or purchase. By 1963, it contolled all the significant mineralization and began an extensive drilling program. By the end of 1965, it had outlined five million tonnes of open pittable ore in six deposits, with an average grade of 1.2 per cent copper. A feasibility study recommended an 1800 tonne-per-day mill and Sumitomo Metal Mining Corp agreed to provide senior financing. Production began in March 1967. Hudson Bay Mining and Anglo American Corp agreed to develop deep ore beneath the Little Chief pit In October 1969.

In 1972, New Imperial changed its name to Whitehorse Copper Mines Ltd and formed a joint venture with Hudson Bay and Anglo to explore the north end of the belt. Between 1973 and 1982, they drilled 35,480 metres in 188 holes at 10 deposits and collected a 4500-tonne bulk sample from the Cowley Park South zone.

Total production between 1967 and 1982 was 10,247,986 tonnes, of which 72.2 per cent was underground ore with an average grade of 1.50 per cent copper from under the Little Chief pit. The other 27.8 per cent was mined from several pits prior to June 1971 and had an average grade of 1.06 per cent copper. The average precious metal grade of the ore was 0.021 ounces-per-ton gold and 0.38 ounces-per-ton silver. The largest mine, Little Chief, had combined production (pit and underground) of 7.25 million tonnes averaging about 1.5 per cent copper. It was the only deposit that exceeded 1.2 million tonnes in size and contained zones exceeding two per cent copper (at depth in iron-rich skarn).

Many of the deposits occurred near irregularities, such as embayments, in the intrusive contact. Mineralization usually occurred near the contact but was sometimes found up to 150 metres from it. Most deposits were lens-shaped or tabular, with steep dips. The best zones had limestone hanging walls and siliceous footwalls. Two main types of skarn were present: Iron-rich, consisting of magnetite and serpentinite with occasional pyrrhotite and pyrite; and iron-poor, consisting of various common calcsilicate skarn minerals. Bornite and chalcopyrite were the most common copper minerals, with minor chrysocolla, native copper, chalcocite, molybdenite and scheelite also present.

New Imperial Mines Ltd

The New Imperial Mines Ltd mine near Whitehorse, 1967.

AME BC Award Recipients

Each year at Mineral Exploration Roundup, AME BC recognizes select individuals or teams of individuals for their outstanding achievements and contributions to the mineral exploration and development industry in BC and globally through its annual awards program, which is overseen by the Awards Committee.

Nominations are solicited from both AME BC members and members of associated mineral exploration and mining organizations. The deadline for submitting nominations each year is September 30. All nomination letters of unsuccessful candidates remain on file to be reconsidered for three years after the original submission date. After nominations are submitted, the committee adjudicates them and in January, the awards are presented at Roundup. To ensure the integrity of the awards, they are presented only if deserving nominees are identified.

*H.H. "Spud" Huestis Award
for Excellence in Prospecting
and Mineral Exploration*

Winners have made a significant contribution, directly or indirectly, to enhance the mineral resources of British Columbia and/or the Yukon Territory, through the original application of prospecting techniques or other geoscience technology.

Past Recipients:

1977 – Spud Huestis

1979 – Karl Springer

1980 – Bern Brynelsen

1981 – Bill Smitheringale Sr.

1982 – Alex Smith

1983 – Egil Lorntzsen

1984 – Andy Robertson

1985 – Tom McQuillan

1986 – Harry Warren

1987 – Jim McDougall

1988 – Stu Barclay

1989 – Ted Chisholm

1990 – Efrem Specogna

1991 – John Stollery

1992 – Mark Rebagliati

1993 – Eric Denny

1994 – Franc Joubin

1995 – Gordon Milbourne

1996 – Bruce Mawer

1997 – Stu Blusson, Chuck Fipke

1998 – Al Archer, Bob Cathro

1999 – Richard Haslinger

2000 – John McDonald, Robert Etzel, Arthur John

2001 – Lorne Warren

2002 – Mark Baknes

2003 – Peter Fox

2004 – Patrick McAndless

2005 – Ed Balon

2006 – Cam Stephen

2007 – John Robins, Lawrence Barry

2008 – Michael Savell

2009 – Shawn Ryan

2010 – David Moore and Myron Osatenko

2011 – Dirk Tempelman-Kluit and Peter Bernier

*E.A. Scholz Award
for Excellence in
Mine Development*

Recipients have made a significant contribution towards the development of mining operation in British Columbia and/or the Yukon.

Past Recipients:

1981 – John Simpson

1982 – Harvey Parliament

1983 – Harold Wright

1984 – Bob Hallbauer

1985 – Edgar Kaiser, Jr.

1986 – Norm Anderson

1987 – Norm Keevil, Jr.

1988 – Don McLeod

1989 – Chester Millar

1990 – Bern Brynelsen

1991 – Albert Reeve

1992 – Clifford Frame

1993 – Tony Petrina

1994 – Hank Ewanchuk

1996 – Ron Netolitzky

1998 – Pierre Lebel

1999 – John Kalmet

2000 – Lawrence "Joe" Adie

2001 – Maurice Ethier, Michael Hibbitts, Terry Lyons, Ken Stowe (Northgate Team)

2002 – Frank Amon, Jim Clark, Rod Killough, Terry Marsten (Highland Valley Copper Team)

2003 – Gary Biles, Ian Cunningham-Dunlop, Dave Kuran, Jim Rogers (Eskay Creek Team)

2004 – David Thompson, Michael Lipkewich (Teck Cominco Team)

2005 – Jim O'Rourke

2006 – Brian Kynoch

2007 – Ron Thiessen

2008 – Scott Broughton, John Mirko, David Skerlec

2009 – Stephen Quin and Bruce McLeod

2010 – John McManus and Robert Rotzinger

2011 – Clynton Nauman and Bradley Thrall

Murray Pezim Award for Perseverance and Success in Financing Mineral Exploration

Recipients are mineral industry financiers who have provided a significant contribution to the British Columbia and/or the Yukon mineral exploration and mining community.

Past Recipients:

1999 – Murray Pezim

2000 – Peter Brown

2001 – Bob Hunter

2002 – John Brock

2003 – John Tognetti

2004 – Ian Telfer

2005 – Ned Goodman

2006 – Adolf H. Lundin

2007 – Rick Rule

2008 – Robert A. Quartermain

2009 – Channing Buckland

2010 – Cal Everett

2011 – Mark O'Dea

Hugo Dummett Diamond Award for Excellence in Diamond Exploration and Development

Recipients have made a significant contribution towards diamond exploration, diamond technology, the diamond discovery process, or diamond mine development.

Past Recipients:

2004 – Hugo Dummett

2005 – Dr. John Gurney

2006 – Buddy Doyle,
Robert (Bob) Hindson,
John Stephenson,
Grenville Thomas

2007 – Dr. John McDonald,
Walter Melnyk,
Dr. Nikolai Pokhilenko,
Randy Turner

2008 – Ken MacNeill,
George Read,
Harvey Bay,
Pieter Du Plessis

2009 – Barbara Scott Smith

2010 – Brooke Clements,
Robert Lucas, and
Pierre Bertrand

2011 – Jon Carlson

Colin Spence Award for Excellence in Global Mineral Exploration

Recipients have made a significant contribution, directly or indirectly, to enhance the mineral resources within Canada (exclusive of British Columbia and/or Yukon) or in foreign countries, through the original application of prospecting techniques or other geoscience technology.

Past Recipients:

2006 – Ross J. Beaty

2007 – Dr. Roman Shklanka

2008 – Charles Forster

2009 – Mark Rebagliati

2010 – David Adamson,
Matthew Wunder,
Ian Russell,
Terry Bursey, and
Crystal McCullough
("The Rubicon Team")

2011 – Recipients: Jeff Pontius
and the International
Tower Hill Mines Ltd.
exploration team

David Barr Award for Excellence in Leadership and Innovation in Mineral Exploration Health and Safety

Recipients have demonstrated one or more of the following: leadership and innovation excellence in exploration safety; improvement in safety records from year to year; and/or demonstrated efficient and compassionate behaviour in dealing with an unfortunate accident.

Adjudicated by the Health & Safety Committee

Past Recipients:

2005 – David Barr

2006 – Imperial Metals Corporation

2007 – Ian Paterson

2008 – Bill Mercer

2009 – Doug Flynn

2010 – Harvey Tremblay

2011 – Michael Gunning

Robert R. Hedley Award for Excellence in Social and Environmental Responsibility

Recipients are AME BC members working globally who have made significant contributions or advances in the realm of social or environmental responsibility.

Past Recipients:

2007 – Anne Ball, Doug Brown, Susan Craig, Rick Van Nieuwenhuyse

2008 – Robert L. Carpenter

2009 – Judi L'Orsa

2010 – Ian Thomson

2010 – The Britannia Mine Museum

Brian Kornichuk

Dwayne Lund prospecting on Lowe Profile's Miya property, Sibola Mountains, B.C.

Frank Woodside Past Presidents' Awards in Recognition of Outstanding Service to AME BC

Presented by the Past Presidents
and Past Chairs of AME BC

Past Recipients:

1994 – David Barr, Fraser Crocker, Ron Stokes

1995 – Dan Pegg, Colin Spence, Geoff Whiton

1996 – Bob Spencer, Cam Stephen,
    Sanford Woodside

1997 – Gavin E. Dirom

1998 – Brian Abraham, John Brock

1999 – Bob and Bruce Brown

2000 – George Cross

2001 – Robert Boyd, Sheila Holmes, Tom Schroeter

2002 – Don Bragg, Ed Kimura, Marilyn Mullan

2003 – Greg Hawkins, Vic Hollister, Art Soregaroli

2004 – John Newell, Wayne Spilsbury,
    Linda Thorstad

2005 – Jeffery P. Franzen, John Thompson,
    Maurice (Moe) J Young

2006 – Lena Brommeland, Jurgen Lau,
    Terry Macauley, Dean Toye

2007 – John Murray, Alastair Sinclair,
    Randy Turner, Randall Yip

2008 – Gerry Delane, Rick Higgs

2009 – Arne Birkeland, Gary Giroux

2010 – Don Coates, Chuck Davis, Chris Graf, Bill Meyer

2011 – Jim Allan, Glen Dickson, Grant Luck,
    and Christine Ogryzlo.

Gold Pan Award

Presented by the AME BC Board of Directors to an individual who has made significant contributions to the mineral exploration community through service to the Association for Mineral Exploration British Columbia.

Past Recipients:

1976 – H.H. "Spud" Huestis

1977 – Walter B. Boucher, Dr. Victor Dolmage, Gardner S. Eldridge, Thomas J. McQuillan, Prof. John M. Turnbull, Prof. Harry W. Warren, George E. Winkler

1979 – Bill Dunn

1980 – Gavin A. Dirom, Thomas Elliott, James A. Pike, George Smith, Dr. William V. Smitheringale, Rick Higgs, Sanford Woodside

1983 – Atholl Sutherland Brown

1995 – Donald Mustard

1996 – Ross M. Deakin, Dirk Tempelman-Kluit

1998 – Jack Patterson

2003 – Bruce McKnight

2004 – Robin Woods

2005 – David Comba

2006 – Shari Gardiner

2007 – Donald McInnes

2008 – David Caulfield

2009 – Jim Gray

2010 – John Murray

2011 – Ed Kimura

Other years:

Dick Athol, John Bonus, Edward H. Caldwell, Jim Fyles, Ralph Macdonald, Rod MacRae, Bill Sirola, Ron W. Stewart

Sources

The 1970s. Payne, Raymond W. *Corporate Power, Interest Groups and the Development of Mining Policy in British Columbia, 1972-77*, B.C. Studies, no. 54, Summer 1982; British Columbia & Yukon Chamber of Mines – numerous documents, briefs, submissions, copies of speeches, letters to the editor et al; Debates of the B.C. Legislative Assembly (Hansard), Victoria.

Britannia. The book's account is adapted from published articles in *Mineral Exploration* magazine by Sarah Efron and Ryan Stuart; it contains a major contribution from Bill Smitheringale.

Cassiar. Asbestos Corporation annual reports; Cassiar Information Booklet; Brinco Limited annual report 1981; James Richardson & Sons research report, December, 1959; B.C. Energy Ministry.

Coal. The Coal Association of Canada – http://coal.ca/content/; Natural Resources Canada – http://www.nrcan.gc.ca/eneene/sources/coacha-eng.phpB.C. Ministry of Energy and Mines – http://www.empr.gov.bc.ca/Mining/Geoscience/Coal/CoalBC/Pages/default.aspx

Eldorado. Mel Stewart recalled his frustrating battle with bureaucracy in an interview with Laurence Thomson for this book.

Endako. The book's account by Julie Domvile, appeared in slightly different form in the Fall 2008 issue of *Mineral Exploration* magazine.

Gibbs. The Canadian Dictionary of Biography, Gibbs' autobiography *Shadow and Light* and the excellent history of Black Pioneers in British Columbia, *Go Do Some Great Thing* by Crawford Kilian.

Granby. Adapted from "The Great Granby" by Mary Hughes (*Mineral Exploration* magazine, Winter 2008) with additional material supplied by John Jewitt, a former president of Granby. Further details were taken from E. S. Moore's *American Influence in Canadian Mining*, pp.75-77, University of Toronto Press, 1941.

Granduc Slide.

"Death Came Silently: the Granduc Mine Disaster" by Murray Lundberg at *explorenorth.com; One Lucky Canuck* by David Barr; *Window in the Rock* by Eugene Peterson; *Uncovering Treasures from the Earth* by Gordon Schnare.

Juniors. *Cashing In* Jane Gaffin, 1980; *Hills of Silver* Aaro E. Aho, 2006; *The Mine Finders* George Lon, 1966; *The McLeod Luck*, Don McLeod with Will Peacock, 2010; *Mining: The History of Mining in British Columbia* G. W. Taylor, 1978; *The New Gold Rush* Frank Keane; *The Discoverers* Monica R. Hanula et al, 1982; *Fleecing the Lamb* Cruise and Griffiths, 1987; *The Vancouver Stock Exchange* Frank Keane, 1996; *The Pez* Jennifer Wells, 1991; *The Wizards* M. Caldwell and Marc Davis, 1996; *The Gold Hustlers* Lewis Green, 1977; *The Wizards* M. Caldwell, 1987; VSE and TSX-V files, 1960s through 2011.

McDame. Ed Kimura "Gold-seekers Rush In" *Mineral Exploration* magazine, Winter 2010; Wikipedia.

Nuggets. The information on gold discoveries was taken from a B.C. Department of Mines report on Placer Mining. It is a 1959 re-print of several earlier government publications. Gold price update: *Daily Telegraph*, London.

Placer. To commemorate its half-century in 1976, Placer Development Ltd. published a detailed account of its growth and impressive reach by R. A. Adams, a specialist in Canadian labour history, then teaching at Simon Fraser University. The first 50 years of our account is adapted from Adams, often reproduced verbatim. Company reports provided much of the story after 1976.

Porphyry Deposits.

Barr, D. A. , Fox, P. E., Northcote, K. E. , and Preto, V. A, (1976). *The Alkaline Suite Porphyry Deposits – a Summary.* in Sutherland Brown, A. , (Ed.), Porphyry deposits of the Canadian Cordillera. Montreal: The Canadian Institute of Mining and Metallurgy, Special Volume 15, p. 359-367.

Cathro, R. J. , (2006). *The Central European (Erzgebirge) tin deposits.* Montreal: Canadian Institute of Mining and Metallurgy Bulletin, vol. 98, no. 1091, p 78-80.

Mustard, D. K. , (1976). *Porphyry Exploration in the Canadian Cordillera.* in Sutherland Brown, A. , (Ed.), *Porphyry deposits of the Canadian Cordillera.* Montreal: The Canadian Institute of Mining and Metallurgy, Special Volume 15, p 17-20.

Newell, J. A. , Carter, N. C. , and Sutherland Brown, A. , (1995). *Porphyry Deposits of the Northwestern Cordillera: A Retrospective* in T. G. Schroeter (Ed.), *Porphyry Deposits of the Northwestern Cordillera of North America.* Canadian Institute of Mining, Metallurgy and Petroleum, Special Volume 46. p 3-19.

Parsons, A. B. (1933). *The Porphyry Coppers.* New York, The American Institute of Mining and Metallurgical Engineers.

Schroeter, T. G., (Ed.) (1995). *Porphyry Deposits of the Northwestern Cordillera of North America.* Canadian Institute of Mining, Metallurgy and Petroleum, Special Volume 46, 888 p.

Sinclair, W. D., (2007). *Porphyry deposits,* in Goodfellow, W. D., (Ed.), *Mineral deposits of Canada: A synthesis of major deposit-types, district metallogeny, the evolution of geological provinces, and exploration methods,* Geological Survey of Canada. St. John's: Geological Association of Canada, Mineral Deposits Division, Special Publication No. 5, p 223-243.

Sutherland Brown, A., (Ed.) (1976). *Porphyry deposits of the Canadian Cordillera.* Montreal: The Canadian Institute of Mining and Metallurgy, Special Volume 15, 510 p.

Titley, Spencer R. and Hicks, Carol A., (Eds.) (1966). *Geology of the porphyry copper deposits, Southwestern North America.* Tucson: The University of Arizona Press, 287 p.

Unger, D, Unger, I, *The Guggenheims – A Family History,* (2005) *A Family History,* New York, Harper Perennial

Rossland.

Various sources available from the Rossland Historical Museum and Archives Assoc. including *Rossland, The Golden City; Rossland's Jurassic Volcano; Historical Guide Map and Story of Rossland;* and *The Story in the Rocks, The Geology of Rossland, BC.* Other sources included J. Mouat's *Roaring Days, Rossland's Mines and the History of British Columbia; Ore Deposits, Tectonics, and Metallogeny in the Canadian Cordillera* (BC MEMPR Paper 1991-4); *Geology of the Rossland-Trail Map Area* (GSC Paper 79-26) and *Geological Setting of the Rossland Mining Camp* (MEMPR Bulletin 74).

Safe Day. Adapted from *To Employ & Protect* by Julie Domvile from the Winter 2005 issue of *Mining Review* (now *Mineral Exploration*).

Recommended Safety Resources:

The Law

Health, Safety and Reclamation Code for Mines in British Columbia – sets out regulatory requirements for exploration programs. Obtain copies from your regional mines inspector or AME BC.

Available at AME BC (also at www.amebc.ca):

Safety Guidelines for Mineral Exploration in Western Canada – 207 pages of important information in a convenient spiral-bound booklet form:

Canadian Mineral Exploration Health & Safety Annual Report 2010/11. The latest annual report tracking trends in mineral exploration health and safety and the most up-to-date health and safety resources. Also includes Health & Safety Policy Guidelines for Junior Mineral Exploration Companies, AME BC Health & Safety Guiding Principles, Basic Emergency Response Guidelines, and http://www. amebc.ca/documents/resources-and-publications/publications/current/full%20h-s%20report%202009.pdf

Handbook for Coal and Mineral Exploration in B.C. Plan and implement your exploration activities with regard for worker health and safety and environmental protection.

http://www.empr.gov.bc.ca/Mining/Exploration/Pages/Handbook. aspx

Staying Safe in Bear Country – the latest, most up-to-date advice regarding bear encounters. Order from www.kodiakcanada.com

Sobering Advice. *Geol. Surv., Canada*, Ec. Geol. Series 7, 1956, "Prospecting in Canada."

Spud Huestis. *Spud's Dream*, Sid Cole, Rand and Sarah Publishing, 1988; The Canadian Mining Hall of Fame; Mining Technology web site: http://www.mining-technology.com/projects/highland; Teck Resources Ltd.; Wikipedia entry on Logan Lake.

Teck. Cominco Ltd. , on-line corporate history; Teck Resources Ltd. for notes on the company's activities since the move of its head office from Toronto to Vancouver in 1972; *Cominco and the Manhattan Project* by C. D. Andrews, BC Studies, No. 11, Fall 1971; additional material supplied by John Hamilton, retired manager, Acquisitions Evaluations.

Wartime. Material relating to wartime activity in the Port of Vancouver relies heavily on James P. Delgado's *Waterfront,* published by Vancouver Maritime Museum and Stanton Atkins & Dosil Publishers. Descriptions of wartime production are found in Margaret A. Ormsby's *British Columbia: a History*, Macmillan of Canada, 1964.

Wells. Richard Thomas Wright, *Barkerville: A Gold Rush Experience*; Wells Historical Society and Museum, *Mining the Motherlode.*

Westmin. *Canadian Encyclopedia; Western Miner*, May 1983; *Investor's Digest*, March 23, 1982; *Westmin Resources Ltd. annual report*, 1996; Westmin Resources Directors' Circular December 9, 1997; Boliden Ltd. short form prospectus June 29, 2001; *Wikipedia* entry on Taseko Mines Ltd. ; Taseko Mines web site; Breakwater Resources web site.

Further Reading

There are many excellent books on the history of British Columbia. Here is some further reading:

Adams, John *Old Square-Toes and His Lady – The Life of James and Amelia Douglas*, Horsdal & Schubart, Victoria, 2001.

Andrews, C. D. *Cominco and the Manhattan Project*, BC Studies, No. 11, Fall 1971.

Barr, David A. *One Lucky Canuck: An Autobiography*, Trafford Publishing, Victoria, 2004.

Brown, Atholl Sutherland *British Columbia's Geological Surveys 1895-1995: A Century of Science and Dedication*, Pacific Section Geological Association of Canada, 1995.

Elliott, Gordon R. *Quesnel – Commercial Centre of the Cariboo Gold Rush*. Cariboo Historical Society, Quesnel Branch, 1958.

Fetherling, George *The Gold Crusaders: A Social History of Gold Rushes*, 1849-1929.

Forsythe, Mark and Dickson, Greg *The Trail of 1858 – British Columbia's Gold Rush Past* Harbour Publishing Co. Ltd. , Madeira Park, B.C., 2007

Gibbs, Mifflin Wistar *Shadow and Light*, autobiography of an enterprising Black pioneer in gold rush British Columbia. Original printed 1902. Reprint New York: Arno Press & The New York Times, 1968.

Green, Lewis *The Gold Hustlers* Alaska Northwest Publishing Company, Anchorage, 1977.

Green, Lewis *The Great Years: Gold Mining in the Bridge River Valley* Tricouni Press, Vancouver, 2000.

Green, Valerie *Above Stairs – Social Life in Upper Class Victoria 1843-1918*. Sono Nis Press, Victoria, B.C. 1995. Good accounts of the hardships encountered by women who travelled to Vancouver Island in the early 1800s.

Higgins, David Williams, *Tales of a Pioneer Journalist – From Gold Rush to Government Street in 19th Century Victoria*, Heritage House Publishing Company Ltd. , Surrey, B.C.,1996. (Selected chapters from *The Mystic Spring* and *The Passing of a Race* – books written by Higgins over a century ago).

Ingersoll, Ernest *Gold Fields of the Klondike*, Mr. Paperback, Langley, 1981. This fascinating book is an abridged paperback edition of *Gold Fields of the Klondike and the Wonders of Alaska*, originally published in 1897.

Joubin, Franc R. and Smyth, D. McCormack *Not for Gold Alone: The Memoirs of a Prospector*, Deljay Publications, Toronto, 1986.

Hill, Beth, *Sappers – The Royal Engineers in British Columbia*, Horsdal & Schubart Publishers Ltd. , Ganges, B.C., 1987.

Historic Yale, The Vancouver Section, British Columbia Historical Association, 1954.

Johnson, Peter *Voyages of Hope – The Saga of the Bride Ships*. Touch Wood Editions, Surrey, B.C., 2002.

Kilian, Crawford *Go Do Some Great Thing – The Black Pioneers of British Columbia*, Douglas & McIntyre, Vancouver, B.C., 1978. A balanced and thoughtful account of the search by coloured immigrants for equality in 19th century British Columbia.

Lavender, David *Land of Giants – The Drive to the Pacific Northwest 1750-1950*. Doubleday, 1956.

Lindsay, F. W. *Cariboo Yarns*, Quesnel, 1962

Lindsay, F. W. *The Cariboo Story*, Quesnel, 1958

Lugrin, N. de Bertrand *The Pioneer Women of Vancouver Island 1843-1866* The Women's Canadian Club of Victoria, B.C., 1928. Interesting anecdotes.

Mayne, Richard Charles *Four Year in B.C. & Vancouver Island*, Printed by W. Clowes and Sons, Stamford St. and Charing Cross, London 1862. First person account of a naval officer's travels during the gold rush, with sharp observations about people, places, wild life, trade etc.

O'Keefe, Betty and Macdonald, Ian *The Final Voyage of the Princess Sophia: Did they all have to die?* Heritage House Publishing Company Ltd. , Surrey, B.C., 1998.

Ormsby, Margaret A. *British Columbia: a History*. MacMillan of Canada, Toronto, 1964. Standard B.C. history. Good on economics and politics. Good material on Fraser Valley/ Cariboo gold rushes.

Pethick, Derek *James Douglas – Servant of Two Empires*. Mitchell Press Ltd., Vancouver 1969. Good biography of Douglas; includes activities of other major players Begbie, Moody etc.

Pethick, Derek *Victoria: The Fort* Mitchell Press Ltd., Vancouver 1968. Good early descriptions of the Hudson's Bay Company fort.

Porcher, E. A. *A Tour of Duty in the Pacific Northwest – E. A. Porcher and H. M. S. Sparrowhawk, 1965-1868*. Ed. Dwight L. Smith. University of Alaska Press, Fairbanks. 2000. Porcher's account of his tour of duty illustrated by the author's fine watercolours.

Ramsey, Bruce *Barkerville, A Guide to the Fabulous Cariboo Gold Camp*, Mitchell Press, Vancouver, 1961.

Ramsey, Bruce *Mining in Focus: An Illustrated History of Mining in British Columbia, 1968*.

Sterne, Netta *Fraser Gold – The Founding of British Columbia*, Washington State University Press, Pullman, Wash, 1998.

Woodcock, George *British Columbia, A History of the Province*, Douglas & McIntyre, Vancouver, 1990.

Epilogue

We have the great fortune to live and work in one of the most beautiful and mineral-rich places on earth. Our responsibility to present and future generations is to respect this amazing land and explore for and develop its riches judiciously.

Our forbearers were great seekers and adventurers. Facing hardship and danger, they set out into the mountains in search of often elusive riches hidden beneath the earth. As eternal optimists, explorationists will continue to head out into the field, live in rough conditions and hike through forests and over mountains in search of mineral wealth to the benefit of society.

Some explorers will be very successful, many not, but the mere act of prospecting and mineral exploration improves our understanding of geology and injects wealth into local economies, engages community members and builds long-term capacity for future generations throughout the province.

B.C.'s mineral wealth has led to the natural development of a large talent pool in the areas of prospecting, geoscience, engineering, environmental stewardship, technological innovation and more. With the addition of public policy, financial and legal experts, B.C. has become a world-renowned centre of excellence in mineral exploration and development.

We should be proud of what we have accomplished, and will continue to accomplish, in these challenging fields. I have no doubt that the industry will attract citizens from a broad cross section of the Canadian population: men and women, Aboriginal citizens and new Canadians; and will continue to develop partnerships between industry and educational institutions to build lasting skills and technical capacity for generations to come.

To operate successfully, B.C.'s mineral explorers rely upon the support of an association to connect with the public at large, liaise with government authorities and Aboriginal communities, and provide a means for members to meet and dialogue about the many shared issues and opportunities facing the industry and, by extension, the public. During much of B.C.'s history, the mineral exploration industry was represented by the B.C. & Yukon Chamber of Mines, which has evolved to become the Association for Mineral Exploration BC (AME BC).

The year 2011 will be remembered for a turbulent global economy and for the prolonged permitting challenges that many explorers faced in B.C. During this time, AME BC was actively engaging with the provincial government about the importance of government geoscientists in land use policy debates and on reforming the mineral exploration notice of work permitting process.

Even with the need for permitting reform, the mineral exploration expenditures in British Columbia reached a record of $463 million in 2011. With more than 350 mineral exploration projects and 20 major mine projects active throughout the province, exploration expenditures over the next five years could substantially increase beyond this peak.

This level of investment should ultimately lead to new discoveries, mine developments, jobs and government revenues as the "open for business" culture is nurtured and embraced. To support this goal, Premier Christy Clark announced in September 2011 that government would be allocating $24 million to expedite the permitting process. This is a very positive investment, as a well-funded permitting process will accrue to the benefit of not only the industry but to all communities and families in British Columbia.

It is clear that balancing the interests of society and our collective need for using minerals in our daily lives while respecting the environment and operating safely are not mutually exclusive goals. It can be done, and must be done in order for us to be responsible stewards of the Earth's mineral resources.

With tremendous pride and joy we celebrated the Association's 100th anniversary in 2012 and the theme of our famous annual conference Mineral Exploration Roundup was aptly named "Celebrating Our First Century of Global Discovery." An all-time record of 8,320 delegates attended Roundup 2012 and Michael McPhie became the Association's new Chair of the Board. We have learned much over the last century but we have much more to discover. As such, we look forward to the next 100 years with a renewed sense of excitement, confidence and opportunity.

I am so pleased to present this book, "Into the Mountains" as a record of the Association's first one hundred years as the primary advocate for B.C.'s prospectors, mineral explorers and developers. On behalf of the staff and board of AME BC, I thank all the volunteers and members of the Association for their valuable contributions in the preparation of this special commemorative book.

Best regards,

Gavin C. Dirom
President & Chief Executive Officer
Association for Mineral Exploration

Index

Past Presidents and Chairs

Robert R. Hedley
President
1912

Hon. Lytton Wilmot
Shatford, President
1913

Dean Reginald W. Brock
President
1914

Prof. John M. Turnbull
President
1915

Nicol Thompson
President
1916 – 1917, 1929

Arthur B. Clabon
President
1918

Arthur M. Whiteside
President
1919

Dr. Edwin T. Hodge
President
1920

J.M. Lay
President
1921

Frank E. Woodside
President
1922 – 1928

Dr. Victor Dolmage
President
1930 – 1934

Dr. William Brenton
Burnett, President
1935 – 1940

Gomer P. Jones
President
1941

Arthur E. "Johnny"
Jukes, President
1942 – 1946

Mel M. O'Brien
President
1947 – 1951

Dr. Harry V. Warren
President
1952 – 1954

Stanley J. Crocker
President
1955

Henry L. Hill
President
1956 – 1957

James A. Pike
President
1958

Dr. Christopher Riley
President
1959 – 1960

R.E. Legg
President
1961 – 1962

Gavin A. Dirom
President
1963 – 1964

Dr. John. A. Gower
President
1965 – 1966

Ralph C. Macdonald
President
1967 – 1968

Len G. White
President
1969 – 1970

Edward Harmon "Ted"
Caldwell, President
1971 – 1972

Edgar A. Scholz
President
1973 – 1974

Robert F. Sheldon
President
1975 – 1976

William St. C. Dunn
President
1977 – 1978

Donald K. Mustard
President
1979 – 1981

R.J. "Bob" Cathro
President
1982 – 1983

Don Rotherham
President
1984 – 1985

Charlie Aird
President
1986 – 1987

Dr. N.C. "Nick" Carter
President
1988 – 1989

W.J. "Bill" Wolfe
President
1990 – 1991

Michael J. Beley
President
1992 – 1993

Gerald G. Carlson
President
1994 – 1995

H. Walter Sellmer
President
1996 – 1997

Lindsay Bottomer
President
1998 – 1999

Donald McInnes
President
2000 – 2001

Shari Gardiner
President
2002 – 2003

Michael Gray
President
2004

David Caulfield
President
2005

Rob Pease
Chairman
2006 – 2007

Dr. Robert Stevens
Chairman
2008 – 2009

Lena Brommeland
Chair
2010

Mona M. Forster
Chair
2011

Michael R.J. McPhie
Chair
2012

Managers and Chief Executive Officers

Arthur B. Clabon
Secretary-Treasurer
1912

F.S. Pilling
Secretary
1913 – 1914

William Gray
Secretary
1918 – 1921

Henry Browning
Secretary
1922 – 1928

Harry Freeman
Secretary
1928

Frank E. Woodside
Manager
1928 – 1955

Thomas Elliott
Manager
1955 – 1975

Frederick G. "Rick"
Higgs, Manager
1975 – 1980

Dave Wilson
Acting Manager
1980

Jack M. Patterson
Manager
1980 – 1998

Bruce McKnight
Executive Director
1998 – 2002

Dan M. Jepsen
President & CEO
2002 – 2008

Gavin C. Dirom
President & CEO
2008 – Present